DATE DUE

OCT 3 1 2010	
Oct. 24, 2012	
APR 09 2014	

BRODART, CO.   Cat. No. 23-221

Criminal Investigative Failures

D. Kim Rossmo

CRC Press
Taylor & Francis Group
Boca Raton   London   New York

CRC Press is an imprint of the
Taylor & Francis Group, an **informa** business

CRC Press
Taylor & Francis Group
6000 Broken Sound Parkway NW, Suite 300
Boca Raton, FL 33487-2742

© 2009 by Taylor & Francis Group, LLC
CRC Press is an imprint of Taylor & Francis Group, an Informa business

No claim to original U.S. Government works
Printed in the United States of America on acid-free paper
10 9 8 7 6 5 4 3 2 1

International Standard Book Number-13: 978-1-4200-4751-6 (Hardcover)

Library of Congress Cataloging-in-Publication Data

Rossmo, D. Kim.
   Criminal investigative failures / D. Kim Rossmo.
      p. cm.
   Includes bibliographical references and index.
   ISBN 978-1-4200-4751-6 (alk. paper)
    1. Criminal investigation. 2. Forensic sciences. 3. Crime scene searches. 4. Evidence, Criminal. 5. Criminal justice, Administration of. 6. Judicial error. I. Title.

HV8073.R725 2008
363.25--dc22
                                                    2008018920

Visit the Taylor & Francis Web site at
http://www.taylorandfrancis.com

and the CRC Press Web site at
http://www.crcpress.com

Dedication

Dedicated to the memory of Constable Candace Anfield (née Mori)
1954–2004
Vancouver Police Department.

She always kept you grounded in the truth.

Contents

Foreword

Investigators, Information, and Interpretation: A Summary of Criminal Investigation Research

Popular entertainment has had a long-running fascination with criminal investigations—in novels, movies, and television—and it shows no sign of letting up. Typically a startling, and often horrific, crime is presented to investigators, who face either a dearth of clues or too many contradictory leads. They then discover some singular facts, often with the help of advanced technology. These facts remain a puzzle until a coincidental encounter with a seemingly unrelated event sparks an intuition that allows the investigators to connect the dots and solve the case. Of course, most of these stories are only distantly connected to typical crimes and how criminal investigations are really carried out. But they do point out an important distinction that has eluded criminal investigation researchers: the importance of information and the need to have the correct interpretation of that information.

The criminal investigative function is one of the two pillars of policing, the other being patrol operations. Although the patrol function provides an incredibly diverse array of services—ranging from maintaining order, ensuring free movement of people, assisting in economic development, preventing crime, establishing justice, and reducing fear of criminal victimization—almost by definition, the criminal investigative function focuses exclusively on crime.

In the late 1970s and early 1980s, there was considerable research into the criminal investigative process. Studies of proactive investigations focused on cases that begin with the identification of serious offenders. These were not studies of "whodunits" but of the effectiveness of "what have they done" investigations. Studies of repeat offender operations suggested that focusing on the most prolific offenders can increase the chances that such individuals will be caught. Logically, it would seem that if we remove the most active offenders, the total number of offenders will decline. Unfortunately, no one has done the research necessary to confirm this proposition.

Reactive investigations are the whodunits. Reactive investigation research examined how information leads to arrests: do cases with a piece of information X have a greater chance of being solved? This research was concerned with where this information came from: citizens, physical evidence, or other sources. And this research was also concerned with who collected the information: patrol officers, detectives, or crime scene analysts.

Like proactive investigations, relatively little social science work has been done on these types of investigations since the early 1980s, yet the findings of the reactive research still stand. This is in part because some of the results seem so obvious (after the research was conducted) and in part because we have not bothered to do the research necessary to confirm the stability of the findings.

These results show that the most important sources of information for the solution of property and violent crime are citizens, particularly victims. If during the first stage of an investigation police cannot locate citizens who have information about suspects, then the chances of solving the crime diminish considerably. Typically, the first investigators are not detectives but uniformed patrol officers who have been dispatched to the crime scene following a call from the victim.

These studies also showed that when victims or witnesses were able to give police information naming or describing the suspect, cases were far more likely to be solved than when victims and witnesses could not provide these types of information. This explains why robberies are more likely to be solved than burglaries; few people see a burglary (aside from the burglar), while every robbery has a witness (the victim). So even if many robbery victims cannot give a good description or a name, more of these victims can than burglary victims.

The results also indicated that physical evidence plays a small, although important role, in the solution to crimes. This finding requires some important qualifications. First, the types of crimes studied in the 1970s were burglary and robbery, for the most part. Homicide and rape, where physical evidence may play a much more important role, were not studied to any great extent. Second, there have been great advances in the methods for collecting, processing, and analyzing physical evidence since these studies were conducted—automated fingerprint identification systems, closed-circuit television, digital imagery and storage, and DNA analysis.

There is a common and unrecognized assumption underlying the criminal investigation research. It is assumed that the critical contribution of investigators is to gather information, and that interpretation and verification of information are relatively unimportant. In some respects, this assumption has merit. In the absence of information, interpretation and verification are impossible. So information collection is clearly a necessary condition. But the assumption that it ends there is clearly invalid. And the findings from the research hint at this. For example, the probability of making an arrest when given suspect information from a witness does not come close to certainty, thus suggesting that much of the information from witnesses cannot be taken at face value.

Kim Rossmo and his colleagues challenge this assumption. Their examination of mistakes made in the interpretation of information is critically important for several reasons.

First, it points out that our myopic concern with police as crime controllers has allowed us to forget that a very important function of policing is to provide justice. Academics and civil libertarians have drawn attention to the possibility of police discrimination against minorities in traffic stops. Racial profiling research has become a cottage industry, although there is considerable debate as to what the findings mean.

Rossmo's concern is more subtle but equally important. Even if racial discrimination and the appearance of racial discrimination are eliminated, we should still be concerned about miscarriages of justice due to cognitive biases inherent in human decision making. He draws attention to the fact that justice is a case-by-case matter, not a matter of percentages. Crime reduction is future oriented, so when we implement a prevention program we are hoping to reduce future victimizations of unknown individuals. If we find that crime has gone down 30%, we know that there is an unknown group of people who would have been victims, but for our actions. But justice is retrospective: we know the names and faces of the victims of injustice. Justice is personal.

Second, Rossmo and colleagues show what police can do to reduce injustices caused by investigative failures. We are used to hearing about new ways to identify offenders, often using the latest technology. But we forget that humans must interpret the results of technology and that these humans must exercise judgment. Over the past two decades, cognitive psychologists have shown that people have built-in reasoning biases, calling to question the ideal of "rational man." Putting these cognitive research findings to practical use in police investigations should be as high a priority as increasing police information collection capabilities.

Finally, Rossmo opens up a completely new area for applied research within policing: how investigators make decisions during the course of investigations. There is already a tradition of research on patrol officer decision making, but there is no comparable research program for investigators. Unlike patrol decision-making research, when the researchers watch and record policing in the field, investigative research will have to be a combination of field observations, systematic interviews, and laboratory experiments using investigative scenarios.

For serious crimes, criminal investigators are the gatekeepers for the rest of the criminal justice system. The information that they collect and their interpretations of this information can have a profound impact on downstream criminal justice outcomes. So it is not just the excitement of the hunt that makes criminal investigators so compelling to the entertainment industry, but the knowledge that they do make a difference. At their best, investigators can protect us from some of society's most dangerous predators.

At their worst, they can create and perpetuate egregious injustices. All the data from our information society and all the results of the latest crime scene investigation technologies must, at some stage, be filtered through the minds of those individuals responsible for investigating crimes. Awareness of investigators' inherent limitations is an important step toward achieving the potential of technological promise. For these reasons, Rossmo's insights into the causes of investigation failures and the ways we can avoid them are critical for investigators, police supervisors, prosecutors, criminologists, and the general public.

John E. Eck

Professor
Division of Criminal Justice
University of Cincinnati
Cincinnati, Ohio

Preface

Solving major crimes is serious business. Successful investigations and prosecutions contribute to improved public safety by incapacitating violent offenders; in doing so, they also build confidence in our justice system, particularly the police. But when investigations fail, the offenders remain free and the public is at risk of further harm. Even worse is when police arrest, and courts convict, an innocent person; not only is a terrible injustice done and the reputation of the justice system harmed, but the real offender remains free to hurt or kill again.

Dr. Kim Rossmo has brought his varied and extensive police experience as a street cop and geographic profiler, his extraordinary academic accomplishments, and his continuing work in criminal investigations to bear in this book on investigative failures. In it, he describes the cognitive biases, biases in evaluation of evidence, probability errors, and organizational traps that lead to investigative failures. Thankfully, he takes what could be difficult-to-understand concepts and explains them in a way that makes this information accessible to police officers, academics, and laymen alike. Most importantly, he describes practical strategies to overcome the challenges posed by the pitfalls he explores, essentially providing a prescription for success. And throughout, he keeps the reader interested and entertained, no small feat given the topic.

The concepts and strategies outlined in this book are invaluable for helping to accomplish an investigator's primary objective: "find the truth." For those of us who care deeply about investigative excellence and justice, particularly police investigators, this book is a "must read."

Doug A. LePard

Deputy Chief Commanding Investigation Division
Vancouver Police Department
Vancouver, British Columbia, Canada

Acknowledgments

This book would not have happened without the hard work and professional dedication of the contributors. I also want to thank Dr. Tony Pinizzotto, FBI Behavioral Science Unit; Dr. John Eck, University of Cincinnati; Dr. Brian Forst, American University; Inspector Ron MacKay (retired), Royal Canadian Mounted Police; and the editorial staff of the *FBI Law Enforcement Bulletin*. I am indebted to Carolyn Spence, Ari Silver, and the professional team at Taylor & Francis for making this book happen. I greatly appreciate the ongoing support of Dr. Quint Thurman, my department chair. Finally, special thanks to my parents, family, and friends for their constant support and encouragement.

My interest in the subject of criminal investigative failures originates from various unsolved major crime cases for which I have consulted. I wish to thank those detectives who were willing to discuss what went wrong in their investigations.

The Author

D. Kim Rossmo is the University Endowed Chair in Criminology and the Director of the Center for Geospatial Intelligence and Investigation (GII) in the Department of Criminal Justice at Texas State University. He earned a Ph.D. in criminology from Simon Fraser University and has researched and published in the areas of environmental criminology, policing, criminal investigations, and offender profiling. Dr. Rossmo was formerly a management consultant with the Bureau of Alcohol, Tobacco, Firearms and Explosives (ATF), the Director of Research for the Police Foundation in Washington, D.C., and the Detective Inspector in charge of the Vancouver Police Department's Geographic Profiling Section, which provided investigative support for the international law enforcement community. He received the Governor General of Canada Police Exemplary Service Medal in 2000.

Dr. Rossmo is a member of the International Association of Chiefs of Police (IACP) Advisory Committee for Police Investigative Operations and the South Carolina Research Authority Integrated Solutions Group Advisory Board. He is an Adjunct Professor at Simon Fraser University, sits on the editorial board for the international journal *Homicide Studies*, and is a Full Fellow of the International Criminal Investigative Analysis Fellowship (ICIAF).

Recently, Dr. Rossmo completed research projects on the geospatial structure of terrorist cells and the applications of geographic profiling to insurgency problems in Iraq. He concluded a study on the geographic patterns of illegal land border crossings between the United States and Mexico to assist Border Patrol interdiction efforts. He is currently working with zoologists, biologists, and epidemiologists from Africa, Great Britain, and the United States, exploring applications of geographic profiling to Great White Shark predation, bat and bee foraging, and malarial mosquito breeding site patterns.

Contributors

John Allore works for the local government in North Carolina and is all too familiar with the inefficiencies of intergovernment relations. When he discovered the true circumstances surrounding the death of his sister Theresa, he went back to school to educate himself on the challenges facing government agencies. In 2008, he graduated from North Carolina State University with a Master's degree in Public Administration, concentrating on justice administration. During his time of study he was the recipient of the Public Administration Alumni Association scholarship and the George Neilson Scholarship awarded by the Government Finance Officers Association. In a former life, he was a film and television actor. His last role was as an FBI agent chasing bank robbers in a forgettable Hollywood movie. In his spare time he runs the blog http://www.whokilledtheresa.blogspot.com. As his heading states, *Life isn't fair, Justice is blind … and dysfunctional, and some cops aren't smart and dedicated like on TV.* He is forever grateful to Patricia Pearson, journalist and writer extraordinaire, who originated the *Who Killed Theresa?* news stories. Without Patricia, his sister would have remained a crime statistic. Through her writing, Theresa was restored to a place of stature and dignity. In the spring of 2008, he applied to the Ph.D. program at North Carolina State University.

Neil Boyd is a professor and associate director of the School of Criminology at Simon Fraser University, educated in psychology at the University of Western Ontario and in law at Osgoode Hall Law School. He is a previous director of the School of Criminology and the author of many academic articles as well as five books: *High Society: Legal and Illegal Drugs in Canada*; *The Last Dance: Murder in Canada*; *Gently into the Night: Aggression in Long-Term Care*; *The Beast Within: Why Men Are Violent*; *Big Sister: How Extreme Feminism Has Betrayed the Fight for Sexual Equality*; and two textbooks, *The Social Dimensions of Law*; and *Canadian Law: An Introduction* (now in its 4th edition); and many academic articles. He is a frequent media commentator on subjects related to criminology, specifically, drug law and policy, and issues of criminal violence and homicide. He has written articles about drug markets, heroin treatment initiatives, injectable drug use, responses to the threats posed by homicide offenders, and the linkage between drug use and homicide. He recently completed a study of the Eron mortgage fraud and is currently conducting an evaluation of Vancouver's supervised injection site and a community impact study of the NAOMI heroin prescription trial in Vancouver.

Elizabeth Campbell is Crown Counsel with the Ministry of the Attorney General, Criminal Appeals and Special Prosecutions office, in Vancouver, British Columbia. She received her LLB from the University of Victoria in 1996. In 1993 and again in 1996, she volunteered at a legal clinic in Durban, South Africa. After clerking with the Supreme Court of British Columbia, she articled and worked as an associate at Harper Grey where her assignments included criminal defense work. She joined the Crown in 1999 and worked as a trial prosecutor in Vancouver before moving to her current section in 2006. In April 2007, she traveled to China with a Canadian Bar Association project as an instructor in a week-long course for legal aid lawyers.

Richard M. Cullen is a graduate student at Memorial University of Newfoundland. He obtained his BSc (Honors) from Memorial in 2005. His general research interests include bounded rationality, forensic psychology, and social cognition. His recent research involves the development of a model that explains how people form beliefs about investigative techniques in the absence of compelling empirical evidence. His graduate work involves a quantitative review of the occurrence of the problem-seeking approach to social psychological research.

Itiel E. Dror (Ph.D. Harvard University) is a cognitive neuroscientist from the University of Southampton, United Kingdom (for details see http://users.ecs. soton.ac.uk/id/). His research focuses on understanding the information processing mechanisms underlying perception, judgment, and decision making. Much of his work is purely theoretical and academic, for example, examining and developing models for risk-taking decisions, time-pressured decision making, and the role of expertise and bias in decision making. He also bridges these theoretical issues to real-world environments. In his applied research, he works with experts on decision making in a variety of domains, such as military (he has worked with the U.S. Air Force for over 15 years), medical, police, and forensics (see http://users.ecs.soton.ac.uk/id/biometrics.html).

Joseph Eastwood is a Ph.D. candidate in experimental social psychology at Memorial University of Newfoundland. He received his Master of Science degree in experimental social psychology from Memorial University in 2007. He was a recipient of a SSHRC Canada Graduate Scholarships Program: Master's Scholarships in 2006–2007. His research interests include police interrogations, bounded decision making, and criminal profiling.

John E. Eck is a professor of criminal justice at the University of Cincinnati. He has served as the evaluation coordinator for the Washington/Baltimore High Intensity Drug Trafficking Area (HIDTA), a regional drug enforcement program. For 17 years he conducted research for the Police Executive Research Forum (PERF), including studies of investigative management. He has been a consultant to the London Metropolitan Police, Royal Canadian Mounted Police, the Police Foundation, and various police organizations. Since 1999 he has served as a judge for the British government's Tilley Awards for Problem-Solving Excellence. He has written extensively on criminal investigations, crime prevention, drug markets, crime mapping, and crime places. He received his Ph.D. in criminology from the University of Maryland in 1994 and his Master's in public policy from the University of Michigan in 1977.

Peter A. F. Fraser-Mackenzie is a Ph.D. student at the University of Southampton, United Kingdom, driven by fundamental questions about cognition and decision making. His doctoral research focuses on exploring the effects of internal predecision biases and external factors (such as time pressure, information load, and risk) on human error. He is also interested in applied domains, such as consumer buying, gambling, and forensics.

Diana M. Havlin is a senior crime analyst with the Washington, D.C., Metropolitan Police Department's Criminal Intelligence and Tactical Crime Analysis Unit. She provides critical insight and analysis on emerging trends and produces daily crime and intelligence products for the command staff, detectives, and patrol officers. She has contributed to a number of investigations in the nation's capital, including a murder-for-hire and a cold serial killer case. She was also responsible for enhancing the department's geographic profiling analysis capabilities by securing much needed federal funding for training and staff certifications. She is an accomplished public speaker, having recently presented to law enforcement and civilian audiences at the Eastern States Investigator's Conference and the Annual i2 User Conference. In addition, she is a regular guest lecturer for detectives and students at both graduate and undergraduate levels. She received her Master of Science in justice, law, and society from American University in 2005. Her primary professional interests include offender travel pattern analysis and offender reentry issues.

John C. House is currently the inspector in charge of the Crimes Against Persons Section of the Royal Newfoundland Constabulary (RNC) in Canada. He has served with the RNC for 27 years, working for most of his career in various units of the Criminal Investigation Division. He has experience investigating large, complex cases and has been the major case manager for investigative homicide teams. He was the inaugural recipient of the Canadian Police College's Police Research Scholarship in 2004 for his study of the attributes of effective major case managers in Canada. He holds a Master of Science degree in investigative psychology from the University of Surrey, United Kingdom. His research interests include offender profiling, intelligence-based policing, and leadership of major case investigative teams.

Doug A. LePard is the Deputy Chief Constable commanding the Investigation Division of the Vancouver Police Department (VPD; British Columbia, Canada), an agency of 1,600 sworn and civilian members. He has been a member of the VPD since 1981, spending much of his career in investigative assignments and in various operational and administrative roles. He holds a Bachelor of Arts degree in criminology from Simon Fraser University as well as certificates from Queen's University, the Banff School of Management, the Canadian Police College, and the Justice Institute of British Columbia. He has lectured extensively locally, nationally, and internationally on various investigative issues and currently instructs new VPD investigators on "preventing wrongful convictions through investigative excellence." He has authored numerous reports for the VPD, including a major review of the "Missing Women" serial murder case, and has coauthored publications on stalking and threat assessment. He has been honored with numerous commendations, including a Lieutenant Governor's Award for bravery. In 2008, Deputy Chief LePard was invested as a Member of the Order of Merit by Her Excellency, the Right Honourable Michaelle Jean, Governor General of Canada.

Gregg O. McCrary entered duty as a Special Agent with the Federal Bureau of Investigation (FBI) in 1969 and retired in 1995. He served in various investigative capacities throughout the United States and as a Supervisory Special Agent with the FBI's Behavioral Science Unit from 1988 to 1995. There, he constructed behavioral profiles and provided analysis regarding a wide range of crimes, including extortions, stalking, product tampering, sex crimes, and homicide. He has conducted research on sex offenders, bombers, extortionists, child killers, and other types of criminals and crimes. He has provided expert witness testimony in North America and Europe and has testified before Select Senate Committees on Sexual Violence in New York State and Massachusetts. He has consulted on thousands of cases throughout North America, Central America, Europe, and Asia. He is the author of *The Unknown Darkness: Profiling the Predators Among Us* (2003) and a contributing author to the *Crime Classification Manual* (1992). His work in violent crime has been highlighted in several television documentaries, including the Emmy-nominated *The Mind of Serial Killer*, produced by NOVA for the Public Broadcasting System. He has provided expert commentary to ABC, NBC, CBS, Cable News Network (CNN), The Discovery Channel, *Larry King Live*, *The New York Times*, *Time*, *Newsweek*, and numerous other national and international media. As the Director of Behavioral Criminology International, he continues to consult on violent crime matters. Gregg is an Adjunct Professor of Forensic Psychology and Criminal Justice at Nova Southeastern University in Ft. Lauderdale, Florida, and at Marymount University in Arlington, Virginia. He also works as an independent contractor for the Threat Assessment Group (TAG) and Park Dietz and Associates, a forensic litigation group, both headquartered in Newport Beach, California.

Patricia Pearson is the author of *When She Was Bad: How and Why Women Get Away with Murder,* an award-winning analysis of female aggression. She has also authored two novels, an essay collection, and the 2008 memoir, *A Brief History of Anxiety—Yours and Mine.* She works as an independent journalist in Toronto and can be reached via her Web site: http://www.pearsonspost.com.

Ken Pease, a forensic psychologist by training, is currently Visiting Professor at University College London, the University of Loughborough, and Chester University. Before retirement, he held chairs at the University of Manchester and the University of Saskatchewan, where he worked in the maximum security Regional Psychiatric Centre (Prairies). He has acted as Head of the Police Research Group at the Home Office, and has been a member of the Parole Board for England and Wales. He is a member of the Home Office Design and Technology Alliance and sits on the Steering Group of the current Department of Trade and Industry (DTI) review of Home Office science. The bulk of his published work over the past two decades has concerned crime reduction, and he was recently flattered by a book published in his honor under the title *Imagination in Crime Prevention.* A candidate for the Green Party for 20 years, his current work includes the integration of security and sustainability in home design, patterns of dog theft, and the application of evolutionary psychology to crime science.

Jason Roach is a senior lecturer in psychological criminology at the University of Huddersfield. Jason graduated in 1992 with a BSc (Honors) in psychology, and in 2000 with an MSc in applied psychology. He is currently finishing a Ph.D. at the Jill Dando Institute of Crime Science, University of London, under the supervision of Professor Ken Pease. In the past, he has been a trainee clinical psychologist at a large psychiatric institution, a researcher for the United Kingdom Home Office, a lecturer and researcher at the University of Manchester, and a tutor at the United Kingdom Police Crime Reduction College. His published work includes the identification of serious offenders via self-selection policing, terrorism, the psychology of police investigations, and the behavioral analysis and profiling of violent offenders. His current work includes coauthoring a book, *Evolutionary Criminology,* with Ken Pease. He continues to work with the United Kingdom police, acting as an advisor on serious crime cases, particularly those deemed "cold."

Brent Snook is an assistant professor in the Department of Psychology and Director of the Bounded Rationality and the Law Laboratory at Memorial University of Newfoundland. He is also a research associate with the Police Research Lab at Carleton University. He obtained his Ph.D. in psychology at the University of Liverpool, United Kingdom. His research primarily involves the study of bounded rationality and the law. He is particularly interested in the types of simple mental rules that people use to make consequential decisions in legal settings, when and why those rules work, succeed, or fail, and the conditions under which those simple rules are used. His research interests also include the use and misuse of psychologically based investigative practices, geographic profiling, offender spatial decision making, and pseudoscience in the criminal justice system.

David Stubbins received a Ph.D. from the Wright Institute, Berkeley, in social-clinical psychology and an A.B. from the University of California, Berkeley. He has consulted for both law enforcement agencies on criminal investigations and attorneys in criminal cases, and has testified as an expert witness. He served as an independent evaluator for California's Sexually Violent Predator and Mentally Disordered Offender programs. As a staff psychologist in high security prisons, he worked with violent offenders, providing psychological assessment and treatment, and was a member of the hostage negotiation team. He has consulted for public and private sector organizations on risk assessment, threat management, and organizational development. He is a member of the International Criminal Investigative Analysis Fellowship (ICIAF). Dr. Stubbins maintains a consulting psychology practice.

Nelson Stubbins received an MFA from the University of California, Davis, and a B.A. from the University of California, Santa Barbara. He has extensive management and professional training experience. He has managed small teams in the software and semiconductor industries, a sheltered workshop, and in the creative arts. He has taught classes to software engineers and scientists on developing real-time programs on an RTOS (real-time operating system), writing low-level graphics programs, and software development on the UNIX operating system. He has written training courses, a technical reference manual, and articles for an online content provider. At a high-tech company, he worked in internal engineer development, which included software reliability, ISO 9000, software testing, management training, team effectiveness, and a variety of organizational development issues. He now focuses on studying and writing about his interest in belief formation and maintenance.

James Trainum has been with the Metropolitan Police Department of Washington, D.C., for 25 years, 15 of those as a homicide detective. In 2001, he created what became the Violent Crime Case Review Project, which utilizes college interns to review old homicide cases and to help prioritize them for additional investigation. He lectures on the topics of interrogation and false confessions to colleges and law enforcement agencies and has been consulted on cases in which there has been an allegation of a wrongful conviction.

The Basics

I

Introduction

D. KIM ROSSMO

1

The police detective is one of the most commonly depicted characters in novels, cinema, and television. He or she resolves complex criminal investigations through deductive skills, high-tech forensics, specialized computer programs, hard work, and luck. Good wins, evil loses, and justice triumphs. But in the real world, things do not always turn out that way. In most crimes, the case is not closed, the criminal is not apprehended, and justice is denied.

The entire investigative process is premised on the assumption that the offender made a mistake. Not all crimes are solvable. In some circumstances, even solvable crimes are not cleared because of incompetence, misfeasance, nonfeasance, resources problems, or simple bad luck. These problems, however, are not the focus of this book. Here, we are concerned with subtle hazards, traps that can cause a criminal investigative failure. Specifically, our focus is on murder and other major crime "whodunits," some of the most demanding cases that detectives must investigate. The question we are interested in is what causes competent and dedicated investigators to make avoidable mistakes, jeopardizing the successful resolution of their cases? If a bridge falls, an airplane crashes, or a building collapses, intensive efforts are made to understand what went wrong (see Bortz, 1995; Levy & Salvadori, 2002). There is evidence gathering, interviews, simulations, analyses, review panels, and hearing boards, followed by the necessary technical, procedural, and policy changes. Unfortunately, with the odd exception of a senate/congressional hearing in the United States or a royal commission in Canada or the United Kingdom, the reasons for criminal investigative failures are rarely examined.[1]

Failures in the criminal investigative process can have serious consequences. Unsolved crimes, unsuccessful prosecutions, unpunished offenders, and wrongful convictions bring the criminal justice system into disrepute. We are all familiar with such notorious cases as JonBenét Ramsey, O.J. Simpson, and Chandra Levy. Moreover, with the cost of some major crime investigations climbing into the hundreds of thousands or, even millions of dollars, wasted effort can be extremely expensive.

---

[1] The *Innocence Protection Act of 2001*, a bipartisan bill that failed to make it through Congress, would have required states to investigate reasons for wrongful convictions, publicize them, and find ways to prevent such errors from reoccurring (Fuller, 2004).

Currently, there are approximately 16,000 murders annually in the United States, with a clearance rate of 63%. This means that every day 16 murders occur that will never be solved, and their perpetrators never arrested.[2] On the other end of the scale, it has been estimated that 0.5% of all felony cases are wrongful convictions (Huff, Rattner, & Sagarin, 1996). The arrest, prosecution, incarceration, or execution of an innocent person is the ultimate failure of justice. Moreover, "when the wrong perpetrator is apprehended, the real perpetrator is left free to roam the streets and victimize others" (Drizin & Leo, 2004, p. 992). By closing the investigation, police have given the offender a "Get Out of Jail Free" card.

The Innocence Project, which only handles cases where postconviction DNA testing can yield conclusive proof of innocence, has helped exonerate 157 wrongfully convicted individuals. Innocence Project personnel have identified 12 factors that lead to wrongful convictions, six of which (affecting 60% of the cases) are related to the investigation or prosecution process. In order of frequency, these include mistaken identification, police misconduct, prosecutorial misconduct, false witness testimony, informants/snitches, and false confessions (Innocence Project, 2005).

The criminal investigative process involves two stages: (1) finding the offender (suspect identification), and (2) proving the offender's guilt (case building) (Rossmo, 2004). Each stage requires different mental processes and actions. The first stage involves information collection, prioritization, and evaluation. The second stage can only be accomplished by means of physical evidence, a witness, or a confession (Klockars & Mastrofski, 1991). Organizational or cognitive pressures to move prematurely from the investigation to the verification mode can lead to injustices (Stelfox & Pease, 2005).

Most investigators are dedicated professionals who want to solve their cases and arrest the right person. So what causes a major crime investigation to fail or a criminal prosecution to focus on an innocent person? Research in the fields of cognitive psychology, forensic statistics, intelligence analysis, law, and the philosophy of science suggests some possible explanations. The key factors can be grouped into three areas: (1) cognitive biases, (2) organizational traps, and (3) probability errors. Like cascading failures in airplane crashes, an investigative failure often has more than one contributing cause.

By outlining some of these "subtle hazards," this book aims toward improving the police investigative process and helping prevent future failures of justice. The contributors to this volume include scholars, police investigators and executives, a crime analyst, a lawyer, a software development manager, a journalist, and the brother of a murder victim. Some common ground is covered, but each author provides his or her own unique perspective.

---

[2] Los Angeles, for example, has 8,000 unsolved homicides from 1960 (Connelly, 2005).

Although there is much agreement, there are also differences of opinion (we would hate to become victims ourselves of tunnel vision or groupthink!).

The chapters follow a logical sequence but can be read out of order or in isolation. In the first section of this book, I provide the foundation for understanding some of the causes of criminal investigative failures. This chapter introduces the rationale for the book. In Chapter 2, tunnel vision, cognitive biases, and common errors in reasoning are examined. In Chapter 3, organizational traps such as rumor, ego, and groupthink are discussed. The Pig Farm serial murder case, an example of a tragic organizational trap, is covered in some detail. In Chapter 4, probability errors in the forensic and profiling contexts are examined, including misunderstanding of coincidences, correlations, and base rates, and the prosecutor's and defense attorney's fallacies.

The second section of the book focuses on cognitive biases in greater detail. In Chapter 5, Itiel Dror and Peter Fraser-Mackenzie study how cognitive biases effect our perceptions, judgments, and decision making. In Chapter 6, taking a bounded rationality approach to criminal investigations, Brent Snook and Richard Cullen argue that heuristics such a tunnel vision are not inherently flawed. And in Chapter 7, David Stubbins and Nelson Stubbins introduce the useful and powerful concept of investigative narrative to explore the influences of cognitive heuristics, biases, and judgment.

The third section of the book contains case studies. In Chapter 8, Gregg McCrary discusses the infamous Michael Crowe case, a deeply flawed investigation that almost resulted in homicide convictions for three innocent boys. In Chapter 9, Neil Boyd and I examine in the investigative and legal issues surrounding the wrongful murder conviction of David Milgaard. In Chapter 10, Jim Trainum and Diana Havlin recount a homicide investigation in which Detective Trainum obtained a false confession from an innocent suspect. In Chapter 11, John Allore and Patricia Pearson tell a sad and frustrating story of the death of John's older sister Theresa, a murder written off by police as a drug overdose. And in Chapter 12, I discuss the other side of wrongful convictions—claims of innocence by guilty criminals, using the Roger Coleman and Benjamin LaGuer matters as case examples.

The fourth section of the book looks at recommendations to help prevent criminal investigative failures. In Chapter 13, Doug LePard and Elizabeth Campbell outline how police departments can introduce organizational changes that will reduce the risk of a wrongful arrest and conviction. In Chapter 14, John House, Joseph Eastwood, and Brent Snook present the results of a research study that identified competencies associated with effective major case police managers and discuss how such leadership can reduce the likelihood of an investigative failure. Jason Roach and Ken Pease argue in Chapter 15 that we need to conduct reviews of unsolved cold cases to better understand how criminal investigations can be improved. Finally, Chapter 16 discusses other recommendations to prevent criminal investigative failures and concludes the book. Additional readings are provided in the bibliography.

The origins of this project begin with my involvement in geographic profiling.[3] From 1995 to 2000, I was the Detective Inspector in charge of the Vancouver Police Department's Geographic Profiling Section with a mandate to provide investigative support to the international police community. As a consequence, I had the opportunity to consult on major crime cases from around the world. Of course, our assistance was only requested in unsolved cases, many of which had been cold for a number of years. Some of these cases were victims of lack of evidence or bad luck. Others, however, were investigative failures. Often the detectives we worked with were very frank about mistakes that had been made and opportunities that had been missed.

These failures were brought home to me in 1998 during Vancouver's Missing Women case. Since 1995, 27 women—most were drug-addicted prostitutes—disappeared from the Low Track stroll of Vancouver's Skid Road. In February 2002, four years after this case was first brought to my attention, Robert "Willie" Pickton was finally arrested at his pig farm in suburban Vancouver. He was subsequently charged with multiple counts of first-degree murder, becoming Canada's worst serial killer. The "Pig Farm Case" was a terrible but not atypical example of a criminal investigative failure—too little, done too late, by a disinterested Major Crime Section. The case is discussed in more detail in Chapter 3.

These experiences prompted me to begin studying cognitive biases, organizational traps, and probability errors, the three main problem areas I thought might be important in understanding the causes of criminal investigative failures. But these were just ideas and theories floating around in my head until September 2003 when I was asked to talk at the annual meeting of the Alberta Crown Attorneys' Association in Banff. They initially wanted a presentation on geographic profiling but then asked if I would also do an after-dinner speech.

The request left me in a bit of a quandary. I had my geographic profiling PowerPoint slideshow all ready to go but had nothing suitable for an after-dinner speech. The idea of discussing criminal investigative failures, my experiences and what I had read, slowly emerged. With some trepidation—after all, I was going to at least obliquely criticize the investigative and trial processes in a room full of prosecutors[4]—I developed a new presentation that pulled together some of these ideas. As it turned out, it was a success; many

---

[3] Geographic profiling is an investigative methodology that analyzes connected crime locations to determine the most probable area of offender residence (Rossmo, 2000). It is typically used for suspect prioritization and information management in serial crime cases.

[4] Canadian lawyers have a tradition of tossing buns at after-dinner speakers if they don't like their talk.

of the Crown counsels came up to me after the speech with their own stories of cases that had gone wrong.

After a subsequent presentation to the International Criminal Investigative Analysis Fellowship (ICIAF) in San Antonio, Texas, Dr. David Stubbins, a forensic psychologist, urged me to put the presentation into writing (see Chapter 7 for a fascinating discussion of the role of judgment, heuristics, and biases in investigative narratives by David and Nelson Stubbins). That led to a paper that was subsequently published in two parts by the *FBI Law Enforcement Bulletin* (Rossmo, 2006a, 2006b). But it became clear that there were too many ideas and cases for a single article. It was also equally clear that other voices from different perspectives could significantly add to this message. From all this came the idea of a book on criminal investigative failures, written for both scholars and practitioners.

The criminal investigation function is an under-researched area in the policing literature, one that has received only limited attention[5] since the Rand study on detectives in the 1970s (Chaiken, Greenwood, & Petersilia, 1976, 1991; see John Eck's comments in the Foreword to this book). Police investigations comprise an important and significant component of the law enforcement function, as the probability of apprehension and sanction is fundamental to the successful operation of the justice system. There is much more to detective work than crime scene forensics. Like scientific research, the investigative process involves a careful and concerted effort to discover the truth, to lay bare the structure of reality. The purpose of this book is to contribute to bettering that search.

References

Bortz, F. (1995). *Catastrophe!: Great engineering failure—and success*. New York: W. H. Freeman.

Chaiken, J. M., Greenwood, P. W., & Petersilia, J. (1976). *The criminal investigation process: A summary report*. Santa Monica, CA: Rand.

Chaiken, J. M., Greenwood, P. W., & Petersilia, J. (1991). The Rand study of detectives. In C. B. Klockars & S. D. Mastrofski (Eds.), *Thinking about police: Contemporary readings* (2nd ed.; pp. 170–187). New York: McGraw-Hill.

Connelly, M. (2005, May 23). Old, but never totally cold. *Los Angeles Times*, p. A1.

Drizin, S. A., & Leo, R. A. (2004). The problem of false confessions in the post-DNA world. *North Carolina Law Review, 82*, 891–1007.

Fuller, A. S. (2004, November). *Wrongful felony convictions in the United States*. Paper presented at the meeting of the American Society of Criminology, Nashville, TN.

---

[5] A survey of papers presented at the 2002 meeting of the Academy of Criminal Justice Sciences (ACJS) found that only 2% concerned the police investigative process (Robinson, 2002).

Huff, C. R., Rattner, A., & Sagarin, E. (1996). *Convicted but innocent: Wrongful conviction and public policy.* Thousand Oaks, CA: Sage.

Innocence Project. (2005). *Causes and remedies of wrongful convictions.* Retrieved April 13, 2005, from http://www.innocenceproject.org/causes/index.php.

Klockars, C. B., & Mastrofski, S. D. (Eds.). (1991). *Thinking about police: Contemporary readings* (2nd ed.). New York: McGraw-Hill.

Levy, M., & Salvadori, M. (2002). *Why buildings fall down: How structures fail.* New York: W. W. Norton.

Robinson, M. B. (2002). An analysis of 2002 ACJS papers: What members presented about and what they ignored. *ACJS Today, 22*(4), 1, 3–6.

Rossmo, D. K. (2000). *Geographic profiling.* Boca Raton, FL: CRC Press.

Rossmo, D. K. (2004). Geographic profiling as problem solving for serial crime. In Q. C. Thurman & J. D. Jamieson (Eds.), *Police problem solving* (pp. 121–131). Cincinnati: Anderson Publishing.

Rossmo, D. K. (2006a). Criminal investigative failures: Avoiding the pitfalls. *FBI Law Enforcement Bulletin, 75*(9), 1–8.

Rossmo, D. K. (2006b). Criminal investigative failures: Avoiding the pitfalls (Part two). *FBI Law Enforcement Bulletin, 75*(10), 12–19.

Stelfox, P., & Pease, K. (2005). Cognition and detection: Reluctant bedfellows? In M. J. Smith & N. Tilley (Eds.), *Crime science: New approaches to preventing and detecting crime* (pp. 191–207). Cullompton, Devon: Willan Publishing.

Cognitive Biases: Perception, Intuition, and Tunnel Vision

2

D. KIM ROSSMO

Habit is stronger than reason.

George Santayana

As Inspector "Dirty Harry" Callahan (Clint Eastwood) of the San Francisco Police Department once said, "A man's got to know his limitations" (*Magnum Force*, 1973). An understanding of human judgment—including the limitations inherent in perception, memory, and decision making—allows us to be aware of and compensate for our cognitive shortcomings. We are then in a better position as investigators to stay grounded in reality and to find the truth.

Perception and Memory Limitations

We are not objective surveyors of our worlds. Rather, the decoding of sensory input (imperfect at best[1]) is influenced by our experiences and expectations, and different people view the world through different lenses (Heuer, 1999). This filtering process creates mindsets. Quick to form, but resistant to change, mindsets are neither good nor bad. They serve a purpose but, under certain conditions, can become problematic. Because perception is based on both awareness and understanding, we often perceive what we expect to perceive. Reaching premature conclusions is therefore dangerous. Communication is doubly subjective as it involves two people. What the speaker means, what he or she says, what the listener hears, and how he or she interprets the communication may not all be the same. Words such as "tall," "young," "likely," and "dangerous" are subjective, with various meanings depending on the situation and experiences of the individual.

What we remember depends on what we believe (Begley, 2005). Our brains do not objectively record data, and our memories are subjective

---

[1] See O'Regan and Noë (2000) for interesting examples of change blindness in visual perception.

interpretations that are seldom reinterpreted, even when circumstances change. New information becomes assimilated with old information, and the old information has more influence on the new information than vice versa. We tend to remember positives (those facts consistent with our theories) and forget negatives (those facts inconsistent with our theories). More weight is placed on evidence that supports our hypothesis than on evidence that weakens it (Heuer, 1999; Schacter, 2001). This is called belief perseverance. Remaining impartial and open minded allows investigators to more accurately assess information.

Our working memory is very limited. Research has shown that we can only hold five to nine items in our conscious memory at one time (Miller, 1956; Schacter, 2001). Data stored in long-term memory can also be difficult to recall. For example, information that is "irrelevant" to our investigative theory may be easily forgotten through lack of use, particularly in a complex case. Even if the information later becomes important, it may remain lost because we failed to develop the neural pathways necessary for retrieval.[2]

Intuition

Most of our cognitive functioning occurs outside of conscious awareness (Heuer, 1999). This is true for perception, information processing, memory, and some methods of decision making. According to Nobel Prize–winning psychologist Daniel Kahneman (2003), humans employ two types of decision-making processes: the intuitive and the rational. Intuition falls between the automatic operations of perception and the deliberate operations of reasoning. Intuition is often misunderstood. We are familiar with the phrases "gut instinct" and "women's intuition," neither of which are good descriptors. "Gut instinct" is, in fact, intuition, not instinct, and it is a mental process, not a digestive one. Moreover, both genders use intuition, although they may acknowledge or respond to it differently. Intuition is not a paranormal ability or a form of extrasensory perception; while it operates at a below-consciousness level, intuition is still based on normal sensory input (Myers, 2002).

Argentinean race car driver Juan Fangio had an interesting intuitive experience during the 1950 Monaco Grand Prix (Ludvigsen, 1999). Fangio braked on the second lap of the race as he exited the long tunnel that is part of the Monte Carlo circuit. Normally, drivers maintain their 170-mile-per-hour speed to maximize the benefits of the long straightaway on the course following the tunnel. Unknown to Fangio, there was a bad accident out of sight around the next corner. Because he had slowed, Fangio, unlike over half

---

[2] Lateral thinking ("thinking outside the box") is one way to help prevent the mental "rust" that can limit our mental abilities.

of the other drivers, avoided crashing into the pile of wrecked cars. He went on to win the race for Alfa Romeo.

Fangio wondered why he had braked, and after much thought figured out what had happened. The crowd in the nearby stands invariably watched the race cars roar out of the tunnel, alerted by the echoing thunder of their engines. On this particular lap, however, they were looking in the other direction, watching the accident. Fangio had fleetingly observed a change in the color of the area of the stands in his peripheral vision. What was normally light, because of the faces of the crowd turned toward the tunnel, was now dark, from the hair at the back of people's heads as they looked the other way. Fangio, concentrating on his driving, only noticed this change at a below-conscious level. At the high speeds of Grand Prix racing, change meant risk, and Fangio automatically slowed down. Intuition helped him avoid the accident and win the race.

Intuition is automatic and effortless, fast and powerful (Kahneman, 2003). It is learned slowly. Because of its implicit nature, intuition is difficult to control or modify. It can be influenced by emotion and is often error prone. Typically, intuition involves the use of heuristics (cognitive shortcuts). Reasoning, by contrast, is slow and effortful, vulnerable to interference, and easily disrupted. However, it is flexible and controllable. Reasoning can overrule intuition.

Different situations require different types of judgment (Stewart, 2002). When the data are unreliable and incomplete, or we need to make decisions quickly under chaotic and uncertain conditions, intuitive decision making is preferable. Such situations occur in street policing or on the military battlefield. However, we certainly do not intuitively fill out our income tax returns. Therefore, when we have reliable and adequate data, and time for proper analysis, reasoning produces the best results. Complex and rule-bound tasks, such as major crime investigations or courtroom prosecutions, require careful analysis and sound logic.

Heuristics and Biases

The test of a first-rate intelligence is the ability to hold two opposed ideas in the mind at the same time, and still retain the ability to function.

F. Scott Fitzgerald (*The Crack-Up*, **1936**)

Clear and rational thinking does not come easily. We sometimes exhibit limited rationality in the face of life's complexities because our brains are not wired to deal effectively with uncertainty. We therefore employ heuristics— rules of thumb that substitute simple questions for more complex ones—to make judgments under such conditions (see Kahneman, Slovic, & Tversky,

1982). Heuristics typically operate at an intuitive level. Although these mental shortcuts work well most of the time, under certain conditions they can lead to cognitive biases.[3] Cognitive biases are mental errors caused by this simplified information processing technique. They are independent of cultural, organizational, political, and self-interest biases (Heuer, 1999). Biases can result in distorted judgments and faulty analyses. Like optical illusions, cognitive biases are consistent and predictable. To add to the problem, research shows a poor correlation between confidence and accuracy. Past a certain point, for example, increased information leads to greater confidence in our analyses, but not necessarily greater accuracy.

Figure 2.1 shows a well-known example of how our perceptual and cognitive shortcuts can lead to errors. (If you are unfamiliar with this illustration, you are encouraged to read aloud the words within the triangle.) This figure is used during my "Criminal Investigative Failures" presentation.

Figure 2.1 Heuristics and errors.

[3] A particular heuristic does not actually have to be right most of the time; as long as it promotes survival, it will be passed on through natural selection (Risinger & Loop, 2002). Although a street police officer's intuition may sometimes be wrong, it is still unwise to ignore (Pinizzotto, Davis, & Miller, 2000, 2004).

Almost invariably when I ask a person in the audience to read it, the person will answer: "Paris in the spring." Eventually, after repeated requests, someone will notice that it actually says: "Paris in the the spring." The phrase is familiar, so once we see the key parts we fill in the blanks. What we do not do is read each letter and word; most of the time, such a process would be slow and inefficient. However, this speed and efficiency come at the cost of accuracy, as errors are more likely to be missed. This is one of the reasons why it is so hard to proofread our own writing. We already know what the words say so we tend to skip over things and consequently often fail to find our typos. Interestingly, when I used this figure during a presentation to a group of English-speaking Italian police officers in Rome, they noticed the mistake right away. The phrase was unfamiliar to them, so they read the slide carefully.

Psychologists have identified many heuristics and biases, some of which are particularly problematic for criminal investigators. The anchoring heuristic refers to the strong influence of the starting point or first approximation on the final estimate.[4] The prevailing situation and the information available at the time determine our first approximation. If we have limited or incorrect information, our starting point will be skewed, jeopardizing the path to a correct conclusion. Unfortunately, there have been many murder cases that first appeared to be something other than what they were. The initial judgment in the JonBenét Ramsey case that the killer was not a family member, despite the statistical reality in child murder cases (see Boudreaux, Lord, & Dutra, 1999; Boudreaux, Lord, & Etter, 2000; Boudreaux, Lord, & Jarvis, 2001; Lord, Boudreaux, Jarvis, Waldvogel, & Weeks, 2002), had serious consequences for the progress and resolution of the investigation.

Tunnel vision (or incrementalism) results when there is a narrow focus on a limited range of alternatives:

> Tunnel vision is insidious. ... It results in the [police] officer becoming so focussed upon an individual or incident that no other person or incident regis-

---

[4] Small deviations in our starting position can be magnified into large deviations over time. In Edgar Allan Poe's *The Gold-Bug*, a code written on a scrap of parchment contains directions to a pirate chest buried on Sullivan's Island: "A good glass in the bishop's hostel in the devil's seat—forty-one degrees and thirteen minutes—northeast and by north—main branch seventh limb east side—shoot from the left eye of the death's-head—a bee-line from the tree through the shot fifty feet out" (Poe, 1975, pp. 66–67). To find the treasure, one must shoot a bullet through the left eye of a skull nailed to a high tulip-tree limb, measure 50 feet out along a line from the tree trunk through the point where the shot hit, and then dig. The story narrator and his colleagues initially dig in the wrong place because they drop a gold beetle (substituted for the bullet) through the skull's *right* eye (left, from a face-on perspective); this error causes them to miss the chest of gold coins and jewels by several yards. The distance between the left and right eye sockets is less than three inches, but this short offset is magnified more than tenfold when measured out 50 feet.

ters in the officer's thoughts. Thus, tunnel vision can result in the elimination of other suspects who should be investigated. Equally, events that could lead to other suspects are eliminated from the officer's thinking. (Cory, 2001, p. 37)

Satisficing is the selection of the first identified alternative that appears good enough. These two heuristics might work well for simple errands, such as buying a hammer, but they are ill suited to the task of solving complex, dynamic investigations. Arresting the first likely suspect, then closing the investigation off to alternative theories, is a recipe for disaster; "tunnel vision has been identified as a leading cause of wrongful convictions" (FPT Heads of Prosecutions Committee Working Group, 2004, s. 4).

Rachel Nickell, an attractive 23-year-old mother, was murdered on Wimbledon Common in July 1992 (Britton, 1997). Her throat had been cut and she had been stabbed 49 times. The only witness to the attack was her two-year-old son. In September, New Scotland Yard detectives received a tip regarding an odd man named Colin Stagg. For the next year, he became their investigative focus, and in August 1993, after a covert operation involving a policewoman who "befriended" Stagg to obtain further incriminating information, he was finally arrested.

The case went to trial in September 1994. The judge quickly threw out most of the prosecution's evidence (of which there was not much to start). He called the covert operation misconceived, commenting, "I would be the first to acknowledge the very great pressures on the police in their pursuit of this grave inquiry, but I am afraid this behavior betrays not merely an excessive zeal, but a substantial attempt to incriminate a suspect by positive and deceptive conduct of the grossest kind" (Britton, 1997, p. 366). The Crown withdrew the charges and Stagg was released.

One New Scotland Yard detective later commented: "Maybe the team got an idée fixe. Maybe they got stuck thinking it had to be Stagg. No one dared to challenge that thinking until it got to the judge. But it's a terrible mess" (Sweeney, 1994, p. 21). Several years later, enhanced DNA from Nickell's clothing pointed toward Robert Napper, a psychopath now detained indefinitely in Broadmoor's secure hospital for murder and rape (Cowan, 2004).

Availability refers to the ease by which previous examples come to mind (Tversky & Kahneman, 1973). However, we make judgments based only on what we remember, not on the totality of our experience. Recent and vivid events are easy to recall, while disagreeable events are difficult to recall. We use the availability heuristic for determining how common or likely something is. Limited experience can therefore result in incorrect estimates of likelihood. The availability heuristic is particularly problematic in investigations of rare crimes, such as child sex homicides.

The presentation of information influences its interpretation. This is called framing (Tversky & Kahneman, 1981), and it implies that information is always understood within a context. An artificial or inappropriate context, however, can distort our understanding of information. Dramatic examples of framing can be seen in the courtroom, where opposing legal counsel present and argue variant positions on the particular events in dispute.

People often estimate the likelihood of an event by recalling a comparable event and then assuming that the likelihoods of the two events are similar. This representativeness heuristic is partly prompted by our urge to categorize things. Similarity in one aspect, however, does not imply similarity in other aspects. For many years, Ted Bundy and his crimes drove the public's image of the typical serial killer case—sexual murders of women committed by a white male, intelligent and mobile. But not all serial murders are sex driven, not all victims are female, many serial murderers are nonwhite or below average in intelligence, and most commit their crimes within their home metropolitan area (Rossmo, 2000).

From 1994 to 2005, northeastern Italy suffered the attacks of a criminal dubbed the Italian Unabomber. Like his American namesake, Ted Kaczynski, he was a serial bomber who randomly attacked strangers over a period of years. But there the similarities end. The Italian Unabomber targeted public places with devices powerful enough to injure but not kill. He appeared to be motivated by generalized social revenge. By comparison, Kaczynski typically mailed his devices, which were designed to kill. He espoused a political/delusional motivation. The Italian media have attempted to understand the motivations and methods of their local bomber by reference to Kaczynski. These misguided efforts are an example of the representativeness heuristic.

Cause and Effect Biases

Our perceptions of cause and effect are susceptible to many mental biases. We err when we fail to differentiate internal (psychological) from external (situational) causes of behavior. For example, the level of force used by a rapist may be contingent on the degree to which a victim resists. If internal and external attributions are confused, an investigator might not connect related crimes to the responsible offender because of apparent differences in the criminal's modus operandi. Also, although we have a tendency to try to explain things, life is full of random events. Random events, by definition, have no explainable cause.

The identity fallacy is our desire to believe that big events must have big causes. Conspiracy theories are often rooted in this belief. Many have found it difficult to accept that a loner like Lee Harvey Oswald, using a $21.45 Mannlicher-Carcano rifle ($12.78 for the rifle, plus the cost of the scope), could assassinate John F. Kennedy, the president of the most powerful nation in the world. Instead, it is more psychologically comfortable to believe in complicated conspiracy theories involving organized crime, the CIA, Cubans, and/or the KGB (for a proper debunking, see Bugliosi, 2007).

Illusory correlations can be misleading on several levels. Events may appear to be correlated when, in fact, they are not. And even if they are connected, correlation does not equal causation. The relation may be spurious or caused by an intervening event. If B appears to cause C, but in reality A is causing both B and C, then the correlation between B and C is spurious. If A appears to cause C, but in reality A causes B, and B causes C, then there is an intervening event. For instance, in a series of burglary rapes on the South Side of Lafayette, Louisiana, police theorized the offender stalked his victims from a local superstore where the women victims had all shopped at one time or another. However, this superstore, the only one in the city, was so big that most people living on Lafayette's South Side likely went there at one time or another. Living on the South Side therefore influenced both shopping and victimization patterns, and there was no direct connection between the two. The relation was strictly spurious. As it turned out, the offender found his victims by prowling residential neighborhoods at nighttime and peeping through windows, looking for women living alone (Rossmo, 2000).

Biases in Evaluation of Evidence

Problems with physical evidence usually result from misinterpretation, and not from the actual analysis. A police shooting that occurred in Alexandria, Egypt, after the First World War (Smith, 1959) provides an intriguing example that also illustrates another issue in evidence evaluation—the risk of ignoring context. A police officer was pursuing a robber who was running, crouched down along a wall. When the robber refused to halt, the police officer shot him (this was then permissible under an existing fleeing felon law). The criminal escaped, only to be found later in a plantation, dead of bullet wounds. The police officer stated he fired only once. During the postmortem examination, however, the local doctor discovered two bullet wounds in the decedent's body. One entered the back and exited the abdomen, consistent with the police officer's story. The other one entered the front of the left thigh, with the bullet still lodged in the leg muscle. The doctor concluded: "'He was shot twice. ... First from the front at rather long range, secondly in the back—probably after he had fallen on his face'" (Smith, 1959, p. 62). Based on the doctor's findings, the police officer was arrested and charged with murder.

Egypt was a British protectorate at this time, and Sir Sydney Smith, the famous professor of forensic medicine, was asked to look at the case. When he examined the shooting victim's clothing, which consisted of a shirt and an outer garment called a galabieh, he expected to find three bullet holes in the latter. Instead, he found only one, in the back. However, there were several holes in the shirt. Smith realized what probably happened. The police officer had told the truth—the single shot had entered the robber's back, penetrated his torso, and exited his abdomen, before finally entering his front thigh. This thigh was lifted high while the robber was bent over running. Smith tested his theory by reconstructing the shooting using a dummy and the clothing. He later confirmed it by exhuming the body of the dead man. This is a classic case of an interpretation error involving physical evidence. Fortunately for the police officer, Smith rectified the local doctor's mistake by examining the robber's clothing and considering context—the influence of body position and posture.

Confirmation bias (also called verification bias) is a type of selective thinking in which an individual is more likely to notice or search for evidence that confirms his or her theory, while ignoring or refusing to search for contradicting evidence (Stelfox & Pease, 2005). Confirming evidence is given more weight, while contradicting evidence is given less weight. Efforts to only verify and not falsify a hypothesis are often inefficient, as a mass of evidence against a suspect can be outweighed by a single item of refuting data.[5] The components of confirmation bias include failure to seek evidence (e.g., a suspect's alibi) that would disprove the theory, not utilizing such evidence if found, refusing to consider alternative hypotheses, and failure to evaluate evidence diagnosticity. Sometimes data that appear to support one theory (or suspect) are actually of little diagnostic value because they also equally support other theories (or suspects).

Guy Paul Morin was accused of the 1984 murder of nine-year-old Christine Jessop, his next-door neighbor in Queensville, Ontario (Makin, 1992). During the trial, the prosecutor suggested Morin's failure to attend Jessop's funeral was evidence of consciousness of guilt. Defense counsel argued that Morin's attendance at the funeral could just as easily been adduced as indicative of guilt, because detectives typically try to identify those who attend a murder victim's funeral in the hope that one of them is the killer (Kaufman, 1998). And this is exactly what happened in the Jessop investigation, where police expended considerable effort in this regard at her funeral. Morin was convicted, but later exonerated through DNA testing of semen stains on Jessop's underwear. Ontario's lieutenant governor in Council ordered a public inquiry, the final report of which found "Mr. Morin's failure to attend the funeral or funeral home was worthless evidence and ought not to have been admitted. ... The leading of this evidence demonstrated that the prosecution sought to squeeze every drop out of the information available to them, to support their case" (Kaufman, "Executive Summary," 1998, p. 34). In other words, the evidence had no diagnosticity.

---

[5] As has been seen many times now with exclusionary DNA evidence in cases involving eyewitness identification and strong circumstantial evidence (see Huff, Rattner, & Sagarin, 1996; Scheck, Neufeld, & Dwyer, 2000).

Studies have shown that we are influenced more by vivid information than abstract data (Heuer, 1999). Personal accounts carry more weight than statistical information, although the latter are actually compilations of many personal accounts. It is not unusual for the vividness of an eyewitness's description to overwhelm other perspectives. For instance, we have seen authorities pursue major investigations based on graphic allegations from "victims" of organized satanic cults. Another example is the "eyewitness" at a Fairfax, Virginia, Home Depot who lied about seeing the DC Snipers. Much weight was put on his account, although an objective evaluation of what he could see over the distance involved strongly suggested caution (see Horwitz & Ruane, 2003; Karem & Napolitano, 2003; Moose & Fleming, 2003; Murphy & Wexler, 2004).

Investigators often fail to account for the absence of evidence, something that can be quite important under certain circumstances. A well-known Sherlock Holmes quotation illustrates this nicely. In *Silver Blaze*, a case involving the theft of a famous race horse, Inspector Gregory asks the fictional detective:

> Is there any point to which you would wish to draw my attention?
> Holmes: To the curious incident of the dog in the night-time.
> Gregory: The dog did nothing in the night-time.
> Holmes: That was the curious incident.

What Holmes meant by this observation was that the dog would have barked at a stranger, and because he did not, the thief was likely a member of the household.

Absence of evidence played an important role in the investigation of the murder of a young woman. An investigator, reviewing photographs of the crime scene in the victim's apartment, carefully examined a picture of her bedroom dresser with a row of neatly lined perfume bottles along the back. There was a space between two bottles. When detectives asked the victim's roommate what was normally in that spot, she told them that a perfume bottle given to the victim by her ex-boyfriend was usually kept there. This pointed investigators to the victim's former boyfriend, who had killed her and taken back his gift because she had jilted him.

As we saw in the discussion on memory, impressions remain in our minds even after the initial evidence they were based on is discounted (Heuer, 1999). This has been termed the "curse of knowledge." The genie cannot be put back into the bottle. A dramatic example is that of David Milgaard, convicted as a teenager of the 1969 sexual murder of 19-year-old nursing assistant Gail Miller in Saskatoon, Saskatchewan, Canada (see Chapter 9). He spent 23 years in prison and was denied parole because of his refusal to admit guilt and "say he was sorry." DNA testing in the

United Kingdom subsequently determined the DNA from a semen stain on the victim's clothing did not match Milgaard, but did match Larry Fisher. Fisher was a convicted serial rapist who caught the same bus at the same stop as Gail Miller did every morning. Milgaard was exonerated, and eventually received $10 million from the Saskatchewan government. Fisher was convicted of first-degree murder and sentenced to life in prison. He has since lost all his appeals. However, there are still people today who cannot accept Milgaard's innocence, "explaining" the DNA by the contrived theory that Fisher and Milgaard knew each other and committed the crime together—despite no evidence to support this idea, and the fact that Fisher and Milgaard lived in different cities.

Such convoluted theories are a classic violation of Occam's razor. Also known as the "Principle of Parsimony," Occam's razor states that when more than one explanation for an event is possible, we should chose the simplest (i.e., the one with the fewest assumptions). In other words, it is best not to make things more complicated than necessary. Occam's razor is an important guiding principle in science. We would be wise to adopt it for criminal investigations. Complex theories make for interesting fiction, but have limited value in the real world.

References

Begley, S. (2005, February 4). People believe a 'fact' that fits their views even if it's clearly false. *Science Journal*, p. B1.

Boudreaux, M. C., Lord, W. D., & Dutra, R. L. (1999). Child abduction: Aged-based analyses of offender, victim, and offense characteristics in 550 cases of alleged child disappearance. *Journal of Forensic Sciences, 44*, 539–553.

Boudreaux, M. C., Lord, W. D., & Etter, S. E. (2000). Child abduction: An overview of current and historical perspectives. *Child Maltreatment, 5*, 63–71.

Boudreaux, M. C., Lord, W. D., & Jarvis, J. P. (2001). Behavioral perspectives on child homicide: The role of access, vulnerability, and routine activities theory. *Trauma, Violence, and Abuse, 2*, 56–78.

Britton, P. (1997). *The jigsaw man*. London: Bantam Press.

Bugliosi, V. (2007). *Reclaiming history: The assassination of President John F. Kennedy*. New York: W. W. Norton.

Cory, P. de C. (2001). *The inquiry regarding Thomas Sophonow*. Winnipeg: Queen's Printer.

Cowan, R. (2004, November 10). DNA points to sex killer in 1992 murder. *The Guardian*, Retrieved July 12, 2008, from http://www.guardian.co.uk/uk/2004/nov/10/ukcrime.rosiecowan.

FPT Heads of Prosecutions Committee Working Group. (2004). *Report on the prevention of miscarriages of justice*. Ottawa: Department of Justice.

Heuer, R. J., Jr. (1999). *Psychology of intelligence analysis*. Washington, DC: Center for the Study of Intelligence, Central Intelligence Agency.

Horwitz, S., & Ruane, M. E. (2003). *Sniper: Inside the hunt for the killers who terrorized the nation.* New York: Random House.

Huff, C. R., Rattner, A., & Sagarin, E. (1996). *Convicted but innocent: Wrongful conviction and public policy.* Thousand Oaks, CA: Sage.

Kahneman, D. (2003). A perspective on judgment and choice: Mapping bounded rationality. *American Psychologist, 58,* 697–720.

Kahneman, D., Slovic, P., & Tversky, A. (Eds.). (1982). *Judgment under uncertainty: Heuristics and biases.* Cambridge: Cambridge University Press.

Karem, B. J., & Napolitano, C. (2003, March). In a room with madness. *Playboy,* pp. 70–74, 84, 146–152.

Kaufman, F. (1998). *The commission on proceedings involving Guy Paul Morin: Report.* Toronto: Ontario Ministry of the Attorney General.

Lord, W. D., Boudreaux, M. C., Jarvis, J. P., Waldvogel, J., & Weeks, H. (2002). Comparative patterns in life course victimization: Competition, social rivalry, and predatory tactics in child homicide in the United States. *Homicide Studies, 6,* 325–347.

Ludvigsen, K. (1999). *Juan Manuel Fangio: Motor racing's grand master.* Sparkford, Somerset, UK: Haynes Publishing.

Makin, K. (1992). *Redrum the innocent.* Toronto: Viking.

Miller, G. A. (1956). The magical number seven, plus or minus two: Some limits on our capacity for processing information. *Psychological Review, 63,* 81–97.

Moose, C., & Fleming, C. (2003). *Three weeks in October: The manhunt for the serial sniper.* Dutton: New York.

Murphy, G. R., & Wexler, C. (2004). *Managing a multijurisdictional case: Identifying the lessons learned from the sniper investigation.* Washington, DC: Police Executive Research Forum.

Myers, D. (2002). *Intuition: Its powers and perils.* New Haven, CT: Yale University Press.

O'Regan, J. K., & Noë, A. (2000, June). *Experience is not something we feel but something we do: A principled way of explaining sensory phenomenology, with change blindness and other empirical consequences.* Paper presented at the meeting of the Association for the Scientific Study of Consciousness, Brussels, Belgium. Also retrieved December 30, 2001, from http://nivea.psycho.univ-paris5.fr/ASSChtml/Pacherie4.html.

Pinizzotto, A. J., Davis, E. F., & Miller, C. E., III. (2000). Officers' perceptual shorthand: What messages are offenders sending to law enforcement officers? *FBI Law Enforcement Bulletin, 69*(7), 1–6.

Pinizzotto, A. J., Davis, E. F., & Miller, C. E. III. (2004). Intuitive policing: Emotional/rational decision making in law enforcement. *FBI Law Enforcement Bulletin, 73*(2), 1–6.

Poe, E. A. (1975). *The complete tales and poems of Edgar Allan Poe.* New York: Vintage Books.

Risinger, D. M., & Loop, J. L. (2002). Three card monte, Monty Hall, *modus operandi* and "offender profiling": Some lessons of modern cognitive science for the law of evidence. *Cardozo Law Review, 24,* 193–285.

Rossmo, D. K. (2000). *Geographic profiling.* Boca Raton, FL: CRC Press.

Schacter, D. L. (2001). *The seven sins of memory: How the mind forgets and remembers.* Boston: Houghton Mifflin.

Scheck, B., Neufeld, P., & Dwyer, J. (2000). *Actual innocence: Five days to execution and other dispatches from the wrongly convicted.* New York: Doubleday.

Smith, S. (1959). *Mostly murder.* New York: Dorset Press.

Stelfox, P., & Pease, K. (2005). Cognition and detection: Reluctant bedfellows? In M. J. Smith & N. Tilley (Eds.), *Crime science: New approaches to preventing and detecting crime* (pp. 191–207). Cullompton, Devon: Willan Publishing.

Stewart, T. A. (2002, November). How to think with your gut. *Business 2.0.* pp. 1–6.

Sweeney, J. (1994, September 18). Why the police hunters took aim at Stagg. *The Observer*, p. 21.

Tversky, A., & Kahneman, D. (1973). Availability: A heuristic for judging frequency and probability. *Cognitive Psychology, 5*, 207–232.

Tversky, A., & Kahneman, D. (1981). The framing of decisions and the psychology of choice. *Science, 211*, 453–458.

Organizational Traps: Groupthink, Rumor, and Ego

3

D. KIM ROSSMO

A criminal investigator operates within an organizational structure that has its own unique dynamics. The powerful police subculture has long been recognized as possessing both positive and negative characteristics. In this chapter, some of the dynamics relevant to major crime investigations are examined, and a particularly dramatic case example is discussed.

Inertia, Momentum, and Roller Coasters

Law enforcement agencies are conservative by nature. They often suffer from bureaucratic inertia—a lethargy or unwillingness to change, evolve, or act. The reluctance of many agencies to adopt the more accurate sequential lineup over the established simultaneous lineup procedure is one illustration of this inertia (*Eyewitness evidence*, 2003). Most police departments cope with many competing demands and have few, if any, spare resources. Change is disruptive, and it requires effort, energy, time, and money. This inertia can also slow a police agency's response to a new crime problem. The temptation exists to adopt an "out of sight, out of mind" approach, particularly for crimes against marginalized victims. Moreover, when a response finally does occur, it is often insufficient, a case of "too little, too late."

The Green River Killer investigation in Washington State is a good example of such foot dragging (Smith & Guillen, 1991). The official response to a series of prostitute murders was slow, and by the time a functional task force was formed, the killer had stopped. Police admitted they had no idea what they were getting into when they began the investigation. Deputy Chief Frank Adamson, King County Police, a member of the Green River Task Force, thought the investigation would be wrapped up in six months (it would actually take over 20 years). "It was a much larger task than I had ever envisioned. ... I think what we really learned was that the task of resolving a very complex serial murder can be a horrendous task" (Griffiths, 1993).

Organizational momentum, the inability to change direction in the midst of a major investigation, is the converse problem. It is difficult for a large investigative effort to redirect and shift its focus from an established theory of a crime or a particular suspect. It is particularly hard when the organization has to admit publicly that the original direction was wrong. A media release of a suspect person's name or description or vehicle information often creates significant organizational momentum. A detective in the Washington, D.C., Sniper case wondered about the response to the mistaken witness report of a suspect white van:

> It begs the question, did we publish composite pictures because witnesses saw the white van, or did we see the white van because we published the pictures? We should've paid more attention to the description of the Caprice and given it as much creditability as the van, but we didn't. In hindsight, it was a mistake made in the emotion of the moment. But with all that we had set in place, we should've done better. (Karem & Napolitano, 2003, p. 146)

Police agencies must strike a balance between stability and responsiveness. Changing gears unnecessarily during an investigation can be costly and demoralizing, but staying the course in light of compelling evidence pointing in a new direction can be catastrophic.

Detectives working high-pressure murder cases often talk about investigative roller coasters, the ups and downs resulting from the pursuit of hot suspects. A problem can occur when suspect Jones comes to the attention of the task force while it is busy pursuing hot suspect Smith. Investigators typically see the viability of a new suspect relative to existing suspects, so if Smith is a prime suspect, then Jones will be considered secondary. When Smith is cleared, what happens to Jones? As was seen in the previous chapter's discussion on cognitive biases, it is unlikely he will be reassessed. At best, Jones remains a secondary suspect; at worst, he will be overlooked altogether. Investigative roller coasters can result in important leads falling between the cracks. These blind spots are often picked up on in cold case murder investigations. Detectives reviewing old files sometimes find the killer figuratively jumping off the pages at them. Initially ignored because they did not fit the dominant theory at the time, these suspects are obvious to the fresh eyes of new observers. Cold case detectives are not subject to the psychological and organizational pressures that may have affected the original investigators (see Walton, 2006).

Red Herrings and Rumors

Red herrings—tips that misdirect an investigation—can be particularly dangerous in high-profile major crime cases. The constant media attention brings forth a flood of public information, some of it relevant, most of it not. During the three weeks of the D.C. Sniper case, for example, 100,000 calls were received by the Joint Operations Center (JOC), and more than 500 investigators pursued 16,000 leads (Karem & Napolitano, 2003). In these situations, the police run the risk of landing a red herring. Witness misinformation, compounded by organizational reluctance to accept that the witness may be wrong, has sent several high-profile investigations down the wrong path (see Campbell, 1996).

Suspect vehicle sightings appear to be particularly problematic. Infamous examples include:

- The car that "looked like a Camaro" observed leaving one of the abduction sites in the "Ken and Barbie" murders in St. Catharines, Ontario (the killers, Paul Bernardo and Karla Homolka, were actually in a Nissan)
- A suspicious white van in the child murder of Mindy Tran in Kelowna, British Columbia (the offender was on foot)
- The white male driving a pick-up truck in the Baton Rouge serial murder case (the killer, Derrick Todd Lee, was black)
- The white box truck/van seen so often during the DC Sniper shootings (the shooters, John Allen Muhammad and John Lee Malvo, drove a blue Chevrolet Caprice sedan).

Sometimes a red herring is the result of mischief or greed. During the Yorkshire Ripper inquiry in England, police investigators received three letters and a cassette tape from a person claiming to be the killer (Doney, 1990). Experts analyzed the voice on the tape and concluded the speaker spoke with a Geordie accent, an indication he was likely from the Sunderland area where the letters had been postmarked. The tape was not from the killer, however, and the police's focus on Sunderland—75 miles north of Bradford, where the real offender, Peter Sutcliffe, lived—hurt the investigation. Once latched onto, red herrings can be very hard to shake. Yet they have been responsible for the waste of millions of dollars of police resources, higher victim counts, and unsolved crimes.

Anyone who has played the game "Telephone" as a child is familiar with how information undergoes distortion as it passes from one source to another. Studies of rumor propagation show that as a rumor spreads, its dramatic components are exaggerated, while its qualifiers diminish or disappear altogether (Shibutani, 1966). In major crime investigations, particularly those involving large numbers of personnel and extending over long periods of time, internal rumors can pose a significant problem. A solidified rumor is gossip that has hardened into "fact" and is taken as such by the investigative team. Those detectives who join an investigation that has been in progress for some time, and therefore receive most of their information secondhand, are most vulnerable.

Investigators must outline their assumptions. If a particular assumption later turns out to be invalid, then everything following from it must be rethought.[1] As the human mind does not automatically reevaluate information, specific organizational procedures are required. Documenting assumptions facilitates this process and protects investigations from "creeping credibility," which occurs when an idea or theory gains credence, not from supporting evidence, but from the passing of time. A possibility hardens into a probability and then crystallizes into "certain fact."

President John F. Kennedy's assassination has provided fertile ground for conspiracy theorists, many of whom have fallen victim to the traps discussed here.[2] They have questioned how Warren Commission Exhibit 399—the "Magic Bullet"—could have exited Kennedy's throat and entered the right shoulder of Texas Governor John Connally, Jr., seated in front of the President in the motorcade limousine. The assumption made here (as shown in Figure 3.1 and depicted in diagrams of the bullet's trajectory; see Livingstone & Groden, 1998) is that Connally was positioned directly in front of Kennedy. In reality, the limousine had been specially altered and had three rows of seats, with two Secret Service agents in the front, the Connallys in the middle, and the Kennedys in the rear. Kennedy's seat was positioned significantly higher and outboard of Connally's (McAdams, 2004). Furthermore, Connally was turned to the right as he waved to the crowd. The bullet also deflected when it traveled through his chest. Consequently, the alignment of the torsos of the two men is not inconsistent with the "Single Bullet Theory" (see Figure 3.2). The trap here is the assumption that the seating in the motorcade limousine had the same arrangement as that found in a normal vehicle.

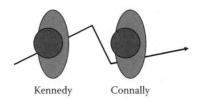

Kennedy   Connally

Figure 3.1 Kennedy assassination "single bullet" trajectory (conspiracy version).

Investigation teams must understand their knowledge base. A question worth asking is how do we know what we think we know? Where is the police report, laboratory analysis, witness statement, or informant tip that is

---

[1] Halberstam (1969) discusses how unquestioned assumptions on the nature of Communism and the viability of the domino theory led the United States deeper into the quagmire of the Vietnam conflict: "These assumptions became realities, became the given" (p. 355).

[2] See Vincent Bugliosi's (2007) thorough and careful analysis of the Kennedy assassination in which he concludes that Lee Harvey Oswald, acting alone, shot the president.

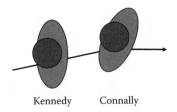

Kennedy   Connally

Figure 3.2 Kennedy assassination single bullet trajectory (actual path).

the basis for the "fact" in question? Validity can be assessed only if the data source is known. If the source cannot be determined, then the information may be a solidified rumor or the product of creeping credibility.

Some investigations have cataloged case information using the following outline:

1. What we know (facts).
2. What we think we know (theories or conjectures).
3. What we would like to know (key issues requiring additional data).

Categorizing and documenting the investigation's knowledge base in this manner facilitates effective information sharing, allowing everyone (both present and future) to work from the same foundation.

Ego and Fatigue

Ego, both personal and organizational, can prevent an investigation from adjusting to new information or seeking alternative avenues of exploration. A homicide sergeant in a large metropolitan area once told me his detectives were very good; they would decide within five minutes of arriving at a crime scene who had committed the murder and would be correct 95% of the time. Although very impressive, one wonders what happens to the remaining 5%. For a jurisdiction their size, this initial error rate equates to more than one misinterpretation every month. A detective must have the flexibility to admit his or her original theory was incorrect and avoid falling into the ego trap inherent in usually being right. Stubbornness, which often coincides with ego, is equally problematic.

Supervisory Special Agent John Douglas of the FBI's Behavioral Science Unit prepared a psychological profile for the sexual killer of nine-year-old Christine Jessop from Queensville, Ontario (Makin, 1992). When police later arrested Guy Paul Morin, who closely matched the profile, Douglas touted the case as a success story (although it has been suggested the profile was "custom fitted" to Morin who was a known suspect). DNA testing of semen stains on

Jessop's underwear later exonerated Morin. In one of his autobiographies, Douglas offered the following explanation: "The DNA evidence might just be a large red herring in this case, as occasionally happens. Whatever the explanation in the Jessop case, I'm afraid this might be one of those tragic instances in which truth and justice will always be elusive" (Douglas & Olshaker, 1995, p. 84). This falls short of convincing. A DNA test is much more likely to be correct than a psychological profile (by a factor of several million). The wisdom in Occam's razor tells us to adopt the simplest explanation—which, in this case, is that the profile was off.

Fatigue, overwork, and stress, all endemic in high-profile crime investigations, can create problems for investigative personnel. Recent research has shown that insightfulness can be significantly improved by sleep (Wagner, Gais, Haider, Verleger, & Born, 2004). Tiredness can dull even the sharpest minds. Critical assessment abilities drop in overworked and fatigued individuals, who start to engage in what has been termed "automatic believing." Dr. James Watson, Nobel Laureate in Medicine and codiscoverer of DNA's molecular structure, commented on the importance of unstructured time in thinking: "It's necessary to be slightly underemployed if you are to do something significant."[3]

Groupthink

Groupthink is the reluctance to think critically and challenge the dominant theory (no one wants to tell the emperor he has no clothes). It occurs in highly cohesive groups under pressure to make important decisions. Yale research psychologist Irving Janis (1982) first suggested the idea of groupthink after the disastrous Bay of Pigs invasion in Cuba. He wondered how some of the most intelligent and talented advisors of the Kennedy Administration could let such a fiasco happen.

The main symptoms of groupthink include:

1. Power overestimation
   - Belief in the group's invulnerability, resulting in unwarranted optimism and risk taking
   - Ignoring the ethical consequences of decisions because of a belief in the morality of the group's purpose
2. Close-mindedness
   - Group rationalizations and the discrediting of warning signs
   - Negative stereotyping of the group's opponents (e.g., evil, stupid, etc.)

---

[3] Retrieved July 10, 2008, from http://creativequotations.com/one/551.htm.

3. Uniformity pressures
- Conformity pressures (those who disagree with the dominant views or decisions are seen as disloyal)
- Self-censorship (the withholding of dissenting views and counter-arguments)
- Shared illusion of unanimity (silence is perceived as consent, and there is an incorrect belief that everyone agrees with the group's decision)
- Self-appointed mindguards (individuals who elect to shield the group from dissenting information).

Groupthink has several negative outcomes. Groups selectively gather information and fail to seek expert opinions (see FPT Heads of Prosecutions Committee Working Group, 2004). They neglect to assess critically their ideas and examine few alternatives, if any. Contingency plans are not developed. For these reasons, groupthink can be a disaster in a major crime investigation.

The Pig Farm

Groupthink and tunnel vision emerged in the police response to what was originally called the Downtown Eastside Missing Women case before it became known as the Pig Farm Serial Murders. In 1998, community workers from the Downtown Eastside in Vancouver, British Columbia, expressed concerns to the police and media over a large number of women who had gone missing from the area (Cameron, 2007). During the previous three years, 27 prostitutes, many of them First Nations women, had disappeared from the Low Track red light district on the edge of Skid Road (Greene, 2001). Were the disappearances a natural part of the transient nature of Skid Row prostitution life or was something more sinister occurring? The first step in assessing any problem of this sort is to obtain an estimate as to what constitutes a "normal" level of such incidents (the base rate). Consequently, the Vancouver Police Department (VPD) reviewed 20 years of data on unfound missing persons from the Downtown Eastside. Surprisingly, all missing persons were eventually found in most of the years from 1978 to 1994; five years had one or two cases of persons still missing (the annual mean was 0.35). However, this changed dramatically in 1995, and by 1998, the number of unfound missing persons had risen to 11 (see Figure 3.3)

To use the language of epidemiologists, this was a statistically significant spatial-temporal cluster. Put more simply, when compared to past trends, there were too many events occurring in too small an area in too short a time for this to just be a random fluctuation. If these numbers represented incidents of tuberculosis, for example, officials would suspect an epidemic and begin searching for the vector (cause) of the disease outbreak. In this

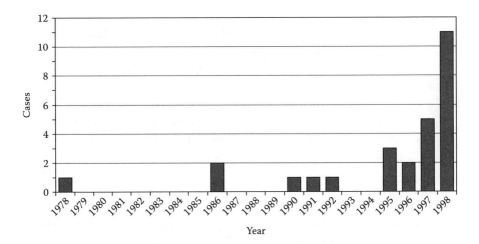

Figure 3.3 Unfound missing persons cases.

situation, it was the responsibility of the police to determine what had happened to the missing women.

However, the inspector in charge of VPD's Major Crime Section (MCS), which is responsible for investigating homicide, sexual assault, robbery, and missing persons cases, argued that the only reason the disappearances were high in recent years was because there had been insufficient time to find the women (see Stelfox & Pease, 2005, regarding the misclassification of murders as missing persons). Over the course of the next few years, he asserted, most of the missing women will be found, and the 1995–1998 peak will drop to the 1978–1994 level. After some debate, a decision was made to test this conjecture empirically. An analysis of national data showed the typical (modal) time from initial missing person report to when the individual was found was two days; after three weeks, 93% of missing persons were found (see Figure 3.4). Using these data to calculate a missing persons case survival curve (i.e., how long a missing person stays missing), it was possible to estimate that over the course of time, on average, only two people out of the 27 would be found. This left 25 missing women, still a statistically significantly high number.

Any theory proposed to explain this cluster of missing women had to be able to answer the following questions:

1. Why was this happening now and not before?
2. Why was this happening in Vancouver's Skid Road and not in any other Canadian urban Skid Road?
3. Why had no bodies been found?
4. Why were only women, and not men, disappearing?

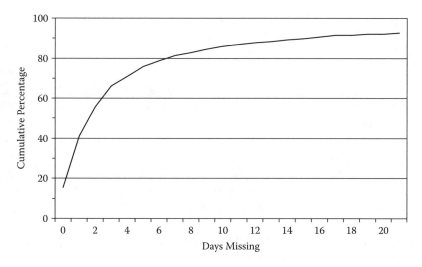

Figure 3.4 Missing persons case survival curve.

The only theory that appeared to answer all these questions was that of a serial killer. As rare as these predators are, Vancouver has had more than its share of them; prostitutes and other marginal members of society are the typical victims (Egger, 2002; Hickey, 2006). Indeed, Lowman and Fraser (1995) estimated the murder rate for street prostitutes to be 60 to 120 times that of nonprostitute women.

Unfortunately, even with this analysis, VPD's MCS and local politicians were reluctant to consider the possibility of a serial killer. When the Vancouver Police Board was asked to offer a reward in the case (similar to a $100,000 reward issued the previous month for information on a series of residential garage robberies on the city's affluent West Side), the response was not sympathetic.

> Mayor Philip Owen says he's not in favor of offering a $100,000 reward to try to find out what happened to 20 prostitutes who disappeared from his city, saying he's not financing a "location service" for hookers. Police and city officials are being pressured by several families of the women to offer cash for information. Social service workers and several of the families believe the women may have been the victims of a serial killer. "There's no evidence that a serial killer is at work. ... No bodies have been found. ... I don't think it is appropriate for a big award for a location service."
>
> He scoffed at claims by relatives of the missing women that the prostitutes had close ties to their families and wouldn't just vanish from the streets.
>
> "That's what they say," Owen said. "... some of these girls have been missing for a year. All of a sudden ... it becomes a major event." (Phillips, 1999)

Within a month, however, the mayor would succumb to political pressure and media criticism. *The Province*, one of the city's two major newspapers,[4] observed: "That reward (and obvious concern) for garages in the city's more affluent areas was the mayor's proud brainchild, but it stood in unfortunately clear contrast to the lack of reward (and apparent lack of concern) for the missing prostitutes in the very poorest neighbourhood" (Stall, 1999). Even when the city begrudgingly agreed to offer a reward in the missing women case, they only put up 30% of the money, the provincial government was responsible for the other 70%.

Avoiding the serial killer explanation, MCS management suggested various alternative theories for what had happened to the missing women. None of these satisfactorily answered the above questions:

- The women are only missing and eventually will be found (does not answer questions 1, 2, or 4).
- Their pimps killed them (does not answer question 3).
- They were drug murder victims (does not answer question 4).
- They died of drug overdoses (does not answer questions 3 or 4).
- They died of natural causes, but problems with hospital record systems have prevented them from being identified (does not answer question 4).
- They were murdered by multiple serial killers (see below).

For some inexplicable reason, the theory of several "little" serial killers became more organizationally palatable than that of one big serial killer— even if it meant that multiple perpetrators now had to be caught. Of course, the likelihood that more than one serial killer was murdering prostitutes in the same area at the same time, and then hiding their bodies, was very remote. Occam would be spinning in his grave.

The initial response of the VPD was to assign one constable from the Missing Persons Unit to the task of finding the missing women. This said much about how MCS management defined the problem. The detective constable was able to locate a few of the women, but she also discovered many more unreported disappearances of sex trade workers in the Downtown Eastside (the list eventually grew to over 60 missing women).

No police officer wants to see a killer go free or a victim not avenged. On the other hand, if the missing women had been from Vancouver's affluent West Side, there is little doubt the police response would have been very different. In all likelihood, the police subconsciously "fooled" themselves into believing what they did. As one homicide detective rationalized, "There are no bodies. So there's nothing we can do." This is equivalent to a fire station refusing to send out trucks because they can only see smoke but no fire.

---

[4] Reporters for Vancouver's other daily newspaper, *The Sun*, deserve much of the investigative credit for the eventual resolution of the Missing Women case.

After much community and media pressure, the Royal Canadian Mounted Police (RCMP) eventually formed a Task Force to review and investigate the missing women case. In February 2002, they arrested[5] Robert "Willie" Pickton, a pig farmer from Coquitlam, British Columbia. Pickton was a suspect known to investigators. He had been the subject of a VPD tip in 1998 by an individual who had seen different women's purses and identification in his farm house (presumably the same items observed four years later by the RCMP constable), and he had been arrested by the RCMP in 1997 for attempted murder after stabbing a prostitute (the case never came to court). A search of Pickton's 14-acre pig farm for body parts took 21 months; excavators dug up 370,000 cubic yards of top soil, with the assistance of 102 forensic anthropologists. The costs of the investigation are estimated at $70 million. To date, over 100 investigators have been involved and at least 100,000 exhibits collected.

Pickton was charged with 27 counts of first-degree murder (one of these was later rejected by the judge); his trial began on January 30, 2006. Prosecutors eventually decided to sever the charges and only proceeded with six counts. On December 9, 2007, almost two years later, the jury found Pickton guilty of second-degree murder and he was subsequently sentenced to life in prison with no possibility of parole for 25 years. It is unlikely the Crown will proceed with the additional 20 charges as further convictions would not increase Pickton's sentence.

Police recovered DNA for 31 women at the pig farm and suspect there is more. Pickton confessed to killing 49 women to an undercover police officer posing as his cell mate. It appears that some of the victim's body parts were fed to Pickton's pigs; after being slaughtered, he gave the pig meat away to friends. Sadly, at least 14 women were murdered after Pickton was first identified as a viable suspect in the disappearances. Police ignored Canada's most prolific sex murderer for over three years because they did not want to believe, despite evidence to the contrary, that a serial killer was responsible for the missing women in the Downtown Eastside.

References

Bugliosi, V. (2007). *Reclaiming history: The assassination of President John F. Kennedy.* New York: W. W. Norton.

Cameron, S. (2007). *The Pickton file.* Toronto: Alfred A. Knopf.

Campbell, A. (1996). *The Campbell Inquiry Report: Bernardo investigation review.* Toronto: Government of Ontario.

[5] Even this arrest was fortuitous, the unintended result of a search for a handgun unrelated to the murders. The RCMP constable executing the search warrant noticed personal effects belonging to several different women in Pickton's farm house.

Doney, R. H. (1990). The aftermath of the Yorkshire Ripper: The response of the United Kingdom police service. In S. A. Egger (Ed.), *Serial murder: An elusive phenomenon* (pp. 95–112). New York: Praeger.

Douglas, J. E., & Olshaker, M. (1995). *Journey into darkness.* New York: Simon & Schuster.

Egger, S. A. (2002). *The killers among us: An examination of serial murder and its investigation* (2nd ed.). Upper Saddle River, NJ: Prentice-Hall.

Eyewitness evidence: A trainer's manual for law enforcement. (2003). NIJ Special Report (NIJ Publication No. NCJ-188678). Washington, DC: U.S. Government Printing Office.

FPT Heads of Prosecutions Committee Working Group. (2004). *Report on the prevention of miscarriages of justice.* Ottawa: Department of Justice.

Greene, T. (2001). *Bad date: The lost girls of Vancouver's Low Track.* Toronto: ECW Press.

Griffiths, R. (Producer). (April 14, 1993). "Murder by number: Inside the serial killers." CNN television special report.

Halberstam, D. (1969). *The best and the brightest.* New York: Ballantine Books.

Hickey, E. W. (2006). *Serial murderers and their victims* (4th ed.). Belmont, CA: Thompson Wadsworth.

Janis, I. L. (1982). *Groupthink: Psychological studies of policy decisions and fiascoes* (2nd ed.). Boston: Houghton Mifflin.

Karem, B. J., & Napolitano, C. (2003, March). In a room with madness. *Playboy,* pp. 70–74, 84, 146–152.

Livingstone, H. E., & Groden, R. J. (1998). *High treason: The assassination of JFK and the case for conspiracy.* New York: Carroll & Graf Publishers.

Lowman, J., & Fraser, L. (1995). *Violence against persons who prostitute: The experience in British Columbia.* Ottawa: Department of Justice.

Makin, K. (1992). *Redrum the innocent.* Toronto: Viking.

McAdams, J. (2004). *The Kennedy assassination.* Retrieved March 27, 2006, from http://mcadams.posc.mu.edu/home.htm.

Phillips, R. A. (1999, April 9). Mayor: No reward in missing hookers case. Vancouver *Downtown Eastside Missing Women.* Retrieved March 10, 2008, from http://www.missingpeople.net/mayor_no_reward-april_9,1999.htm.

Shibutani, T. (1966). *Improvised news: A sociological study of rumor.* Indianapolis: Bobbs-Merrill.

Smith, C., & Guillen, T. (1991). *The search for the Green River Killer.* New York: Penguin Books.

Stall, B. (1999, April 25). Mayor to propose skid-row reward. *The Vancouver Province.* Retrieved March 10, 2008, from http://www.canada.com/theprovince/news/story.html?id=6b6fec98-13e6-4dc0-8901-13cb5c2a1131.

Stelfox, P., & Pease, K. (2005). Cognition and detection: Reluctant bedfellows? In M. J. Smith & N. Tilley (Eds.), *Crime science: New approaches to preventing and detecting crime* (pp. 191–207). Cullompton, Devon: Willan Publishing.

Wagner, U., Gais, S., Haider, H., Verleger, R., & Born, J. (2004). Sleep inspires insight. *Nature, 427,* 352–355.

Walton, R. (Ed.). (2006). *Cold case homicides: Practical investigative techniques.* Boca Raton, FL: CRC Press.

Errors in Probability: Chance and Randomness in Forensics and Profiling

4

D. KIM ROSSMO

Anyone who has spent a few hours watching the tables in Las Vegas will realize that probability is a difficult concept for the human mind. We often use heuristics—and suffer from biases—when dealing with probability. Police officers find it particularly hard to think probabilistically. Because of their street experiences, they prefer black and white rather than shades of gray. Probability errors in criminal justice most often occur in the forensic sciences, but they can also happen in criminal profiling.

Language and Uncertainty

Whenever we discuss chance, likelihood, risk, or forecasting—indeed, predictions of any uncertain future event—by necessity, we are talking probability (Bernstein, 1996; Orrell, 2007). However, we often use words to describe mathematical probabilities: "always," "likely," "common," "risky," "infrequently," "never." Unfortunately, these words are not well matched to underlying numbers; they also mean different things to different people and even to ourselves at different times (Heuer, 1999, pp. 152–156). What you mean by "frequent" might be very different from what I mean by "frequent." Part of the confusion is that the time frame may not be specified. Furthermore, we often do not know the real probability of an event.

Take the statement: "John Smith will likely commit another crime." What does this mean? What is the probability associated with "likely"—30%, more than 50%, over 90%? And what time period does this forecast refer to—in the next week, sometime this year, in his lifetime? Different people will interpret such a statement in different ways under different circumstances.

This ambiguity can become a problem during an investigation or criminal trial. A good example of this confusion occurred during testimony for the prosecution by a pathologist in the trial of David Milgaard, accused of the sexual murder of a young nursing assistant (*R. v. Milgaard*; see Chapter 9).

Sperm recovered at the crime scene contained type A antigens. When Milgaard's saliva was tested, however, the results showed he was a nonsecretor.[1] To circumvent this problem, the Crown advanced the possibility of blood contamination, a theory supported by the pathologist in his testimony:

> Q. Are there conditions under which human blood as such can get into seminal fluid or spermatozoa in the male person?
> A. Yes.
> Q. Could you tell the Court what they are please?
> A. One would be local injury to the male genitals. A second and *quite common* occurrence would be any inflammation, either internal or external, of the male genitals [emphasis added].[2]

What, exactly, did the pathologist mean when he said "quite common"? Let us consider this in the context of the following questions related to the probability of burglary:

- How likely is it that Jim, a police officer, will be called to investigate a burglary in a month?
- How likely is it that Susan has been burgled in her life?
- How likely is it that George will be burgled today?

Jim sees burglary as a common event, Susan much less so, while George considers the risk of burglary to be extremely low. We do not know what was in the pathologist's mind when he said the occurrence was quite common, but one would suspect, considering his professional medical background, that he was using Jim's perspective. What was relevant for Milgaard's guilt, however, was George's perspective.[3]

Coincidences

Skeptics often say they do not believe in coincidences. However, when looking for patterns within large numbers of items (i.e., events, suspects), coincidences are inevitable. Let us examine the well-known comparison of Presidents Kennedy and Lincoln:

- Abraham Lincoln was elected president in 1860, John F. Kennedy in 1960.
- The surnames Lincoln and Kennedy each contain seven letters.

---

[1] A secretor is a person whose saliva, semen, and other bodily fluids contain ABO antigens from which their blood type can be determined; nonsecretors do not possess this genetic trait (Cunliffe & Piazza, 1980). About 80% of the North American population are secretors.

[2] Direct examination of Dr. H. E. Emson, Trial transcript, pp. 1157–1158.

[3] It turns out that such a condition is exceedingly rare, perhaps even nonexistent.

- Both presidents were particularly concerned with civil rights.
- Both men lost children while in the White House.
- Both men were shot on a Friday.
- Both men were shot in the head.
- Both presidents were succeeded by Southerners named Johnson.
- John Wilkes Booth ran from a theater and was caught in a warehouse, while Lee Harvey Oswald ran from a warehouse and was caught in a theater.
- Booth and Oswald were both assassinated before their trials.

What do these remarkable similarities mean? The answer is nothing. They are strictly the product of chance. First, there have been 43 U.S. presidents (as of 2008), resulting in 903 possible president-to-president comparisons. Second, these particular comparisons have been cherry picked. Third, only the similarities—not the differences—have been listed. For example, Lincoln was assassinated in April 1865, Kennedy in November 1963. Abraham has seven letters, John only four. And so on.

What role does coincidence play in major crime investigations? Mark Kennedy, a St. Louis sex crimes detective pursuing a serial rapist responsible for numerous crimes in several jurisdictions over many years, once commented to me—half-seriously—that he could have convicted three people if it were not for DNA. What he meant was the task force had looked at so many suspects that some of them, by sheer chance, circumstantially appeared guilty—until they were cleared by DNA testing. A few people will just be in the wrong place at the wrong time. A coincidence with one chance in a hundred of occurring is more than likely to happen if even just 70 suspects are examined. Efforts to solve a crime by "working backward" (i.e., from the suspect to the crime, rather than from the crime to the suspect) are susceptible to errors of coincidence. If you look hard enough, you can usually find some sort of connection. These types of errors are often seen in the proffered "solutions" to such famous cases as Jack the Ripper.

The Dreyfus Affair

Probability played an interesting role in the infamous Dreyfus Affair (Gigerenzer, 2002). In 1894, the French Army court-martialed Captain Alfred Dreyfus for treason in a case that became an international cause célèbre because of its anti-Semitic injustice (Kaye, 2007). Before it was over, a colonel who forged evidence against Dreyfus would commit suicide, the chief of the Army's General Staff and the Minister of War would resign, and the government would fall. The matter all began when a handwritten letter containing information on French artillery and troops was recovered from the wastebasket in the military attaché office of the German embassy. French intelligence officers focused their investigation on Captain Dreyfus, an unpopular Alsatian[4] from a wealthy Jewish family. The investigators collected and fabricated evidence against Dreyfus and suppressed all conflicting information.

The closed trial was riddled with procedural errors and corruptions of justice. A secret dossier was given by the prosecution to the judges but illegally withheld from the defense. Dreyfus was convicted of transmitting military secrets to Germany and sentenced to life imprisonment on Devil's Island, the notorious penal colony off the coast of French Guyana.

Influential French novelist Émile Zola, risking his career, wrote the famous "*J'accuse ... !*" open letter to the president of the French Republic, published on the front page of the Paris daily, *L'Aurore*, on January 13, 1898. Zola accused the highest levels of the Army of obstruction of justice and anti-Semitism. This proved to be a turning point in a case about which many had grave doubts.

Following revelations of evidence fabrication by the military, France's highest Court vacated the verdict. Dreyfus was tried a second time in 1899. In a bizarre compromise judgment, the Court again found him guilty, but he was quickly pardoned. In 1906, finding no credible evidence of his guilt, the Court annulled the verdict.[5] Now a major, Dreyfus returned to the Army and was soon made a Knight of the *Légion d'honneur*. He was eventually promoted to Lieutenant Colonel and served against Germany during the First World War.

One of the witnesses during Dreyfus's court-martial was Alphonse Bertillon, the developer of the anthropometry system of body measurement used by police to identify criminals before the adoption of fingerprinting (Brandl, 2004). Bertillon provided expert testimony regarding his analysis using an "infallible and transcendent method of graphology" (Kaye, 2007, p. 833). This pseudoscientific technique compared the treasonous letter with correspondence written by Dreyfus. Bertillon tried to estimate the probabilities associated with the length of certain words, combinations of initial and final letters, and the spacing and positions of letters, to show joint authorship.

The famous French mathematician Henri Poincaré found "colossal errors" in Bertillon's analysis, which he told the court completely lacked merit. The supposedly improbable coincidences that "confirmed" Dreyfus's authorship were common to all written documents. Bertillon (who had no background in handwriting analysis) failed to understand the nature of

---

[4] Alsace-Lorraine is a border territory with a contested history, occupied by both German- and French-speaking people. Alsace was part of France when Dreyfus was born but was occupied by Germany by the time of his court-martial, having been annexed in 1871 following the Franco-Prussian War.

[5] A French officer named Esterhazy was the actual writer of the letter sent to the German military attaché (Kaye, 2007).

probability and random patterns. In a way, he fell victim to the coincidences of the Lincoln–Kennedy comparison. Another witness, analyzing a page of Bertillon's own report using these methods, "proved" it too was a forgery. Fortunately, the court found this evidence largely unintelligible (Kaye, 2007).

"The Law of Small Numbers"

One of the most common problems with probability has been called "The Law of Small Numbers." This tongue-in-cheek label is a reference to the risks associated with looking for patterns in, or drawing inferences from, a small number of incidents. An analyst examining the dates for a series of 15 street robberies may observe that there have been no crimes on a Thursday. Is this a meaningful pattern? Probably not. With only 15 crimes, chances are at least one day of the week will be free of robberies. Similarly, a detective working on his third child homicide would be unwise to place too much weight on his limited past experience. The two previous crimes may not be representative of the current case.

Similar Fact Evidence

Coincidences can be a trap when offender modus operandi and similar fact evidence are used for crime linkage purposes. Trawl search problems occur when only similarities, and not differences, are examined (Risinger & Loop, 2002). Furthermore, comparisons of common similarities lack utility. For example, vaginal intercourse is typical of most rapes and therefore serves as a poor modus operandi variable for the purposes of discriminating between different sex offenders.

How a crime scene variable is defined is also important. At first glance, the two crimes depicted in Table 4.1 appear to have several similar characteristics, suggesting they are likely connected. When we look at these characteristics in more detail (shown in Table 4.2), however, important differences appear. It now appears less likely these crimes were committed by the same person.

Table 4.1 Crime Scene Variables

Crime 1	Crime 2
child murder	child murder
sexual assault	sexual assault
strangulation	strangulation
transportation of victim	transportation of victim
concealment of body	concealment of body

Table 4.2   Detailed Crime Scene Variables

Crime 1	Crime 2
three-year-old male victim	14-year-old female victim
anal sexual assault	vaginal sexual assault
manual strangulation	ligature strangulation
victim transported 100 yards	victim transported 20 miles
body found in a dumpster	body dumped into river

Conjunction Fallacy

The conjunction fallacy occurs when a higher probability is assigned to the overlap of two events than to either event separately. Probabilities are combined by multiplying them together.[6] This means the product must be smaller than either initial probability, given noncertainty. Conjunction fallacies have occurred in DNA matching, offense linkage analysis, and crime forecasting ("Crime analysis challenge," 2002).

The following example illustrates how probabilities should be combined. A witness reports seeing a vehicle flee the scene of a nighttime gas station robbery in which the clerk was shot and killed. He states he only had a quick glimpse of the vehicle, but is reasonably sure it was a gray Chrysler minivan. How much weight should be placed on this description?

There are two parts to this question. First, we need to know the probability that he actually saw the robber's vehicle. In major crime cases involving significant publicity, the desire for members of the public to be helpful (or to become part of the investigation) is high, but often their information is not reliable. Assume there is a 75% chance that this witness actually saw the robber's vehicle. The second part of the question concerns the accuracy of the vehicle description. The witness provides three descriptive elements: (1) vehicle make (Chrysler); (2) type (minivan); and (3) color (gray). Let us assign witness accuracy probabilities of 70% to vehicle make, 90% to vehicle type, and 60% to vehicle color (under sodium vapor street lights, blue looks gray). Therefore, the likelihood the vehicle seen by the witness was a gray Chrysler minivan is only 38% (70% x 90% x 60%). The probability that the offender was driving such a vehicle is only 28%—the probability that the witness actually saw the vehicle, multiplied by the probability of witness accuracy (75% x 38%). This does not mean the witness's information is not valuable. Obviously, suspect vehicles that are gray Chrysler minivans should still be prioritized and investigated. A problem occurs, however, when other suspect vehicles (e.g., blue Toyota sports utility vehicles) are ignored.

---

[6] Assuming the events are independent.

Double Counting and Correlations

Double counting refers to extracting two elements of a crime from a common source and then erroneously treating them as separate aspects. A rumor heard from more than one person does not necessarily verify the information, as both individuals may have received it from the same source. Double counting can mislead a criminal investigation. Let us suppose that a sexual assault victim has described her attacker as a Vietnamese male, 25 to 30 years of age, black hair, moustache, five feet six inches tall, with a slim build. Although the victim provided seven different physical characteristics for comparison against suspects, in reality only four of these have utility. Virtually all Vietnamese people have black hair. Furthermore, many of them are slim in build. So in this instance, hair color, and to some extent physical build, flows from the offender's racial ethnicity and should not be treated as independent factors for comparison purposes.

Consider also the example of a behavioral profile of a child murderer. Among other details, the profile estimated the offender's age and type of vehicle owned. The latter was determined from automobile insurance data, which provide information on the vehicles most commonly owned by specific age groups. Armed with the profile, investigators evaluate two suspects, one who matches both the age and vehicle criteria, and the other who only matches the age criteria. Who is the better suspect vis-à-vis the profile?

The answer is they are equal. The vehicle type was derived from the age estimate, and therefore is not an independent profile element drawn from the crime scene (as opposed to, say, a vehicle sighting by a witness). To consider the age and vehicle type as two separate match points would be double counting.

The prosecution committed this type of error in *People v. Collins*, a California case involving a purse snatching that occurred on June 18, 1964, in the San Pedro area of Los Angeles (Gigerenzer, 2002). A witness to the crime described the assailant as a blonde woman with a ponytail, seen climbing into a yellow car driven by a black man with a beard and moustache. Police arrested Janet and Malcolm Collins, who fit this description. At their trial, the prosecutor brought in a mathematics instructor to testify to the probability that the couple was guilty given their match to the witness's description.

To do this, the expert witness determined the probability that a given couple randomly selected from the general population would match the following characteristics (the associated probabilities were provided by the prosecution) (Koehler, 1997):

- woman with blond hair   1/3
- woman with ponytail   1/10
- man with moustache   1/4
- black man with beard   1/10

- interracial couple   1/1,000
- yellow automobile   1/10.

By multiplying these numbers together (see previous section), the expert witness calculated the random match probability to be one in 12 million. The prosecutor then informed the jury that the likelihood the couple was innocent was, conservatively, only one in 12 million. The jury convicted the defendants of robbery. On appeal, however, the California Supreme Court reversed their conviction for the following reasons:

1. The probabilities were only estimates, and not based on empirical data.
2. It was assumed the characteristics were certain (i.e., the witness was reliable) when there was specific reason for doubting this.
3. The assumption that the characteristics were independent was highly unlikely—for example, most men with beards have moustaches.
4. The probability estimation was flawed because of an error known as the prosecutor's fallacy.[7]

By double counting correlated characteristics, the expert witness inflated his probability estimate. The correlations in the Collins case were obvious, but they are sometimes more subtle and invidious.

In November 1999, British solicitor Sally Clark was convicted of smothering her two infant sons, who had died a year apart from sudden infant death syndrome (SIDS, also known as crib or cot death). At her murder trial, a pediatrician, Sir Roy Meadow, testified the probability of two crib deaths occurring in a single family of affluent means was "vanishingly small," approximately one in 73 million (Hall, 1999). He calculated this number by squaring 1/8,543, the probability of a single SIDS case in England.

There were several problems with Meadow's analysis. First, he made the incorrect assumption that crib deaths are independent within a single family, ignoring the possibility of a genetic effect (see Chapter 5). Second, he committed an ecology fallacy in treating individual-level risk as equivalent to average overall population risk. And third, because crib deaths are relatively common but nonrandom events, recurrence happens somewhere in England about once every 18 months (Hall, 1999). The Royal Statistical Society took the unusual action of issuing a press release stating there was no statistical basis for Meadow's estimation.

In January 2003, upon her second appeal, Clark's conviction was quashed, but only after she had served more than three years in prison. The case is considered a great miscarriage of justice in Britain and a tragic example of the misrepresentation of statistical evidence.

---

[7] The correct probability is the random match probability multiplied by the number of couples in the population. The prosecutor's fallacy is discussed in detail below.

Base Rates

A lack of understanding of base rates can lead to the misinterpretation of research findings and forensic results (Robertson & Vignaux, 1995; Tversky & Kahneman, 1982). Consider the oft-quoted fact: "Serial killers are usually white males." Although this statement is technically correct, at least for the United States, it is incomplete. To understand it properly, we must also consider the relevant base rates. Four different studies of serial murderers found black offender proportions of 16%, 20%, 20%, and 28% (mean equals 21%), and female offender proportions of 4%, 9%, 10%, and 16% (mean equals 10%) (Kraemer, Lord, & Heilbrun, 2004; Rossmo, 2000). The results of the 2000 U.S. Census showed 75% of the U.S. population was white and 49% male. This means that serial killers are disproportionately male (as is true of murderers generally) but not disproportionately white. The only reason most serial killers in the United States are white is because most of the population in the United States is white. In South Africa, serial killers are primarily black. In Japan, they are Japanese. More importantly, all else being equal, serial killers are less likely to be white in predominantly black or Hispanic areas in the United States, such as Baltimore, Maryland, or Laredo, Texas.

Criminal profiling infers offender characteristics from offense characteristics and then uses this information to help prioritize suspects. Consider the research finding that 61% of sex murderers had adolescent rape fantasies (Ressler, Burgess, & Douglas, 1988, p. 24). But what, exactly, does this figure mean? If 3% of the noncriminal male population has adolescent rape fantasies, this number takes on one meaning. However, if 87% of the noncriminal male population has adolescent rape fantasies, then it means something entirely different. Without knowing the appropriate base rate, we cannot properly interpret the research finding and do not know how to use it to help prioritize suspects in a sex murder case.

Errors of Thinking

Two errors have been identified related to the understanding of probability within the court context—the prosecutor's fallacy and the defense attorney's fallacy (Robertson & Vignaux, 1995).

The Prosecutor's Fallacy

The prosecutor's fallacy occurs when the probability of the evidence given guilt is equated to the probability of guilt given the evidence. When the evidence is highly probable given the hypothesis, we must avoid the trap of believing that the hypothesis itself must be highly probable. Put simply, although all cows are four-legged animals, not all four-legged animals are cows. This error (known as transposing the conditional) can occur in both forensic science and behavioral profiling.

The case of the Birmingham Six in England is an infamous example of the prosecutor's fallacy (Robertson & Vignaux, 1995; Woffinden, 1988). In 1974, horrendous bomb explosions in two central Birmingham pubs killed 21 people and injured 182. The bombings were attributed to the Provisional IRA. Special Branch police officers detained a group of six men traveling to a funeral in Belfast. Their hands were swabbed, and the swabs subsequently analyzed for traces of nitroglycerine using Griess, thin-layer chromatography (TLC), and gas chromatography multiple spectrometry (GCMS) tests. A forensic scientist later testified, during what became the largest mass murder trial in Britain, that he was "99% certain" the defendants had handled explosives, based on the results of these tests. It was later disclosed, however, that many other substances could produce positive test results, including nitrocellulose, which is found in paint, lacquer, playing cards, soil, gasoline, cigarettes, and soap. The defendants were playing a game of cards on the train shortly before their arrest. The convictions of the Birmingham Six were overturned on appeal, partly as a result of the forensic evidence being discredited. During his testimony the scientist had transposed the conditional.

The prosecutor's fallacy can also occur in behavioral analysis. If a behavioral profile on a violent crime indicates a specific personality profile with a 90% degree of confidence, it is not correct to assume that someone with that same personality profile is 90% likely to be guilty. This is what happened during the investigation of the 1996 Atlanta Centennial Park Olympics pipe bombing. Security guard Richard Jewell became a major suspect in the investigation simply because he fit the psychological profile of a certain type of bomber. Effectively branded guilty, it took several weeks before he was ultimately cleared of a crime later attributed to the notorious fugitive Eric Rudolph (Reid, 1996; Schuster & Stone, 2005; Walls, 2003).

Consider the following expert testimony of a psychologist during a child sexual abuse trial in New Zealand (R. v. S., 1989, 1 NZLR 714; Robertson & Vignaux, 1995):

> Prosecutor: Did [the complainant] exhibit any characteristics which were consistent with what you had come to know as the characteristics of sexually abused children?
> Psychologist: Very definitely. [lack of eye contact, self-mutilation, unwillingness to talk about home life]

What was missing in this testimony is an estimate of how common these characteristics are in children who have not been sexually abused. The New

Zealand Court of Appeal rejected the psychologist's evidence for this and other reasons. If we are to evaluate properly the importance of a particular piece of evidence, whether it is a forensic test or a behavioral characteristic, we need to know both its sensitivity (based on the number of true positives) and its specificity (based on the number of true negatives).

The Defense Attorney's Fallacy

The defense attorney's fallacy occurs when evidence is considered in isolation, rather than in totality. This type of error happened during O.J. Simpson's preliminary hearing. The prosecution presented evidence that blood found at the murder scene, when analyzed using conventional grouping techniques, matched that of the accused, with characteristics shared by one in 400 people. The defense argued that an entire football stadium could be filled with those people in Los Angeles who would also match the blood grouping, and therefore the evidence was useless (Robertson & Vignaux, 1995). Although the first part of the defense argument regarding the number of matches is correct, only a limited number of those people had relationships with Nicole Brown Simpson or Ronald Goldman, and even fewer had any reason for wanting to kill them. The probability of an individual being in all three categories (equal to the individual probabilities multiplied together, as discussed above) is very low. Consequently, the second part of the argument—that the evidence is useless—is not correct.

Answering the Wrong Question

The defense attorney's fallacy was not the only probability error to arise in the context of the O.J. Simpson case. Harvard law professor Alan M. Dershowitz testified for the defense at the murder trial in regards to Simpson's previous domestic assault on Nicole Simpson. He concluded that "Battery, as such, is not a good independent predictor of murder" (Dershowitz, 1996, p. 104):

> Because of my academic expertise in this area,[8] I was placed in charge of writing the legal briefs on this and related issues. We told the court that … in 1992, according to the FBI Uniform Crime Reports, a total of 913 women were killed by their husbands, and 519 were killed by their boyfriends. In other words, while there were 2½ to 4 million incidents of abuse, there were only 1,432 homicides. Some of these homicides may have occurred after a history of abuse, but obviously most abuse, presumably even most serious abuse, does not end in murder. In fact, the ratio of murders to batterings is somewhere between .0006 to 1 (1,500 murders to 2,500,000 "batterings") and .000375 to 1

---

[8] Presumably his legal, not mathematical or statistical, expertise.

(1,500 murders to 4 million "batterings"). ... The relationship between battery and murder is a complex one, and we argued that the jury could easily become confused and ascribe too much weight to the history of spousal discord in this case. (Dershowitz, 1996, pp. 104–105)

The jury members were not the only ones who were easily confused. Dershowitz's analysis is fundamentally flawed. At issue is not the probability that a battered woman will be murdered by her abuser, but rather the probability that a *battered and murdered* woman was killed by her abuser (Good, 1995, 1996). Dershowitz answered the wrong question.

Figure 4.1 shows this error graphically by outlining the following groups:

- All battered women (A, the circle);
- All murdered and battered women (B, the square); and
- All battered women who were killed by their batterers (C, the white area within B).

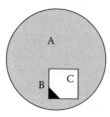

Figure 4.1 Probability of a battered woman being murdered.

What Dershowitz calculated was the probability of B/A. But what actually is of interest is C/B. The former probability is less than 0.04%; this was the evidence given at trial. The latter, correct probability, however, is almost 90% (Gigerenzer, 2002; Good, 1996). Unbelievably, the prosecution let this "probability evidence" go unchallenged.

Unfortunately, this confusion over probative probability still lingers. In *Law and Human Behavior*, the official journal of the American Psychology–Law Society of the American Psychological Association (APA), Davis and Follette (2002) mistake the probability of an unfaithful husband murdering his wife with the probability of a murdered woman having been killed by her unfaithful husband. At one point, they argue:

Imagine, for example, that the prosecution has presented evidence against a male defendant accused of killing his wife including motives of infidelity and insurance benefits (as in our case), and an eyewitness who saw a man with hair color and approximate height matching the defendant walking away from the site of the murder within the appropriate time frame. ... Given the low base rate of uxoricide, this combined evidence would demonstrably fall short of proof of murder beyond a reasonable doubt. Thus, given prosecution reliance solely on the listed evidence, the defense could justifiably argue for dismissal. (p. 155)

Davis and Follette (2002, p. 156) observed: "There is no doubt that it will be difficult for courts to adapt to the ideas presented here." It was not just the judiciary who had difficulty. Scholarly peers were quick to point out the mathematical and conceptual errors in their paper. Friedman and Park (2003, p. 643) concluded: "Frankly, we hope our response helps to prevent testimony based on the Davis-Follette analysis from being received into evidence. ... The judge presiding in the Franklin case was clearly correct in excluding Professor Davis's testimony as prejudicial" (see also Kaye & Koehler, 2003; Wells, 2003; see rebuttal by Davis & Follette, 2003).

The Infallibility of DNA?

DNA profiling has become one of the most powerful tools in the police investigative arsenal (Brown, 1994; Kelly, Rankin, & Wink, 1987; Rudin & Inman, 2002). Since its initial introduction in the Narborough murder inquiry in the United Kingdom, the use of DNA analysis has both grown and advanced ("DNA profiling," 1995; Gaudette, 1990; Miller, 1991; U.S. Department of Justice, 2000; Wambaugh, 1989). The technology has also been responsible for helping free a number of wrongfully convicted individuals (Connors, Lundregan, Miller, & McEwen, 1996; Drizin & Leo, 2004; U.S. Department of Justice, 1999).

Forensic DNA testing, however, is not entirely unproblematic (Gigerenzer, 2002; Goldscheider & Kessis, 2006). Despite claims by the FBI and other agencies that DNA is infallible, it does have an error rate.[9] Testing has shown false-positive matches ranging from 2% to 0.5% (Gigerenzer, 2002). Problems result from enzyme failures, mislabeling, pattern interpretation errors,

[9] Even the venerable fingerprint has come under close scrutiny. The U.S. Supreme Court has ruled that a known error rate is one of the requirements for the trial admissibility of scientific evidence (*Daubert v. Merrell*, 1993). The error rate (random match probability, or RMP) for DNA can be determined, but fingerprinting fails the Daubert test because no error rate has ever been established. Instead, fingerprint experts insist that two prints either match or they do not—in other words, there is no possibility of error. The Brandon Mayfield case and research by Dror and others have called that claim into question (Dror & Charlton, 2006; Dror & Rosenthal, 2008; see Chapter 5). One of the problems is the testing that has occurred to date has only involved the comparisons of known prints, which tend to be of high quality. In the real world, known prints are usually compared against latent prints, many of which are of poor quality. Human judgment—and error—therefore plays a role. Also, the fewer features of similarity found between two prints, the less certain the match. Courts are increasingly demanding information on fingerprint error rates (Neufeld & Scheck, 2002).

contamination, and other human mistakes. Furthermore, separate laboratories analyzing the same evidence have produced different random match probabilities because of sample corruption, environmental degradation, or substandard laboratory practices. There can also be database errors (Ballard, 2007).

DNA probabilities are often misunderstood. It is important to understand the difference between random match probability (RMP) and source probability (SP): "the *random match probability* is the probability that a person randomly selected from a population would match the trace evidence as closely as the suspect.[10] The *source probability*, in contrast, is the probability that the suspect is actually the source of the recovered trace evidence" (Gigerenzer, 2002, pp. 165–166). RMP is a function of the number of loci matches. SP is a function of the RMP and the number of potential suspects. These two probabilities are often confused (the prosecutor's fallacy), and more than one case has been successfully appealed because the prosecutor used RMP as an index of guilt.[11]

DNA can only show presence, and other evidence is necessary to establish guilt in a criminal court. Let us use as an example the case of a woman raped and murdered in her home. A male neighbor is linked to the scene through DNA from saliva on a cigarette butt found at the scene. By itself, this evidence has limited probative value, as all it does is establish the man's presence in the house at some point—not unusual for a neighbor. A DNA match from a drop of blood at the scene is more useful, especially if there is evidence the victim fought her assailant. However, the neighbor could still explain this by claiming he suffered a nose bleed during a visit. A DNA match from semen recovered from the victim's vaginal vault, which showed signs of trauma, is much more compelling. Establishing the victim had a monogamous relationship with her boyfriend or that the neighbor had been stalking her completes the case.

As DNA technology advances and the testing becomes more sensitive, the potential for identifying large numbers of potential suspects increases. But imagine, for instance, DNA evidence collection techniques so sensitive that they can detect slough cells from anybody who has ever been in a particular room—including all current and former residents, all visitors, and every delivery person and maintenance worker. Our case example of the woman raped and murdered in her home illustrates how this increased sensitivity could become an issue.

Cold hits from a DNA databank present another probability issue (McCue, Smith, Diehl, Dabbs, McDonough, & Ferrara, 2001; Schubert, 2006,

---

[10]The RMP value assumes no one in the population is related. The probability is significantly higher for family members.

[11]This was part of the probability confusion in *People v. Collins* (see above).

p. 139; *Using DNA to solve cold cases*, 2002). It is important to remember that a cold hit is a starting point and not the end of an investigation. Key considerations are the RMP, the number of people in the databank, and where the identified suspect lives. If we have a suspect RMP of one in one million, but there are five million people in the database,[12] then the source probability is only 20% (one in five) because of the number of other individuals (on average, four) who could be expected to have the same DNA profile with that number of loci matches. The likelihood of false matches, particularly for lower RMPs found with mitochondrial DNA, will only increase as the size of the DNA databank grows.

Obviously, a cold DNA hit on an individual who lives in the same city as the victim is of much greater significance than a match to someone living on the other side of the country.[13] Evidence of a relationship and/or motive also helps. Coincidences do happen, so consideration has to be given to the size of the suspect population as well as how unlikely the coincidence. This very situation arose during a homicide investigation in Wuppertal, Germany, in which serological evidence closely matched a suspect whose car was found 12 miles from the crime scene (Gigerenzer, 2002). However, this distance covered an area of almost 500 square miles, and about 100 thousand men, so even a blood type RMP of over 97% represented hundreds of suspects. Charges were dropped when the court found conclusive evidence the suspect was in his hometown, 60 miles from the crime, at the time of the murder.

References

Ballard, M. (2007, May 17). 100,000 'erroneous' records on DNA database. *The Register*.

Bernstein, P. L. (1996). *Against the gods: The remarkable story of risk*. New York: John Wiley and Sons. Retrieved July 12, 2008, from http://theregister.co.uk/2007/05/17/dna_v_rozzers.

Brandl, S. G. (2004). *Criminal investigation: An analytical perspective*. Allyn and Bacon: Boston.

Brown, J. R. (1994, March). DNA analysis: A significant tool for law enforcement. *The Police Chief*, pp. 51–52.

Connors, E., Lundregan, T., Miller, N., & McEwen, J. T. (1996). *Convicted by juries, exonerated by science: Case studies in the use of DNA evidence to establish innocence after trial* (National Institute of Justice Research Report No. NCJ-161258). Washington, DC: U.S. Government Printing Office.

[12] As of October 2007, there were a total of 5,070,473 convicted offender profiles on the U.S. National DNA Index System (NDIS) (NDIS Statistics, 2007).

[13] Most criminals travel less than two miles to offend (see Costello & Leipnik, 2003; Groff & McEwen, 2005; Phillips, 1980; Rengert, 2004; Rossmo, 2000).

Costello, A., & Leipnik, M. R. (2003). Journeys to crime: GIS analysis of offender and victim journeys in Sheffield, England. In M. R. Leipnik & D. P. Albert (Eds.), *GIS in law enforcement: Implementation issues and case studies* (pp. 228–231). London: Taylor and Francis.

"Crime analysis challenge." (2002). *Crime Mapping News, 4*(3), 9–13.

Cunliffe, F., & Piazza, P. B. (1980). *Criminalistics and scientific investigation.* Englewood Cliffs, NJ: Prentice-Hall.

Davis, D., & Follette, W. C. (2002). Rethinking the probative value of evidence: Base rates, intuitive profiling, and the "*post*diction" of behavior. *Law and Human Behavior, 26,* 133–158.

Davis, D., & Follette, W. C. (2003). Toward an empirical approach to evidentiary ruling. *Law and Human Behavior, 27,* 661–684.

Dershowitz, A. M. (1996). *Reasonable doubts: The criminal justice system and the O.J. Simpson case.* New York: Simon and Schuster.

"DNA profiling." (1995, January). *DNA Database,* p. 2.

Drizin, S. A., & Leo, R. A. (2004). The problem of false confessions in the post-DNA world. *North Carolina Law Review, 82,* 891–1007.

Dror, I. E., & Charlton, D. (2006). Why experts make errors. *Journal of Forensic Identification, 56,* 600–616.

Dror, I. E., & Rosenthal, R. (2008). Meta-analytically quantifying the reliability and biasability of forensic experts. *Journal of Forensic Sciences, 53,* 900–903.

Friedman, R. D., & Park, R. C. (2003). Sometimes what everybody thinks they know is true. *Law and Human Behavior, 27,* 629–644.

Gaudette, B. D. (1990). DNA typing: A new service to Canadian police. *RCMP Gazette, 52*(4), 1–7.

Gigerenzer, G. (2002). *Calculated risks: How to know when numbers deceive you.* New York: Simon and Schuster.

Goldscheider, E., & Kessis, T. (2006, August 17). Quest for certainty: Is forensic DNA foolproof? *Northampton Valley Advocate.*

Good, I. J. (1995). When batterer turns murderer. *Nature, 375,* 541.

Good, I. J. (1996). When batterer becomes murderer. *Nature, 381,* 481.

Groff, E. R., & McEwen, J. T. (2005). Disaggregating the journey to homicide. In F. Wang (Ed.), *Geographic information systems and crime analysis* (pp. 60–83). Hershey, PA: Idea Group Publishing.

Hall, C. (1999, December 31). "Statistical error" in child murder trial. *Telegraph.* Retrieved July 12, 2008, from http://telegraph.co.uk/htmlcontent.jhtml?html=/archive/1999/12/31/nsa/31.html.

Heuer, Jr., R. J. (1999). *Psychology of intelligence analysis.* Washington, DC: Center for the Study of Intelligence, Central Intelligence Agency.

Kaye, D. H. (2007). Revisiting *Dreyfus*: A more complete account of a trial by mathematics. *Minnesota Law Review, 91,* 825–835.

Kaye, D. H., & Koehler, J. J. (2003). The misquantification of probative value. *Law and Human Behavior, 27,* 645–659.

Kelly, K. F., Rankin, J. J., & Wink, R. C. (1987). Method and applications of DNA fingerprinting: A guide for the non-scientist. *Criminal Law Review, 2,* 105–110.

Koehler, J. J. (1997). One in millions, billions, and trillions: Lessons from *People vs. Collins* (1968) for *People vs. Simpson* (1995). *Journal of Legal Education, 47,* 214–223.

Kraemer, G. W., Lord, W. D., & Heilbrun, K. (2004). Comparing single and serial homicide offenses. *Behavioral Sciences and the Law, 22*, 325–343.

McCue, C., Smith, G. L., Diehl, R. L., Dabbs, D. F., McDonough, & J. J., Ferrara, P. B. (2001). *Criminal histories of sex offenders identified through DNA "cold hits."* Unpublished manuscript, Virginia Division of Forensic Science, Richmond, VA.

Miller, J. V. (1991). The FBI's forensic DNA analysis program. *FBI Law Enforcement Bulletin, 60*(7), 11–15.

NDIS Statistics. (2007). Retrieved March 12, 2008, from http://www.fbi.gov/hq/lab/ codis/clickmap.htm.

Neufeld, P., & Scheck, B. (2002, March 9). Will fingerprinting stand up in court? *New York Times.* Retrieved July 12, 2008 from http://query.nytimes.com/gst/ fullpage.html?res=9C03E0D71130F93AA35750C0A9649C8B63.

Orrell, D. (2007). *The future of everything: The science of prediction.* New York: Thunder's Mouth Press.

Phillips, P. D. (1980). Characteristics and typology of the journey to crime. In D. E. Georges-Abeyie & K. D. Harries (Eds.), *Crime: A spatial perspective* (pp. 167–180). New York: Columbia University Press.

Reid, P. (1996, October 13). Fit the profile, pay the price. *The Edmonton Journal,* p. F5.

Rengert, G. F. (2004). The journey to crime. In G. Bruinsma, H. Elffers, & J. de Keijser (Eds.), *Punishment, places and perpetrators: Developments in criminology and criminal justice research* (pp. 169–181). Cullompton, Devon: Willan Publishing.

Ressler, R. K., Burgess, A. W., & Douglas, J. E. (1988). *Sexual homicide: Patterns and motives.* Lexington, MA: Lexington Books.

Risinger, D. M., & Loop, J. L. (2002). Three card monte, Monty Hall, *modus operandi* and "offender profiling": Some lessons of modern cognitive science for the law of evidence. *Cardozo Law Review, 24*, 193–285.

Robertson, B., & Vignaux, G. A. (1995). *Interpreting evidence: Evaluating forensic evidence in the courtroom.* Chichester: John Wiley and Sons.

Rossmo, D. K. (2000). *Geographic profiling.* Boca Raton, FL: CRC Press.

Rudin, N., & Inman, K. (2002). *An introduction to forensic DNA analysis* (2nd ed.). Boca Raton, FL: CRC Press.

Schubert, A. M. (2006). The prosecution of cold case murders. In R. Walton (Ed.), *Cold case homicides: Practical investigative techniques* (pp. 131–144). Boca Raton, FL: CRC Press.

Schuster, H., & Stone, C. (2005). *Hunting Eric Rudolph.* New York: Berkley Books.

Tversky, A., & Kahneman, D. (1982). Evidential impact of base rates. In D. Kahneman, P. Slovic, & A. Tversky (Eds.), *Judgment under uncertainty: Heuristics and biases* (pp. 153–160). Cambridge: Cambridge University Press.

U.S. Department of Justice. (1999). *Postconviction DNA testing: Recommendations for handling requests* (National Institute of Justice Research Report No. NCJ 177626). Washington, DC: U.S. Government Printing Office.

U.S. Department of Justice. (2000). *The future of forensic DNA testing: Predictions of the Research and Development Working Group* (NIJ Publication No. NCJ-183697). Washington, DC: U.S. Government Printing Office.

Using DNA to Solve Cold Cases. (2002). NIJ Special Report (NIJ Publication No. NCJ-194197). Washington, DC: U.S. Government Printing Office.

Walls, K. (2003). *Man hunt: The Eric Rudolph story.* Crescent City, FL: Global Authors Publications.

Wambaugh, J. (1989). *The blooding*. New York: Bantam Books.

Wells, G. L. (2003). Murder, extramarital affairs, and the issue of probative value. *Law and Human Behavior, 27*, 623–627.

Woffinden, B. (1988). *Miscarriages of justice*. London: Hodder and Stoughton.

Cognitive Biases

II

Cognitive Biases in Human Perception, Judgment, and Decision Making: Bridging Theory and the Real World

5

ITIEL E. DROR AND
PETER A. F. FRASER-MACKENZIE

Scientific research into human cognition is well established by decades of rigorous behavioral experimentation, studies of the human brain, and computer simulations. All of these converge to provide scientific insights into perception, judgment, and decision making (Dror & Thomas, 2005; Kosslyn & Koenig, 1995). Many of these theoretical insights play an important role in our understanding of how humans behave in the real world. The scientific research has important bearings on how human perception, judgment, and decision making can be enhanced, as well as how both lay people and experts can (and do) make mistakes. Bridging scientific theory to the real world can assist our understanding of human performance and error and help us evaluate the reliability of humans. Furthermore, it has implications on how to minimize such error through proper selection and training, best practices, and utilizing technology (Dror, 2007, in press). In this chapter, scientific findings about human cognition are discussed and linked to practical issues in the real world of investigations.

We first must understand the theoretical and conceptual framework of perception, judgment, and decision making (Lindsay & Norman, 1977; Marr, 1982; Rumelhart & McClelland, 1986). Information comes to us from the outside world via sensory input (vision, hearing, touch, etc.). As information is received, it is processed; for example, we try to identify and make sense of it, interpret and assign it meaning, compare it to information already stored in memory, and so on. One of the fundamental and established cornerstones of human cognition is that people do not passively receive and encode information. *The mind is not a camera.* We actively interact with the incoming information in a variety of ways. What we see not only reflects the pure and raw data from the input provided by the external world, but it is, to a large degree, a product of how we interpret and interact with the incoming data. *Perception is far from perfection* (Dror, 2005) because our perception and judgment are influenced by a variety of cognitive processes that are not dominated by the actual data.

In this regard, it is important to distinguish between bottom-up data-driven processes versus top-down processes that are guided and driven by factors distinct from the actual data provided by the external world. The existence and power of such top-down processes in shaping the identification of visual and other patterns has been demonstrated time and again in a number of different studies using a variety of different scientific methodologies, all confirming subjective effects on perception and judgment (e.g., Balcetis & Dunning, 2006; Humphreys, Riddoch, & Price, 1997; McClelland & Rumelhart, 1981; Zhaoping & Guyader, 2007). Top-down influences include, among other things, contextual information, expectation, what we already know (or think we know), hope, motivation, and state of mind. Although top-down processing is essential for human cognition and is a sign of expertise, it can also interfere and contaminate our perception, judgment, and decision-making processes. These biases and distortions arise from a long and well-studied list of cognitive and psychological phenomena (e.g., Evans, 1989; Gilovich, Griffin, & Kahneman, 2002; Hogarth, 1980; Kahneman, Slovic, & Tversky, 1982; Nickerson, 1998; Nisbett & Ross, 1980). These well-established cognitive and psychological phenomena (e.g., confirmation bias, cognitive dissonance, self-fulfilling prophecies, motivated reasoning, hindsight bias, escalation of commitment, etc.) cause people to lose objectivity.

Subjectivity arises when we no longer examine data purely by itself, evaluating it on its own merit without cognitive influences. When we examine information in light of such influences, we unavoidably and unconsciously perceive and judge it differently. When cognitive biases exist, we interact differently and subjectively with the information. This is manifested in a variety of ways. For example, during our examination of the data we are more likely to notice and focus on characteristics that validate and conform to extraneous information or context, a belief or a hope. Thus, the way we search and allocate attention to the data is selective and biased. Confirming data are emphasized and weighted highly, and when data quality is low (and therefore ambiguous and open to different interpretation), the existence of an extraneous influence will make people interpret the data in ways that are consistent with them. We tend to avoid and ignore data that conflict and contradict such biases, and disconfirming data that we notice are ignored. Finally, data that do not fit the bias or context and cannot easily be ignored are dismissed and explained away, and weighting of disconfirming data is low.

These and other manifestations of bias and cognitive influences can make perception, judgment, and decision making unreliable. They are well researched and documented by many scientific studies (e.g., Balcetis & Dunning, 2006; Cordelia, 2006; Ditto & Lopez, 1992; Edwards & Smith, 1996; Evans, 1989; Gilovich et al., 2002; Haselton, Nettle, & Andrews, 2005; Hogarth, 1980; Kahneman et al., 1982; Koriat, Lichtenstein, & Fischhoff, 1980; Kunda, 1990; Nickerson, 1998; Nisbett & Ross, 1980; Tversky & Kahneman, 1974; Zhaoping & Guyader, 2007). The criminal justice system, for example, has in many ways adopted and taken on board these and other cognitive and psychological findings to improve investigations (e.g., Ask & Granhag, 2005; Risinger & Loop, 2002; Stelfox & Pease, 2005). A clear case is the way in which line-ups are conducted. Rather than biasing eyewitnesses by presenting them with the suspect (the target), eyewitnesses are presented with a range of targets that include the suspect as well as numerous decoys. The line-up procedures have been drastically improved by taking into account issues of bias and other cognitive and psychological influences (e.g., Charman & Wells, 2006; Turtle, Lindsay, & Wells, 2003; Wells & Olson, 2003). In this chapter we present cognitive theory and bridge it to practical situations in the real world of investigations. Of course, within the scope of this chapter we can only bring examples, as illustrations, to convey the complex issues at hand.

Initial Impressions and Accountability

Research indicates that early impressions have considerable influence on our final evaluations. Indeed, it is common for people to maintain preexisting beliefs despite dissonant or even contradictory evidence. Nisbett and Ross (1980) describe the phenomenon as *belief perseverance*. It has been demonstrated in many areas, including problem solving (Luchins, 1942), and attitudes to change, as well as stereotype perseverance (Allport, 1954; Hamilton, 1979). Tetlock (1983) provides an example of one such study. In his experiment, participants viewed evidence from a criminal case and then assessed the guilt of a defendant. The information provided was identical in content; however, the order of the presented information was manipulated between participants. The results showed that the participants who were given the prosecution evidence first were more likely to find the defendant guilty than the participants who were given the evidence for defense first. Interestingly, this effect disappeared when participants were initially told that they were expected to justify their decision or that they would be held accountable for their decision. However, if the participants were shown the information and were only told afterward that they would have to justify their decision, then the order effect persisted. This suggests that our judgments are strongly influenced by initial information. Furthermore, influences and effects prior to information collection appear to strongly affect the way the information is perceived and interpreted, and hence how it is remembered and judged. All of this is further influenced by issues of accountability.

During the early 1990s, it was generally considered that the police were immune from their actions when they were engaged in the detection and suppression of crime. Indeed, in the case of *Hill v. Chief Constable of West Yorkshire* (1989), the mother of one of the victims of the Yorkshire Ripper sought damages in response to the police's failure to apprehend Peter Sutcliffe prior to the murder of her daughter. The House of Lords found that no duty of care arose where there is no special relationship between the victim of crime and the police, and as a result there is no liability in negligence. Moreover, it was considered dangerous as it diverted police resources from fighting crime. However, the cost of error has been shown to increase accuracy in judgment and reduce the effect of biasing factors such as order effects, ethnic stereotyping, and anchoring (Freund, Kruglanski, & Shpitzajzen, 1985; Kruglanski & Freund, 1983). However, it also increases deliberation time (McAllister, Mitchell, & Beach, 1979). Indeed, Kunda (1990) argues that accuracy is a product of deeper processing, resulting from accuracy motives that affect the initial encoding and processing of information. Tetlock (1983, 1985) showed that accuracy-promoting manipulations reduce bias when they are delivered before information presentation, but not after.

Time pressures can increase biasing effects (Freund et al., 1985; Kruglanski & Freund, 1983), perhaps because information selectivity is higher and decision criteria thresholds are lower (Dror, Busemeyer, & Basola, 1999). Although accuracy motivation through accountability appears to increase the quality of decision making, in several studies the biases are not entirely eliminated (Fischhoff, 1977; Kahneman & Tversky 1972; Lord, Lepper, & Preston, 1984; Tversky & Kahneman, 1973). These, as well as other biasing countermeasures, most often reduce and minimize bias but do not eliminate it altogether. Accountability plays a major role in a variety of domains that rely on perception, judgment, and decision making, for example, in the perception of risk and the decision to use force by police (Dror, 2008). In sum, it appears that initial impressions and preconceptions can bias our perception and judgment, which can be detrimental to achieving high-quality, evidence-based decisions. This problem can be reduced by accountability and the cost of error; however, it is never entirely eliminated, and time pressure in particular has a detrimental effect on the ability to ignore biasing factors. It is important to note that these biasing effects are examples of honest mistakes brought about by our cognitive build, which affect us all and are not representative of a conscious, malicious desire to draw one conclusion over another. On the contrary, many times the motivation to "help" and solve a case, to "do justice," clouds our judgments and our ability to reach objective conclusions.

Confirmation Bias

The tendency to confirm an initial theory or preconception and avoid disconfirming information is known as confirmation bias. An example of this is demonstrated by Wason's (1960) selection task. Participants were given a three-number sequence that followed a certain rule. They were required to deduce this rule by proposing potential sequences. They were then given feedback as to whether their proposed sequences followed the rule. The rule was simply "any ascending sequence," yet the rules suggested by participants were generally far more complex. Participants appeared to formulate a potential rule and then only generate sequences that conformed to their rule. If enough sequences were accepted, then the theory would be accepted. Surprisingly, participants tended not to try to falsify their theories.

This phenomenon has also been observed in other areas. We often appear to prefer information that is biased toward previously held beliefs, desired outcomes, or expectations (Jonas, Schulz-Hardt, Frey, & Thelen, 2001) or appear to support our expectations in negotiations (Pinkley, Griffith, & Northcraft, 1995), our outlooks and attitudes (Lundgren & Prislin, 1998), our self-serving conclusions (Frey, 1981), or our social stereotypes (Johnston, 1996). Our mind does not seem to be designed to optimize and find the perfect solution to any given problem. Instead, it merely aims to feel sufficiently satisfied with a solution (Simon, 1956, 1982). Therefore, decision makers have a criterion level, a threshold that must be met before a conclusion can be reached. Once this threshold has been reached, it is a *winner takes all* process in which a final and decisive decision is reached (Dror et al., 1999). Investigators will search for and process information until this threshold is reached (Busemeyer & Townsend, 1993; Nosofsky & Palmeri, 1997; Ratcliff & Smith, 2004). Moreover, decision factors such as time pressure can influence this threshold level (Dror et al., 1999).

In the investigative process this means that once a conclusion is reached—for example, who committed the crime—it is cognitively adopted. Additional information is then gathered to confirm the decision (for example, build the best case possible against the person believed to have perpetrated the crime). At this stage, all information is weighted in a biasing context, which means, for example, that information proving the innocence of the person may be ignored or explained away. This is in addition to the problem that the initial determination can be biased because of preconceptions, initial theory, contextual evidence, or even just a hunch. It is quite possible for the initial theory to only be corroborated by confirmatory investigative search patterns and never be truly challenged. This chain of cognitive influences may render the investigative conclusions questionable, if not altogether unreliable.

Forensic Examination: We See What We Expect to See

Interestingly, initial information affects how we perceive visual information as well as facts and figures. Bruner and Potter (1964) provided participants with blurred images that were gradually brought into focus. If the image was initially extremely blurry, it was harder for participants to finally identify the image, even when it was fully brought into focus, than if it began less blurry. People who use weak evidence to form initial hypotheses have difficulty correctly interpreting subsequent, more detailed, information. This has implications for a wide range of forensic evidence, such as fingerprints and closed-circuit television images, where initial information can be of low quality. Top-down processing uses past knowledge, current emotional state, and/or expectations to facilitate perception and judgment, resulting in faster but more subjective impressions. An example of this is waiting for a friend in a crowd and mistaking a stranger for the friend. In this case, our expectations cause us to interpret visual information in a certain way, and what we see conforms to our expectations. Dror and Rosenthal (2008) established that expert forensic examiners can have their judgments biased by extraneous contextual information (see also Dror & Charlton, 2006; Dror, Charlton, & Peron, 2006; Dror, Peron, Hind, & Charlton, 2005). In a number of studies, fingerprint experts were asked to compare prints that had been presented in a biased context. The circumstance affected their judgments, resulting in most of the examiners reaching differing conclusions on identical prints that had been presented within differing contexts. The visual information was processed in a way that conformed to their expectations.

These effects were not due to the experts having varying philosophies, training, or procedures because the conflicting conclusions were reached by the same experts on the same prints; the only difference was the context in which the prints were presented. Indeed, such biases occurred in the investigation of the 2004 Madrid train bombings. Brandon Mayfield's fingerprints were alleged to have been identified against those found on a bag of detonators found in Spain. A senior fingerprint expert from the FBI matched the latent print from the crime scene to Mayfield, who was a Muslim convert and had a military background (see Figure 5.1). The identification was further verified by two additional senior FBI fingerprint experts. Even an independent expert appointed by the court on behalf of the defense matched the print to Mayfield. All experts concluded with 100% certainty that the latent print was Mayfield's (see Stacey, 2004). After the incorrect identification was exposed by coincidence, the FBI's report on this error, as well as a report by the U.S. Department of Justice's Office of the Inspector General, concluded that circular reasoning and confirmation bias played a role in the erroneous identification.

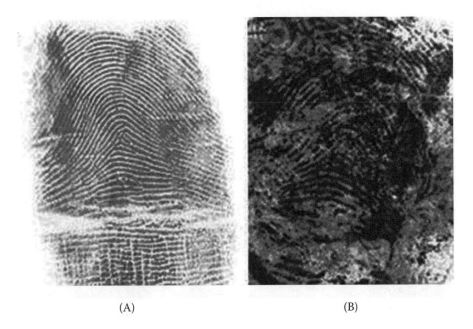

(A)   (B)

Figure 5.1 Print A on the left belongs to Brandon Mayfield. Print B on the right was found at the crime scene.

Motivation is another element that can introduce bias. Charlton, Dror, and Fraser-Mackenzie (2008) highlighted the potential of motivational bias in a study in which they interviewed forensic examiners to explore motivational and emotional experiences in routine and high-profile cases. Examiners reported a heightened emotional state both during the search for and on the finding of a match, especially during serious and high-profile cases. For example: "that [the feeling] was, that was great, I mean, to be involved in such a high profile case and finally get a match" and "oh it's a buzz. It's a definite buzz. ... When you get one, especially from the search, the buzz is there" (Charlton et al., 2008).

The research suggests that this could quite possibly have contributed to the erroneous matching of Brandon Mayfield's prints. Such failures may be more likely in serious, high-profile cases than in high-volume, day-to-day crimes. Moreover, such crimes carry the heaviest penalties and thus the greatest cost of making an error. Indeed, the Menezes Case highlights this precise point.

The Menezes Case: Context Can Kill

On July 22, 2005, Jean Charles de Menezes, an innocent man, was shot dead at Stockwell Station on the London Underground because he was incorrectly

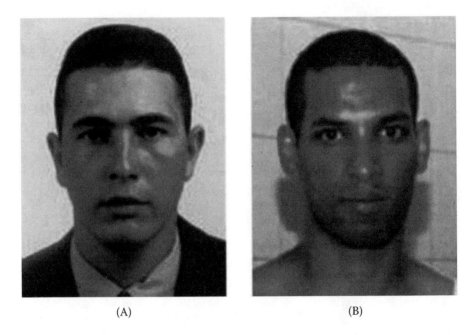

(A)   (B)

Figure 5.2 Photograph A on the left is of Jean Charles de Menezes. Photograph B on the right is of Hussain Osman.

identified as a suicide bomber (see Figure 5.2). His housing complex was under police surveillance because Hussain Osman, suspected of being a potential suicide bomber, lived there. As Menezes left his home, he was followed by police officers who thought he may be their suspect, Osman. Menezes took a bus to a tube station, where he was observed getting off the bus and then getting on another bus. The surveillance team interpreted his actions as an attempt to lose them, when in fact he was going to another tube station only because this one was closed. At Stockwell Station, he boarded a train that had pulled up to the platform. Officers were convinced that he was a suicide bomber and shot him numerous times.

Initial contextual information suggested that Menezes could be the terror suspect. Subsequent neutral information and even disconfirming information was present but appears to have been processed incorrectly. Furthermore, the potential threat of a suicide bombing on a crowded Underground would have induced stress and time pressure. Stressors such as time pressure can affect our decision-making threshold (Dror et al., 1999) as well as increase the biasing effect of erroneous initial information (Freund et al., 1985; Kruglanski & Freund, 1983). Many people will be surprised to learn such mistakes can happen; however, for cognitive experts, it is clear why such errors are made, especially when police officers do not receive proper training on cognitive issues.

The Presentation of Evidence and Emotional Effects

Due to the importance of information context and framing, it follows that the presentation of evidence is vital. The impression of forensic evidence is that it is infallible, scientifically proven, undeniable truth. It therefore has considerable impact on judges and juries. For instance, Sir Roy Meadow's evidence in the Sally Clark sudden infant death case suggested that the chance of Sally Clark having two sudden infant deaths in the family was one in 73 million (see Chapter 4). The probability of a sudden infant death is 1 in 8,543, and Meadows simply squared this value to calculate the probability of two sudden infant deaths in the same household. Statistically, however, this would only be valid if both cases were independent of each other. The findings of a sudden infant death gene rendered the evidence invalid. Nevertheless, the expert evidence had great impact on the case. Forensic evidence in particular is seen under this golden halo effect when in reality "there can be genuine disagreement between forensic scientists just as there can be disagreement between nuclear physicists or art historians" (Roberts & Willmore, 1993).

The presentation of erroneous information not only biases judgments, but seemingly innocuous changes in the way evidence is presented during a trial can have dramatic outcomes on the verdict. For example, descriptions of a psychiatric patient might affect expert forensic psychologists' and psychiatrists' evaluations of whether the patient should be released from a hospital. These descriptions can either be given in frequency terms (e.g., "of every 100 patients similar to Mr. Jones, ten are estimated to commit an act of violence to others") or in statistical terms (e.g., "patients similar to Mr. Jones are estimated to have a 10% chance of committing an act of violence to others"). Research revealed that clinicians who were given such information in frequency terms labeled the patient as being more dangerous than when the same information was presented in statistical terms (Slovic, Monahan, & MacGregor, 2000). Thus, it appears as though alternative ways in which information can be represented, which have no logical or numerical difference, can result in different judgments. This suggests that in some cases, and perhaps more than we are aware, it is not the information itself that is important as much as how it is packaged and processed by the human cognitive system.

An important determinant of how we package information is our emotional state. Research has suggested that the interpretation and selection of information can be greatly influenced by affect. For example, the processing of facial expressions corresponds to the emotional state of the perceiver (Niedenthal, Halberstandt, Margolin, & Innes-ker, 2000; Shiffenbauer, 1974). Even lexically ambiguous sounds are interpreted in a way that conforms to the person's own emotional state (Pincus, Pearce, & Perrott, 1996). This demonstrates that a person's internal context affects how information is perceived and judged, as well as the decision making that follows.

Research by Zajonc (1980, 1984a, 1984b), Bargh (1984), and LeDoux (1996) shows that affective reactions to stimuli are often more basic than cognitive evaluations (Loewenstein, Weber, Hsee, & Welch, 2001). However, these very processes can be responsible for the erroneous processing of information. Therefore, the emotional context of an investigation could potentially influence the processing of evidence and investigative decision making.

Logic versus Believability

Despite all the research described above, it might still be argued that we can use logical reasoning to override such cognitive and psychological biases. For example, investigators could be made aware of these issues and be asked to keep an open mind, listen only to the facts, free themselves from bias, prejudice, and sympathy, and remain uninfluenced by preconceived ideas and extraneous information. Unfortunately, even logical reasoning is not immune to psychological effects. Evans, Barston, and Pollard (1983) attempted to compare directly the extent to which context and past knowledge interfere with logical thought in simple reasoning tasks. In their experiment, they gave participants statements and conclusions that were either believable or unbelievable and either valid or invalid by logic and reasoning. Participants were asked to decide whether they agreed with the conclusions, using only strict logic and reasoning. Table 5.1 shows how participants were more inclined to support believable conclusions and ignore logic and reasoning.

Table 5.1   Evidence of Belief Bias in Syllogisms with Percentage of Acceptance of Conclusions as Valid

Conclusion	Acceptance
Logically Valid and Believable	89%
Logically Valid but Unbelievable	56%
Logically Invalid but Believable	71%
Logically Invalid and Unbelievable	10%

Source: Evans, Barston, & Pollard, 1983.

It appears that people use past experience more so than logic and rationality to guide their decision making. These systematic deviations from logic are unavoidable cognitive performance restrictions and errors (Johnson-Laird & Byrne, 1991; Kahneman et al., 1982; Oaksford, & Chater, 2001; Rips, 1994). People avoid cognitively taxing processes, preferring the faster and less cognitively involved process of relying on what is believable. Police often encounter inaccurate information presented as fact, for example, conscious misdirection by a guilty party or erroneous evidence from a witness. Accordingly, to the investigator or examiner, the believability heuristic is forefront in their cognitive processing.

Concluding Thoughts

In this chapter, we discussed the influence of extraneous contextual information on data. Scientific research as well as actual cases (such as the Brandon Mayfield and Menezes incidents) have demonstrated time and again how cognitive bias can cause errors in real world situations. Our minds are not designed to optimize, and it is important to ensure that we have reached a correct conclusion instead of just adopting a "satisfactory" solution. Changes have already occurred in the investigative profession. Dixon (1999) found that detectives who arrest on a hunch or give weak cases "a run" have less status than those who collect conclusive evidence prior to making an arrest. However, many forensic examiners and police officers have not received proper training in cognitive biases, and appropriate procedures and best practices to deal with these issues are needed. Although it is impossible to avoid the influence of extraneous factors on our perception, judgment, and decision making, there is plenty of room to drastically reduce such biases (Dror, in press).

References

Allport, G. W. (1954). *The nature of prejudice*. Reading MA: Addison Wesley.

Ask, K., & Granhag, P. A. (2005). Motivational sources of confirmation bias in criminal investigations: The need for cognitive closure. *Journal of Investigative Psychology and Offender Profiling, 2*, 43–63.

Balcetis, E., & Dunning, D. (2006). See what you want to see: Motivational influences on visual perception. *Journal of Personality and Social Psychology, 91*, 612–625.

Bargh, J. A. (1984). Automatic and conscious processing of social information. In R. S. Wyer & T. K. Srull (Eds.), *Handbook of social cognition* (Vol. 3, pp. 1–43). Hillsdale, NJ: Erlbaum.

Bruner, J., & Potter, M. (1964). Inference in visual recognition, *Science, 44*, 424–425.

Busemeyer, J. R., & Townsend, J. T. (1993). Decision field theory: A dynamic-cognitive approach to decision making in an uncertain environment. *Psychological Review, 100*, 432–459.

Charlton, D., Dror, I. E., & Fraser-Mackenzie, P. A. F. (2008). *A qualitative study investigating the emotional rewards and motivating factors associated with forensic fingerprint analysis*. Technical report, University of Southampton, School of Psychology, Southampton, UK.

Charman, S. D., & Wells, G. L. (2006). Applied lineup theory. In R. C. L. Lindsay, D. F. Ross, J. D. Read, & M. P. Toglia (Eds.), *Handbook of eyewitness psychology: Memory for people* (pp. 219–254). Mahwah, NJ: Lawrence Erlbaum.

Cordelia, F. (2006). *A mind of its own: How your brain distorts and deceives.* Cambridge, UK: Icon Books.

Ditto, P. H., & Lopez, D. F. (1992). Motivated skepticism: Use of differential decision criteria for preferred and nonpreferred conclusions. *Journal of Personality and Social Psychology, 63,* 568–584.

Dixon, D. (1999). Police investigative procedures: Changing legal and political contexts of policing practices. In C. Walker & K. Starmer (Eds.), *Miscarriages of justice: A review of justice in error* (pp. 65–82). Oxford: Oxford University Press.

Dror, I. E. (2005). *Perception* is far from *perfection*: The role of the brain and mind in constructing realities. *Brain and Behavioural Sciences, 28,* 763.

Dror, I. E. (2007). Land mines and gold mines in cognitive technologies. In I. E. Dror (Ed.), *Cognitive technologies and the pragmatics of cognition* (pp. 1–7). Amsterdam: John Benjamin Press.

Dror, I. E. (2008). Perception of risk and decision to use force. *Policing, 1,* 256–272.

Dror, I. E. (in press). How to manage cognitive biases. *Forensic sciences policy and management.*

Dror, I. E., Busemeyer, J. R., & Basola, B. (1999). Decision making under time pressure: An independent test of sequential sampling models. *Memory and Cognition, 27,* 713–725.

Dror, I. E., & Charlton, D. (2006). Why experts make errors. *Journal of Forensic Identification, 56,* 600–616.

Dror, I. E., Charlton, D., & Peron, A. (2006). Contextual information renders experts vulnerable to making erroneous identifications. *Forensic Science International, 156,* 74–78.

Dror, I. E., Peron, A., Hind, S., & Charlton, D. (2005). When emotions get the better of us: The effect of contextual top-down processing on matching fingerprints. *Applied Cognitive Psychology, 19,* 799–809.

Dror, I. E., & Rosenthal, R. (2008). Meta-analytically quantifying the reliability and biasability of forensic experts. *Journal of Forensic Sciences, 53,* 900–903.

Dror, I. E., & Thomas, R. D. (2005). The cognitive neuroscience laboratory: A framework for the science of the mind. In C. Erneling & D. Johnson (Eds.), *The mind as a scientific object: Between brain and culture* (pp. 283–292). Oxford: Oxford University Press.

Edwards, K., & Smith, E. E. (1996). A disconfirmation bias in the evaluation of arguments. *Journal of Personality and Social Psychology, 71,* 5–24.

Evans, J. St. B. T. (1989). *Bias in human reasoning: Causes and consequences.* Hillsdale, NJ: Erlbaum.

Evans, J. St. B. T., Barston, J. L., & Pollard, P. (1983). On the conflict between logic and belief in syllogistic reasoning. *Memory and Cognition, 11,* 295–306.

Fischhoff, B. (1977). Perceived informativeness of facts. *Journal of Experimental Psychology: Human Perception and Performance, 3,* 349–358.

Freund, T., Kruglanski, A. W., & Shpitzajzen, A. (1985). The freezing and unfreezing of impressional primacy: Effects of the need for structure and the fear of invalidity. *Personality and Social Psychology Bulletin, 11,* 479–487.

Frey, D. (1981). The effect of negative feedback about oneself and the cost of information on preferences for information about the source of this feedback. *Journal of Experimental Social Psychology, 17*, 42–50.

Gilovich, T., Griffin, D., & Kahneman, D. (2002). *Heuristics and biases: The psychology of intuitive judgment.* New York: Cambridge University Press.

Hamilton, D. L. (1979). A cognitive attributional analysis of stereotyping. In L. Berkowitz (Ed.), *Advances in experimental social psychology* (Vol. 12, pp. 53–84). New York: Academic Press.

Haselton, M. G., Nettle, D., & Andrews, P. W. (2005). The evolution of cognitive bias. In D. M. Buss (Ed.), *Handbook of evolutionary psychology* (pp. 724–746). Hoboken, NJ: Wiley.

Hill v. Chief Constable of West Yorkshire (1989). AC 53.

Hogarth, R. (1980). *Judgement and choice.* New York: John Wiley.

Humphreys, G. W., Riddoch, M. J., & Price, C. J. (1997). Top-down processes in object identification: Evidence from experimental psychology, neuropsychology, and functional anatomy. *Philosophical Transactions of the Royal Society, London, 352*, 1275–1282.

Johnson-Laird, P. N., & Byrne, R. M. J. (1991). *Deduction.* Hillsdale, NJ: Erlbaum.

Johnston, L. (1996). Resisting change: Information-seeking and stereotype change. *European Journal of Social Psychology, 26*, 799–825.

Jonas, E., Schulz-Hardt, S., Frey, D., & Thelen, N. (2001). Confirmation bias in sequential information search after preliminary decisions: An expansion of dissonance theoretical research on "selective exposure to information." *Journal of Personality and Social Psychology, 80*, 557–571.

Kahneman, D., Slovic, P., & Tversky, A. (1982). *Judgment under uncertainty: Heuristics and biases.* Cambridge: Cambridge University Press.

Kahneman, D., & Tversky, A. (1972). Subjective probability: A judgment of representativeness. *Cognitive Psychology, 3*, 430–454.

Koriat, A., Lichtenstein, S., & Fischhoff, B. (1980). Reasons for confidence. *Journal of Experimental Psychology: Human Learning and Memory, 6*, 107–118.

Kosslyn, S. M., & Koenig, O. (1995). *Wet mind: The new cognitive neuroscience.* New York: Free Press.

Kruglanski, A. W., & Freund, T. (1983). The freezing and unfreezing of lay-inferences: Effects on impressional primacy, ethnic stereotyping, and numerical anchoring. *Journal of Experimental Social Psychology, 19*, 448–468.

Kunda, Z. (1990). The case for motivated reasoning. *Psychological Bulletin, 108*, 480–498.

LeDoux, J. (1996). *The emotional brain.* New York: Simon and Schuster.

Lindsay, P. H., & Norman, D. A. (1977). *Human information processing.* New York: Academic Press.

Loewenstein, G. F., Weber, E. U., Hsee, C. K., & Welch, E. S. (2001). Risk as feelings. *Psychological Bulletin, 127*, 267–286.

Lord, C. G., Lepper, M. R., & Preston, E. (1984). Considering the opposite: A corrective strategy for social judgment. *Journal of Personality and Social Psychology, 47*, 1231–1243.

Luchins, A. S. (1942). Mechanisation in problem solving: The effect of Einstellung. *Psychological Monographs, 54*, 1–95.

Lundgren, S. R., & Prislin, R. (1998). Motivated cognitive processing and attitude change. *Personality and Social Psychology Bulletin, 24*, 715–726.

Marr, D. (1982). *Vision.* New York: W. H. Freeman.

McAllister, D. W., Mitchell, T. R., & Beach, L. R. (1979). The contingency model for the selection of decision strategies: An empirical test of the effects of significance, accountability, and reversibility. *Organizational Behavior and Human Performance, 24*, 228–244.

McClelland, J. L., & Rumelhart, D. E. (1981). An interactive activation model of context effects in letter perception: Part 1. An account of basic findings. *Psychological Review, 88*, 375–407.

Nickerson, R. S. (1998). Confirmation bias: A ubiquitous phenomenon in many guises. *Review of General Psychology, 2*, 175–220.

Niedenthal, P. M., Halberstandt, J. B., Margolin, J., & Innes-ker, A. H. (2000). Emotional state and the detection of change in facial expressions of emotion. *European Journal of Social Psychology, 30*, 211–222.

Nisbett, R. E., & Ross, L. D. (1980). *Human inference: Strategies and shortcomings of social judgment.* Englewood Cliffs, NJ: Prentice-Hall.

Nosofsky, R. M., & Palmeri, T. J. (1997). An exemplar based random walk model of speeded classification. *Psychological Review, 104*, 266–300.

Oaksford, M., & Chater, N. (2001). The probabilistic approach to human reasoning. *Trends in Cognitive Sciences, 5*, 349–357.

Pincus, T., Pearce, S., & Perrott, A. (1996). Pain patients' bias in the interpretation of ambiguous homophones. *British Journal of Medical Psychology, 69*, 259–266.

Pinkley, R. L., Griffith, T. L., & Northcraft, G. B. (1995). "Fixed pie" a la mode: Information availability, information processing, and the negotiation of suboptimal agreements. *Organizational Behavior and Human Decision Processes, 62*, 101–112.

Ratcliff, R., & Smith, P. L. (2004). A comparison of sequential sampling models for two-choice reaction time. *Psychological Review, 111*, 333–367.

Rips, L. (1994). *The psychology of proof.* Cambridge, MA: MIT Press.

Risinger, D. M., & Loop, J. L. (2002). Three card monte, Monty Hall, *modus operandi* and "offender profiling": Some lessons of modern cognitive science for the law of evidence. *Cardozo Law Review, 24*, 193–285.

Roberts, P., & Willmore, C. (1993). The role of forensic science evidence in criminal proceedings. *Royal Commission on Criminal Justice Research, Study No 11.* London: HMSO.

Rumelhart, D. E., & McClelland, J. L. (1986). *Parallel distributed processing: Explorations in the microstructure of cognition.* Cambridge, MA: MIT Press.

Shiffenbauer, A. (1974). Effect of observer's emotional state on judgments of the emotional state of others. *Journal of Personality and Social Psychology, 30*, 31–35.

Simon, H. A. (1956). Rational choice and the structure of the environment. *Psychological Review, 63*, 129–138.

Simon, H. A. (1982). *Models of bounded rationality.* Cambridge, MA: MIT Press.

Slovic, P., Monahan, J., & MacGregor, D. G. (2000). Violence risk assessment and risk communication: The effects of using actual cases, providing instruction, and employing probability versus frequency formats. *Law and Human Behavior, 24*, 271–296.

Stacey, R. B. (2004). Report on the erroneous fingerprint individualization in the Madrid train bombing case. *Journal of Forensic Identification, 54,* 706–718.

Stelfox, P., & Pease, K. (2005). Cognition and detection: Reluctant bedfellows? In M. J. Smith & N. Tilley (Eds.), *Crime science: New approaches to preventing and detecting crime* (pp. 191–207). Cullompton, Devon: Willan.

Tetlock, P. E. (1983). Accountability and the perseverance of first impressions. *Social Psychology Quarterly, 46,* 285–292.

Tetlock, P. E. (1985). Accountability: A social check on the fundamental attribution error. *Social Psychology Quarterly, 48,* 227–236.

Turtle, J. W., Lindsay, R. C. L., & Wells, G. L. (2003). Best practice recommendations for eyewitness evidence procedures: New ideas for the oldest way to solve a case. *Canadian Journal of Police and Security Services, 1,* 5–18.

Tversky, A., & Kahneman, D. (1973). Availability: A heuristic for judging frequency and probability. *Cognitive Psychology, 5,* 207–232.

Tversky, A., & Kahneman, D. (1974). Judgment under uncertainty: Heuristics and biases. *Science, 185,* 1124–1131.

Wason, P. C. (1960). On the failure to eliminate hypotheses in a conceptual task. *Quarterly Journal of Experimental Psychology, 12,* 129–140.

Wells, G. L., & Olson, E. (2003). Eyewitness identification. *Annual Review of Psychology, 54,* 277–295.

Zajonc, R. B. (1980). Feeling and thinking: Preferences need no inference. *American Psychologist, 35,* 151–175.

Zajonc, R. B. (1984a). The interaction of affect and cognition. In K. R. Scherer & P. Ekman (Eds.), *Approaches to emotion* (pp. 239–246). Hillsdale, NJ: Erlbaum.

Zajonc, R. B. (1984b). On primacy of affect. In K. R. Scherer & P. Ekman (Eds.), *Approaches to emotion* (pp. 259–270). Hillsdale, NJ: Erlbaum.

Zhaoping, L., & Guyader, N. (2007). Interference with bottom-up feature detection by higher-level object recognition. *Current Biology, 17,* 26–31.

Bounded Rationality and Criminal Investigations: Has Tunnel Vision Been Wrongfully Convicted?[1]

6

BRENT SNOOK AND
RICHARD M. CULLEN

Cognition is the art of focusing on the relevant and deliberately ignoring the rest.

Gerd Gigerenzer and Peter Todd

A substantial portion of judgment and decision-making research has led to the conclusion that using *heuristics*—simple mental strategies that people use to deal with our uncertain world—result in erroneous decisions. The message that "heuristics are bad" primarily stems from a wealth of research showing that human decision making deviates from idealistic, statistics-based decision-making models that strive for optimality (Kahneman, Slovic, & Tversky, 1982; Nisbett & Ross, 1980). In particular, it has been argued that heuristics ignore apparently relevant information, whereas complex models examine everything. A negative view of heuristics has spread to many domains (see Gilovich, Griffin, & Kahneman, 2002, for some examples), including criminal investigations, where the use of heuristics by police officers is thought to produce reasoning errors that contribute to criminal investigative failures (e.g., Findley & Scott, 2006). One heuristic-like model that is cited frequently as an explanation for criminal investigative failures is *tunnel vision*. If investigating officers, for example, stop searching for additional suspects after locating a viable suspect, they may be accused of using tunnel vision. Despite a complete absence of empirical research on tunnel vision in criminal investigations, there have been calls to eradicate this mental "virus" (Cory, 2001) by employing more deliberate and careful decision-making strategies (e.g., Findley & Scott, 2006).

[1] Support for the research reported in this chapter was provided to the first author by the Natural Sciences and Engineering Research Council of Canada, and to the second author by the Social Sciences and Humanities Research Council of Canada.

71

Although this solution is intuitively appealing, its feasibility is questionable given (1) the constrained context of criminal investigative decision making and (2) the processing limitations of the human mind.

In this chapter, we outline a psychological framework called *bounded rationality* and illustrate how it applies to investigative decision making. Applying the bounded-rationality perspective involves outlining the actual context where police officers work and determining whether the heuristics that officers use are efficient and effective decision-making strategies within that context. In taking an ecological view, we hope to gain some insight about when and why heuristics are likely to succeed and fail in the criminal investigative environment. We use tunnel vision as a primary example of how heuristics in policing have been vilified (see Lerner [2005] for a more detailed discussion of how police heuristic-led judgments are criticized in the criminal justice system). Tunnel vision appears to consist of a set of heuristics, which are arguably adaptive mechanisms that have evolved in the mind to allow people to make smart decisions. As with all judgments and decisions, decisions made at various points in the investigative process are constrained by time, knowledge, and mental capacity. It is unrealistic, not to mention impossible, for police officers to investigate *all* possible suspects, collect evidence on *all* of those suspects, explore *all* possible avenues concerning the circumstances surrounding a crime, search for disconfirming and confirming evidence of guilt for every suspect, and integrate all of this information to make an "optimal" decision.

Has Tunnel Vision Been Wrongfully Convicted as a Flawed Mental Tool?

Cases of wrongful conviction are being uncovered at an increasing rate and have rightfully received much public scrutiny (Huff, 2004; Huff, Rattner, & Sagarin, 1986; Rosen, 1992; Scullion, 2004). Such cases have devastating effects on wrongfully convicted individuals (see Campbell & Denov, 2004; Grounds, 2004), allow guilty offenders to go free, and bring disrepute to the administration of justice. In recognition of the need to prevent wrongful convictions, the Canadian Federal-Provincial-Territorial Heads of Prosecutions Committee (hereafter referred to as the FPT Committee) established a Working Group on the Prevention of Miscarriages of Justice in 2002 to identify the factors that contribute to these justice system errors. The mandate of the FPT Committee was to, among other goals, ascertain why wrongful convictions were occurring, how criminal investigations were failing, how police resources could be used more efficiently, and how to facilitate the timely resolution of cases. The FPT Committee concluded that criminal investigative failures were sometimes the result of unethical conduct by investigators who assigned blame to the wrong individuals. In other cases, the FPT Committee added that investigators failed to use best practices (e.g., having knowledge about recent research on eyewitness identification and testimony, line-up methods, interviewing and interrogation strategies, jailhouse informants, and DNA technology). In addition, the FPT Committee identified police tunnel vision as a factor that leads to criminal investigative failures. Tunnel vision in this context involves (1) identifying a primary suspect, (2) gathering evidence about that suspect, and (3) ignoring information that might disconfirm that the primary suspect is the culprit, including information about other plausible suspects.

The FPT Committee provided a series of policy recommendations aimed to eliminate, or at least reduce, future miscarriages of justice. They recommended that police agencies should implement training, screening, and disciplinary policies to deal with unethical conduct; that police officers should be educated on best practices; and that police officers should avoid tunnel vision. Although we wholeheartedly agree with the first two recommendations, we take issue with the third one.

Those who argue that tunnel vision is a cause of wrongful convictions seem to believe that bad outcomes (the conviction of an innocent suspect) only result from either bad decision-making strategies or bad investigators. But good strategies and good investigators can also be associated with bad outcomes. Heuristics are normally effective and efficient strategies for handling complex information and drawing conclusions from that information, but in some instances they can lead to poor decisions. The heuristics that make up tunnel vision are no exception. For example, even the most decorated police officer can be led astray by "misleading information" such as a fabricated eyewitness account (although its falsity would not be known to that officer until after the fact). And whereas bad (e.g., malicious, indifferent, or "nobly corrupt") investigators may indeed be the cause of some investigations going awry, tunnel vision is an altogether different process.

The recommendation to "avoid," "correct," or "prevent" tunnel vision is therefore premature. Not enough is known about tunnel vision to make such recommendations. More specifically, such a recommendation is as likely to be ineffective as it is to be effective because (1) tunnel vision is an ambiguous concept, (2) there has been no systematic study of the proportion of successful cases where police officers used tunnel vision, and (3) there has been no valid evaluation of the contribution of tunnel vision to wrongful convictions. Given that current complaints about tunnel vision are based on retrospective analysis of investigative fiascos (Findley & Scott, 2006), the recommendations to correct tunnel vision appear to be based on nothing but "bad common-sense reasoning" (see Gendreau, Goggin, Cullen, and Paparozzi [2002] for how bad common-sense–based policy recommendations, as opposed to those based on empirical evidence, can lead to the implementation of ineffective policies).

The idea that police officers should be wary of tunnel vision mirrors an ongoing debate in psychology about human rationality. Policy makers and researchers who have prematurely focused on tunnel vision as a flawed mental process might be able to increase the likelihood of reducing the occurrence of investigative failures by considering the issues that are at the heart of this debate, particularly the arguments that have been put forth since bounded rationality theory originated in the 1950s. Consequently, the primary goal of this chapter is to expose readers to the relatively recent developments in the wider rationality debate and illustrate how this debate is applicable to the understanding of heuristic-led judgments in criminal investigations.

We begin with an overview of the rationality debate. Put simply, researchers on one side focus disproportionately on the instances where heuristics produce errors. These researchers argue that using heuristics is irrational because heuristics are suboptimal to complex decision-making models that supposedly define the best possible way to make decisions. The other side argues that heuristics lead to good decisions. According to the latter view, tunnel vision might be helpful to police officers on a psychological level, for example, by allowing them to focus their thoughts in a complex investigative environment. We then describe the criminal investigative environment and argue that it is impossible for officers to use what are commonly referred to as fully rational decision-making models. This will be followed by an attempt to operationalize tunnel vision using existing heuristics that have been outlined and tested in the psychological literature.

The Rationality Debate in Psychology

The rationality debate is primarily about whether people make good decisions. Arguably, the most contentious issue in this debate is about how to best measure good decisions. Over the years, psychologists have varied the decision-making benchmark between how people perform in the real world to achieve their goals and objectives (referred to as "rationality$_1$," by Mantkelow [1999]) and whether people live up to normative standards (referred to as "rationality$_2$," by Mantkelow [1999]). In order to be judged rational$_2$, a person would have to search indefinitely for endless amounts of information, have knowledge of every relevant aspect, weigh all the available information according to importance, and finally perform intractable mathematical and statistical calculations. (Such a person has been called *Homo economicus*, or economic man.) If rationality is thought to be synonymous with optimality—which has often been the case—then unbounded models of this sort become the definition of rational thinking. People are doomed to appear irrational if such an unattainable standard is maintained.

Bounded-rationality researchers have challenged the view of the human mind as a statistical software package (Gigerenzer, 2000; Kahneman & Tversky, 1973; Simon, 1955, 1956) by arguing that the natural constraints on decision making must be taken into account when assessing human rationality. These researchers proposed that heuristics are more psychologically plausible models of human decision making than those that involve a high degree of information integration and abstract mathematical assignments and calculations. Most recently, Gerd Gigerenzer and his colleagues (e.g., Gigerenzer, Todd, & The ABC Research Group, 1999; Gigerenzer, 2001; Todd & Gigerenzer, 2000) have shown that heuristics are rational because they work well in natural environments.

We therefore adopt the rationality$_1$ definition and measure rationality by how well people make decisions in the real world, where decision making is limited by available time, information or knowledge, and mental resources.

Historical Developments

Although it is generally acknowledged that people use heuristics to make all sorts of decisions, the debate continues over whether their use leads to good or bad decisions. There were three especially influential contributions to this debate in the second half of the past century (see Gilovich & Griffin, 2002; Goldstein & Hogarth, 1997). First, Paul Meehl (1954) empirically compared the judgments of expert clinicians (which were presumably made with heuristics) with judgments reached by actuarial models and made two important discoveries. First, the actuarial methods almost always outperformed the experts. Second, the experts thought they performed better than they actually did. These two findings inspired further research on ways that the mind produces convincing but erroneous judgments. This further research generally supported Meehl's conclusions (e.g., Goldberg, 1965; Sawyer, 1966) that humans cannot reason as well as they should be able to.

Nobel Prize–winning economist and cognitive scientist Herbert Simon (1955, 1956) refuted this conclusion because it suggested that humans are irrational. Simon thought that it might be the definition of rationality, and not human performance, that was the problem regarding judgment and decision-making tasks. Simon is now credited with developing the argument that the level of rationality$_2$ suggested by rational choice models was an impractical standard for assessing human rationality. Proponents of rational choice models assume that people make judgments by evaluating the probability of each outcome, determining the utility to be gained from each outcome, combining these two evaluations, and then choosing the option that offers the optimal combination of probability and utility (Gilovich & Griffin, 2002). Simon was opposed to this classical criterion of full rationality and proposed the principle of bounded rationality as a more realistic standard. According to

Simon's view, judgment and decision making are constrained by the processing limitations of the mind, so humans have evolved to use "simple" strategies that can handle complex information (see also Kahneman, 1973; Miller, 1956). Simon believed that humans are in fact rational, considering that they make decisions under limited mental capacity and within the complexities of our uncertain world. He compared heuristics to a pair of scissors, where one blade represents the environment and the second represents the mind. Simon asserted that one must study how the two fit together, like the blades of the scissors, in order to appreciate how heuristics work.

The third important contribution to the rationality debate was the inception of Bayesian statistical analyses, a form of probability calculus, into the field of psychology by Ward Edwards (Edwards, Lindman, & Savage, 1963). The Bayesian models set a normative standard to which heuristic-led judgments could be compared (e.g., Edwards, 1968). Normative standards are those that establish how things should be, which things are good or bad, or which actions are right or wrong. Through such comparisons, it appeared that heuristic-led judgments were less than optimal because people never performed the way they should according to the idealistic benchmarks. An interest in the causes of this shortcoming subsequently emerged, as well as interest in determining ways to correct the apparent "flaws" of human cognition (Gilovich & Griffin, 2002).

Heuristics and Biases

Following these developments, Daniel Kahneman and Amos Tversky published a series of papers about how heuristics can sometimes lead to errors and biases (e.g., Kahneman & Tversky, 1972, 1973; Tversky, 1972; Tversky & Kahneman, 1971, 1973, 1974, 2002). A collection of their works, along with articles of other like-minded researchers, appeared in a now classic book titled *Judgment Under Uncertainty: Heuristics and Biases* (Kahneman, et al., 1982). Its main message is that people often use heuristics rather than fully rational models to make judgments under uncertainty. The contributors proposed that heuristics can yield both good and bad decisions, challenged whether complex normative models of human judgment accurately described the underlying mental strategies, and attempted to explain the range of observed human errors as the systematic result of cognition without implying that humans are irrational (Gilovich & Griffin, 2002). This program of research became known as the *heuristics and biases* program.

They discovered that everyday judgments do not adhere to the laws of probability or to statistical principles and argued that the underlying processes in decision making were altogether different from those implied by rational choice models. They subsequently proposed that people employ a limited number of simple cognitive rules, or heuristics, that evaluate the likelihood of options using basic computations that the mind can perform. They proposed three judgmental heuristics—the *representativeness heuristic*, the *availability heuristic*, and the *anchoring and adjustment heuristic*—that are commonly used to estimate probabilities, frequencies, and values; are cognitively cheap; and are usually effective (see Chapter 2 of this book for a discussion of how these heuristics have been observed in criminal investigative failures). Heuristics were defined as any automatic or deliberate strategy in which a natural assessment is used to estimate or predict something. The representativeness heuristic, for instance, involves the classification of things based on how similar they are to a typical case. It is supposedly used when trying to determine the probability that object A belongs to class B. The subjective probability judgment rests on how representative object A is of class B. To use a criminal investigative example, when inferring whether a particular person is likely to be guilty, police officers might mentally compare the suspect to their perception of a prototypical guilty offender. A person who is unremorseful, for example, might seem to be particularly heinous and immoral (see Weisman [2004] for a discussion of how showing remorse is interpreted by officials in the criminal justice system).

Kahneman and Tversky argued that *biases* occur because heuristics denote a tendency to make a choice that is inaccurate. For instance, the representativeness heuristic could yield an incorrect judgment if a suspect did not show remorse but was actually innocent, because a lack of remorse may not always indicate guilt (an innocent suspect would not show remorse). It was the tendency for different people to make remarkably similar errors on similar judgment tasks, relative to the normative models, that led to the conceptualization of the three aforementioned judgmental heuristics. The predictability of the biases invoked research into the cognitive mechanisms that caused them—heuristics. However, the biases continued to receive most of the scholarly attention in the immediate years to follow. Although it was apparently not Kahneman and Tversky's intention (see Gilovich & Griffin, 2002), the disproportionate focus on the instances where heuristics lead to error, rather than the instances where they lead to good decisions, combined with the continued scholarly acceptance that normative models were the most superior method of making decisions, appears to have produced the belief that heuristics are bad, a belief that still exists today. A negative image of human cognition was thus cast and the "cognitive miser" image was born (Fiske & Taylor, 1991). According to this image, humans are thought to deliberately sabotage their own accuracy by using heuristics because they are too lazy (or cheap) to carry out extensive computational strategies. Research illustrating the fallibility of heuristics has now gained a strong foothold in many areas, including economics, medicine, politics, sports, and justice (see Myers [2002] and Piattelli-Palmarini [1994] for a list of the many documented heuristic-led biases).

The ABCs of Bounded Rationality

In recent years, Gigerenzer and his colleagues (e.g., Gigerenzer et al., 1999; Gigerenzer & Selten, 2001; Gigerenzer & Todd, 1999; Todd & Gigerenzer, 2003) at the Centre for Adaptive Behavior and Cognition at the Max Planck Institute for Human Development (hereafter referred to as the ABC Research Group) have been challenging the unbalanced view that heuristics are bad. Gigerenzer and Todd (1999) claim there is an unquestioned assumption in much of psychology "that the more laborious, computationally expensive, and *nonheuristic* the strategy, the better the judgments to which it gives rise" (p. 20, italics added). Those who compare human reasoning to the unrealistic benchmarks set by rationality$_2$ promote this "more-is-better ideology." The ABC Research Group does not believe that more is always better; in fact, they have argued that less is more in certain situations (Goldstein & Gigerenzer, 1999, 2002; Todd & Gigerenzer, 2003). In a compilation of their experimental findings and theoretical essays, titled *Simple Heuristics That Make Us Smart*, Gigerenzer et al. (1999) maintain that the image of humans as irrational, resulting from years of comparing human rationality to normative models, can be mended by considering the real and inherently uncertain environments in which people make decisions. Essentially, the ABC Research Group maintains that heuristic reasoning strategies have evolved over time not as suboptimal decision-making strategies, but as effective strategies that we can use to make everyday judgments and decisions in a complex world.

Two of the ABC Research Group's core concepts—bounded rationality and ecological rationality—capture their central ideas. *Bounded rationality* originated with Simon's (1955, 1956) notion of satisficing, which involves the mental or physical search through a series of alternatives until one is found that meets a certain predefined level—called the aspiration level. If you were searching for a house to buy, for example, you would satisfice because it is nearly impossible to look at all available houses everywhere and then select the best option. You might decide that you want a clean house in a suburban area that is below $300,000, and, by satisficing, buy the first house that meets these requirements.

Fundamental to the ABC Research Group's bounded rationality theory, and the most intriguing contribution to the ongoing debate about the validity of heuristics, is a metaphor that views the mind as an *adaptive toolbox*. Like a carpenter's toolbox, the mind is equipped with a repertoire of simple mental tools that are specially suited for certain judgments and decisions. These mental tools are *fast and frugal* heuristics that have evolved to allow people to make smart decisions. The heuristics are fast because they do not involve much calculation or integration of information, and frugal because they ignore some of the available information, thus sparing mental resources.

The simplest tool in the adaptive toolbox is the recognition heuristic, which leads people to choose something they recognize over something they do not recognize (Goldstein & Gigerenzer, 1999). As an example of how the recognition heuristic might be used to make a decision, consider this question: Which of these two National Hockey League players has achieved the highest total career points—Mark Messier or Eric Cairns? If you only recognize one player and not the other, you will use the recognition heuristic. Did you choose Mark Messier? Was it because you recognized Messier and not Cairns? If so, you made a correct inference by using the recognition heuristic (see Snook & Cullen, 2006). Given a set of options, the heuristics in the adaptive toolbox specify how people search through the attributes that are associated with the options, stop that search, and then make a choice. From this toolbox perspective, human decision making is adaptive because the mind is equipped with heuristics that meet the demands of a variety of decision tasks.

Ecological rationality is concerned with the structure and representation of information in the environment and how well heuristics match that structure. To the extent that such a match exists, heuristics allow people to make an accurate decision quickly (i.e., the heuristic is ecologically rational). By focusing on the match between the environment and the mind, the ABC Research Group has placed human reasoning into an evolutionary framework that is omitted from most decision-making theories. It does not define errors by how far the outcome and model deviate from rules specified by rational choice models. By contrast, it considers the ecological rationality of a strategy to assess whether it is effective in a particular situation. To continue with our hockey player example, the recognition heuristic is ecologically rational for this particular decision because good hockey players are more recognizable than mediocre hockey players. In addition to receiving media attention for being a good player, Messier also received wide media exposure through his endorsement of Lay's Potato Chips. Of course, Lay's would not have hired an unrecognizable player in the first place. Essentially, people are able to capitalize on the fact that media exposure is a reflection of hockey greatness because the best players receive relatively more media exposure and thus have a greater likelihood of being recognized.

Bounded rationality is based on the premise that our minds construct simplified models of the complex world in order to deal with uncertainty. The performance of these heuristics has been compared to complex methods in a series of studies. In perhaps the most comprehensive study, Czerlinski, Gigerenzer, and Goldstein (1999) compared the performance of simple heuristic models against multiple regression—a complex statistics-based model—in 20 decision environments (e.g., predicting average attractiveness ratings of famous men and women). They found that the heuristic models provided an equally good fit to a range of data sets and tend to do so with fewer cues (i.e., they are more frugal). Similar results have been reported by Dhami and Harries (2001) in their study of how a group of general practitioners would decide to prescribe blood pressure medication, by Snook, Taylor, and Bennell (2004) in their study of how people predict offender home locations, by Dhami (2003) in her study of how judges make bail decisions, and by Smith and Gilhooly (2006) in their study of practitioners' decisions to prescribe antidepressant medication. Taken together, these studies have shown that the fast and frugal heuristic models provide a psychologically plausible account of how people make all sorts of judgments and decisions.[1]

In sum, the rationality debate has a long history and is deeply entrenched in the field of psychology. Some researchers examine rationality by comparing human reasoning to lofty benchmarks that they believe people should achieve and, because people fall short of these normative benchmarks, conclude that cognition is flawed and people are unavoidably irrational (see Kahneman et al., 1982; Piattelli-Palmarini, 1994). The natural response to this observed "irrationality" has been to prescribe corrective procedures to allow people to get closer to the benchmark. By contrast, the bounded-rationality perspective is concerned with describing how decision-making strategies allow people to function in the real world. Bounded-rationality researchers use ecological standards (accuracy, speed, frugality), rather than normative standards, to evaluate human rationality. By considering the nature of the situation in which a decision is made, it is possible to gain an understanding of when and why a particular heuristic is likely to succeed or fail in that situation.

Components of the rationality debate are clearly evident in the recent criminal justice literature that cites tunnel vision as a flawed mental process that produces criminal investigative failures. The basis of the specific arguments that tunnel vision is a mental virus is the same as that for the argument that heuristics lead to poor decisions—these strategies are too simple or they ignore information. Furthermore, in the current concern about tunnel vision, as well as in the broader debate, there has been a recognized need for corrective measures against heuristic use. Because the bounded-rationality perspective has provided some insight for the greater rationality debate, it can also shed light on the way tunnel vision is currently viewed by criminal justice professionals.

---

[1] Other researchers have also suggested that research on cognitive accomplishments has been "crowded out" by research on cognitive errors, and that statistical analyses typically focus on bias to the exclusion of accuracy. Krueger and Funder (2004), for example, argue that many "biases" can be beneficial, and that when an analysis stops without asking "why" such a behavioral or cognitive tendency exists, or what general purpose it might serve, the development of integrative theory and sensible advice is stymied.

Bounded Rationality and Criminal Investigations

Police officers work in an environment where they are expected to be fully rational.[2] This is especially the case when investigative failures come under direct public and legal scrutiny. When searching for suspects or through information about a set of existing suspects, police officers are expected to investigate all possible evidence and all possible suspects, explore all possible avenues concerning the circumstances surrounding a crime, search for disconfirming and confirming evidence, and make an optimal decision based on the information found (Forst, 2004; Goff, 2001; Innes, 2002). These expectations are similar to those placed on human decision making by proponents of rational choice models that assume that people have infinite time and ability to acquire and process all the information relevant to a particular decision. As previously mentioned, setting implausible information processing expectations can lead to the conclusion that the decision maker, in this case the police officer, is irrational, lazy, or used a flawed mental strategy. In other words, the expectation of optimal processing makes it seem like police officers are not doing their jobs properly.

According to the bounded-rationality perspective, however, people always use heuristics to make decisions. To apply the bounded-rationality framework to police decision making, one must consider whether a particular heuristic meets the demands of the policing environment.

The Bounded Investigative Environment and the Mind

The criminal investigative environment can be best characterized as a naturalistic decision setting. Such settings typically involve time pressures, high stakes, experienced decision makers, inadequate (e.g., missing or uncorroborated) information, ill-defined goals, poorly defined procedures, stress, dynamic conditions, team coordination, interruptions, distractions, noise, and other stressors (see Klein, 2001; Orasanu & Salas, 1993). When a crime is reported, police officers begin a search for information to identify and locate a primary suspect through physical (e.g., canvassing, interviewing witnesses), mental (e.g., linking related cases), and/or archival (e.g., searching police files) sources (de Poot & van Koppen, 2004; Innes, 2002; Sanders, 1977).[3] In a world without limits, an officer could conduct an infinitely large search of all information available in the universe. In reality, however, police officers do not have the luxury of unlimited search time. There are limitations, for example, on how many houses can be canvassed, how much comparative analysis can be done, and how much effort can be spent searching police records.

---

[2] Or at least parrot the overtones of full rationality (Lerner, 2005).
[3] See Maguire (2003) and de Poot and van Koppen (2004) for a discussion of how different types of crimes demand different search strategies that vary in complexity.

Criminal cases become harder to solve with time (Keppel & Weis, 1994; Mouzos & Muller, 2001), so many investigations are a race against the clock. *Time*, therefore, is the first major constraint on police decision making. Time constrains the search for information by influencing how resources are allocated, most notably the manpower required to manage investigative teams, interview witnesses, interact with other agencies, organize information coming into the investigation, respond to the media, and follow lines of inquiry (Eck, 1979). Police officers simply do not have time to search for all the information that is relevant or necessary to make an optimal decision. In the end, time-limited searches influence the quality and quantity of information that is collected, organized, and processed.

The *resources* that are available during an investigation are also limited. Resource allocation in a police agency must be prioritized to ensure that all important functions of the agency continue to operate properly. There are limited financial resources available, and a balance must be struck between, for example, personnel (e.g., overtime), equipment (e.g., radios), and new technology (e.g., forensic capabilities). Although agencies can sometimes obtain new resources at the start of a major investigation, these cannot be sustained indefinitely. As with time, resource limitations constrain the search for information that is used to make investigative decisions.

Similarly, there are limitations on *cognitive ability*, or constraints on the mental processing of information (e.g., Kahneman, 1973; Miller, 1956), that limit the decisions made by investigators. At the most basic level, information processing involves encoding, storing, and recalling information (Atkinson & Shiffrin, 1968). In order for relevant and novel information to be encoded and stored in the first instance, one must pay attention to that information. If attention is interrupted, by distraction, for example, the encoding process can be disrupted and the information will not become stored in memory. In addition to inattention, there are several other limitations on information processing. For example, people can only hold an average of seven pieces of information in their short-term, working memory store at any given time (Baddeley, 1992; Miller, 1956). The human mind, therefore, does not have the capacity to consider every piece of information, weight the importance of each piece of information, and integrate the information in a computationally expensive way. It is unrealistic, then, to expect a police officer's mind to act like a computer processor.

Nor should we expect police officers to have unlimited *knowledge* about every aspect of criminal investigations or have access to all of the information that is required to make a perfect decision. It is clearly impossible for police officers, or anyone else for that matter, to be fully familiar with, aware of, or completely understand criminology, forensics, psychology, law, biology, sociology, anthropology, linguistics, chemistry, statistics, ethics, politics, management, and other areas that could be required to effectively investigate crimes. Knowledge is gained through experience or study. Police officers accumulate their criminal investigative knowledge through experience gained from working a range of different cases, through training and self-study, and by interacting with and listening to other investigators.

The decisions that detectives reach are also contingent upon both the quantity and the quality of information about the current investigation. Police officers, for example, may have only one eyewitness account of a crime but must use that limited, and often ambiguous, information to make investigative decisions (see Manning, 1977; Sanders, 1977). Even if numerous eyewitnesses come forward, the knowledge they provide is still limited by the fallibility of human memory (Sporer, 1996).

In addition to the four major constraints, police officers experience pressure from internal and external sources that can influence the types of decision-making strategies that work well in the investigative environment (Findley & Scott, 2006; Maguire, 2003). For example, Crego and Alison (2004) conducted electronic focus groups with 28 senior investigating officers (SIOs) in the United Kingdom for a range of different types of serious inquiries (e.g., child abductions, stranger rapes). The officers reported the types of issues they believed were important features of the critical incidents that they had managed. Of the wide range of issues the SIOs reported having to deal with, several of them were identified as placing considerable stress on the inquiry process. The officers felt pressure because of the consequential nature of the decisions they make that can affect people's lives, the complexity of the case, the local community's concerns, the involvement and scrutiny of the press, the inability to influence other individuals that can have an impact on the investigation, the management of the investigative team, the ever-changing nature of the investigation, and their belief that they will be blamed for anything that goes wrong. Furthermore, police are expected to deal with these pressures amid the regular constraints of the political and legal systems (Goff, 2001; Lyons & Truzzi, 1991; Young, 1996).

Now that the constraints on investigative decision making have been highlighted, it is necessary to develop a clear definition of tunnel vision in order to determine whether it is likely to be an effective strategy in the investigative environment.

Tunnel Vision: Narrow-Mindedness or Focused Determination?

In biological terms, tunnel vision refers to a reduced field of vision—as from within a tunnel looking out—that results from the loss of peripheral vision with retention of central vision (Williams, 1985). A Google search of "tunnel vision" retrieves over 14 million hits; however, a quick scan of these shows that the term is often used metaphorically to describe how people in a range of domains (e.g., medicine, politics, law, and business) search for information. Tunnel vision in this sense is generally seen as a negative or undesirable process, as it refers to the narrow-minded pursuit of evidence that supports a decision that has already been made while ignoring evidence that may contradict that initial decision. The main argument against tunnel vision is that some of the ignored evidence may be valid, and people should therefore allow their beliefs to change in accordance with that evidence. Like the proponents of rationality$_2$, some criminal justice pundits appear to believe that a different investigative process, involving the collection and consideration of all available evidence, is superior to this "narrow-mindedness." But tunnel vision can also be cast in a positive light; it can be interpreted as an adaptive process whereby people focus on important, relevant evidence while ignoring evidence that distracts them from making a decision and acting upon it (Lewicka, 1998). This optimistic view implies "focused determination," a desirable human characteristic. Regardless of whether one takes a pessimistic or an optimistic stance, the metaphorical tunnel vision appears to be referring to a cognitive strategy, albeit an ambiguous one, that guides the search for alternatives and information.

Tunnel vision has become a convenient catchphrase in the field of criminal justice to refer to how the police locate suspects and build a case against them. Published articles, books, and judicial inquiries about wrongful convictions in Canada, such as the Donald Marshall, David Milgaard, Wilbert Coffin, Steven Truscott (Anderson & Anderson, 1998), Guy Paul Morin (Anderson & Anderson, 1998; Epp, 1997), and Thomas Sophonow (Anderson & Anderson, 1998; Cory, 2001; Wilson, 2003), all cite police or prosecutorial "tunnel vision" as a contributing factor. In addition, tunnel vision was discussed several times in a special issue of the *Canadian Journal of Criminology and Criminal Justice* (2004, v. 46, n. 2) that was dedicated to research on wrongful convictions, and the FPT Committee, discussed earlier in this chapter, also identified "tunnel vision" as one of the contributors to wrongful convictions.

Although these different published works defined tunnel vision in slightly different ways, most of the definitions assume that tunnel vision is a form of police misconduct. Even authors who have attempted to define tunnel vision objectively, by referring to it as a natural way of processing the information gathered during an investigation (e.g., Findley & Scott, 2006; Wilson, 2003), have still cast tunnel vision in a negative light by implying that it is a suboptimal or flawed investigative strategy. No one appears to have considered that tunnel vision might be a cognitive strategy that serves a useful purpose for criminal investigators. Below are some of the definitions that have been provided, which illustrate two things: (1) a lack of agreement about what, exactly, tunnel vision is and (2) the confounding of police misconduct with systematic cognitive processing.

Perhaps the most widely cited definition of tunnel vision is that provided by Justice Cory (2001) in relation to the wrongful conviction of Thomas Sophonow. Cory stated that:

Tunnel vision is insidious. It can affect an officer or, indeed, anyone involved in the administration of justice with sometimes tragic results. It results in the officer becoming so focussed upon an individual or incident that no other person or incident registers in the officer's thoughts. Thus, tunnel vision can result in the elimination of other suspects who should be investigated. Equally, events which could lead to other suspects are eliminated from the officer's thinking. Anyone, police officer, counsel or judge can become infected by this virus. (p. 37)

Kennedy (2004), a defense lawyer who has assisted with the exoneration of several wrongfully convicted individuals, argued that "police misconduct, which takes the form of overzealous and shoddy investigative practices, and specifically 'tunnel vision'" (p. 200) are the most significant factors leading to wrongful convictions. To this, Kennedy added:

Tunnel vision can result from incompetence, negligence, or simply a desire to secure a conviction at any and all costs. It may occur when a police officer, Crown counsel, or judge believes, prior to the presentation of all the evidence, that the defendant is guilty. ... Tunnel vision leads to the use of worthless evidence, the consideration of erroneous forensic science, and a reliance on the testimony of jailhouse informants. (pp. 200–201)

According to the FPT Committee (2004), tunnel vision is:

the single minded and overly narrow focus on an investigation or prosecutorial theory so as to unreasonably colour the evaluation of information received and one's conduct in response to the information. Tunnel vision, and its perverse by-product "noble cause corruption," are the antithesis of the proper roles of the police and Crown Attorney. Yet tunnel vision has been identified as a leading cause of wrongful convictions in Canada and elsewhere. (p. 35)

MacFarlane (2006) suggested that tunnel vision occurs when the:

investigative team focuses prematurely, resulting in the arrest and prosecution of a suspect against whom there is some evidence, while other leads and potential lines of investigation go unexplored. (p. 40)

Findley and Scott (2006) argued that tunnel vision is:

a natural human tendency that has particularly pernicious effects in the criminal justice system. By tunnel vision, we mean that "compendium of common heuristics and logical fallacies," to which we are all susceptible, that lead actors in the criminal justice system to "focus on a suspect, select and filter the evidence that will 'build a case' for conviction, while ignoring or suppressing evidence that points away from guilt." The process leads investigators, prosecutors, judges, and defence lawyers alike to focus on a particular conclusion and then filter all evidence in the case through the lens provided by that conclusion. Through that filter, all information supporting the adopted conclusion is elevated in significance, viewed as consistent with the other evidence, and deemed relevant and probative. Evidence inconsistent with the chosen theory is easily overlooked or dismissed as irrelevant, incredible, or unreliable. Properly understood, tunnel vision is more often the product of the human condition as well as institutional and cultural pressures, than of maliciousness or indifference. (p. 292)

Martin (2004) stated that tunnel vision is:

a set of preconceptions and heuristics that causes police investigators to select evidence to build a case for the conviction of their chosen suspect while suppressing or ignoring information and interpretations that point away from guilt.

Lastly, Wilson (2003) stated that:

We have to remember that wrongful convictions do not happen out of malice. I have never met a policeman who has deliberately tried to frame an innocent man—this is not how wrongful convictions occur. Instead, investigators become convinced of the guilt of people like Mr. Sophonow because the evidence itself appears to be so convincing. It is crucial to remember that the case against an accused, on the evidence, can be extremely compelling and yet the accused may be innocent. (p. 5)

Some of these definitions clearly imply police misconduct, as evidenced from the phrase "noble cause *corruption*" in the FPT Committee's report, where a conviction is knowingly obtained under falsehoods or improper procedures because the police and/or prosecutor believe the accused to be guilty. By observing in hindsight a case that ended in a wrongful conviction and noticing that information was ignored during the investigation, it is not surprising that police misconduct and tunnel vision might be viewed synonymously. Ignoring information certainly could be the result of either misconduct or tunnel vision. However, it does not necessarily follow that misconduct is to blame each and every time an investigator ignores a piece of information. It is our contention that these are two totally separate concepts that have been confounded. Whereas malicious investigators may intentionally build a case against a suspect irrespective of his or her guilt, detectives using tunnel vision really believe their primary suspect is responsible for the crime. It is this belief that causes investigators to ignore some information—that which simply does not register in their thoughts because it does not fit with the story they developed through their interpretation of the evidence. Or if it does register, it might be "explained away" on the basis of the investigator's experience or the other evidence in the case. Tunnel vision, in our view, guides an information search in complex, uncertain, and pressure-filled situations. Ignoring some information is an integral part of all heuristic strategies. Once it is agreed that misconduct and tunnel vision are separate, we can begin to understand whether tunnel vision is really a flawed cognitive process.

Despite the ambiguities surrounding tunnel vision, there have been several recommendations to remove tunnel vision from the investigative process (Cory, 2001; Findley & Scott, 2006; FPT Committee, 2004; MacFarlane, 2006). Such recommendations and concerns, however, have been raised despite any compelling empirical evidence that tunnel vision is maladaptive or even that it *can* be avoided. This type of recommendation is referred to as "common-sense" based (Gendreau et al., 2002). Before such policy recommendations can be implemented with any degree of confidence, they must be validated by systematic research. Indeed, there are many questions about tunnel vision that remain unanswered. For example, how often is tunnel vision used? When does tunnel vision lead to good decisions? When does tunnel vision lead to bad decisions? Why does it work? Why does it fail? How often does tunnel vision lead to successful criminal investigative outcomes? How often does tunnel vision lead to criminal investigative failures? Is it realistic to expect the police to follow all lines of inquiry even if they have a viable suspect identified? How many suspects should the police consider? When should they stop searching for suspects? How much evidence is required to define a prime suspect? How should police officers choose between equally viable suspects? Perhaps to start we should determine what, exactly, tunnel vision is.

Operationalizing Tunnel Vision

Although the occurrence of tunnel vision has often been blamed for investigations going awry, the concept has not been defined in a way that allows it to be meaningfully studied and scrutinized. Cognitive strategies are normally modeled in a way that clearly outlines the steps that lead to a decision (e.g., an algorithm). This has never been done for tunnel vision, however.[4] In this section, we will discuss a number of mental strategies that could potentially comprise tunnel vision. Each heuristic may serve as a useful function in human cognition—and in criminal investigations.

Judgment and decision-making research provide at least four heuristics that may account for a portion of the process that is commonly referred to

---

[4] Although Findley and Scott (2006) argue that tunnel vision is multidimensional and allude to the idea that it is made up of heuristics, they draw upon vague cognitive tendencies in their attempt to operationalize tunnel vision.

as tunnel vision: (1) the *satisficing heuristic*, (2) the *take-the-best heuristic*, (3) the *elimination-by-aspects heuristic*, and (4) *confirmation bias*. Satisficing is a heuristic that may potentially be used to guide the search for a primary suspect by ignoring some of the available information. The next two heuristics, which also ignore some of the available information, can potentially be used to select a suspect from a list of known suspects. Each of these three heuristics forms part of the adaptive toolbox in the bounded-rationality framework, and each involves rules for how to search for information, stop that search, and make a decision. Bounded-rationality researchers have proposed these as alternatives to rational$_2$ models. In experiments where decisions made with these models are compared to decisions made using complex models, the simple models perform at least as well and even better in some situations (e.g., Dhami, 2003; Gigerenzer, 2000). Confirmation bias is involved during the building of a case against a suspect who is believed to be the offender. This is a psychological tendency that occurs when people attempt to support and defend their decisions, but it can also be viewed as a component of the decision-making process. Arguably, each of these psychological mechanisms (and other seemingly irrational strategies) serves adaptive functions in human cognition. Evolutionary psychologists maintain that, otherwise, these mental tools would have been eliminated from our minds.

Satisficing, briefly discussed earlier, is a term that was introduced to the decision-making literature by Simon in the 1950s. It is actually a term that conveniently combines "satisfy" and "suffice" and essentially means looking for a good enough option rather than the best option when making a decision. The satisficing heuristic involves the sequential consideration of options until one is found that appears to meet certain aspiration level. Once that option is chosen, no further options are considered. Within the context of a criminal investigation, suspects are usually discovered one at a time and considered in that order. Police officers will compare all relevant evidence on each suspect to the predefined level of evidence that, in the police officers' experience, is an indication of guilt. Any suspect that does not meet the aspiration level is rejected, and one primary suspect (the first suspect that meets all the aspiration levels) emerges. If no suspects meet all the desired levels of evidence, the level of evidence required may be relaxed and the strategy repeated, or the suspect who comes closest to the aspiration level may be chosen. For example, a detective investigating a murder may determine that the likely offender is a white male between 18 and 25 years of age, who lives near the crime scene, has a previous conviction for burglary, and knows the victim. According to the satisficing heuristic, the first suspect encountered *that satisfies all these bits of information* (not simply the very first suspect who is encountered) will suffice as the primary suspect, and the search for other suspects is then ceased. In actuality, however, more than one suspect might meet the aspiration level.

Other heuristics might be used to choose the best suspect from that set of possible suspects.

In the example about purchasing a house presented earlier in this chapter, it can be seen that satisficing may not always lead to the best possible choice. After you purchase a house that meets all of your criteria, you may continue to browse the market only to find a better house with a nicer view than your new home. This is a prime example of the type of situation that is the basis of the rationality debate. Satisficing is a rational$_1$ strategy that allows us to make decisions in complex situations where there are so many factors involved that it would be impossible to integrate them all into a decision. Yet using it might cause one to make a suboptimal (irrational$_2$) choice. So a rational strategy produces an apparently irrational result. But, satisficing allowed the home buyer to reach a good enough decision, which meant that the primary goal of buying a house was achieved. Only in hindsight can it be learned that this house may not have been the best choice. In criminal investigations, however, the situation is different. There is a "right answer," that is, there is normally just one suspect who is responsible for a crime in question. But police officers probably use this heuristic nonetheless. It involves setting standards and making sure those standards are met before coming to a final conclusion. The standards are based on training and experience with similar crimes. This allows investigators to make a decision and move the case forward. What better strategy is there? If the evidence points to a suspect and the police wrongly conclude the suspect is the rightful offender, this may be an error, but it is not an irrational conclusion because the detective followed the evidence. In such a situation, it would be interesting to determine whether other investigators (or anyone else) would also have followed the same line of inquiry and chosen the wrong suspect.

The *take-the-best heuristic* (TTB) involves making decisions on the basis of just a few pieces of data and ignoring the rest of the available information (Gigerenzer, 2000; Gigerenzer, Hoffrage, & Kleinbölting, 1991). The recognition heuristic, described earlier in this chapter, is a simplified form of TTB in which decisions are based on recognition. Options that are not recognized are eliminated as potential choices. Recall that the recognition heuristic is only used to make a final decision when only one option is recognized. In other situations, recognition is used as a preliminary cue to eliminate some options before additional information is considered. Informational cues pertaining to the remaining options are then considered in a manner that involves considering the "best" (most subjectively valid) cue first, then the second best, and so on, until a cue is found that discriminates between the options.

For police officers assessing whether a case can be built against a suspect, these cues might include motive, alibi, and prior criminal record, although the specific factors will vary from case to case. It is assumed that the list of all potential suspects is available prior to determining the primary suspect. The police would then evaluate the motives of the potential suspects, eliminating any who had no motive. They would then do the same for alibi, then prior criminal record, and other information, until only one suspect remains. This description of TTB assumes that all cues are binary (present or not present), but the heuristic can also be generalized in such a way that it considers the values of the cues (Gigerenzer, 2000), such as the strength of the alibi or the degree of prior criminal activity. In any case, TTB involves making a decision by only considering enough information to distinguish between options. Some information is simply not used, although it may be available; hence, TTB is often referred to by the slightly longer name, "take the best, ignore the rest."

The elimination-by-aspects (EBA) heuristic, originally proposed by Tversky (1972), is similar to TTB except that it considers the values of the cues (e.g., degree of prior criminal activity). The most important piece of evidence is determined, a cut-off value is set, and suspects are rejected if they do not surpass the cut-off level. This strategy is repeated with the second most important piece of evidence, and so on, until only one suspect is left. For example, the major crime investigator may have four possible suspects, and they may all have alibis (which the investigator believes to be the most important piece of evidence in the case), but one may have a weaker alibi than the rest. Like TTB, this heuristic does not require considering all pieces of information when choosing a primary suspect.

Once a primary suspect has been selected, the objective of an investigator is to build a case against that person for the prosecution. Attempting to find information to support a belief is commonly referred to as *confirmation bias*. Confirmation bias, by definition, is a type of information search strategy whereby people look for information to confirm their beliefs, theories, or hypotheses, and avoid or misinterpret contradictory evidence so that it does not disconfirm their beliefs (Arkes & Harkness, 1980; Evans, 1989; Lewicka, 1998; Nickerson, 1998; Wason, 1960). The confirmation bias as it is currently explained in the literature, then, refers to two separate mechanisms: (1) selective (confirmatory) information search and (2) biased interpretation of information (so that it does not disconfirm our beliefs).

Confirmation bias has been called both a "ubiquitous phenomenon" (Nickerson, 1998) and the primary bias (Klein, 2001). These authors have observed that all people have a tendency to search for information that confirms their beliefs—a tendency that appears to play a role in many aspects of human cognition. Indeed, the scientific method is designed as an attempt to overcome confirmation bias—by teaching scientists to seek evidence that disconfirms theories. Klein (2001), however, noted that one of the most common strategies of scientific research is to derive a prediction from a theory and attempt to support it with evidence, thereby strengthening the reputation of that theory. Interviews with prominent and successful National Aeronautics and Space Administration (NASA) scientists (Mitroff, 1974) revealed that a number of them were committed to confirming their theories and saw this type of strategy as both desirable and necessary. These scientists claim that seeking confirmatory evidence is necessary for the development and refinement of new theories. Other researchers have also shown that scientists and other expert professionals do not always search for disconfirmatory evidence (Greenwald, Pratkanis, Leippe, & Baumgardner, 1986; Haverkamp, 1993; Mahoney & DeMonbreun, 1977). Mahoney and DeMonbreun (1977), for instance, revealed that the reasoning skills of 15 psychologists and 15 physical scientists (all with Ph.D.s) did not differ from the reasoning skills of 15 conservative Protestant ministers. When successful scientists use confirmation-seeking strategies, we perceive those strategies as a sign of persistence or focused determination. Ironically, however, some scientists criticize their research subjects for using similar strategies on judgment and decision-making tasks.

These arguments can similarly be applied to the criminal investigative context. Officers who build *a successful case* by searching for evidence that supports their belief while ignoring evidence that contradicts their belief would likely be applauded for being persistent, focused, determined, and dedicated. Those who use the same strategy in *a case that ends in a wrongful conviction*, on the other hand, might be accused of using confirmation bias (or perhaps tunnel vision), as though they neglected to properly fulfill their duties. The confirmation bias is said to violate the "fully rational" expectation that police officers should search for endless amounts of evidence or falsifying evidence in a totally objective manner, weigh and combine it all, and then make the best decision. It appears that the outcome of the investigation (rather than how well it was conducted) is the primary determinant of whether or not the investigative process is criticized.

If confirmation bias is a conscious strategy, then it should be possible to teach people not to use it. However, people may seek confirmatory evidence unconsciously rather than consciously. Mynatt, Doherty, and Tweney (1977, 1978) trained participants on a falsification technique and an alternate hypotheses technique and found that it did not decrease the prevalence of confirmatory-seeking behavior when testing hypotheses. The researchers also discovered a counterintuitive finding—a few participants were actually led astray by the search for disconfirming evidence (i.e., the falsification technique). Such research suggests that even individuals who are explicitly trained to make decisions and test hypotheses in a fully rational manner, using normative strategies, often fail to do so, and training people to use "optimal" search strategies can sometimes result in worse decisions. Mynatt et al. further found that promising, but partially incorrect, hypotheses were quickly abandoned when disconfirmation was received, and participants turned to other hypotheses that were much further from the solution they were trying to find. So, while searching for confirmatory evidence might increase the likelihood of supporting a prior belief, it does not completely rule out the possibility that disconfirmatory evidence might also be discovered.

Tunnel vision appears to consist of a set of heuristics because, by definition, some of the available information is ignored. There are many documented heuristics that people can use to search for information, end that search, and make a decision. We have proposed just four that may comprise the concept of tunnel vision, as currently used in the criminal justice literature, to illustrate the importance of operationalizing concepts in a way that allows them to be empirically tested. Experimental methods already exist for testing the four strategies we have presented, whereas tunnel vision appears to be an ambiguous catchphrase that currently cannot be subjected to the appropriate testing that would be required to determine its actual role in criminal investigative successes and failures.

Conclusion

There is a gap between the reality of how police officers make decisions and how the criminal justice system (and the general public) expects them to make decisions. Given the uncertain, dynamic, and pressure-filled nature of criminal investigations and the demands of the adversarial justice system, it is not reasonable to recommend that police officers use "optimal" decision-making strategies. Just like a substantial number of psychological researchers over the past several decades, those who cite tunnel vision as a cause of wrongful convictions have made a very important oversight—investigative decisions are made by humans in the real world, not by supercomputers in some ideal place where time, knowledge, and resources are unlimited. Decision-making models that involve ignoring information, including the heuristics that comprise tunnel vision, are thus more psychologically and ecologically plausible than those that strive for optimality.

Unfortunately, policy recommendations to eliminate wrongful convictions by eradicating mental viruses are not based on any hard facts. Empirical research on the nature of tunnel vision needs to be conducted before concluding that it causes criminal investigative failures. Comparative research is required to examine, for example, the prevalence of tunnel vision in criminal investigations that resulted in both wrongful *and* rightful convictions. Only then can it be stated with any certainty whether using tunnel vision is a poor way to approach investigative decision making. Perhaps tunnel vision is used by investigators in every case, but only a very small percentage of these result in wrongful convictions. This cannot be determined from the present criminal justice literature because only investigative fiascos have been examined. That is not to say that the analysis of investigative fiascos is not a useful starting point for identifying the possible causes of wrongful convictions. Before the apparent use of tunnel vision is used to drive policy recommendations, however, systematic research demonstrating the role of tunnel vision in criminal investigative failures is required.

Ironically, it seems that everyone uses tunnel vision, including those who have argued that tunnel vision is a flawed mental process (by presenting only anecdotes that seem to support their arguments). Some of the authors that we cite seem to have ignored research that might disconfirm or weaken their arguments. Findley and Scott (2006), for example, made an argument about tunnel vision that was similar to ours. Like us, they argued that tunnel vision does not result from malice and is a set of heuristic strategies. They made their argument by focusing on the heuristics and biases literature, however, and appear to have ignored, or perhaps did not search, the bounded rationality literature. The former generally claims that heuristics are bad, while the latter argues their use can lead to smart decisions. Findley and Scott then criticize police officers for using tunnel vision and recommend that officers think more critically when making investigative decisions. This is where our views deviate from that of many other researchers. By incorporating bounded-rationality research into the picture, we have argued that heuristics, including tunnel vision, might be adaptive strategies that allow people to function in a complex world. According to this view, asking police officers to avoid tunnel vision might not be a feasible recommendation. Moreover, because tunnel vision helps police officers achieve the positive goal of remaining focused, avoiding tunnel vision may not even be desirable.

We admit that even we used what some might call tunnel vision when we wrote this chapter. Our approach was to come to a conclusion regarding the use of tunnel vision through our psychological and legal knowledge, and then proceed to construct a rationale for these conclusions by searching for evidence that supported them. But we were not intentionally trying to mislead anyone when we chose not to include arguments from some sources. It is simply not feasible to incorporate every argument that could potentially have an impact on this chapter. We strongly believe, furthermore, that the bounded-rationality approach currently holds the most promise for understanding human decision making. Of course, if you read this chapter and give it a positive evaluation, then you will probably conclude that our approach was good; whereas, if you do not agree with our position, you will probably accuse us of being biased. Although we may be criticized for doing so, we openly admit that we used a tunnel-vision approach to build our argument because our knowledge of this area allows us to believe that we are presenting a valid argument, and confirmatory strategies have been argued to serve an adaptive purpose in human reasoning.

In conclusion, the main goal of this chapter is to stop the spread of the idea that heuristics are inevitably flawed. We recommend that people always consider the positive objectives that heuristics might serve before concluding that people are irrational, lazy, or mentally inept. We hope this chapter will help contribute to the larger, ongoing counter-revolution aimed at balancing the view of the role and value of heuristics in human decision making.

References

Anderson, B., & Anderson, D. (1998). *Manufacturing guilt: Wrongful convictions in Canada*. Blackpoint, NS: Fernwood.

Arkes, H. R., & Harkness, A. R. (1980). The effect of making a diagnosis on subsequent recognition of symptoms. *Journal of Experimental Psychology: Human Learning and Memory, 6*, 568–575.

Atkinson, R. C., & Shiffrin, R. M. (1968). Human memory: A proposed system and its control processes. In K. W. Spence & J. T. Spence (Eds.), *The psychology of learning and motivation* (Vol. 2, pp. 89–195). New York: Academic Press.

Baddeley, A. D. (1992). Working memory. *Science, 255*, 556–569.

Campbell, K., & Denov, M. (2004). The burden of innocence: Coping with a wrongful imprisonment. *Canadian Journal of Criminology and Criminal Justice, 46*, 139–163.

Cory, P. (2001). Commission of inquiry regarding Thomas Sophonow. Manitoba Justice, Province of Manitoba. Retrieved July 1, 2008, from http://www.gov.mb.ca/justice/sophonow/index.html.

Crego, J., & Alison, L. (2004). Control and legacy as functions of perceived criticality in major incidents. *Journal of Investigative Psychology and Offender Profiling, 1*, 207–225.

Czerlinski, J., Gigerenzer, G., & Goldstein, D. G. (1999). How good are simple heuristics? In G. Gigerenzer, P. M. Todd, & the ABC Research Group (Eds.), *Simple heuristics that make us smart* (pp. 97–118). New York: Oxford University Press.

de Poot, C. J., & van Koppen, P. J. (2004). *Police detectives at work: On the nature and consequences of problem solving strategies in police investigations*. Manuscript submitted for publication.

Dhami, M. K. (2003). Psychological models of professional decision making. *Psychological Science, 14*, 175–180.

Dhami, M. K., & Harries, C. (2001). Fast and frugal versus regression models of human judgment. *Thinking and Reasoning, 7*, 5–27.

Eck, J. E. (1979). *Managing case assignments: The burglary investigation decision model replication*. Washington, DC: Police Executive Research Forum.

Edwards, W. (1968). Conservatism in human information processing. In B. Kleinmuntz (Ed.), *Formal representation of human judgment* (pp. 17–52). New York: Wiley.

Edwards, W., Lindman, H., & Savage, L. J. (1963). Bayesian statistical inference for psychological research. *Psychological Review, 70*, 193–242.

Epp, J. A. (1997). Penetrating police investigative practice post-Morin. *UBC Law Review, 31*, 95–126.

Evans, J. St. B. T. (1989). *Bias in human reasoning: Causes and consequences*. Hove, UK: Laurence Erlbaum.

Findley, K. A., & Scott, M. S. (2006). The multiple dimensions of tunnel vision in criminal cases. *Wisconsin Law Review, 2,* 291–397.

Fiske, S. T., & Taylor, S. E. (1991). *Social cognition.* New York: McGraw-Hill.

Forst, B. (2004). *Errors of justice: Nature, sources and remedies.* New York: Cambridge University Press.

FPT Heads of Prosecutions Committee Working Group. (2004). *Report on the prevention of miscarriages of justice.* Ottawa: Department of Justice.

Gendreau, P., Goggin, C., Cullen, F. T., & Paparozzi, M. (2002). The common-sense revolution and correctional policy. In J. Maguire (Ed.), *Offender rehabilitation and treatment: Effective programmes and policies to reduce re-offending* (pp. 359–386). Chichester, UK: Wiley.

Gigerenzer, G. (2000). *Adaptive thinking: Rationality in the real world.* New York: Oxford University Press.

Gigerenzer, G. (2001). The adaptive toolbox. In G. Gigerenzer & R. Selton (Eds.), *Bounded rationality: The adaptive toolbox* (pp. 37–50). Cambridge, MA: MIT Press.

Gigerenzer, G., Hoffrage, U., & Kleinbölting, H. (1991). Probabilistic mental models: A Brunswikian theory of confidence. *Psychological Review, 98,* 506–528.

Gigerenzer, G., & Selton, R. (2001). *Bounded rationality.* London: MIT Press.

Gigerenzer, G., & Todd, P. M. (1999). Fast and frugal heuristics: The adaptive toolbox. In G. Gigerenzer, P. M. Todd, & the ABC Research Group (Eds.), *Simple heuristics that make us smart* (pp. 3–34). New York: Oxford University Press.

Gigerenzer, G., Todd, P., & The ABC Research Group. (1999). *Simple heuristics that make us smart.* New York: Oxford University Press.

Gilovich, T., & Griffin, D. (2002). Heuristics and biases: Then and now. In T. Gilovich, D. Griffin, & D. Kahneman (Eds.), *Heuristics and biases: The psychology of intuitive judgment* (pp. 1–18). Cambridge, UK: Cambridge University Press.

Gilovich, T., Griffin, D., & Kahneman, D. (2002). *Heuristics and biases: The psychology of intuitive judgment.* Cambridge, UK: Cambridge University Press.

Goff, C. (2001). *Criminal justice in Canada.* Scarborough, Ontario: Nelson Thomson Learning.

Goldberg, L. R. (1965). Diagnosticians vs. diagnostic signs: The diagnosis of psychosis vs. neurosis from the MMPI. *Psychological Monographs, 79*(9, Whole No. 602), .

Goldstein, D. G., & Gigerenzer, G. (1999). The recognition heuristic: How ignorance makes us smart. In G. Gigerenzer, P. M. Todd, & the ABC Research Group (Eds.), *Simple heuristics that make us smart* (pp. 37–58). London: Oxford University Press.

Goldstein, D. G., & Gigerenzer, G. (2002). Models of ecological rationality: The recognition heuristic. *Psychological Review, 109,* 75–90.

Goldstein, W. M., & Hogarth, R. M. (1997). Judgment and decision research: Some historical context. In W. M. Goldstein & R. M. Hogarth (Eds.), *Research on judgment and decision making: Currents, connections, and controversies* (pp. 3–65). Cambridge: Cambridge University Press.

Greenwald, A. G., Pratkanis, A. R., Leippe, M. R., & Baumgardner, M. H. (1986). Under what conditions does theory obstruct research progress? *Psychological Review, 93,* 216–229.

Grounds, A. (2004). Psychological consequences of wrongful conviction and imprisonment. *Canadian Journal of Criminology and Criminal Justice, 46,* 165–182.

Haverkamp, B. E. (1993). Confirmatory bias in hypothesis testing for client-identified and counselor self-generated hypotheses. *Journal of Counseling Psychology, 40,* 303–315.

Huff, C. R. (2004). Wrongful convictions: The American experience. *Canadian Journal of Criminology and Criminal Justice, 46,* 107–120.

Huff, C. R., Rattner, A., & Sagarin, E. (1986). Guilty until proven innocent: Wrongful conviction and public policy. *Crime and Delinquency, 32,* 518–544.

Innes, M. (2002). The 'process structures' of police homicide investigations. *British Journal of Criminology, 42,* 669–688.

Kahneman, D. (1973). *Attention and effort.* Upper Saddle River, NJ: Prentice-Hall.

Kahneman, D., Slovic, P., & Tversky, A. (1982). *Judgment under uncertainty: Heuristics and biases.* Cambridge, UK: Cambridge University Press.

Kahneman, D., & Tversky, A. (1972). Subjective probability: A judgment of representativeness. *Cognitive Psychology, 3,* 430–454.

Kahneman, D., & Tversky, A. (1973). On the psychology of prediction. *Psychological Review, 80,* 237–251.

Kennedy, J. P. (2004). Writing the wrongs: The role of defense counsel in wrongful convictions—A commentary. *Canadian Journal of Criminology and Criminal Justice, 46,* 197–208.

Keppel, R. D., & Weis, J. G. (1994). Time and distance as solvability factors in murder cases. *Journal of Forensic Sciences, 49,* 386–401.

Klein, G. (2001). *Sources of power: How people make decisions.* Cambridge, MA: MIT Press.

Krueger, J. I., & Funder, D. C. (2004). Towards a balanced social psychology: Causes, consequences and cures for the problem-seeking approach to social behavior and cognition. *Behavioral and Brain Sciences, 27,* 313–376.

Lerner, C. S. (2005). *Reasonable suspicion and mere hunches.* George Mason Law and Economics Research Paper No. 05-20.

Lewicka, M. (1998). Confirmation bias: Cognitive error or adaptive strategy of action control? In M. Kofta, G. Weary, & G. Sedek (Eds.), *Personal control in action: Cognitive and motivational mechanisms* (pp. 233–258). New York: Plenum.

Lyons, A., & Truzzi, M. (1991). *The blue sense: Psychic detectives and crimes.* New York: Mysterious Press.

MacFarlane, B. A. (2004). Convicting the innocent: A triple failure of the justice system. Retrieved July 14, 2008, from http://www.canadiancriminallaw.com/articles/articles%20pdf/convicting_the_innocent.pdf.

Maguire, M. (2003). Criminal investigation and crime control. In T. Newburn (Ed.), *Handbook of policing* (pp. 379–393). Devon, UK: Willan.

Mahoney, M. J., & DeMonbreun, B. G. (1977). Psychology of the scientist: An analysis of problem-solving bias. *Cognitive Therapy and Research, 1,* 229–238.

Manktelow, K. (1999). *Reasoning and thinking.* Hove, Sussex: Psychology Press.

Manning, P. K. (1977). *Police work: The social organization of policing.* Cambridge, MA: MIT Press.

Martin, D. L. (2004). Lessons about justice from the "laboratory" of wrongful convictions: Tunnel vision, the construction of guilt and informer evidence. *The Canadian Review of Policing Research.* Retrieved December 13, 2004, from http://crpr.icaap.org/index.php/crpr/index.

Meehl, P. E. (1954). *Clinical versus statistical prediction.* Minneapolis, University of Minnesota Press.

Miller, G. A. (1956). The magic number seven, plus or minus two: Some limits on our capacity for processing information. *Psychological Review, 63,* 81–93.

Mitroff, I. (1974). *The subjective side of science.* Amsterdam: Elsevier.

Mouzos, J., & Muller, D. (2001). Solvability factors of homicide in Australia: An exploratory analysis. *Trends and Issues in Crime and Criminal Justice* (no. 216). Australian Institute of Criminology, Canberra.

Myers, D. G. (2002). *Intuition: Its powers and perils.* New Haven, CT: Yale University Press.

Mynatt, C. R., Doherty, M. E., & Tweney, R. D. (1977). Confirmation bias in a simulated research environment: An experimental study of scientific inference. *Quarterly Journal of Experimental Psychology, 29,* 85–95.

Mynatt, C. R., Doherty, M. E., & Tweney, R. D. (1978). Consequences of confirmation and disconfirmation in a simulated research environment. *Quarterly Journal of Experimental Psychology, 30,* 395–406.

Nickerson, R. S. (1998). Confirmation bias: A ubiquitous phenomenon in many guises. *Review of General Psychology, 2,* 175–220.

Nisbett, R. E., & Ross, L. (1980). *Human inference: Strategies and shortcomings of social judgment.* Englewood Cliffs, NJ: Prentice-Hall.

Orasanu, M., & Salas, D. (1993). Team decision making in complex environments. In G. A. Klein, J. Orasanu, R. Calderwood, & C. E. Zsambok (Eds.), *Decision making in action: Models and methods* (pp. 327–345). Norwood, NJ: Ablex.

Piattelli-Palmarini, M., & K. Botsford, Trans (1994). *Inevitable illusions. How mistakes of reason rule our minds.* New York: Wiley.

Rosen, P. (1992). *Wrongful convictions in the criminal justice system.* Ottawa: Research Branch of the Library of Parliament.

Sanders, W. B. (1977). *Detective work: A study of criminal investigations.* New York: Free Press.

Sawyer, J. (1966). Measurement and prediction, clinical and statistical. *Psychological Bulletin, 66,* 178–200.

Scullion, K. (2004). Wrongful convictions and the criminal conviction review process pursuant to Section 696.1 of the Criminal Code of Canada. *Canadian Journal of Criminology and Criminal Justice, 46,* 189–195.

Simon, H. A. (1955). A behavioral model of rational choice. *Quarterly Journal of Economics, 69,* 99–118.

Simon, H. A. (1956). Rational choice and the structure of the environment. *Psychological Review, 63,* 129–138.

Smith, L., & Gilhooly, K. (2006). Regression versus fast and frugal models of decision-making: The case of prescribing for depression. *Applied Cognitive Psychology, 20,* 265–274.

Snook, B., & Cullen, R. M. (2006). Recognizing national hockey league greatness with an ignorance-based heuristic. *Canadian Journal of Experimental Psychology, 60,* 33–43.

Snook, B., Taylor, P. J., & Bennell, C. (2004). Geographic profiling: The fast, frugal, and accurate way. *Applied Cognitive Psychology, 18,* 105–121.

Sporer, S. L. (1996). Psychological aspects of person descriptions. In S. L. Sporer, R. S. Malpass, & G. Köehnken (Eds.), *Psychological issues in eyewitness identification* (pp. 53–86). Mahwah, NJ: Earlbaum.

Todd, P. M., & Gigerenzer, G. (2000). Précis of simple heuristics that make us smart. *Behavioral and Brain Sciences, 23*, 727–780.

Todd, P. M., & Gigerenzer, G. (2003). Bounding rationality to the world. *Journal of Economic Psychology, 24*, 143–165.

Tversky, A. (1972). Elimination by aspects: A theory of choice. *Psychological Review, 79*, 281–299.

Tversky, A., & Kahneman, D. (1971). Belief in the law of small numbers. *Psychological Bulletin, 76*, 105–110.

Tversky, A., & Kahneman, D. (1973). Availability: A heuristic for judging frequency and probability. *Cognitive Psychology, 5*, 207–232.

Tversky, A., & Kahneman, D. (1974). Judgment under uncertainty: Heuristics and biases. *Science, 185*, 1124–1131.

Tversky, A., & Kahneman, D. (2002). Extensional versus intuitive reasoning: The conjunction fallacy in probability judgment. In T. Gilovich, D. Griffin, & D. Kahneman (Eds.), *Heuristics and biases: The psychology of intuitive judgment* (pp. 19–48). Cambridge, UK: Cambridge University Press.

Young, A. N. (1996). The Charter, the Supreme Court of Canada, and the constitutionalization of the investigative process. In J. Cameron (Ed.), *The charter's impact on the criminal justice system* (pp. 1–33). Scarborough, Ontario: Thomson Canada Limited.

Wason, P. C. (1960). On the failure to eliminate hypotheses in a conceptual task. *Quarterly Journal of Experimental Psychology, 12*, 129–140.

Weisman, R. (2004). Showing remorse: Reflections on the gap between expression and attribution in cases of wrongful conviction. *Canadian Journal of Criminology and Criminal Justice, 46*, 121–138.

Williams, L. J. (1985). Tunnel vision induced by a foveal load manipulation. *Human Factors, 27*, 221–227.

Wilson, P. J. (2003). Wrongful conviction: Lessons learned from the Sophonow Public Inquiry. *Canadian Police College.*

On the Horns of a Narrative: Judgment, Heuristics, and Biases in Criminal Investigation

7

DAVID STUBBINS AND
NELSON STUBBINS

All observation must be for or against some view if it is to be of any service.

[Without a theory, a geologist] might as well go into a gravel-pit and count the pebbles and describe the colors.

Charles Darwin[1]

The "story" is what geologists call a hypothesis for the causal sequence by which things got put together. ... To construct a casual narrative is what it means to understand something.

Steven Vick[2]

Hic sunt dracones. [Here be dragons.]

Phrase used by ancient and medieval cartographers to indicate dangerous or unknown regions.[3]

Narratives are the stories we tell about how the world works. We are story-telling creatures who evolved to see the world in terms of cause and effect. Identifying causal connections gave us a huge survival advantage, both to avoid predators and to improve our effectiveness as predators. Story telling, passing information from person to person or generation to generation, compounds this advantage.

Creating narratives is unavoidable in criminal investigations (as it is in understanding anything). From the first exposure to a crime scene, an investigator begins applying common sense and criminological models to

---

[1] Quoted by Shermer (2006, p. 2). The first quote comes from an 1861 correspondence with Henry Fawcett. The second quote is from Francis Darwin, *The Life and Letters of Charles Darwin*, Vol. 2, John Murray (1887, p. 121).

[2] Vick (2002, pp. 186–187).

[3] The phrase appears on the Lenox Globe (ca. 1503–1507).

construct a story or theory of the crime or what we shall call a narrative.[4] There is a reciprocal relationship between narrative and evidence: the evidence suggests the narrative, and the narrative identifies and selects the evidence. To paraphrase Charles Darwin, without a narrative an investigator might as well go to a crime scene and count the blood spatters and describe the colors.

When a bullet is sent to the crime lab, it is because there is a story about how the world works that selects that piece of evidence as significant. A .30 caliber bullet does not leap up and fly off at 2,700 feet per second when the moon is in Aquarius. It is shot by pulling the trigger of a firearm, an act that, at least in the context of a crime scene, is performed with the intent to do harm. Investigators share a common-sense model of the relationship between bullets and firearms. With these forensic models in hand, a story surfaces: "the perpetrator shot the victim with a .30-caliber pistol while the victim was attempting to flee." A narrative about how the crime transpired emerges.

An investigator does not go to a crime scene empty handed. The notion that the skilled investigator arrives with an open mind—a *tabula rasa*— without beliefs or preconceptions, is a charade. He or she brings a set of stories (theories or models) about how the world works. Some are common sense, some artifacts of culture, and some specialized, unique to criminology and forensic science. The emerging crime scene narrative is a product of the investigator's expertise, intuition, and understanding, reciprocally interacting with the bits and pieces of the world that are becoming evidence. The narrative transforms a dead body into a homicide, a suicide, a death by natural causes, or an accident victim.

A good narrative is a good story. It is comprehensive. It respects the laws of physics, the rules of logic, and the complex and often bizarre ways we have of being human. A good narrative explains the physical evidence, the behavioral events, and the rich constellation of motives, goals, and meanings that comprise a complex crime. It is, first and foremost, a story we are compelled to believe.

A good narrative adjusts as evidence presents itself and as the reciprocal relationship between evidence and narrative is put under the cold scrutiny of rational thought. Like a plan, even the best narrative may need revision as the investigator gathers evidence, confirms and disconfirms hypotheses, and gains new insights into the players and situation. There is a tendency, however, for a narrative, once constructed, to develop a life of its own. Like the carnivorous plant in the film *The Little Shop of Horrors*, a narrative can, whatever benefits it brings, also get out of control.

---

[4] We will use the term *model* or *theory* to refer to general stories about how the world works and *narrative* to refer to specific stories that are used to explain specific events.

One need look no further than our daily dose of gossip or journalism to see how narrative can both inform and misinform. A "good" story, even when told without malicious intent, is not always good with the truth.

In the context of criminal investigative failure, the *meaning conferring* and *bidirectional* nature of narratives are its two most pertinent characteristics. A narrative of the crime confers meaning on evidence. Evidence without a narrative is mute. It is stuff, what Aristotle called *hyle*.[5] It is the narrative that tells us that stuff is evidence and presents it as meaningful. But the adoption of a narrative also carries risk. Once a narrative is accepted or institutionalized—taking on the imprimatur of an agency—it becomes increasingly more difficult to look outside its box, that is, to see alternative explanations or generate alternative narratives. Without a narrative the crime is senseless. Like turning off the headlights while driving at night, discarding the narrative throws an investigation into darkness. Compounding this problem is that narratives are seductive and easy to fall in love with. The longer the narrative has been operational, the longer egos have been invested in it, the more difficult it can be to divorce oneself from it. Like a bad marriage, a bad narrative can deteriorate over time, and adapting to what you have can seem preferable to the alternatives.

A narrative points both backward and forward in time—backward in explaining evidence and forward in suggesting investigative actions. The bidirectional nature of a narrative is fundamental to its usefulness, but it can also lead to errors in either direction.

The meaning-conferring and bidirectional nature of the narrative can cause a problematic narrative to have undesired consequences. A shoddy narrative can misinterpret evidence or cause potential evidence to be ignored. Such narratives suggest unproductive directions, wasting time and resources and ultimately sending the investigation on a wild goose chase.

A poorly constructed narrative may stink (and everybody knows it) or appear attractive and appealing. The good-looking narrative seduces the unwary into explaining away evidence. The foundation of a narrative erodes after the repeated rationalizing away of evidence. Like a game where each player removes a block from the stack until the whole pile tumbles, a narrative can become increasingly unstable. But unlike such a game, the unstable foundation of a narrative is not always visible until the whole thing crumbles. At times, investigators can become so wedded to their narrative that they see a viable structure long after the blocks have toppled.

Often a narrative is only questioned when the leads it had so auspiciously offered shrivel away. Worse, a bad narrative can lead to a dogged quest for

---

[5] Before Aristotle, there was no word in Ancient Greek for undifferentiated stuff. Aristotle borrowed the Greek word *hyle*, "lumber," for this purpose. Hence, it is building material from which things emerge.

the nonexistent evidence that will save it. We are all subject to becoming, like Don Quixote de la Mancha, entranced in a fantasy that impels ineffective deeds, whether tilting at windmills in a futile search for clues or camping by the phone in a never-ending wait for the tip that breaks the case.

This chapter examines the formation and maintenance of criminal investigative narratives, how they can contribute to investigative failure, and ways of mitigating these problems. It is based on the work of researchers in cognitive psychology, none of whom, to the best of our knowledge, ever studied investigators. What follows assumes that investigators function cognitively like everyone else. Although we have no reason to believe otherwise, research is needed to confirm this assumption.

Our discussion centers on an area of cognitive psychology concerned with the study of heuristics and biases. A heuristic is a rule of thumb used to make judgments and decisions. A bias is the way in which everyday application of these rules can lead to errors. For example, one heuristic we use to judge the distance of an object is its clarity (Tversky & Kahneman, 1982b, p. 3). A less distinct object is judged to be farther away, whereas one seen more sharply is judged to be closer. Although this heuristic works most of the time, it can lead to bias and error. On a hazy day we tend to judge objects to be farther away than they in fact are; on particularly clear days we judge them to be closer.[6]

The goal of the criminal investigative function is typically seen as the apprehension and prosecution of an offender. Investigative failures include arresting and prosecuting the wrong suspect, an incomplete or flawed investigation that can be exploited by the defense, or not arresting and prosecuting anyone (an unsolved case). To reach a positive outcome, to meet professional and ethical standards, and to avoid an investigative failure, we suggest there must be an ongoing examination of the operative narrative. The narrative itself must be explicitly considered, analyzed, and reviewed.

The problems associated with narrative formation and maintenance differ. To the experienced investigator, the context and the evidence (or lack of evidence) suggest narratives. This intuitive process, with its strengths and weaknesses, transforms evidence into a story of the crime. Expertise plays a major part in this transformation. The narrative, like a flashlight, illuminates areas worthy of exploration and casts shadows on unprofitable areas. Examining how narratives are formed, the role of intuition and expertise, and the models, mindsets, and perceptions of detectives are all critical to understanding investigative failures.

---

[6] Pilots are probably more familiar with this bias insofar as they are more reliant on the heuristic: observers on the ground use intermediate objects to establish an object's distance, whereas pilots in flight typically have no intermediate objects to assist them in judgment. One of the authors, while a student sailplane (glider) pilot, misjudged the distance to the airport on a particularly clear day and nearly had to land in a local park. For a novice pilot, an unintended off-field landing is particularly humiliating.

As a narrative emerges, it tends to develop a life of its own through the gathering of confirming evidence. Examining the often subtle, unintuitive, and suspect ways in which the mind sustains a narrative once created is also key to understanding investigative failures. An expert investigator usually gets the narrative right the first time. When he or she does not—due to the unusual nature of the crime, the paucity of evidence, or misleading evidence—a separate set of skills and actions is needed to test the narrative and generate alternatives.

Narrative Formation

Narratives vary considerably—in detail, comprehensiveness, speed of formation, origin, and credibility. At times the crime is so familiar to the investigator, the setting and sequence of events so routine, that the narrative appears immediately almost in its entirety. In such cases, rarely does the obvious narrative deceive, especially when the narrative comes with expectations that can be met or violated. Anomalies can lead the investigator to question and reappraise the narrative.

In other cases, no comprehensive narrative emerges from the crime scene. The investigator can construct only the rudiments of a story. A comprehensive narrative may not be formed until days or weeks later, or may never emerge.

A third possibility is that the investigator considers multiple narratives with no compelling evidence or rationale to select one over the other.

Expertise and Intuition

When an expert investigator arrives at a crime scene, evidence appears in ways that seem mysterious to the noninvestigator or novice investigator. Even what is not present may be relevant (as in Sherlock Holmes and the famous non-barking dog, mentioned in Chapter 2). From this disorder, the intuition of the expert investigator begins forming a narrative.

The two key elements in the formation of a criminal investigative narrative are intuition and expertise. By intuition, we are not implying some mystical process. Intuition is based on experience, or more accurately, expertise. We all have intuition about other people because we all are, to a greater or lesser extent, experienced on the subject. Some people are better at interpersonal relationships, have greater expertise, and therefore possess more valid intuitions.

Unlike the commonly held view that intuition is something certain people have and others do not, the research indicates that intuition is something developed specific to a domain of expertise (Klein, 2003). Just as an expert investigator has no intuition as to why a species of warbler has declined in an ecosystem, an expert biologist is clueless at a crime scene.

Intuition, experience, and expertise are inexorably intertwined. Although the research on how these pieces fit together is ongoing, the implications for criminal investigation suggest that experience and knowledge are a necessary, but not sufficient, condition for expertise. Experts have rich sources of patterns, processes, and stories that are readily accessible to them. The difference between experience and expertise seems related to not just their quantity but also to their complexity, particularly the creative and nuanced ways in which they are applied. An experienced investigator may have the same formal knowledge as an expert investigator, but an expert applies this knowledge in more subtle and thoughtful ways.

Intuition involves matching evidence and situation to these stored experiences and knowledge (patterns). Intuitive thinking is thinking by analogy. At a high level (Bereiter & Scardamalia, 1993), expert investigators have formal knowledge (forensic science, criminology, "book learning"), informal knowledge (how to "get things done"), and self-regulatory knowledge (understanding of personal strengths and weakness and how to manage them).

At a more detailed level, expert investigators have the following characteristics (adapted from Ross, Shafer, & Klein, 2006, pp. 405–406):

- Perceptual skills—ability to make fine discriminations and notice clues missed by novices
- Mental models—more sophisticated models of how things work in their domain, allowing faster processing of information and understanding of situations
- Sense of typicality and associations—a large set of patterns for recognizing what is typical and hence what is expected and what is anomalous
- Routines—a repertoire of tactics for getting things done
- Declarative knowledge—knowledge of more facts and details, but also tacit knowledge
- Mental simulation—use of mental simulations to explore courses of actions as well as theorize how a situation may have developed
- Assessing the situation—more time spent in assessing dynamic situations than novices and less time in deliberating over the appropriate course of actions
- Finding leverage points—experts identify the key issues (evidence) in a situation that will have the greatest impact
- Managing uncertainty—experts have more strategies for managing uncertainty in critical field situations
- Understanding one's own strengths and limitations—experts are better at self-monitoring

A novice investigator may become overwhelmed by a crime scene and is likely to resort to performing some memorized procedural steps, such as going through a checklist. He or she is less likely to spot meaningful clues and will be distracted by "noise," leading to an inability to distinguish the relevant and significant from the irrelevant.

Narratives formed by nonexperts may be subject to best-fit errors. In a study of expertise in medicine, Bereiter and Scardamalia report:

> What did the nonexpertlike medical students do when faced with a difficult diagnostic problem? They tended to use a best-fit strategy—in other words, to treat the difficult problem as if it were an easy one that could be solved by matching symptoms with known patterns. Even though they knew relatively few patterns—just some of the classical ones presented in text-books—they tended to choose whichever one of those few provided the best fit. One thing about the best-fit strategy is that it always yields an answer. (1993, p. 158)

Using such a method to choose a narrative will always produce a narrative, albeit one of dubious validity.

Experts sort the relevant from the irrelevant. They are not overwhelmed by the mass of data. Their intuitions come more readily and are more complex than those of investigators with less expertise. They know what is important, what to look for, what is missing—what is consistent and inconsistent with the various possible narratives.[7]

For example, the homicide victim in an apparent carjacking/robbery was found in a high-crime area, shot and bludgeoned. Gregg McCrary, a retired FBI special agent who consulted on the case, described her as "a bloody mess." The anomaly that transformed the case was that, although her socks were blood soaked, the inside of her sneakers were not. "That changed every-thing," said McCrary. Investigators reassessed their narrative built around a crime of opportunity or a random act of violence. Their subsequent con-struction of narratives consistent with victim's redressing—an organized, considered act—lead to the arrest of her husband (G. McCrary, personal communication, February 9, 2008).

---

[7] A good example of the role of expertise and intuition is recounted by Klein (1999, pp. 31–33). An experienced fire fighter commander responded to a kitchen house fire. After assessing the situation, the commander led his team into the kitchen. When the fire did not respond to their efforts, he pulled his men out. Soon after, the kitchen floor collapsed. Recalling the team probably saved their lives. The commander had no idea what prompted him to take this action and came to believe he might have some kind of extrasensory perception. After deconstructing the events, the commander came to realize he had subconsciously identified anomalies (the fire was not responding like a normal kitchen fire, the floor was unusually warm, and so forth) that lead him to realize his initial assessment of the cause of the fire was incorrect. In fact, the fire had started in the basement, which, at the time, he did not even know existed. His narrative—that this was a normal kitchen fire—conflicted with his expert intuition about how these fires should behave. For a firefighter, having the wrong narrative can spell disaster.

In the formation of a narrative, the expert brings a set of expectations and an attention to anomalies that alerts to false trails. Depending on the nature and availability of evidence, the resulting narrative may be sketchy and provisional or full featured and comprehensive.

Decision-Making Models

There are two basic models of judgment and decision making: Naturalistic Decision Making and Rational Decision Making. The Naturalistic Decision-Making (NDM) model was developed by studying how people make decisions in real-life, ambiguous, time-critical, and dynamic situations. The NDM research focuses on expertise and intuition. NDM is often referred to as a satisficing[8] method because the results of this approach do not necessarily produce optimal solutions, but rather "good enough" solutions.

When a patrol officer responds to a crime scene, he or she uses knowledge and intuition about the city to decide on the best route. The shortest route in terms of distance may not be shortest route in terms of time. Knowledge of traffic patterns and time of day (rush hour versus off hours) may influence the route selected. It is likely, however, the route will not be the optimum choice, but will simply be good enough. It makes no sense to spend ten minutes determining the optimum route to save two minutes of travel time.

The Rational Decision-Making (RDM) model takes a different approach by focusing on how we should make decisions to reach optimum outcomes. RDM compares alternatives by examining them against some objective criteria (ideally quantitative), and the best choice emerges from the process. The everyday version of the RDM model is to "add up the pros and cons."

Most people have been exposed to some form of the RDM model. There are a number of variants, but they all go something like this:

1. Define the problem.
2. Gather all the available information.
3. Generate all possible solutions.
4. Create objective assessment criteria.
5. Select the best solution.

Critics of RDM contend that this method has little to do with how most decisions are made in real-life situations. Anyone who has applied this approach to everyday decision making has experienced frustration. It is often unclear how to quantify value criteria and the complexities of their interrelationships. Do I want to live downtown or in the suburbs? The decision

---

[8] The term was coined by Herbert Simon in *Models of Man: Social and Rational* (1957).

will depend on a host of interrelated factors: the cost of housing, accessible amenities, traffic congestion, availability of mass transit, and so forth. Proponents of the RDM model argue that if you cannot define the problem and measure the criteria, you cannot make rational choices.

Given these two fundamentally different models, which one should guide the decision making and judgment of the criminal investigator? The answer is both.

In the earlier stages of an investigation, it is clear that time constraints, ambiguity of the crime scene, and the dynamic nature of a police inquiry demand the expert's intuition. However, there are two reasons this approach by itself is inadequate:

- The heuristics (rules of thumb) used in everyday judgments are subject to well-known biases.
- A narrative generated by intuition merely suffices in explaining evidence and thus is insufficiently reliable.

These problems are the subject of the remaining part of this section.

Perception, Persistence of Vision, Mindsets, and the Self-Fulfilling Nature of Narratives

Our perception of the world is less reliable than we might think. Errors can be more insidious than the interesting, but rare, *trompe-l'œil* or optical illusion. Perception is intentional; we tend to see what we expect to see (Heuer, 1999, pp. 7–14). Anyone who has tried to proofread his own writing is familiar with this phenomenon.

Perception is influenced by our models and mindsets. We use the term model synonymously with theory. A model is conscious or can readily be made so: The Law of Gravitation is a model of the world. A mindset is unconscious or poorly articulated: Racism is a mindset (unless it is conscious and explicit). We are unable, or at least find it difficult, to articulate our mindsets. Simply put, models are explicit, and mindsets are implicit.

Our models may or may not be correct. Often they are half-truths. Models have the advantage over mindsets in that being explicit they can be called into question and subject to scrutiny. Models and mindsets influence how detectives interpret evidence, human motivations, and other factors that go into crime narrative formation.

The more ambiguous the evidence, the more likely models and mindsets will predominate in narrative construction. As in the formation of rumor, in the absence of evidence, models and mindsets tend to fill in the missing pieces to generate a coherent story.

The more vague or ambiguous an image appears, the more likely that intentions, models, and mindsets influence those perceptions. It takes longer to correctly see an object that is initially perceived incorrectly.[9] To the extent that evidence in a criminal investigation accumulates over time, a faulty narrative is more apt to develop; it will then take more time, more evidence, and less ambiguous evidence to correct it.

An investigator arrives at a crime scene with models and mindsets about how the world works, how criminals behave, and how crimes occur. If a death is perceived as a murder, there are consequent expectations—at the very least, that there is a murderer and that the death was not by accident, suicide, or natural causes. A narrative, however partial or ill-formed, emerges; it provides the investigator with expectations that serve to focus his or her efforts. At the same time, this focus and set of expectations serve to obscure that which is inconsistent with the narrative and thus not expected. The narrative illuminates and obscures, creating the visible and the invisible. The creator of a murder narrative is disposed to find evidence of murder.

Memory is reconstructive and affected by what is subsequently experienced (Fischhoff, 1982). As a narrative becomes more comprehensive and detailed, and thus more credible and persuasive, it influences recollection (memory) of events and evidence.[10]

Models, Folklore, and Groupthink

The narratives that investigators build are based on their scientific models, folklore, and individual experiences. Science, pseudoscience, and folklore form a spectrum in which the distinction between where one ends and the other begins is not always clear. Further, the distinctions themselves are often more folklore than anything else. Fingerprinting has been employed for over 100 years, and yet its scientific basis and accuracy are still in question. (Will the reliability of a seven-point identification of a latent print please stand up?) As the *Amici* brief of the New England Innocence Project (2005, p. 5) in the *Commonwealth of Massachusetts v. Patterson* put it, "human friction

---

[9] Bruner and Potter (1964) report an experiment in which they purposefully blurred an image and then slowly brought it into focus. They were interested in how clear the image needed to become before the experimental subjects could correctly identify the image. They found that the more ambiguous and unclear the image was where it started, the more information the experimental subject needed (see Heuer, 1999, Chap. 2, for additional examples of perceptual problems).

[10] An example of how details and specificity work can be seen in an experiment in which people were asked to rate the likelihood of a thousand people dying from a natural disaster or an earthquake. People rated the earthquake as more likely to kill a thousand people. As an earthquake is just one kind of natural disaster, this obviously makes no sense. By describing a more concrete situation, it automatically became more probable in people's minds (see Rottenstreich & Tverksy, 2004, p. 383).

ridge skin is unique—but this in no way demonstrates the reliability of latent fingerprint individualization any more than the uniqueness of human faces demonstrates the reliability of eyewitness identification."

Groupthink affects groups attempting to reduce conflict and arrive at consensus without critically testing and evaluating ideas.[11] It tends to arise when a group is isolated from outside opinion, lacks diversity, and has no clear rules for decision making. As in any cult, social and self-imposed pressures—not wanting to anger or embarrass other group members or appear foolish—can cause the group to lose its ability to think effectively, reality-test ideas, and make moral judgments. The decision making of John F. Kennedy's cabinet during the Bay of Pigs fiasco and the National Aeronautical and Space Administration's (NASA) *Challenger* disaster are cited as examples of groupthink (Plous, 1993, pp. 203–207).

The Persistence of Memory: Anchoring Bias and Discredited Evidence

Not only are our perceptions fallible, but so too are our memories. Once an idea or experience becomes a memory, it affects us in ways that are not intuitive and are difficult to undo or remove. Unlike computers, humans do not have access to a delete key. Memories involve synaptic connections in the brain, and it is only through disuse of these neurobiological connections that memory fades.

Research suggests that we use information even after it has been discredited. "[T]here is much evidence that people continue to rely on misinformation even if they demonstrably remember and understand a subsequent retraction" (Lewandowsky, Stritzke, Oberauer, & Morales, 2005, p. 190). This is more likely if the original information is consistent with our beliefs and less likely if we are suspicious about the motives of the source of the original information. If an investigator uncovers evidence that supports the operative narrative, but this evidence is later discredited, the evidence will likely continue to bolster the narrative's perceived legitimacy.[12]

Anchoring refers to the tendency to make judgments relative to the first thing encountered, thus creating a kind of mental anchor. A witness who is asked if the suspect was over or under 180 pounds will use 180 pounds as the

---

[11] The term groupthink was first coined by Irving L. Janis (1972, 1982). See Chapter 2.

[12] See also Heuer (1999, pp. 124–125). A possible explanation for this phenomenon is that information does not enter our minds in a clean, pristine, and unconnected manner, but rather as a web of interrelationships (such as a cause-effect relationship or as confirming some hypothesis about the world). This may account for the persistence of urban folklore. The urban legend of alligators in the sewers of New York City may have as much to do with people's preconceived ideas of New York as anything to do with alligators (we suspect the legend would not have persisted if the story arose in Duluth or Bakersfield).

"anchor" and will give an answer closer to 180 pounds than if the anchor was 150 or 200 pounds.[13] People tend to make insufficient adjustments once an anchor is introduced.

The problem of discredited evidence exists in specific investigations as well as in the folklore and legends of the investigative community. As Heuer (1999, p. 125) said, "once information rings a bell, the bell cannot be unrung."

Induction and Confirmation Bias

If it looks like a duck, walks like a duck, and quacks like a duck, then it is probably a duck. But let us take for a moment the bird's point of view. Suppose you are a turkey and everyday around 3:00 p.m., a human shows up and feeds you. This goes on for months and months. You would have pretty good evidence that humans are deeply concerned about your well-being—at least until the day before Thanksgiving.[14]

Induction or inductive reasoning involves drawing conclusions (generalizations) from data or observations. Inductive reasoning is necessary, but never fail-safe.[15]

Fingerprint identification is an inductive method. The issue of how many points are needed to identify a print is a still a debated question. The more points of identification, the more reliable the identification. The role of disconfirming evidence is recognized in the "one-dissimilarity doctrine," wherein one unexplained difference is adequate to establish that two prints are not identical (Thornton, 1977). Of course, what is "unexplained" can be in the eyes of the beholder. The difference between an "explanation" and a "justification" for ignoring inconvenient evidence is not always clear.

Criminal investigative narratives are formed inductively and are therefore subject to these same problems. How much evidence is needed to be reasonably certain that the narrative is accurate? Regardless of how much

---

[13]For example, in one study, two groups of experienced real estate agents were asked to estimate the value of a house. The first group was told that a similar house recently sold for $300,000, while the second group was told $350,000. The first group's estimates were closer to $300,000 and the second group's estimates were closer to $350,000 (see Plous, 1993, pp. 148–149).

[14]This example is from Taleb (2007, p. 40). The original version of the story (with a chicken instead of a turkey) comes from British philosopher Bertram Russell.

[15]Inductive reasoning can be contrasted with deductive reasoning, which is going from a known principle to a specific case. Deductions are provable, that is, if the premises or assumptions are true, the conclusion must be true (all squares have four sides, this is a square, therefore it must have four sides). Conclusions reached from inductive reasoning can never be proven. They can have sufficient confirmatory evidence to be considered believable or almost certainly true (for example, the sun rises in the east). Conclusions reached by induction can be falsified by discovering a counter-example. All swans are white—until you build ocean-going ships and the navigation skills and equipment to reach Australia and find black swans (see Taleb, 2007).

evidence accumulates, we need only one piece of evidence to disconfirm the narrative (for example, a valid alibi that places the suspect in a different city at the time of the crime).

As such disconfirming evidence is much more probative than confirmatory evidence, the logical conclusion is that we should test our beliefs by searching for disconfirming evidence rather than confirming evidence. But this is not what people typically do. Once a narrative has been created, there is a tendency, a "confirmation bias," for investigators to focus exclusively on gathering confirmatory evidence.[16]

Not only do we tend to seek out only confirmatory evidence, but we tend to overvalue the evidence that we do have.

The Strength and Weight of Evidence

Griffith and Tverksy (2004) looked at two aspects of evidence: strength and weight. Strength is the unusualness or extremeness of evidence, its significance, while weight refers to its credibility or reliability. For example, if you are trying to determine if a coin is "fair" you could flip it a number of times. The proportion of heads is the strength of evidence and the sample size is the weight. If the percentage of heads was 50%, the strength of evidence suggests a "fair" coin. If the sample size was large, the weight of the evidence would suggest a "fair" coin.

People tend to overvalue strength and undervalue weight when evaluating evidence. "The extensive experimental literature on judgment under uncertainty indicates that people do not combine strength and weight in accord with the rules of probability and statistics" (Griffith & Tversky, 2004, p. 276). We seem to evaluate the strength of the evidence and then adjust for the evidence's weight. "Because such an adjustment is generally insufficient ... the strength of the evidence tends to dominate its weight in comparison to an appropriate statistical model. Furthermore, the tendency to focus on the strength of the evidence leads people to underutilize other variables that control predictive validity, such as base rate and discriminability. This treatment combines judgment by representativeness, which is based entirely on the strength of an impression, with an anchoring and adjustment process that

---

[16] Wason and Johnson-Laird (1972) conducted the following confirmation bias experiment with 128 university students. Students were shown four cards marked E, K, 4, 7, and informed that a card with a vowel on its face has an even number on the other side. Students were then asked to identify which cards they needed to turn over to determine if the statement was false. The most common response was E and 4 (59 students), and the next most common response was E (42 students). Only five students gave the correct answer. People turn over the E card to confirm the statement. Turning over 4 actually tells us nothing. Few people attempt to disconfirm the statement. Turning over E and 7 (the correct answer) are the two possible cards that can disconfirm the statement (see Plous, 1993, pp. 231–232).

takes the weight of the evidence into account, albeit insufficiently" (Griffith & Tversky, 2004, p. 276).

Take, for example, a witness who identified a suspect he saw at a crime scene from a distance of 100 yards. This evidence has significant strength, but how much weight does it have? Or take the recent issue with compositional analysis of bullet lead (CABL). The National Research Council (2004) reported on the legitimacy of the science, but expressed concerns that the significance of a match was overstated by expert witnesses. It was not the strength of the evidence that was at issue, but its weight.

When evidence has strength (significance in confirming the narrative), there is a tendency to give it more credence than it deserves. This is especially true when the weight of the evidence (its reliability) is low. The weight or reliability of evidence is often related to the probability of its truthfulness. Unfortunately, our handling of probability is also problematic.

Randomness, Probability, and the "Law of Small Numbers"

Detectives are suspicious of nonrandom events—coincidences—and their identification is an important part of the criminal investigative process. Unfortunately, people have poor intuitive concepts of randomness.[17] "People's intuitive conceptions of randomness do not conform to the laws of chance" (Tversky & Gilovitch, 2004, p. 257).[18] People often see events as correlated when they are not and correlated events as indicators of causation when they are not (Heuer, 1999, pp. 141–143).

In a parody of the statistic's law of large numbers (the larger the sample size, the more reliable the results), Tversky and Kahneman (1982a) used the term "the law of small numbers" to refer to people's tendency to draw inappropriate conclusions from small samples. Even social scientists familiar with statistics

---

[17] In one study, participants were asked to write down a random sequence as one would find from the toss of a fair coin. Ninety % of the participants alternated the heads and tails more frequently than chance would dictate (Plous, 1993, pp. 159–160).

The Birthday Problem is an example of a question on coincidence few people correctly answer:

(a) How many people would you need to gather in one room for there to be a 50/50 chance that two of them share a birthday?

(b) What is the probability that in a group of 365 people (you being one of them) one or more people share your birthday?

The answers are: (a) 23 people; and (b) 63% (see Aczel, 2004, pp. 69–75).

Another common but mistaken probability belief is called the Gambler's Fallacy. Many people think there is a greater chance of a head coming up after a string of tails in a fair coin toss. In fact, each coin flip is an independent event. "Deviations are not "corrected" as a chance process unfolds, they are merely diluted" (Tversky & Kahneman, 1982b, p. 7).

[18] Tversky and Gilovitch (2004) studied basketball statistics and concluded that the "hot hand" is an illusion. Streak shooting can be reasonably explained by normal variations in a frequency distribution.

are prone to make inappropriate inferences from small sample sizes. A corollary to this is people's tendency to expect small samples to conform to some known distribution.[19] As investigators often deal with small sample sizes, they are particularly prone to these types of errors.

Determining whether a sequence of events is random (that is, a coincidence) or nonrandom (meaningful) is dependent on how the question is framed. If the question is framed as "what is the probability of me winning the lottery?" the answer is the chances are infinitesimally small. But if the question is "what are the odds of someone winning the lottery?" then the answer is 100% or certainty.

The probability of an event is related to its base rate, the prevalence of an event or condition in a population (the denominator in a probability computation). For example, if one out of 100 Americans is a physician, then the physician base rate would be 1% (the chances of randomly finding a doctor in a crowd of Americans). The base rate is highly sensitive, however, to the population under consideration. The base rate for physicians is higher at a hospital than in a Christian Science Reading Room.

People often incorrectly incorporate base rates into their judgments, and these judgments are highly sensitive to the way questions are framed. Tversky and Kahneman (1982c, pp. 156–158) posed the following problem:

A cab was involved in a hit and run accident at night. Two cab companies, the Green and the Blue, operate in the city. You are given the following data:

(a) 85% of the cabs in the city are Green and 15% are Blue.

(b) A witness identified the cab as Blue. The court tested the reliability of the witness under the same circumstances that existed on the night of the accident and concluded that the witness correctly identified each one of the two colors 80% of the time and failed 20% of the time.

What is the probability that the cab involved in the accident was Blue rather than Green?

The median answer to this question was typically 80%. The correct answer, however, is 41%:

$$\frac{80\% \times 15\%}{(20\% \times 85\%) + (80\% \times 15\%)} = 41\%$$

[19] For example, given a coin toss sequence of H-T-H-T, people overrate the chance that the coin is fair. On the other hand, given a fair coin, people expect a sequence of tosses to look more like H-T-H-T than is warranted. There is a greater chance of a fair coin producing a sequence like H-T-T-T than our intuitions believe is likely.

These issues seem to be sensitive to framing. Tversky and Kahneman (1982c) modified condition (a) above to:

> Although the two companies are roughly equal in size, 85% of cab accidents in the city involve Green cabs and 15% involve Blue cabs.

Although the problem is logically the same, the median answer now changed to 60%. It seems people were more likely to incorporate base rate information when the problem was framed in this manner. Tversky and Kahneman believe the different response is due to the ease with which one can draw a causal inference in the second case.

Our view of the world is colored by the availability of information, the extent to which it is readily at hand. This availability bias is reflected in people's overestimation, due to media reporting, of the likelihood of being a victim of violent crime. Conversely, dangers that are less frequently reported but are, in fact, more likely, tend to be underestimated. Our "mental base rate" is built on the availability of information—often informally acquired or based more on folklore than rigorous research—and may be poorly aligned with realities. Even when there is sound empirical evidence of a probability, Koehler and Macchi (2004) have demonstrated an "exemplar availability" bias; the easier the quantitative information is to imagine, the more available it is to us.[20]

When an investigator encounters potentially random events, he or she should be aware of the following:

- If we know the probability of an event or sequence of events occurring and we have a small sample size, we are likely to believe it is nonrandom even if it is random.
- If we encounter a sequence of events with a small sample size, we are likely to see a pattern even if it is really random.
- In determining the probability of an event, attention should be paid to the selection of the appropriate base rate.

Diagnosticity

There is a tendency to attribute diagnostic value to facts even when they have none. Evidence that supports all narratives has no diagnostic value because it does not help us select one. If a data point is consistent with Tom having

[20]For example, the easier a low probability event is to imagine, the more weight people place on it. It is easier to imagine 1 in 20 people than a 5% probability or two people out of one thousand rather than 0.2% probability. Although these pairs have the same numerical value, the first in the pairs have greater influence on people.

committed the crime and Bill having committed it, it does not serve to differentiate whether Tom or Bill did it. But while a particular data point or story element may have no diagnostic value insofar as it is consistent with all available narratives, it can still increase the perceived credibility and validity of the narrative already chosen.

Another example of zero evidence diagnosticity is the "Barnum statement." A Barnum statement is a vague description that appears to be significant but which can apply to just about anyone. For example, the statement, "While you have some personality weaknesses you are generally able to compensate for them,"[21] is a typical Barnum statement. Astrologers and psychics are known for Barnum statements, and even criminal profilers have been accused of using them (e.g., Gladwell, 2007). The power of these statements is their apparent meaningfulness. A Barnum statement may seem to confirm a narrative while having no diagnostic utility.

Formal and Informal Logical Fallacies

Formal and informal logical fallacies can be difficult to identify. Although the ones that look odd are easy to discard, it is the ones that appear valid that are pernicious. To borrow a concept from sociobiology, it is only the fallacious, valid-appearing arguments that evolve and spread. Those that are unsuccessful at mimicking a valid argument suffer an early death. Like gossip, only the good ones survive. The following logical fallacies may be relevant to criminal investigators.[22]

Affirming the Consequent
If all X-type crimes are committed by Y-type criminals and the suspect is a Y-type, does that prove that the suspect committed the crime? For example, we know that if a homicide was unplanned, it was likely committed with a weapon of opportunity. If the murder weapon was a fireplace poker normally found in the home, can we assume the homicide was unplanned? Looking at this line of reasoning as a logical syllogism makes it easier to see. Consider the following:

---

[21] This example is part of the Barnum statement that was used by B. R. Forer in his original 1949 study. Sometimes referred to as the "Forer effect" or the personal validation fallacy, the "Barnum effect" is named after the famous circus man and master practical psychologist P. T. Barnum, who once claimed "we have something for everyone" (see Carroll, 2003, pp. 146–148).

[22] There are many books available on the subject; see, for example, Whyte (2004) or Gula (2002).

If the homicide was unplanned, the murder weapon was a weapon of opportunity.

The murder weapon was a weapon of opportunity.

Therefore, the murder was unplanned.

This is the logical fallacy of affirming the consequent. Because the murderer used a weapon of opportunity does not necessarily mean the murder was unplanned. The murderer could have brought a revolver to kill the victim but happened to change his mind. You cannot have an unplanned murder and plan ahead what the murder weapon will be, but you can plan ahead and change your mind.

False Cause Fallacy: Post hoc ergo propter hoc

There is a tendency to see cause-effect relationships when things happen sequentially. The cue ball strikes the four ball, then the four ball goes spinning into the corner pocket; therefore, the cue ball caused the four ball to go into the corner pocket. But not all sequential events are causal. Because cause-effect relationships do have this same temporal sequencing, we tend to reason incorrectly that anything that happens after something else is its cause.

If Mr. Big and Mr. Small had an argument, and then Mr. Small was murdered, can we assume that Mr. Big is the murderer? If arguments caused murder like cue balls cause four balls to move, we would not have an issue with overpopulation. The argument between the two speaks to motivation. The events may be correlated, but it is incorrect to say that an argument per se caused the murder. An argument is not a necessary and sufficient condition for murder, although a particular violent argument with a particular type of person in a particular type of situation may be.

The More Evidence Addiction

People confronted with uncertainty often see the problem as a lack of evidence. But if an abundance of evidence already exists, particularly if it is conflicting, the solution will rarely be found by obtaining more of the same. Additional evidence may add weight to a particular narrative, but it can never confirm it. On the other hand, disconfirming evidence can eliminate a narrative.

Once enough information is received to make an informed decision, new information (that is not substantially different) tends to increase confidence without increasing reliability. People tend to overrate the amount of information that they use in their judgments, relying more on key data they have identified. "Experts overestimate the importance of factors that have only a minor impact on their judgment and underestimate the extent to which their decisions are based on a few major variables" (Heuer, 1999, p. 56). People, including experts, tend to use simpler heuristics than they think they do and are "typically unaware not only of which variables *should* have the greatest influence, but also which variables *actually* are having the greatest influence" (Heuer, 1999, p. 56, italics in the original). More is not always better, but more sometimes leads to overconfidence.

In a study of medical diagnoses, physicians "who stressed thorough collection of data as their principal analytical method were significantly less accurate in their diagnoses than those who described themselves as following other analytical strategies such as identifying and testing hypotheses. Moreover, the collection of additional data through greater thoroughness in the medical history and physical examination did not lead to increased diagnostic accuracy" (Heuer, 1999, p. 41).

Often too much time and effort are devoted to searching for more evidence and not enough is focused on how to test the information already available. Time and resources would be more productively spent determining the quality and diagnostic value of the evidence at hand.[23]

The Problem of the Hasty Narrative

Investigators are often confronted with competing and conflicting needs. On the one hand, they need to delay formation of a comprehensive narrative until all relevant information is gathered, and, on the other, they need to rapidly construct a narrative in order to make progress with the investigation. Obviously, premature narrative development can lead to mistakes; speed and accuracy are often competing requirements. Ideally, the investigator would wait until all the data are in before committing to a narrative; however, real-world exigencies require judgments and decisions prior to having all the data in place. Invariably, the investigator is placed in the position of having to construct the structure while still figuring out what kind of structure it needs to be. Data often do not make sense until the narrative is developed and completed. In the investigator's world, narrative formation is inherently dynamic.

Identifying a dead body as a murder victim is already taking the first steps down the narrative path. Building a narrative in the course of an investigation is inevitable, however rudimentary or ill-formed it may be. The issues are always to what extent other potentially probable narratives are being

---

[23]In a study of how people manage complex, dynamic systems, a key factor that distinguished performance was focus on testing narratives/hypotheses. "The good participants differed from the bad ones, however, in how often they tested their hypothesis. The bad participants failed to do this. For them, to propose a hypothesis was to understand reality; testing that hypothesis was unnecessary. Instead of generating hypotheses, they generated 'truths'" (Dörner, 1996, p. 24).

excluded and to what extent the narrative obscures as well as illuminates recognized and unrecognized evidence.

A number of forces may push toward rapid narrative formation:

- Speed is critical because evidence decays: witnesses disappear, memories fail, and crime scenes cannot be secured indefinitely.
- Organizational pressures may result from departmental resource limitations and political demands in high-profile cases. Ambitious investigators may be motivated to draw conclusions prematurely in order to be the first one with the answer.
- People have different levels of comfort for tolerating and managing uncertainty or ambiguity. Those with lower thresholds are predisposed to quickly adopt narratives.
- Personality (ego-strength) differences among investigators vary with regard to their comfort level in admitting ignorance or uncertainty. People are sensitive about being perceived as stupid, incompetent, or indecisive.
- Social issues such as one's status in the organization may play a role. Seeing oneself or being seen by others as an unproven team member (such as someone new to a section), being newly promoted, or being a novice are risk factors for hasty narrative development. The crusty old investigator who has proved his worth in countless investigations is more likely to feel comfortable saying he does not have a clue than is the newly promoted investigator who is not sure he or she can cut the mustard. Organizational cultures differ with regard to their tolerance of uncertainty and ambiguity. In groups with low tolerance, members may lose status or be seen as lacking competence if they do not have answers to questions or they admit they do not know something. Such pressures—whether self-imposed or in combination with external pressures, real or imagined—may lead to hasty narrative development.
- We may have a motivational or confirmation bias to see certain types of individuals as more likely to commit crimes. These biases may also have organizational support. Mindset (prejudices, common and received ideas) can cause narratives to form a little too quickly and easily. Holding the view, "If his lips are moving, he must be lying," affects these kinds of errors. A belief that everyone is a liar—particularly in an organizational culture that causes status to accrue to those who hold this view (or act like they do)—will adversely impact one's error rate, at least to the extent that everyone is not a liar.
- There may be unsubstantiated folklore that points to a suspect.
- Having a narrative enhances self-esteem, while not having one is ego deflating. Particularly in cases that appear simple, an investigator may be tempted to embrace the first or most obvious narrative. What may

seem to be a small and natural step for an investigator may appear to be a leap of faith to an outside observer.

The main countervailing force is the need to apprehend the correct suspect.

Summary

Narratives come into being through the interaction of crime scene evidence and the investigator's mindsets, models, and experiences—that is, the investigator's intuition. Intuition provides a rapid, first-order approximation of the solution to the crime. These narratives are unavoidable, necessary, and fallible. Research on the heuristics used in judgment and decision making oblige investigators to recognize the cognitive errors to which narratives are vulnerable. Reducing these errors is the responsibility of the professional investigator.

Narrative Maintenance

Like a snowball racing down a mountain slope, once a narrative has formed, it tends to build momentum, weight, and credibility. Investigators must be wary of such a natural course of events, alert to the symptoms, aware of the consequences, and able and willing to intervene when necessary.

Implicit versus Explicit Narratives

Implicit narratives or narratives that are poorly articulated are more likely to conceal errors. By explicitly owning and documenting the narrative, investigators are more likely to identify inconsistencies and discrepancies.

Implicit narratives are verbal, vague, and nonspecific. The more casually they are communicated, the more they are subject to wide-ranging interpretations. Like the perception of an indistinct object, what is seen in an implicit narrative is in the eye of the beholder. An implicit narrative can inadvertently become a "Barnum narrative" with something for everyone.

Making a narrative explicit means to document:

- The description of the narrative as a theory of the crime
- The assumptions and any causal inferences made in the narrative
- The evidence that supports the narrative (confirming evidence)
- The evidence that raises questions about the narrative (disconfirming evidence).

Experts differ from novices in their ability to question the operant narrative and adapt it to changes. Expert investigators are more likely to spot anomalies and modify or discard a narrative as the investigation progresses. Experts may be more flexible because they have the resources to modify or re-create a narrative and do not need to hold on to one "for dear life." They may allow themselves to be adrift because they have the confidence that it won't be so for too long—that a new narrative will emerge.

Anomalies

Evidence that points in a different direction may be explained away. This is not just an issue in criminal investigations; it is a problem confronted by all professionals who have to make decisions based on limited or unreliable information. A physician confronted with a symptom not typically associated with the hypothesized diagnosis may either explain it away or take it is as disconfirming evidence. Either might be true. Identifying anomalies and being attentive to disconfirming data provide critical opportunities to clarify one's judgment and decision making.

In what is called the *normalization of deviance* (Vaughan, 1996), anomalies are ignored or explained away. When a narrative surfaces and begins to have official status, it is easily reified. Investigators can fall into cognitive lock (Chiles, 2002, p. 41), where they focus on narrative confirmation and exclude or ignore evidence that might point elsewhere. Research suggests that experts are better at spotting anomalies. Less experienced investigators, especially the interpersonally or organizationally weaker members, are less likely to call attention to inconsistencies. A narrative needs no coronation for it to appear in the sanctioned robes that bully the unwary. To suggest "the Emperor has no clothes" is often not the best career move.

Procedural or other demands for consistency, inspired by past lessons, legal requirements, or organizational needs, may also obscure anomalies. Criminal procedures that demand consistent approaches, although designed to ensure reliable results, may obscure rather than illuminate. These problems are not found solely in criminal investigation. Vick (2002) describes the problem of consistency in the context of geotechnical engineering:

> But consistency is indifferent to truth. One can be entirely consistent and still be entirely wrong ... [like] the paranoid who finds perfect consistency in the world's actions. The implied promise of consistency in method is correctness of result, and this promise might even be fulfilled were it not for the awkward circumstance that the problems are not consistently the same. Because geology is never constant, each geotechnical problem differs in diagnosis and interpretation, so that applying uniformly consistent solution techniques will guarantee that some answers will be consistently right. And others consistently wrong. (p. 69)

The complexities of people, culture, and crime scenes are huge. Using a procedure that was effective in the past or comparing the present crime to a similar, successfully solved, past crime is no guarantee of success. Reliance on past experience, while often a useful technique, can also lead to explaining away anomalies.

A Narrative Is a Commitment: Necessary, but Not Necessarily Reliable

A narrative is a way of seeing the world and, as such, precludes alternative interpretations. One story about a set of relations—physical and behavioral—precludes others. If Professor Plum committed the crime in the study with a knife, then Miss Scarlet did not do it in the kitchen with a gun.

Once a story starts to form, it is increasingly more difficult to step back and see how alternative narratives also explain the evidence. A narrative takes on a life of its own. There is a twofold danger to fixing on a single narrative: if it is proven incorrect, time and opportunities are lost in not pursuing alternative investigative paths; if it is not proven incorrect (but is still wrong), there is the danger of accusing the wrong person.

To the extent we are committed to a narrative, that we have a stake in its success, we are prone to a self-serving bias. This is not to question the fairness or morality of investigators, but is a reflection of the research on how people make decisions. "The self-serving bias exists because people are imperfect information processors. One of the most important subjective influences on information processing is self-interest. People tend to confuse what is personally beneficial with what is fair or moral" (Bazerman, 2002, p. 2).[24]

The narrative often suggests or even dictates the ways in which questions are framed, which also affects how they are answered.[25] This not only influences the way witnesses are questioned (and hence their responses), but the way investigators ask themselves questions. This reciprocity between how questions are framed and the answers received can lead the narrative toward self-fulfilling prophecy.

Fixing on a Narrative

There is a tendency for investigators to fix on a narrative, to use an explanatory story to the exclusion of all other possible stories. A narrative that is initially ill-formed and tentative—a hypothesis—becomes reified over time. The narrative demands that reality conform to the story. Like ephemeral

[24]See also the related section on egocentrism in Bazerman (2002, pp. 70–72).
[25]The same question asked in different ways may produce different answers. For example, there was a 20% difference in how people responded when asked if public speeches against democracy in the United States should be "allowed" or "forbidden" (see Plous, 1993, p. 69; Bazerman, 2002, pp. 46–51).

snowflakes that quietly pile up on a mountain slope, a narrative tends to transform into something that looks solid, dependable, and trustworthy.[26]

There are internal and external forces that lead investigators to hunker down with one narrative (it may not be the best one, but it may be the only one).

Internal Forces

People have an aversion to ambiguity. A narrative in hand is better, as it were, than two in the bush. One characteristic necessary for an expert investigator is "self-regulatory knowledge" (Bereiter & Scardamalia, 1993) of how to manage ambiguity and uncertainty. Without it, an investigator is too prone to fix prematurely on a narrative. This is part of the "knowledge" of how to be a good investigator.

Once a narrative begins to be trusted, other believable narratives or conflicting evidence may be experienced as *cognitive dissonance*. A conflict associated with two beliefs that cannot both be true must be resolved one way or the other. Ideally, this is experienced as an opportunity to approach the truth; more commonly, one side of the dilemma is simply explained away.

Conspiracy theorists and pseudoscientists are two groups with strong skills in dissipating cognitive dissonance. Conspiracy theorists can always say, "Of course, the government would say that!" Pseudoscientists can always say, "Of course, the scientist establishment will never listen to the truth!"

The sunk-cost effect can lead us to stubbornly hold on to a narrative (see below).

External Forces

"The truth will make you free" (John 8:32). It will also allow you to arrest the perpetrator and get on with the next case. On the other hand, you can just tell your boss what you think of her and her narrative and that will also set you free. If the organization has fixed on a narrative, it may be difficult, if not career impairing, to suggest or argue for an alternative narrative. Those who propose alternative narratives may be seen as "not getting it," "wandering off in the weeds," or "rocking the boat."

There can be an illusory consensus among investigators. Sometimes people do not speak up because they assume others have better information, are more knowledgeable, or have more experience. Sometimes they remain silent for reasons related to their personal psychology or because they do not want to be held accountable for mistakes. Dealing with consensus explicitly can be tricky and difficult for managers.

Organizations may also implicitly or inadvertently suppress dissent. Pressure to be a "good team player" can be used to suppress dissenting voices

[26]For a comprehensive case example, see Gregg McCrary's chapter in this book (chap. 8), "Who Killed Stephanie Crowe?"

that might be raised against the prevailing narrative. Limited investigative resources or external pressures in high-profile cases may prematurely close or fix a narrative. Narrowing an investigation to a single narrative has implications for allocation and expenditure of resources. It may also provide the appearance of progress. Organizations, strapped for resources, may therefore implicitly pressure an investigation to focus on a single narrative.

Organizations differ with regard to their tolerance for diversity of opinion. Within an organization, some opinions—depending on either the ideological content or the speaker—may have more volume or credibility. Some organizations and managers view all good ideas as only coming from the top down.

Organizations also differ with regard to how much chaos they tolerate. Overly ordering or prematurely ordering an investigation may be limiting and counterproductive. Intuition and creativity may lead to productive thinking and revised or new narratives. On the other hand, chaos and disorganization may result in lack of progress, running in circles, wheel-spinning, and poor communication. It is possible that what is effective in the first 48 hours is counterproductive in cold case investigations, and vice versa.

Overconfidence

Research indicates that people tend to be overconfident in their assessment of their subjective probabilities and predictions. Although this is true for both novices and experts, there appears to be differences among professions. Meteorologists exhibited the least overconfidence of the professions studied, probably due to the frequency and regularity of feedback. Investigators, like other professionals not blessed with regular and immediate feedback, need to be wary of overconfidence.

Griffith and Tverksy (2004) attribute overconfidence to the way people misassign the strength and weight of evidence. Vick (2002, p. 210) attributes overconfidence to the "hard-easy effect," suggesting confidence increases relative to difficulty for the simple reason that the less we know the less we know what we do not know. Both explanations may be right.

There are a number of ways in which overconfidence can be expressed in a criminal investigation:

- Overconfidence in the narrative itself.
- Overconfidence in the significance and diagnosticity of specific evidence.
- Overconfidence in the attribution of motives or in understanding the psychological and/or behavioral dynamics of suspects, witnesses, and victims.
- Overconfidence in the reliability and accuracy of an eyewitness.

As a narrative becomes more detailed, its salience and believability increase. Most U.S. police detectives will remember the infamous search for the nonexistent white van seen everywhere during the DC Sniper case. One way to decrease overconfidence is to provide an alternative hypothesis. The act of examining and comparing alternative crime scenarios decreases the subjective probability of the original narrative and should reduce overconfidence (Rottenstreich & Tverksy, 2004, pp. 383–402).

Halo Effect

The halo effect (Thorndike, 1920) refers to a cognitive bias that attributes qualities commensurate with our judgment of someone or something. Is high employee morale a cause of corporate success? Or do successful companies tend to have high morale? Most of the business bestsellers that claim to reveal the "hidden secrets" of successful companies are only reporting halo effects. Rosenzweig (2007) observes that while these companies have many positive characteristics as a byproduct of their success—high morale, low turnover, environmental concerns, and so on—there is no real evidence these are, in themselves, the causes of the success. He argues that what it takes to be a corporate success is far more complicated and involves many unpredictable elements (a good business gamble, ineffective competitors, the right product at the right time, and so forth). A business selling horseshoes at the start of the twentieth century was not going to be successful for long—except perhaps by getting into the automobile tire business.

In an analogous manner, investigators evaluating suspects are vulnerable to the halo effect (although it may be more apt to label it the devil effect). Investigators may be quick to attribute negative characteristics, not all of which may be warranted, to criminals. Although past behavior can be a good predictor of future behavior, and while many offenders are versatile in their offense history, it is not valid to lump all criminal behaviors together. A burglar with a long record for auto theft, shoplifting, and fraud, but no violence, is probably no more likely (or unlikely) to commit a crime of violence as someone without a criminal past.

The halo effect may also cause positive attributions of investigative prowess to accrue to detectives with positive attributes unrelated to criminal investigative skill, such as being "one of the boys," proficient in sports, or a generous drinking buddy.

Sunk-Cost Effects

Once action has been taken involving the expenditure of time, effort, money, or prestige, it becomes difficult to withdraw from a continuing commitment, even when evidence fails to support the validity of the ongoing pursuit.

Human nature is such that we all too often throw good money after bad. Investors tend to hold on to losing investments, and government agencies continue programs even after they have been shown to be ineffective. Sunk-cost effects may be a factor in investigators holding on to a narrative long after it has lost contact with evidence and reality. Research suggests that once an action has been taken, there is a tendency to evaluate it more positively and see the choice as more justified than beforehand (Plous, 1993, p. 29), presumably because there is now a psychological investment in the decision.

Summary

Narratives, however ill-formed or incomplete, attract supporting structures that may be less solid than they appear or tainted with cognitive biases:

- Implicit narratives are more likely to be supported by vague and insubstantial evidence than explicit narratives.
- Anomalies may be explained away rather than be seen as disconfirming evidence.
- A narrative, although providing a way of seeing the crime, also restricts the way questions are framed and the way investigators think about the crime.
- There may be both internal and external forces that encourage prematurely fixing on a narrative.
- Investigators are subject to overconfidence not only in their judgment of a narrative but also in the value, significance, or diagnosticity they attach to evidence.
- Narratives are subject to sunk-cost effects, particularly after substantial effort has been expended.

Techniques for Managing Narratives to Reduce Failure

Narratives, like the opposite sex, are one of those things you cannot live with and you cannot live without. To make sense of evidence requires constructing a narrative. And yet the very narrative that gives sense to the crime scene and the investigation also carries within it an encumbrance of potential error that can lead to investigative failure. The narrative is constructed from evidence, but then itself becomes load bearing in interpreting and valuing evidence.

The heuristics of everyday life and criminal investigations usually work—generally, they are good rules of thumb. But in some sense they are like drinking and driving: it is inconvenient to call a cab and most of the time the drive home is uneventful. But drunk driving, like everyday heuristics, can result in spectacular failures.

The cognitive errors and biases detailed in the previous sections are not unique to criminal investigations. All professions share these same challenges. The specific ways in which errors manifest may differ among professions, but the underlying problem is that they are all staffed by humans with their corresponding biological, neurological, and psychological strengths and weaknesses. What differentiates professionals from amateurs or dilettantes is not just experience, but how well they attend to and mitigate the skewing effects of cognitive errors.

Therefore, the professional investigator needs to address the following two questions: (1) what processes, methods, and techniques are available to mitigate the risk of error, and (2) what level of risk mitigation is appropriate?

This section addresses the first question by presenting procedures that can be implemented by a detective or small team to investigate the narrative itself. These procedures can have immediate impact, cost little, and jeopardize nothing. They are actions that may be applied to a specific investigation without organizational support. Not all techniques will be appropriate for all investigations.

The following section takes a broader, organizational perspective. These higher-level, organizational approaches tend to have higher costs, delayed impact, and may be of more interest to senior managers than to line investigators.

The second question (level of reliability) will be addressed in our concluding remarks.

Make Narratives Explicit

It is easy to fall in love with a narrative and not see its flaws. The reciprocity of narrative and evidence forms a bond of mutual support. The naive belief that objectivity will surmount all obstacles and produce a true and accurate account is founded on the incorrect view of how narratives are constructed and how evidence is interpreted. "Objectivity is gained by making assumptions explicit so that they may be examined and challenged, not by vain efforts to eliminate them from analysis" (Heuer, 1999, pp. 41–42).

To make a narrative explicit means to document carefully the narrative, including listing: (1) assumptions, (2) confirmatory evidence, explicitly stating how this evidence supports the narrative, (3) anomalies or disconfirming evidence, (4) causal inferences, and (5) actions performed to disconfirm evidence.

Constructing Alternative Narratives

Narratives are constructed through the use of intuition, which uses satisficing heuristics (see above) that are prone to failure. Investigators should explicitly and consciously attempt to generate alternative narratives in complex cases with ambiguous evidence or wherever plausible alternatives can be reasonably constructed. It is dangerous to rely on the first narrative that "works" or suffices. *Hic sunt dracones* (Here be dragons).

There are several benefits to developing alternative narratives. Evidence that had been overlooked may become visible in light of a different narrative. Having alternative narratives provides a yardstick to measure the quality and diagnosticity of evidence (see above). The diagnostic paucity of a once-cherished piece of evidence may only become apparent when seen in comparison with alternative narratives. When evidence is consistent with and supportive of all operative narratives, it has no diagnostic value. A high fever is useful in indicating that a patient is ill, but it has little or no diagnostic value in identifying the specific disease. The most useful evidence is that which addresses the probability of one narrative over another.

Vetting a Narrative

Narratives form by the reciprocal interaction of evidence, expertise, and intuition. To the extent that this follows the NDM model, it is inherently a satisficing heuristic. Investigators should not accept a "good enough" narrative. A correct narrative is needed—or at least the best that can be developed given available resources and evidence.

A narrative, like a race horse, should be vetted.[27] It needs to be checked for health and soundness before being allowed to race in public. At some point, the investigator must stop gathering evidence and subject the favored horse to examination. This requires leaving behind intuition and applying analytical methods.

The concern in vetting a narrative is not to apprehend the perpetrator of the crime, but to apprehend false or misleading conclusions, deductions, and suppositions that buttress the narrative. It is to investigate the narrative itself. Becoming too invested in catching the bad guy is the road to investigative perdition. Professional investigative teams resist the modus operandi of children's soccer. Just as there is more to soccer than going after the ball, there is more to a criminal investigation than catching the bad guy. The goal must be to get the story right. This can only be accomplished by stepping out of the favored narrative and examining the crime from a perspective beyond the implications of the narrative.

The narrative should be transformed into a testable hypothesis. It can then be examined by identifying and seeking disconfirming evidence, which has more diagnostic value than confirming evidence. Narratives should be periodically reviewed for their viability. A narrative that once appeared promising may, over time and through the appearance of new evidence, lose its viability.

---

[27]The term originally meant to be checked by a veterinarian.

The following queries and actions are relevant to the vetting of a narrative:

- Are anomalies recognized, or are they explained away or morphed into evidence? As a narrative becomes fixed, it becomes more difficult to notice anomalies. A narrative can become like a totalitarian ideology— it keeps the truth from emerging.
- Does the evidence have diagnosticity?
- Are Barnum statements functioning as evidence?
- Has some evidence been double counted?
- What assumptions have been made?
- What models or mindsets are being used to draw causal inferences? How reliable are they? Are they a product of folklore passed from one investigator to another, or is there actual scientific evidence to support these suppositions?
- To avoid anchoring bias, consider items of evidence in an order different from the one in which they were obtained.
- Identify key evidence. Recall that people (including experts) tend to make judgments and decisions based on a few key data points. Explicitly identifying the most important evidence and removing the distraction of less salient evidence permits focus on the central issues.
- Rate the key evidence for its strength and weight. Be wary of evidence high in strength and low in weight, as there is a tendency to overestimate its evidentiary value. Conversely, evidence low in strength and high in weight is likely to be underestimated.
- List evidence that was discredited or disconfirmed. This list should be carefully examined as its items may still be inappropriately influencing the investigator's evaluation of the credibility of the narrative.
- What actions can be taken to ensure that disconfirming data are recognized and confirmation bias minimized?
- If the case involves probabilities or statistics, convert percentages into frequencies. They are easier to understand and less prone to cognitive errors (Gigerenzer, 2002). Investigators who are not familiar with statistics and probability should consider consulting an expert to assist their understanding, and question such issues as whether the appropriate base rate is being applied.
- Be wary of aspects of the narrative based on intuitions about statistics or other computationally intensive evidence, including forensic technologies.
- Check for hasty generalization (i.e., making inductive conclusions from too small a sample). Beware the "Law of Small Numbers."
- Check for attribution errors. Do not undervalue the influences of situation and circumstance on an individual's behavior. Are there situational factors that would cause an individual to behave as the narrative prescribes? Beyond personality traits, what would cause an individual (victim, witness,

or suspect) to behave as he or she did? Be wary of explanations that rely solely on character traits devoid of a supporting situational context.

Another vetting technique is to perform a "narrative premortem" (adapted from Klein, 2003, pp. 98–101). Examine the narrative with the assumption that it is wrong. List the "evidence" that *if* existed would make the narrative fail. Keep in mind the goal here is not to (directly) solve the crime but to critique vigorously the narrative. When Klein uses premortems, he begins by saying, "I am looking into a crystal ball and, oh no, I am seeing that the project [narrative] has failed. It is a total, embarrassing, devastating failure." After describing the failure—perhaps the wrong suspect arrested and convicted—he says, "Things have gone as wrong as they could. However, we could only afford an inexpensive model of the crystal ball so we cannot make out the reason for the failure." Then he asks, "What could have caused this?"

This technique may help identify weakness in the narratives, suggest investigative actions or alternative narratives, and reduce the risk of investigative failure.

Managing Multiple Narratives

Typically multiple narratives evolve because the evidence is uncertain or the meaning of the evidence is unclear. A murder with signs of a great deal of emotion does not necessarily reveal which emotions were involved. The creation of alternative narratives promotes exploration of various possibilities, avoiding the tunnel vision to which a single narrative is prey. The most likely narrative or narratives are pursued by the investigation. Premature selection of a narrative, when other narratives are equally probable, is more likely to result in investigative failure. Narratives, like tools, suggest actions. If it is true that "to a man with a hammer, everything looks like a nail," then adopting a single narrative is problematic.

When an investigation has multiple narratives, traditional RDM methods can be applied to compare narratives. These optimizing techniques are designed to identify the best narratives and to avoid accepting a quick and dirty (good enough) story. Investigators use intuition to generate the most promising narratives. These alternative hypotheses need to be compared not just by scrutinizing evidence for their comparative value in confirming the narratives, but, like a scientist, by actively seeking out and evaluating disconfirming evidence.

Here is a suggested technique adapted from Heuer (1999):

1. List possible narratives. Ideally, this is a team effort as one person can rarely generate a comprehensive list. Elicit input from senior investigators, detectives with varied backgrounds and experiences, and those who tend to think differently about things. At this step, the goal should

be diversity of opinion and creativity (how can these pieces, the evidence, be put together to form a coherent story?).

2. List the narratives in columns (see Table 7.1). If there are too many narratives to manage, group similar ones or eliminate the least likely. List the facts of the case (the evidence) in rows.

3. For each item of evidence, evaluate the diagnosticity for every narrative. Work across the table, column by column, row by row, noting evidence as confirming (C), disconfirming (D), or neutral (–). If preferred, evidence could be weighted from 1 to 10 for confirming, –1 to –10 for disconfirming, and 0 for neutral. Use whatever symbol is preferred. When evaluating the evidence, keep in mind strength versus weight issues.

4. Compare the narratives by columns. If a data point supports all narratives, it has no diagnostic value—cross it out. A narrative develops unwarranted believability by accumulating "evidence" that has no particular diagnostic value. Examine the evidence for possible intercorrelations or double counting. For example, if one of the facts of a murder case is that Mr. Big had an argument with the victim, and another that he said he was angry with the victim, then these are really the same evidence (Mr. Big had a motive). More attention should be paid to disconfirming evidence, as it has more diagnostic value.

Table 7.1 Analysis of Competing Narratives

Evidence	Narrative 1	Narrative 2	Narrative 3
Motive			
Means			
Opportunity			
Witness Smith			
Witness Jones			
Trace physical evidence			
Total			

Develop an Appropriate Stance or Attunement toward Narratives

The investigator's attitude toward the narrative determines what can be made visible and what remains veiled. Most people find they cannot be creative and critical at the same time. Whether this involves neurological issues regarding utilization of different parts of the brain or a haberdashery problem of not being able to wear two hats at the same time, humans have learned to separate these activities in order to be more creative and more critical.

Most investigators have difficulty forcefully and aggressively pursuing the implications of a narrative while retaining awareness of the narrative's strengths and weaknesses. It is difficult to be both creatively involved in everyday implications and at the same time take a critical, spectatorial stance toward our actions and their biases. These stances are often best performed as separate and distinct activities, or even better, by different people. Awareness of one's limitations is the first step toward compensating for them.

The investigation of the narrative should be ongoing. Periodic examination of the narrative itself should become as much a part of the investigative process as sending evidence to the lab. This can be accomplished by using one of the more formal processes described above, or by simply soliciting the opinion of outside experts not immersed in the investigation.

The narratives that experts build tend to come with a set of expectations. The discovery of evidence that conflicts with these expectations is often a surprise. Such surprises are an important warning that an expectation is not being confirmed. They should be duly noted, taken as evidence against the narrative and a warning that the narrative may be faulty.

Investigating a crime without a comprehensive narrative is confusing and frustrating. It can engender feelings of hopelessness and powerlessness. A narrative provides a feeling of power and control; this is a strong enticement to most of us. The professional investigator, alert to the self-regulatory demands of expertise, must be cautious that such feelings do not seduce him or her into accepting substandard narratives.

Individuals, as well as organizations, have a range of comfort in handling uncertainty and ambiguity. Some individuals and organizations tolerate higher levels of confusion and chaos than do others. When these levels of comfort are exceeded, there will be a tendency to rush to a hasty narrative. Detailing the process that will be used to generate or abandon a narrative can mitigate these tendencies.

Smaller teams or organizations tend to be better at coping with uncertainty than larger ones. This is due, in part, to organizational pressures on larger teams to stay coordinated. A trip to the store is always more efficient when done alone than as a family project. The acceptable level of chaos is greater for small teams that can easily regroup and reorganize. For larger groups, the reorganization process is more difficult and time consuming.

Feedback

Feedback is a critical element in the development of expertise, particularly for the accurate assessment of the likelihood of predictions. The evidence suggests that feedback alone is insufficient; it must be reflected upon and integrated to be useful. The key question is what lessons can be learned? Taking feedback at face value can be deceptive. It needs to be processed to differentiate the typical cases from those in which anomalies are present. It is critical that investigators and investigative teams develop mechanisms to acquire feedback and perform the requisite processing.

Every profession needs to concern itself with how ideas come to be accepted as canon. Where did the procedures, guidelines, and directives used in criminal investigation originate? Are they the results of empirically validated research or folklore passed through an oral tradition? Whether the investigative culture has embraced and implemented the requisite feedback mechanisms to correct errors of general theory and practice warrants further scrutiny. For example, the known risk of obtaining false confessions from prolonged interrogations, especially of juveniles, seems to be slow in reaching the police community (see Chapters 8 and 10).

Perform Postmortems

What was learned? What was the key evidence that led to the correct narrative? What anomalies were there? What errors were made, and what lessons can be learned from them? What could the team have done better? Did errors made suggest systemic problems requiring systemic solutions?

The key to a successful postmortem is not to assign blame, but rather to capture lessons that can be learned from the experience. The measure of a successful investigation should not solely be that the defendant was convicted; what happens in court is a problematic metric. There must also be concern with the quality of the investigation itself.

The term *learning organization* has fallen into almost cliched status. Like apple pie, no one is against it, yet few organizations are really able to effectively and consistently learn. The assumption underlying the concept is that organizations, like individuals, can develop expertise by learning, retaining, and applying these lessons to improve future performance.

The motivations and time frame involved in developing expertise are reasons organizational learning is so difficult. Experts make long-term investments to improve their expertise. Most organizations are short sighted. They are often judged on short-term goals, and our culture tends to readily forget or disregard an organization's past successes. Given this time horizon, it is not hard to see why organizations struggle to invest in activities with uncertain and long-term payoffs.[28]

Given these challenges, waiting for organizational support for activities such as postmortems may be long in coming. Nonetheless, teams or

---

[28] Years ago, one of the authors was a strong proponent of Health Maintenance Organizations (HMO). His reasoning was that only with an HMO would there be a financial incentive for health organizations to invest in sorely underfunded preventative medicine. He was quite perplexed when this did not happen. The reason was twofold: (1) American job and geographic mobility means that most people do not stay in the same HMO for very long; and (2) the payoff for preventative medicine is long term. The bottom line is that it simply does not pay for HMOs to invest in preventative medicine because the payback period exceeds the average membership term.

individuals can still benefit by initiating these activities, regardless of the organizational context. Ideally, postmortems should be ingrained in the organizational culture. But even if they are not, an informal lunch reviewing a past case can reap many of the same benefits.

Managing the Organization to Promote Best Practices

Criminal investigations take place within an organizational context which can promote or frustrate best narrative practice. Organizations need to reinforce those behaviors and practices that are desired and avoid inadvertently reinforcing those that are undesirable or problematic. Effective organizations are fertile ground for the development of expertise and intuition; they recognize and avoid cognitive errors and biases and become self-correcting, highly reliable operations. Investigative organizations need to develop, maintain, support, reward, and transmit expertise and intuition.

We believe the following practices will support positive narrative outcomes with minimal risk:

- Nurture diverse opinions and avoid groupthink. Recognize and affirm divergent ideas, perspectives, and ways of thinking. Someone's "stupid idea" may trigger a good idea in someone else. Castigating bad ideas can send the message that introducing ideas contrary to the prevailing orthodoxy is unacceptable behavior. The cost of entertaining a bad idea is low, whereas the cost of missing a good one is high. Avoid placing value on conformity. The use of Red Teaming,[29] devil's advocates,[30] and narrative safety officers[31] are some of the possible approaches to implementing these ideas in an organization.
- Hire and respect diversity. By "diversity," we do not mean racial diversity—although that could be part of it—but diversity of experience,

[29]Red Teaming involves an independent review of and challenge to existing practices. The term comes from the U.S. Army where the Red Team is the group taking the opposing side (versus the Blue Team) in a war game.

[30]A devil's advocate is someone who takes an opposing view for the sake or argument or to serve an organizational purpose. We mean it in the sense of someone who questions the prevailing narrative. The term comes from the Roman Catholic Church where an *advocatus diaboli* was appointed by the Church to argue against the canonization of a candidate for sainthood.

[31]The safety officer is a role from search and rescue, specifically high-angle rock rescue. The safety officer observes the rigging activity of the team without actually participating. His job is to watch for mistakes and not become directly involved in the rescue, so he is in a better position to notice anything that might have been missed in the press of the moment. In the context of criminal investigations, we use this term in the sense of someone not directly involved in the investigation, who observes the progression of the narrative as it forms, and pays attention to errors or biases that may be invisible to the investigators themselves.

perspective, and ways of thinking about and approaching problems. A team reflecting professional diversity is more productive and less likely to fail. Homogenous teams, in which everyone thinks alike, are less likely to spot their group-based errors and biases and are more prone to groupthink. In criminal investigations, this might involve broadening the team to include detectives from other investigative sections or civilian professionals who have useful expertise.

- Keep the focus on the goal of developing the correct narrative, not apprehending a suspect or confirming any one narrative. The right narrative will lead to the apprehension of the right person. Being blindly wedded to a narrative is not necessarily bad if it is the correct one, but it can be catastrophic if it is the wrong one. Narratives should be evaluated as they develop and guide an investigation, rather than later, as a "lesson learned" following a failure.

- Promote team cohesiveness by focusing on the goal of constructing the right narrative and not on yea-saying. The most effective teams are not ones in which everyone always agree, but those in which members are dedicated to the same goal. Avoid cohesiveness based on an external organizational enemy.

- Appreciate and value respectful argumentation. Respecting divergent opinions serves to build a culture of creativity. Prematurely shutting off divergent opinion in order to "get on with it" may have short-term benefits but long-term costs. An unorthodox opinion may help identify investigative errors, suggest alternative narratives, or open new lines of inquiry. The organizational culture—and management—must ensure that disagreements remain respectful. Build trust and constructive feedback mechanisms to allow the free creation of competing narratives and the criticism of prevailing orthodoxies. Individuals need to assume a duty to speak up regarding problems, concerns, errors, and anomalies. When an airplane engine is on fire, the pilot wants the crew to speak up. The pilot does not want the crew wondering whether it is normal or whether saying anything will cause embarrassment.[32] Getting the narrative right is everyone's job, not just the lead investigator's responsibility.

- Promote an organizational culture that focuses on doing a professional, reality-based, scientifically informed investigation, rather than on

[32]In general (private) aviation, the authors have never heard of a pilot being dismissive in word or tone of a passenger pointing out the presence of another aircraft in flight. Pilots recognize that they can become distracted, miss spotting another aircraft, and the potentially high costs of not seeing what ought to be seen. The hardest airplane to spot is the one heading straight towards you. Our eyes are best at noticing movement. Aircraft on a head-on collision course will not move against the background–which would make them easier to see–they just get bigger.

"getting the bad guy off the street." This emphasis can help minimize the chances of a wrongful conviction. The organization and its members should derive satisfaction from doing a professional job rather than from the case's judicial outcome. Bringing a malefactor to justice should be a rewarding byproduct rather than the goal-in-chief.

- Do not positively reinforce unprofessional investigative actions. Such behavior is usually rewarded implicitly rather than explicitly, hence the difficulty in rooting it out.
- Be attentive to errors that may be embedded in investigative practice. Become preoccupied with mistakes rather than successes. Do not become complacent in the belief that a disastrous failure could not occur here. Thinking that the spectacular blunder only happens to someone else is a dangerous mindset. Be aware that no one is perfect and be cognizant of the possibility—even probability—of errors of omission and commission. "Be glad when you're having a bad day! When things go wrong, you uncover more details and learn more about how things work..." (Weick & Sutcliffe, 2001, p. 161).
- Professional organizations have what Weick and Sutcliffe (2001) call "mindfulness." Being mindful means that "you stop concentrating on those things that confirm your hunches, are pleasant, feel certain, seem factual, and explicit—and that others agree on. You start concentrating on those things that disconfirm, are unpleasant, feel uncertain, seem possible, are implicit—and are contested" (U.S. Department of Agriculture, 2004, p. 17).
- Defer to expertise rather than hierarchy. Seek out individuals with knowledge rather than title; do not be bound by rigid organizational hierarchies.
- Try to understand why the system failed instead of seeking out scapegoats to blame. "How many times have we seen executives and administrators attempt to manage the unexpected after-the-fact by blaming someone—usually someone else" (U.S. Department of Agriculture, 2004, p. 7). Rarely are failures in professional organizations due entirely to one person's incompetence or misdeed; more often the failures are related to a complex of organizational problems. Focusing on the identification of the individual most proximate to the failure often has the appearance of "dealing with the problem," while leaving the underlying problem unresolved.
- All the members of the organization should take responsibility for the quality of the narrative and be attentive to potential errors within it. These issues are not just management's responsibility. Conversely, the organization should reward those who raise unpleasant issues and concerns, rather than viewing them as disloyal, not team players, or poor for morale. Messengers with bad news often find themselves

shunned. These "malcontents" either learn their lesson and get with the program or they leave—taking their expertise and mindfulness with them.

Conclusion

Verily at the first Chaos came to be ...

Hesiod, *The Theogony* **(E. White, Trans.)**

In the beginning was the Word ...

John 1:1

The narrative does not emerge unaided, Phoenix-like from the ashes of a crime scene. It is born from the union of the chaos and the models and mindsets of the investigator. The narrative metamorphoses the chaos into evidence, and the evidence in turn validates the narrative.

As the word is spoken, the narrative, like the plot in a drama, reveals the story. The investigator and suspects have their roles. The setting and the props are provided by victim and perpetrator. The narrative as plot connects, interprets, and mediates the drama; it explains how things came to be and foretells the future. Unlike a stage play, the investigator as director cannot suffice with a plausible story, nor allow the plot to push the drama to some seemingly inevitable climax. A narrative qua story has a world and logic of its own. The investigator must be vigilant that the story remains grounded in the events and facts of the case, that the *dramatis personæ* are three-dimensional people, not caricatures, and that the heuristics used to explain the actions in the drama are believable and free of cognitive bias.

No responsible investigator is indifferent to a bad or false narrative. The questions we raised were: (1) What can be done to prevent these errors and (2) How much risk mitigation is appropriate in a criminal investigation?

In this chapter we have described possible actions that investigators or investigative organizations can take:

- Explicitly documenting the narratives.
- Constructing alternative narratives.
- Vetting narratives (questioning the diagnosticity of evidence, seeking disconfirming evidence, searching for cognitive biases, performing a "narrative premortem").
- Using analytic techniques to compare competing narratives.
- Developing a more questioning stance toward narratives and a mindfulness of investigative failures.

- Using feedback.
- Performing postmortems.
- Promoting investigative best practice on an organizational level.

Before the question of risk mitigation can be addressed, we must first ask what criteria is used to evaluate the narrative itself. Is a good narrative one that leads to the apprehension and conviction of an offender? Is a bad narrative one that produces no results? Is a narrative, however inconsistent with the facts of the case, still good if it gets the bad guy—or a "bad guy"? Or is a good narrative one that was soundly built (best reflects the "truth" of the case as the evidence permits us to see the truth), whether or not it produces results?

Another way of framing the question is should narratives be judged by their outcome or by the process used to create them? Outcomes, by themselves, are not completely in the hands of the investigator. Chance plays a role. The detective who sits by the Crime Stoppers telephone waiting for the tip that will break the case may get lucky, whereas the diligent field investigator working all angles may come up empty handed. However, to divorce process completely from outcome is to elevate it so high into the ivory tower as to render it meaningless. By definition, a good process must, on average, produce good results. We believe that a good narrative—comprehensive, self-consistent, accordant with the rules of logic, laws of science, and empirically supported models of human behavior—will produce, over the long term, the best investigative result and the fewest failures.

This perspective on the role narratives play in the criminal investigative process runs counter to the image detectives may have of themselves, as well as how they are viewed by their organizations and the larger community. Investigators who define their role as "getting bad guys off the street" may view themselves as playing the part of the lawman in a Hollywood western, riding into town to restore peace and order—not as a professional investigator struggling with the complex issues of evidentiary diagnosticity, confirmation bias, and the like. We all want to see our work, in some fashion or other, as a noble quest (the authors of this chapter being no exception). These are strong inducements; however, if they are not linked to an equally strong sense of professional ethics, they can result in investigative failure.

The sociopolitical context in which investigations take place involves, on the one hand, an adversarial system of justice in which the prosecution's task is to do what it takes to convict wrongdoers (albeit within ethical and legal constraints), and on the other, a larger community whose members simply want the police to quickly catch criminals. For the most part, neither party to the process is particularly concerned with or wishes to be involved in the details or problems associated with the identification of evidence and the formation of accurate and complete criminal narratives.

The police are caught in the middle. The experience of being caught between a rock and a hard place is a dilemma shared by others professionals. Physicians find themselves pressured between organizations preoccupied with cost saving and patients who just want to get better. Engineers struggle to balance organizational pressure to complete projects "on time and within budget" and their responsibility to produce safe and reliable products. How professionals define their roles, both to themselves and within their organizations, determines how they navigate these difficult choices.

Criminal investigations range from the straightforward slam-dunk case to the "whodunit" with ambiguous evidence pointing in many directions. Investigations can be comprised of a single individual, a team, or a multi-agency task force. Procedures for narrative management appropriate to one set of circumstances may be inappropriate for another. Research is needed to assist investigators in identifying which cases and circumstances require what procedures. It would be useful to know how particular investigative failures relate to specific cognitive errors. Absent this research, we must use the same heuristics to choose procedures to address the problem of cognitive errors and biases that were themselves the cause of the problem in the first place.

References

Aczel, A. D. (2004). *Chance*. New York: Avalon.

Bazerman, M. H. (2002). *Judgment in managerial decision making* (5th ed.). New York: Wiley.

Bereiter, C., & Scardamalia, M. (1993). *Surpassing ourselves: An inquiry into the nature and implications of expertise*. Chicago: Open Court.

Bruner, J. S., & Potter, M. C. (1964). Interference in visual recognition. *Science, 144*, 424–425.

Carroll, R. T. (2003). *The skeptic's dictionary*. Hoboken, NJ: Wiley.

Chiles, J. R. (2002). *Inviting disaster: Lessons from the edge of technology*. New York: HarperCollins.

Dörner, D. (1996). *The logic of failure* (R. Kimber & R. Kimber, trans.). New York: Henry Holt. (Original work published 1989).

Fischhoff, B. (1982). For those condemned to study the past: Heuristics and biases in hindsight. In D. Kahneman, P. Slovic, & A. Tversky (Eds.), *Judgment under uncertainty: Heuristics and biases* (pp. 335–351). Cambridge: Cambridge University Press.

Gigerenzer, G. (2002). *Calculated risks: How to know when numbers deceive you*. New York: Simon and Schuster.

Gladwell, M. (2007, November 12). Dangerous minds: Criminal profiling made easy. *New Yorker*, pp. 36–45.

Griffith, D., & Tversky, A. (2004). The weighing of evidence and the determinants of confidence. In E. Shafir (Ed.), *Preference, belief, and similarity: Selected writings* (pp. 275–299). Cambridge, MA: MIT Press.

Gula, R. J. (2002). *Nonsense*. Mount Jackson, VA: Axios Press.

Heuer, R. J., Jr. (1999). *Psychology of intelligence analysis*. Washington, DC: Center for the Study of Intelligence, Central Intelligence Agency.

Janis, I. L. (1972). *Victims of groupthink: A psychological study of foreign-policy decisions and fiascoes*. Boston: Houghton Mifflin.

Janis, I. L. (1982). *Groupthink: Psychological studies of policy decisions and fiascoes* (2nd ed.). Boston: Houghton Mifflin.

Klein, G. (1999). *Sources of power: How people make decisions*. Cambridge, MA: MIT Press.

Klein, G. (2003). *The power of intuition*. New York: Doubleday. (Originally published as *Intuition at work*).

Koehler, J. J., & Macchi, L. (2004). Thinking about low-probability events [Electronic version]. *Psychological Science, 15*, 540–546.

Lewandowsky, S., Stritzke, W. G. K., Oberauer, K., & Morales, M. (2005). Memory for fact, fiction, and misinformation [Electronic version]. *Psychological Science, 16*(3), 190–195.

National Research Council. (2004). *Forensic analysis: Weighing bullet lead evidence* (Report in Brief) [Electronic version]. Washington, DC: National Academies Press.

New England Innocence Project. (2005). *Amici brief,* Commonwealth of Massachusetts v. Patterson [Electronic version]. Supreme Judicial Court, Suffolk County, No. 09478.

Plous, S. (1993). *The psychology of judgment and decision making*. New York: McGraw-Hill.

Rosenzweig, P. (2007). *The halo effect: ... and the eight other business delusions that deceive managers*. New York: Free Press.

Ross, K. G., Shafer, J. L., & Klein, G. (2006). Professional judgments and "naturalistic decision making." In K. A. Ericsson, N. Charness, R. R. Hoffman, & P. J. Feltovich (Eds.), *The Cambridge handbook of expertise and expert performance* (pp. 403–419). Cambridge: Cambridge University Press.

Rottenstreich, Y., & Tverksy, A. (2004). Unpacking, repacking, and anchoring: Advances in support theory. In E. Shafir (Ed.), *Preference, belief, and similarity: Selected writings* (pp. 383–402). Cambridge, MA: MIT Press.

Shermer, M. (2006). *Why Darwin matters*. New York: Henry Holt.

Simon, H. A. (1957). *Models of man: Social and rational*. New York: Wiley.

Taleb, N. N. (2007). *The black swan: The impact of the highly improbable*. New York: Random House.

Thorndike, E. L. (1920). A constant error in psychological ratings. *Journal of Applied Psychology, 4*, 25–29.

Thornton, J. I. (1977). The one-dissimilarity doctrine in fingerprint identification. *International Criminal Police Review, 306*, 89–95.

Tverksy, A., & Gilovich, T. (2004). The cold facts about the "hot hand" in basketball. In E. Shafir (Ed.). *Preference, belief, and similarity: Selected writings* (pp. 257–265). Cambridge, MA: MIT Press.

Tversky, A., & Kahneman, D. (1982a). Belief in the law of small numbers. In D. Kahneman, P. Slovic, & A. Tversky (Eds.), *Judgment under uncertainty: Heuristics and biases* (pp. 23–31). Cambridge: Cambridge University Press.

Tversky, A., & Kahneman, D. (1982b). Judgment under uncertainty: Heuristics and bias. In D. Kahneman, P. Slovic, & A. Tversky (Eds.), *Judgment under uncertainty: Heuristics and biases* (pp. 3–20). Cambridge: Cambridge University Press.

Tversky, A., & Kahneman, D. (1982c). Evidential impact of base rates. In D. Kahneman, P. Slovic, & A. Tversky (Eds.), *Judgment under uncertainty: Heuristics and biases* (pp. 153–160). Cambridge: Cambridge University Press.

U.S. Department of Agriculture. (2004). *Managing the unexpected in prescribed fire and fire use operations: A workshop on the high reliability organization* (General Technical Report RMRS-GTR-137). Fort Collins, CO: Rocky Mountain Research Station.

Vaughan, D. (1996). *The* Challenger *launch decision: Risky technology, culture, and deviance at NASA.* Chicago: University of Chicago Press.

Vick, S. G. (2002). *Degrees of belief: Subjective probability and engineering judgment.* Reston, VA: American Society of Civil Engineers.

Wason, P. C., & Johnson-Laird, P. N. (1972). *Psychology of reasoning: Structure and content.* Cambridge, MA: Harvard University Press.

Weick, K. E., & Sutcliffe, K. M. (2001). *Managing the unexpected.* San Francisco: Jossey-Bass.

Whyte, J. (2004). *Crimes against logic.* New York: McGraw-Hill.

Case Studies III

Who Killed Stephanie Crowe?

8

GREGG O. MCCRARY

Investigators understand the importance of conducting their analyses in a manner that will lead to the arrest and prosecution of the guilty while at the same time protecting the innocent. Most investigators are competent, dedicated professionals who want to solve their cases and arrest the right people (Rossmo, 2006), but sometimes they can become ensnared in the subtle hazards and traps to which all investigations are exposed. The chances for a miscarriage of justice increase proportionately with the degree that reliable investigative and analytical methodologies are ignored, marginalized, or subverted. This case demonstrates how a flawed investigation led to the indictment of three innocent teenagers. A subsequent thorough investigation prevented the ultimate miscarriage of justice by bringing the true killer to justice, but not before the original investigators and the FBI, experiencing a type of institutional folie à deux, devastated the lives of three young men and their families. It took years to reveal how a cascading series of errors, including anchor traps, tunnel vision, groupthink, belief perseverance, ego, and other pitfalls, put the initial investigation on the wrong course and then locked it into a fatal tail spin. I have been involved in this case for a number of years and have provided expert testimony regarding many of the issues. I offer the following assessment in an attempt to present an educational note to law enforcement on how to identify, understand, and, hopefully, avoid these errors.

Introduction

In January 1998, 12-year-old Stephanie Crowe was stabbed to death in the bedroom of her Escondido, California, home. Murder is uncommon in Escondido. In the year Stephanie was murdered, there was only one other homicide in this city of about 120,000. Investigators from the Escondido Police Department quickly concluded that Stephanie's murder was an inside job and focused on the victim's 14-year-old brother Michael. They isolated him from his parents and subjected him to a series of psychologically coercive interrogations over a two-day period until Michael "confessed" to killing his sister. Police implicated two other ninth-graders, Michael's best friend Joshua Treadway and Aaron Houser, an acquaintance of Michael's. Treadway also "confessed" after caving in to the same type of psychologically abusive interrogation techniques used on Michael. Houser did not succumb and maintained his innocence. However, at the request of his interrogators, Houser was encouraged to offer a hypothetical scenario about how knives could have been used to murder Stephanie. He did so, and that was good enough for the investigators. Although their "confessions" contradicted one another on important points such as who stabbed Stephanie and were inconsistent with the forensic evidence, San Diego County prosecutors charged all three boys with Stephanie's murder.

The night of the murder, Richard Tuite, a mentally ill transient, was prowling the area near the Crowe home, behaving bizarrely, looking for a girl who resembled Stephanie. Police marginalized him as a suspect because they were familiar with Tuite and thought he was incapable of pulling off a "no-trace-evidence" murder. They also believed Stephanie's homicide was an "inside job," and they had the evidence and confessions to prove it. Over the course of the next year as their case against the three teens unraveled, prosecutors sought the help of the FBI's National Center for the Analysis of Violent Crime (NCAVC) to shore up their case. The NCAVC wrote a report in support of the original investigation and was prepared to testify against the teenagers. The results of an independent laboratory analysis requested by one of the teens' defense attorneys struck like a bombshell, blowing the case against the three teens completely apart. Up to that point, there was no physical evidence linking the victim with any suspect, including the three boys. But a DNA lab found Stephanie Crowe's blood spattered on the clothing that Richard Tuite wore the night of the murder. The Escondido Police Department seized that clothing within hours of Stephanie's murder, and it had been in their care, custody, and control since then. The bloodstains were visible to the naked eye, but investigators never requested they be tested. As a result of this evidence, the charges against the three teens were dropped with the provision they could be refiled. Escondido police were tasked with explaining how the victim's blood came to be spattered on Richard Tuite's clothing if the three teens had murdered her.

A year went by with no developments in the case when the San Diego County Sheriff's Office took over the investigation from the Escondido Police Department. Led by Detective Victor Caloca, their investigation developed probable cause to believe that Richard Tuite murdered Stephanie Crowe. When the San Diego County District Attorney failed to prosecute Tuite, the Attorney General's Office for the State of California stepped in and charged him. The case went to trial and the jury convicted Richard Tuite for the murder of Stephanie Crowe. An objective inquiry into the initial investigation and attempted prosecution of three innocent teens, as supported by the FBI, reveals a number of troubling errors. The subsequent responses of those involved in the initial investigation raise additional concerns.

An Ordinary Night

In January 1998, Stephen and Cheryl Crowe and their three children, Michael (14), Stephanie (12), and Shannon (10), lived in a modest home in Escondido, California (see Figure 8.1). Cheryl's mother Judith Kennedy was also living with them at that time. Tuesday evening, January 20, was a fairly typical night. Stephen and Cheryl Crowe got home from their respective jobs, had a dinner of Hamburger Helper, and watched television. Michael helped Stephanie with her homework, and then the two of them huddled together on the floor beneath a comforter, watching television. They giggled so persistently that their grandmother, Judith Kennedy, and Shannon retreated to the bedroom they shared to watch TV. Cheryl's brother, Michael Kennedy, stopped by around 8:00 p.m. and left at 8:45 p.m. through the laundry room door, which led to the driveway. Michael Crowe spoke with his friend Joshua Treadway who called to ask why he had not been in school that day. Michael had the flu, but assured Joshua that he would be in school the next morning as it was finals week.

Although things were normal inside the Crowe residence, several neighbors had called the police to report a disoriented stranger prowling about, knocking on doors and looking for his former girlfriend, Tracy, who had previously lived in the area. There had been several calls to 9-1-1 between approximately 7:30 and 9:30 p.m. Some witnesses described the individual as looking like Charles Manson. Even earlier, around 7:00 p.m., Sharon Thomas encountered this individual in the church parking lot when she picked up her daughter. He kept yelling, "I'll kill you, you fucking bitch!" She said to him, "Come on, you're in a church parking lot," but he was nonresponsive. His demeanor appeared hostile and threatening. The Reverend Gary West made the last call to 9-1-1 that night concerning this prowler. He told the dispatcher that the man was looking for some girl, had "spooked" everybody, and had no business being there.

Officer Scott Walters of the Escondido Police Department responded to the call from Reverend West. Walters headed west up the stem of a T-shaped driveway with spot, alley, and "take down" lights ablaze. He turned left at the "T" and slowly headed for West's house. After reaching it and not observing anything unusual, he turned and headed toward the house at the other end of the driveway where the Crowe family lived. At the time he approached with all of his lights on, Stephanie Crowe was in her bedroom on the phone with her friend Amanda Riedy. Stephanie had received the phone as a Christmas gift and had wired it through her bedroom window. During that conversation Stephanie exclaimed that her cat just came in through her window. At approximately 10:00 p.m., Amanda's mother and father told her it was time to hang up. The rest of the Crowe family were in their bedrooms.

Figure 8.1 Aerial view of Crowe house, Escondido, California.

Figure 8.2 Laundry room door at Crowe residence.

As Walters approached the Crowe house, he saw the laundry room door, which was initially open, close in a normal fashion (see Figure 8.2). Concluding there was nothing unusual at either the West or Crowe residences, he drove away, entering "GOA" ("gone on arrival") into his mobile data terminal (MDT) at 9:56 p.m. He then took his dinner break.

Discovering the Crime

At 6:30 the next morning, Judith Kennedy crossed the hallway to Stephanie's bedroom to see why her alarm clock kept ringing. She saw Stephanie lying on her right side on the floor inside the room, partly against the door. Thinking the girl had fallen, Judith checked her, mistaking the blood on her body for mud. She immediately knew something was terribly wrong. She cried out and Stephen and Cheryl responded. Horrified at the condition of his daughter, Stephen made a desperate call to 9-1-1. While waiting for help to arrive, he moved Stephanie's head to keep it off the cold floor, and Cheryl stretched out over her to try to warm her. Stephen unbolted the laundry room door to go outside to wait for the paramedics. He was surprised to find it dead-bolted, as the family did not use this lock. When paramedics arrived they had to pull Cheryl off of Stephanie because she was clinging to her so tightly. There was nothing the paramedics could do for Stephanie. She had been stabbed to death in her bedroom as the rest of the family slept close by.

No one else in the home that night had been harmed, but some family members reported hearing noises in the night, which could assist with the reconstruction of the crime. Little did anyone know just how a seemingly minor mistake about a door could lead the investigation so dramatically astray.

Initial Investigation

The Crowe residence was a single-level, four-bedroom home in rural Escondido. There was heavy brush on all sides, isolating it from view from the street. Emergency medical personnel arrived by 6:37 a.m., followed soon by police. Stephanie was pronounced dead at the scene. She was still fully clothed from the night before; even her hair was still tied the same way. The evidence suggested that, after being stabbed, she crawled across the floor to her bedroom door before succumbing to the loss of blood. Detectives turned up few leads: no biological fluid, fingerprints, fibers, or murder weapon—only a partial smudge that might be a footprint. Stephanie's clothing, head, hands, and feet were bagged before she was transported from the crime scene.

Under questioning, Cheryl Crowe recalled that she had heard pounding during the night, but had thought she was dreaming. She also recalled that her internal bedroom door had moved twice, but she assumed it was from the cats. Stephen Crowe reported that when he woke up, the bedroom door was wide open, but he had had little time to think about it as he rushed toward Judith Kennedy's alarming cry. Independently, Michael reported hearing pounding and recognized it as coming from the laundry room door because of the way the glass rattled. When it stopped, he assumed someone had answered the door. He did not go check it himself. He said the dog, which was in the garage, had not barked, something the family indicated was not unusual.

Shortly after 6:50 a.m., Pat Green, the son-in-law of Reverend Gary West, told an officer about the "obstinate ... belligerent" transient they encountered the night of the murder;[1] the officer noted this in his report. Barry Sweeney was the first detective on the scene. Ralph Claytor, a 23-year veteran who would be the lead detective in the case, arrived shortly thereafter. They determined that all the doors and windows had been locked except for Stephanie's window and the sliding door in the parents' bedroom. As the screens on Stephanie's window were intact, and it seemed unlikely that anyone could have entered through the master bedroom sliding door undetected, investigators decided there had been no forced entry. However, they did not take into account Officer Walters's report that he observed the laundry room door closing at a time when all the family members were in bed. That should have raised the salient question of who was closing the laundry room door. Unfortunately, investigators had already concluded it was an inside job.

Investigators thus made their first and most significant misstep. Initial information and impressions can influence all subsequent thoughts and judgments. An *anchoring effect* occurs when disproportionate weight is given to first theories or beliefs. Limited or incorrect data can lead investigators down the wrong path. As Rossmo (2006, p. 8) states, "Small deviations in the starting position can become large ones over time." One needs all the data before developing any working hypotheses. This phenomenon is sometimes referred to as *threshold diagnosis*, determining what happened from early impressions.

After reviewing all police reports, it is clear that investigators did not take into account the possibility the laundry room door was open at the time of the murder when they checked for points of entry. Detective Claytor testified he "didn't attach any real significance to [Officer Walters's crucial observation]" and concluded he must have been mistaken.[2]

Due largely to this erroneous assessment, the detectives developed a working hypothesis that the murder was an inside job. Michael became their most likely suspect. The only other people in the home were Stephanie's parents, grandmother, and her 10-year-old sister. The detectives then interpreted Michael's demeanor on the morning of the murder as being inappropriate, playing a hand-held video game as the police questioned members of the alarmed and grief-stricken family. Prosecutor Summer Stephan would later say that she thought this behavior revealed a dark, distant side, and she would base her hypothesis about the murder motive on this behavior. This is an example of the halo effect (Thorndike, 1920), a cognitive bias whereby the perception of one trait (e.g., propensity to murder) is influenced by the perception of former traits (e.g., inappropriate game playing) in a sequence of interpretations. In actuality, there is no standard profile of how someone should behave when their little sister has been stabbed to death. People exposed to serious trauma react in a number of different ways.

---

[1] Deposition of Patrick Green, pp. 16–18, 23, 43.
[2] Deposition of Ralph Claytor, pp. 87–90.

Other witnesses denied that Michael had behaved in this manner, but the image, once seized, carried enough power to become entrenched in the belief systems of investigators and prosecutors. It would prove to also be another anchoring effect, framing the subsequent thoughts and actions of both groups. Investigative momentum was picking up and detectives were starting to fall into other traps such as tunnel vision, belief perseverance, and confirmation bias, leading them to ignore, discredit, or marginalize the disconfirming reports and evidence that continued to be developed.

Indeed, there was more behavior that investigators and prosecutors believed implicated Michael, who had been home sick that day. He said that he got up during the early morning hours to take a Tylenol for a headache. Although his sister's room was across from his and she was already dead at that time, he said he did not see her body in the doorway. His statement was viewed as highly improbable. In fact, it was actually very likely as the family described Stephanie as being inside her room when they first discovered the body. It also seems unlikely Michael would admit he had walked around the home at that hour if he had actually killed his sister. The logical act of an organized killer would be to stay quiet or claim to have slept through the night.

All the family members were taken to the police station where they were interviewed, stripped, and photographed in the nude. About 5:30 p.m. that afternoon, Michael was allowed to make a phone call from the police station. He called Joshua Treadway and while crying, told his best friend that his sister was dead, that somebody may have broken into the house and killed her. Numerous witnesses spoke with Detective Sweeney about the transient they had seen the evening of the murder. A patrol officer gave Detective Sweeney a picture of Richard Tuite on the afternoon of January 21.

At 7:00 p.m., police told the Crowes that their two surviving children were being taken to the Polinsky Children's Center for abused and neglected children. Stephen Crowe erupted, demanding that his children be brought to him. Several officers rushed in to quiet him down. He recalls being told, "We were going to let you say goodbye to them, but you have lost that privilege" (Haunting questions, 1999). Cheryl was allowed to briefly say goodbye to her sobbing children. She told them to be strong, to trust the police because they were there to help. The police decided to put the Crowes in a motel overnight as they were far from finished searching and processing the house.

Police officers located Richard Tuite at a laundromat and brought him in for questioning. Detective Barry Sweeney interviewed him for about half an hour, while other officers collected fingernail scrapings and clippings from Tuite and photographed him and his clothing (see Figure 8.3). They found that he had scrapes on his body and a 1- to 1.5-inch cut on his right palm. Detective Sweeney confiscated his clothing, black jeans, black Nikes, a white T-shirt, and a red turtleneck sweatshirt. The police gave Tuite new clothes and sneakers and then released the schizophrenic drifter. Detective Sweeney

Figure 8.3 Police photograph of Richard Tuite, taken within hours of the Crowe murder.

did not run a criminal history check on Tuite. This was a fundamentally flawed decision. It was also contrary to standard law enforcement policy and practice when interviewing criminal suspects, especially in a murder case. Had Detective Sweeney checked, he would have learned that Tuite had numerous prior contacts with law enforcement, including several arrests on drug charges, one for possession of a loaded firearm, one for vandalism, several for prowling, and at least one for burglary. Tuite had assaulted a fellow inmate while institutionalized and had attacked another individual with a knife, stabbing the victim in the head and neck area in a manner similar to the attack on Stephanie Crowe. Tuite also had knives in his backpack during a previous arrest, and his parole had been revoked because he was found in possession of a knife.

Detective Sweeney testified that, although he considered Tuite a suspect in the murder of Stephanie Crowe, he did not ask Tuite if he had murdered her because he thought someone else would get around to it later.[3] And while he looked at what Tuite had in his pockets—three one-dollar bills, some loose change, two plain matchbook covers, and some other small items—he did not process them for fingerprints on the chance that Tuite had taken them from the Crowe residence. He photographed and returned the items (see Figure 8.4). Although Tuite lied about having contact with people in the area of the murder scene, he was not challenged on this point.

The following day a patrol officer was sent to find Tuite as Detective Sweeney and his colleagues had neglected to fingerprint him during the interview. Three days later a patrol officer was summoned to the Best Western Motel where a transient had been seen looking into car windows. The transient was Tuite. When asked what he was doing at the motel, he replied that he thought "the family of the kid who got killed" might be staying there.[4] Coincidentally, the Crowes were going to be lodged there, but the motel was full and they had to stay elsewhere.

Dr. Brian D. Blackbourne performed the autopsy the day after the homicide and determined Stephanie had sustained nine knife wounds. He estimated the length of the blade of the weapon at five to six inches. All of the wounds were around her head, neck, shoulder, and chest. Two wounds had been deep enough to be fatal, severing arteries, others were more superficial. There was no evidence of sexual assault. Dr. Blackbourne estimated her time

Figure 8.4 Contents of Tuite's pockets.

[3] Deposition of Barry Sweeney, pp. 399–400.
[4] San Diego Regional Officer's Report #01421.

of death somewhere between 9:00 p.m. and 12:30 a.m. Other facts about her activities that evening placed her death at sometime after 10:00 p.m.

Physical Evidence at the Residence

The only fingerprints found in Stephanie's room suitable for comparison were hers. There was blood on the bed, bedding, window curtains, floor, and bedroom door. Most of it was concentrated near the head of Stephanie's bed, as if she had been attacked there as she lay beneath the comforter. It appeared the killer pulled the comforter up and then stabbed through it, perhaps to protect himself from being spattered with blood. It showed defects consistent with the pattern of wounds found on her body when torn areas of the comforter were gathered together. The trail of blood indicated she had been alive after the stabbing and had dragged herself to her bedroom door, probably in an effort to get help, although no one heard her cry out.

Stephanie was attacked inside her home with five family members close by. She was left alive and was able to make her way as far as the bedroom door. The killer could not have known she would die before she could get help, which was a real possibility considering the size of the modest 1,800-square-foot house. The murder was limited to a single room. The offender did not abduct the victim or move her body. The offender approached her in an unsophisticated manner by using a blitz attack rather than employing a con, ruse, subterfuge, or ploy to lure her elsewhere. Almost any other location would have been less risky and would have provided the offender more control.

Investigators collected blood and hair samples, fingerprints, bedding, and other items, totaling 280 pieces of evidence. Five crime scene technicians arrived to process the scene, returning each day for the rest of the week. A blood spatter analyst was brought in, as well as a team from the San Bernardino Sheriff's crime lab. Investigators pulled apart stereo speakers, cut holes in the walls, brought in plumbers who uprooted two toilets and ran a camera through the sewer lines. There was no evidence of blood in any sink or drain. There was no knife. No bloody clothes. Nothing.

The Interrogations

Michael and Shannon were isolated from their parents at the Polinsky Center, but they had other visitors. Detectives came and talked to them. Over the next two days an interrogation team was assembled including Detectives Claytor, Wrisley, and Anderson, Oceanside Police Detective Chris McDonough, and forensic psychologist Dr. Lawrence Blum.

Investigators interviewed all members of the Crowe family, but gave only Michael a Miranda warning. He was isolated and interrogated by detectives on January 22 and 23, 1998, for a total of nine hours. There was no evidence linking him to the crime. Instead of recognizing that this supported Michael's innocence, the police concluded he must have had accomplices. They focused on Michael's friend, Joshua Treadway, and an acquaintance named Aaron Houser. Aaron's mother told police that a knife was missing from her son's collection. Police searched Joshua's room, located the missing knife beneath his bed, and concluded that this must be the missing murder weapon.

On January 27, both Joshua Treadway and Aaron Houser were questioned. Joshua was also interrogated the next day and again on February 10. Aaron was questioned a second time on January 28 and encouraged by detectives to offer a hypothetical scenario involving murdering someone with a knife.

The boys were interviewed for hours at a time. In effect, they were threatened with jail if they did not confess and promised leniency if they did. Michael denied any knowledge or involvement over 80 times during the initial interviews. He agonized over his sister's murder and was profoundly distressed about being separated from his family. He eventually broke after police repeatedly lied to him about the evidence. There was no evidence that even suggested that Michael might have been involved, but Detective Claytor told him: "we're going to prove every minute detail. There [are] fifty-some odd people right now with experts as far north as Los Angeles with consultations as far east as Maryland that is going to bury you and your story, an avalanche of evidence. It's all going to come tumbling down."[5] Michael eventually caved in and told the police what he thought they wanted to hear.

Joshua's first interrogation began at 9:45 p.m. on January 28 and ended at 8:00 a.m. the following morning. His second interrogation lasted 11.5 hours. Joshua eventually provided a lengthy and detailed description of how he, Michael, and Aaron had perpetrated the crime. However, Treadway's statement was strikingly inconsistent with Michael's statement. Houser never confessed, and only with prompting provided a hypothetical scenario on how someone could be killed with a knife. This was good enough for investigators. Despite the lack of evidence and the contradictory statements, Escondido authorities charged all three boys with the murder of Stephanie Crowe.

But how valid were these confessions? False confessions are more common than most people think (see Chapter 10). In more than 25% of the DNA exonerations from the Innocence Project,[6] defendants made incriminating statements, confessed, or pled guilty. They tend to occur under certain facilitating conditions: sleep deprivation, threats, feigned friendship,

---

[5] Crowe Transcript, Vol. III, p. 162.
[6] Retrieved July 10, 2008, from http://www.innocenceproject.org/understand/false-confessions.php.

isolation, use of leading questions, exposure to graphic crime scene photos, and suggestions that police already have evidence against the person. Also, if promises are made in exchange for a confession, or if a way out is offered through blaming an accomplice, an individual may well confess to relieve the stress and end the interrogation. At the time, the long-range consequences of what the individual says may not occur to him or her.

Those most likely to give a false confession have one or more of the following characteristics: youth; low intelligence; mental illness or confusion; a high degree of suggestibility; a trusting nature; low self-esteem; high anxiety; poor memory; and/or recent bereavement. Some of these traits are exacerbated by the fatigue of a lengthy interrogation, and anxiety has been confused for guilt.

Dr. Richard Leo, Associate Professor of Criminology, Law and Society and Associate Professor of Psychology at the University of California at Irvine, an expert on police-induced false confessions, evaluated the conditions under which the boys were interrogated and offered his report in November 2002. He reviewed the videotapes and transcripts of all three boys.

To set the context, Dr. Leo distinguished between a coerced-compliant confession, in which a suspect knowingly confessed falsely in order to terminate the interrogation, and a persuaded false confession (coerced internalized), in which the suspect comes to accept that what he is confessing is true. The suspect doubts his own memory. Juveniles are highly susceptible to the latter.

> Michael Crowe: Why are you doing this to me? I didn't do this to her. I couldn't. God, God. Why? [Indiscernible]. I can't even believe myself anymore. I don't know if I did it or not. I didn't though.
>
> Detective Claytor: Well, I think you're on the right track. Let's go ahead and think through this now.
>
> Michael Crowe: I don't think if I did this, I don't remember it. I don't remember a thing.
>
> Detective Claytor: You know what, that's possible.[7]

Dr. Leo found that the police used several techniques on Michael, including isolation and a machine called a Computer Voice Stress Analyzer (CVSA). They convinced him that the machine was highly accurate, although independent studies by the U.S. Department of Defense have shown it to be no more reliable than chance.[8] Detectives lied to him about the evidence, lied about his performance on the CVSA, and pressured him

---

[7] Crowe Transcript, January 22, 1998, p. 89.
[8] Detective McDonough told Michael Crowe that the Voice Stress Analyzer has an accuracy rate that is phenomenal and that is what made it such a great tool (Crowe Transcript, Vol. I, p. 42).

to take the heat off other family members.[9] They suggested he had multiple personality disorder and, perhaps most troubling of all, promised him leniency if he confessed.

When Michael told detectives that he was afraid he was going to be locked up for a long, long time for something he could not even remember, Detective Claytor responded: "You have to trust me on this. ... I think we have ways of helping this situation. ... I'm not really sure that locking you up is the answer. ... We don't do that to 14-year-olds." When Michael asked what was done, Detective Claytor responded: "We look for understanding and we try to help."[10] He told Michael: "You're a child. You're 14-years-old. Nobody is going to hold you to the same standards that they would some criminal on the street. Okay. You're going to need some help through this."[11]

Detective Claytor asked Michael to write Stephanie a letter, seeking her forgiveness. Alone in the interview room, Michael wrote the following [errors in original]:

> Dear Stephanie,
> I'm so sorry that I can't even remember what I did to you. I feel that it is almost like I am more being convinced of this than really knowing it. I will always love you and can still remember you in life.
> You have always given so much that [you] likely must be an angel. I tried to be as loving as possible to you. I'm still crying for you and I pray to God that you forgive me for what they say I did.
> Sometimes I think it would be better if I could remember but I don't really want to try. The fact that I can't remember is a blessing from God. I only want to remember the way you were when you were with us. I hope that you love me forever and that I never forget what you were, a truly loving person. They are putting me through hell and I think this is what I [UNCLEAR].
> I will always hold you dear to my heart. If I did do this then I am insane, I hope both you and God will forgive me for this. We all miss you and I feel that I am being ripped from everything I know.
> I never meant to hurt you and the only way I know I did it is because they told me I did. I hope you understand that I don't know what I was thinking when I did this. I hope I never remember because I don't think I could ever forgive myself if I know what I did.
> I want you to know that I was not myself when I did this they want me to help them but I can't I feel because of that that I am letting you down. I should help you but I simply can't.

---

[9] The investigators' tunnel vision and belief perseverance that Stephanie's murder was an inside job are abundantly evident as Detective Claytor tells a sobbing Michael, "It was either Shannon, or it's your Grandma, or it's your Mom, or it's your Dad, or it's you."

[10] Crowe Transcripts, Vol. III, pp. 80–81.

[11] Crowe Transcripts, Vol. III, p. 73.

If you don't forgive me then I can understand. You showed me what God could do for you and now I have excepted him myself. I shall one day see you in heaven and I hope that I shall have an eternity to serve you for this.

Never forget that I always loved you.

Love, Michael

Michael's "confession" was a self-admitted lie. He could not provide any detail as to how the crime actually was committed for the simple reason that he did not know. Michael told his interrogators that he "would have to make up a story."[12]

Michael Crowe: If I tell you a story, the evidence is going to be a complete lie.
Detective Wrisley: Well, then, tell us the story.
Michael Crowe: Well, I'll lie. I'll have to make it up.
Detective Wrisley: Tell us the story, Michael.
Michael Crowe: You want me to tell you a little story?
Detective Wrisley: Tell me the story. What happened that night?
Michael Crowe: Okay. I'm going to warn you right now. It is a complete lie.

*****

Detective Claytor: You let me know when you get to the lie part.
Michael Crowe: Okay. Here's the part where I'll start lying. That night I got pissed off at her. I couldn't take it anymore, okay. So I got a knife went into her room, and I stabbed her. After I was done, I pulled her off the bed, picked her up off the bed, dropped her ...
Detective Claytor: How many times did you stab her?
Michael Crowe: This is going to be a lie, three times.
Detective Claytor: How many?
Michael Crowe: Three. It's a lie ...
Detective Wrisley: When you went in to do that, Mike, was she on her back or on her stomach or on her side when she was in bed?
Michael Crowe: On her side, that's a lie. I don't know I told you it was going to be a lie.
Detective Wrisley: Well, tell me what the truth is.
Michael Crowe: The only reason I'm trying to lie here is because you presented me with two paths, one I'm definitely afraid of. I'd rather die than go to jail.[13]

Dr. Leo concluded this interrogation to be the most psychologically brutal interrogation and tortured confession that he has ever observed. He determined much the same about the interrogation of Joshua Treadway, although he called this one a coerced compliant confession, the result of more than 20 hours of interrogation.

---

[12]Crowe Transcripts, Vol. III, pp. 77, 129–130, 142.
[13]Crowe Transcripts, Vol. III, pp. 160–162.

Dr. Leo concluded that detectives coerced Aaron Houser by telling him Treadway had already confessed, and that he should get revenge by telling investigators what Treadway's role was. They falsely claimed that they had evidence against Aaron and ignored his repeated requests to leave. They also told him that if he did not confess, he would be causing his mother a great deal of suffering. Leo found the approach inept and reckless. Aaron was not advised of his rights and was not allowed to end the sessions when he said he wanted to.

Collectively, the three interrogations appeared to Dr. Leo to be a textbook case of police misconduct, psychological coercion, and illegality. The presiding judge excluded most of these statements, ruling that they had been obtained either illegally, through coercion, or both. Even prosecutor Summer Stephen later admitted that at least parts of Michael Crowe's confession had been coerced, were "unfair," and had not been done properly. She stated that had she been in the monitoring room she would have told the police to stop.

In their review of the literature on the psychology of false confessions, Kassin and Gudjonsson (2004), widely regarded experts in the field, note several points salient to this case. If an interrogator holds a strong belief in a suspect's guilt, his or her frame of mind can influence the interaction. Once an individual has formed a belief, confirmation bias can set in as the interrogator seeks only information that confirms his or her opinion while ignoring contradictory evidence. Research indicates that when people view a specific outcome as inevitable, they tend to allow their cognitive processes to move in that direction so that they can accept the situation. Juries are not well equipped to recognize a false confession. Unfortunately, this is also true for some interrogators. A case can be quickly solved with a confession; this tends, in some situations, to alleviate the responsibility of both investigators and jurors to carefully weigh the evidence. Confessions can be incredibly powerful because most people believe that an innocent person would never confess to a crime he or she did not commit.

It is well established that the mere authority of the police, the isolation of an individual, especially a juvenile, and the uncertainty and anxiety surrounding an interrogation, in particular one that occurs over an extended time, may lead to a false confession. "Two studies have investigated the suggestibility scores of boys between the ages of 11 and 16. The results from both studies indicate that youths are no more suggestible than adults, unless their answers are subjected to negative feedback (i.e., interrogative pressure). Then they become markedly more suggestible than adults" (Gudjonsson, 1992, p. 182).

The interrogations of Crowe, Treadway, and Houser were not a search for truth, but rather attempts to manipulate the teens into confessing and thus validating the investigators' hypothesis of how the murder occurred. The police decided that Joshua acted as the lookout, while Michael and Aaron went into Stephanie's bedroom. They believed that Michael told her to be quiet while

Aaron stabbed her to death. Then all three left the house, and Aaron later gave the knife to Joshua, but instead of getting rid of it he tossed it under his bed. It was a simple plan, but not one that correlated with either logic or the facts.

To be considered reliable, a confession must have both internal and external validity; that is, it must be consistent with itself and consistent with the external evidence. Professional law enforcement investigators understand that a confession is not an end to the investigation, as it must then be subjected to a vigorous follow-up investigation. A true confession typically contains a wealth of specific details that not only are consistent with the crime and the crime scene, but also includes new information beyond what is known by investigators. A confession's validity is strengthened through corroboration; it is weakened when the evidence does not support its claims. There were conflicting statements and contradictory evidence in the "confessions" of Michael Crowe and Joshua Treadway. The Escondido detectives did not conduct the type of postconfession investigations necessary to resolve these discrepancies fairly and objectively. No one else in either the Treadway or the Houser families was questioned. Amazingly, either no attempts were made to compare the "confessions" with the facts, or, if the investigators did so, they ignored the numerous inconsistencies and contradictions. Shortly after admitting, directly or indirectly, their involvement in the murder, the boys recanted their confessions and claimed they had made them up because of the unrelenting pressure from their interrogators and the fear of going to jail if they did *not* confess.

In setting forth probable cause for the arrest of Michael Crowe, Detective Claytor swore that "Chemical tests done in the house also revealed that a large quantity of blood had been washed down a bathroom drain."[14] In fact, no blood had been found in that or any other drain in the house. Prior to testifying before the grand jury, Detective Claytor received a report from a DNA laboratory clearly stating that there was no blood or DNA present on the knife seized from Joshua Treadway. Detective Claytor then proceeded to tell the grand jury that this lab reported finding blood on the knife, but that there was an insufficient amount to determine any DNA factors.[15] The grand jury indicted the three boys for the murder of Stephanie Crowe.

Heading to Trial

As the trial[16] approached, the case against the boys rapidly unraveled. Not only had the presiding judge ruled that the majority of the boys' statements

---

[14]Declaration and Determination, which identified Detective Claytor as the arresting officer.
[15]Grand Jury Transcript of Detective Claytor's testimony, p. 588.
[16]*People of the State of California v. Joshua David Treadway,* case no.: SCD130983.

were inadmissible,[17] but it also became clear how deceptive Detective Claytor had been. There was no "avalanche of evidence." There were no 50 experts. There was no blood on the knife or in any of the drains.

However, when Detective Claytor told Michael that "It's all going to come tumbling down," he was prescient. It was just that the case was about to tumble down in a manner Detective Claytor did not anticipate. For Assistant District Attorney (ADA) Summer Stephen, the lead prosecutor, Claytor's prediction was morphing into a painful reality. On November 27, 1998, with the trial only weeks away and in desperate need of help, ADA Stephen contacted Supervisory Special Agent (SSA) Mary Ellen O'Toole at the FBI's NCAVC.

SSA O'Toole's handwritten notes of that conversation indicate that ADA Stephen wanted a report followed by testimony in January 1999 regarding the crime scene and forensic evidence. In those notes O'Toole underlined: "Don't refer directly to transient [Richard Tuite]". Making such a decision prior to reviewing any material is problematic. It suggests that SSA O'Toole and her colleagues at the FBI accepted without question the dominant theory that the boys did it. SSA O'Toole testified she spent 500 hours reviewing case documents and materials, but never reviewed the videotaped interviews and interrogations of the three teens or their written transcripts. However, her handwritten notes contained numerous specific references to those interviews and interrogations. In addition, she and her colleagues were either unaware or accepted as proper police procedure Detective Claytor's misrepresentation of evidence to the grand jury that indicted the teens. These, among other factors, suggest that tunnel vision, confirmation bias, groupthink, and organizational momentum had dangerously combined.

If SSA O'Toole and her FBI colleagues at the NCAVC had conducted an independent and unbiased analysis of this case, these errors might have been detected and the investigation put on the right track. But they did not. There are additional issues, which will be delineated below. As SSA O'Toole and her FBI colleagues began their review and analysis, the attorneys for the three boys were pursuing their own leads.

Public defender Mary Ellen Attridge, who represented Joshua Treadway, was convinced that Richard Tuite was a much more viable suspect than were the three boys. She requested a complete analysis of the clothing that Richard Tuite had worn the night of the murder, surprised that over the course of the last year the police had not already done so. They sent Tuite's clothing to Dr. Edward Blake who completed his analysis in early January 1999.

About this time SSA Mary Ellen O'Toole submitted her three-and-a-half-page peer-reviewed report, which supported the prosecution's theory that the murder was an "inside job." She concluded:

---

[17] After the District Court ruling, Michael Crowe's confession was listed as one of the top 10 false confessions in the United States in the preceding 20 years (Davis, 2005).

This crime scene indicates there was a familiarity, comfort and knowledge of the victim's residence … [the murder was] a controlled assault and controlled scene. … A certain degree of planning is evident in all three phases of this crime, pre-offense phase, the crime itself, and the post-offense phase … the scene was controlled and carefully managed.[18]

SSA O'Toole was prepared to testify against the three boys, but Dr. Blake's findings were about to change everything.

On January 14, 1999, the results of Dr. Blake's examination of Richard Tuite's clothing hit the courtroom like a bombshell. He had found three spots of Stephanie Crowe's blood on the right sleeve of Tuite's red sweatshirt (see Figure 8.5). Judge Thompson stopped the trial, gagged the attorneys, and gave the prosecution six weeks to explain how Stephanie's blood came to be found on Tuite's shirt.

Escondido police and San Diego County prosecutors came up with a host of reasons to explain away this blood evidence. They speculated that it was a contact smear from evidence mishandling; however, it was airborne spatter, not a contact smear. They suggested defense attorney Attridge planted Stephanie's blood on the garments, but she had only taken the case after Stephanie was buried and had no access to her blood. Besides, police photographs showed blood already on Tuite's red sweatshirt, which had been in police custody within hours of the homicide. Detectives and prosecutors pursued the idea that Tuite had come into contact with the boys and had picked up the

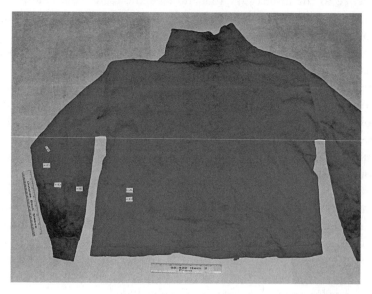

Figure 8.5 Locations of Stephanie Crowe's blood on Richard Tuite's red sweatshirt.

[18] Report of SSA O'Toole, January 7, 1999, pp. 3–4.

bloodstained shirt after they had discarded it. The problem with that theory is Tuite was seen wearing the red shirt *before*, as well as after, the murder.

On February 25, 1999, the San Diego County District Attorney dropped charges against the three teens with the proviso they could be filed again. The teenagers, who had been in custody for six months, were released. The boys and their families found it ironic that in the motion to dismiss, the prosecution quoted Sherlock Holmes in *A Scandal in Bohemia*. "It is a capital mistake to theorize before one has data. Insensibly one begins to twist facts to suit theories instead of theories to suit facts."

A task force was formed to review the evidence. The boys and their families preferred a new, independent team, but the task force was comprised of Escondido detectives Ralph Claytor, Barry Sweeney, and Mark Wrisley and others who had already concluded the boys were guilty. While reinvestigating Stephanie's murder, Detectives Claytor and Sweeney interviewed a prison inmate who alleged that Richard Tuite had been involved in a drug-related murder, that he often carried a "Buck"-type knife and fantasized about stabbing a person in the head and neck. When being deposed, both detectives denied ever interviewing anyone who had made such allegations and denied ever visiting a prison to talk to anyone about this allegation. Their memories improved markedly when the plaintiff's attorney provided them with copies of Detective Claytor's report of that interview. When asked if he "buried" the report, Detective Claytor responded, "Well it couldn't have been buried very deep." He then stated, "But no I didn't bury the report."[19]

On February 5, 2000, with no movement in the case, the Escondido Police Department, citing a need for "fresh eyes," turned the investigation over to the San Diego County Sheriff's Office. Sheriff Koelander told his cold case team to leave no stone unturned. Led by Detective Victor Caloca, the Sheriff's Office conducted an exhaustive investigation and spent countless hours interviewing witnesses and reinvestigating the crime. Nearly $50,000 was expended on sophisticated DNA testing alone.

Detective Caloca carefully reviewed the boys' videotaped confessions and found glaring problems with the interrogation methods used; he also noted discrepancies between the stories they told and the case facts—something the interrogators had failed to document or even bother to check. At the end of their investigation, Detective Caloca and his team came to the conclusion that the evidence showed probable cause to believe that Richard Tuite murdered Stephanie Crowe. The San Diego County District Attorney refused to charge Tuite with the murder so the Sheriff's Office presented the facts to Special Assistant Attorney General David Druliner of the State of California Attorney General's Office.

---

[19]Deposition of Detective Claytor, pp. 196–197, 351–354; deposition of Detective Sweeney, pp. 294–302.

Druliner evaluated the case and thought Tuite should be arrested even though the San Diego County DA told him a case against Tuite could not be won because the boys' confessions would provide reasonable doubt (personal conversation with David Druliner). Druliner rejected this reasoning, and on May 15, 2002, over four years after the murder, Tuite was arrested. In announcing the arrest, the representatives of the San Diego County Sheriff's Office and the State of California Attorney General's Office took the unusual step of publicly exonerating the three boys.[20]

I knew none of this when Milton Silverman, an attorney representing the boys in their subsequent civil suit against the Escondido Police Department, first contacted me in 2002. He asked if I would conduct a crime analysis of the homicide and offer an opinion regarding the efficacy and reasonableness of the investigation conducted by the police. I told him that I would, but obviously could not know what my opinions would be until I had reviewed the material. That was exactly what he was seeking. An ocean of materials arrived shortly thereafter, and I began analyzing the crime, the crime scene, the evidence, the interrogations of the boys, the sworn testimony, and all the expert reports.

Crime Scene Analysis

A proper crime scene analysis requires recognizing and considering the five types of crime scene evidence: transient, conditional, pattern, transfer, and associative. Transient evidence is temporary and includes such things as odors and temperatures, which quickly change. Conditional evidence, such as the state of a victim's body, is produced by an event or action. Pattern evidence includes imprints, trajectory patterns, and glass fractures. Transfer or trace evidence is the result of contact between a person and the crime scene, wherein something is left behind or taken away. Associative evidence can be anything that associates a victim or a suspect with a crime or a crime scene and includes testimonial as well as physical evidence.

It is also important to conduct a thorough victimology (study of the victim). This is done to determine what, if anything, elevated that individual's risk for becoming the victim of violence. The analysis looks at the victim's lifestyle, relationships, records, and all situational variables, including everyone with whom the victim may have crossed paths, in order to develop potential suspects. It is proper to avoid considering suspect information when constructing a *profile* because suspect information can impair an analyst's objectivity about who committed the crime. However, when conducting a *crime scene analysis*, one must consider and integrate all data, including suspect information,

---

[20]*People of the State of California v. Richard Raymond Tuite,* case no: CD166932.

especially when the latter is the result of eyewitness evidence. Overlaying and correlating suspect and eyewitness statements with independent evidence is the only way for investigators to determine if they may be dealing with a false confession or a false allegation. The totality of evidence involves examining all the information found in these categories. The victim, suspects, crime scene, and evidence are then linked in a four-way analysis in which each part is informed by what is known of the other parts. To the degree that any of these components is ignored, the analysis becomes unreliable.

Analysis of the Crowe Murder

There was no credible evidence of any skillful planning in the preoffense phase of Stephanie Crowe's murder. Attacking a victim in her residence with five other family members present is not a well thought-out plan. It would be more likely for an organized offender to have devised some type of con or ruse to lure the victim to an area where it would be safe to attack her, rather than do so in her home with adults present. This was clearly a reckless and high-risk act.

It could be argued that one indication of "organization" evident during the crime was the fact that the offender covered the victim with a comforter from the bed during part of the assault. This would likely have muffled any screams from the victim and minimized the amount of cast-off blood, blood spatter, or transfer blood.

The crime was perpetrated against a 12-year-old child who was a victim of opportunity. She was someone whom a violence-prone offender encountered while "on the hunt." The attack on the victim was limited to nine stab wounds, with no blunt force trauma, facial battering, or sexual assault. There is no indication the offender interacted with this victim in any way either prior to, or after, stabbing her. The offender surprised the victim and carried out a "blitz" attack that is more consistent with a *disorganized* than an *organized* offender. This is because disorganized offenders typically lack the interpersonal skills necessary to use a con, ruse, subterfuge, or ploy to gain and maintain control over a victim. Rather they rely on the immediate application of injurious physical force.

It is common in domestic or familial homicides for there to be an escalation from verbal to physical to homicidal behavior. What begins as an argument escalates to pushing, shoving, grabbing, slapping, and hitting, which in turn progresses to homicide. This type of escalation was absent at the Crowe crime scene and in the precrime family situation.

There is a correlation between the amount of time an offender spends at a crime scene (especially an indoor scene) and his or her degree of comfort with that location. Offenders may be familiar with a scene because they live or work there or have some other legitimate reason for being at that location. Conversely, the less time an offender spends at a scene, the more likely it is he or she has no legitimate reason for being there. They quickly want to leave to avoid detection. The fact that there was no blood anywhere in the house other than in the victim's bedroom and the conclusion that the offender fled while the victim was still alive are consistent with someone who was not familiar or comfortable enough with the Crowe home to spend time "cleaning up," removing evidence, or staging the crime scene. This suggests an outside intruder, not a family member.

Twigs found at the scene suggest the offender may have walked through brush or shrubbery prior to entering the home, consistent with someone who was peeping and prowling outside. Although one cannot rule out the possibility that the twigs were artifact, possibly brought to the scene by medical or emergency personnel, it is unlikely the first responders were wandering through brush or shrubbery before entering the house. However, police apparently did not investigate that possibility. In summary, the totality of the circumstances supports an interpretation of an impulsive, high-risk crime, typical of a more disorganized offender.

Suspects

Michael Crowe, a reputedly quiet, bookish boy, was isolated from his family and subjected to over nine hours of psychologically abusive interrogation over a two-day period. Michael's ninth-grade friends, Joshua Treadway and Aaron Houser, were also interviewed and interrogated. Finally, after initial denials, Michael and Joshua broke down, while Aaron, when pressured, offered a hypothetical scenario about how to use his collection of knives—a gift from his grandfather—to wound someone. Treadway gave a very detailed confession, even returning to add more details as detectives asked ever more leading questions. Michael said he did not know how he had done the murder and could not recall committing it, but believed the investigators when they told him that he had. Perhaps most importantly, their confessions were inconsistent with the physical and forensic evidence, and they contradicted one another. Michael never implicated Treadway or Houser. Treadway said Houser stabbed Stephanie and the bloody knife was washed off in the sink, but no blood was found in any sink or drain. Houser denied everything.

Regardless, all three were charged with conspiring to kill Stephanie Crowe. The police pegged Michael's motive as competition between him and his sister, which by his own admission, made him feel worthless. The boys went to jail to be held for trial while their families hired attorneys.

An issue that seemed to be of some interest to investigators and prosecutors was Michael Crowe's involvement with "fantasy"-based video games that had some violent content, the inference being that this was predictive of violence. But such a connection is not supported by the research. Dr. Stanton

Samenow, a respected criminal psychologist who works with violent juveniles, has observed: "Critical is not what is shown on the screen, but what is in the mind of the viewer. ... The program or movie is not what 'causes' the viewer to behave in a criminal manner. The seeds were there long before..." (1998, pp. 21). In other words, it is an individual's predisposition to violence that is critical. There is no direct causal relationship between playing violent video games and violent behavior. An individual who is predisposed to violence may find some validation or stimulation through violent video games or other violence-oriented media, but the latter do not *cause* one to become violent.

Michael Crowe, Josh Treadway, and Aaron Houser had no history of violence nor is there any credible indication that they were predisposed to violence. Any inference that Michael Crowe's interest in violent video games was predictive of homicidal behavior is unfounded. Also of significance is the fact that juveniles who murder are most likely to target acquaintances or strangers and least likely family members (U.S. Department of Justice, 1999).

The fact that Michael Crowe and his friends had none of the antecedent risk markers for violence, had no history of violence, and are statistically among the group (juveniles) least likely to target family members made them unlikely suspects. These facts stand in marked contrast to those surrounding Richard Tuite, who had an extensive mental health and criminal history. On the evening of the murder, Tuite was agitated, pounded on doors, and tried to enter the homes of people he did not know who lived in the immediate vicinity of the Crowe residence.

Detective Ralph Claytor gave "incorrect" testimony on several key points to the grand jury on May 20, 1998. He said:

- All of the biological evidence had been submitted for analysis; in fact, 48 items had not been.
- Blood was discovered on the knife believed to be the murder weapon but in an amount insufficient to test for DNA; 20 days earlier, however, he had received the lab report indicating there was no blood on the knife.
- Blood found in the room could have been either Stephanie's or Michael's; this was not true.

He later admitted in a deposition that these statements were "incorrect." He also said he did not place any significance on Officer Walters's report about seeing someone go in through the laundry room door. He decided that Officer Walters had been at another home, despite the fact that Walters double checked his location and affirmed that it was the Crowe house. And when Claytor showed a photo of Tuite to people who called police the night of the murder, he used one that was eight years old, although he had access to more recent high-quality photos of Tuite.

The Escondido police rushed to judgment. Their investigation was incomplete, they missed key information, and consequently the investigation suffered from errors in logic. Detectives closed their minds and subsequently lacked the flexibility to recognize other suspects. Due to the resulting tunnel vision, Richard Tuite was not thoroughly checked out. In the end, a DNA analysis, along with persuasive circumstantial evidence, made Tuite the most viable suspect for Stephanie's murder. Missteps during the investigation obscured this reality, irreparably harmed three families, and unnecessarily put the community at risk.

The FBI's analysis should have been a safety net that helped identify these problems. In this instance, it did not. In their hygienic seclusion, the FBI analysts used just enough facts to support the erroneous conclusion that three innocent teens committed the murder. Forensic evidence, such as DNA, is the most scientific and reliable. Blood spatter pattern analysis, trace evidence analysis (in this case, hairs and fibers), and crime scene profiling all involve subjective interpretation and consequently are less scientific. The investigation must consider compelling associative crime scene evidence—such as a victim's blood found on a suspect's clothing. But in the Crowe case, the DNA evidence proved to be an inconvenient truth for FBI analysts. They chose to dismiss it and the possibilities it opened up. The agents appeared to believe in the infallibility of their analysis and its invulnerability to any and all future case developments. They were definitely singing off the same sheet of music as the original investigating and prosecution team.

Troubled not only by the Escondido authorities' investigation and conclusions, but also by the FBI's apparent full support of the original investigation, I contacted Larry Ankrom, a former FBI colleague of mine, who was Mary Ellen O'Toole's immediate supervisor. Larry stated that when he approved O'Toole's January 1999 report, he was unaware of many of the details of the original investigation, such as the coercive interrogations or the fact that the lead investigator had misled the grand jury about the evidence. Although he knew that Stephanie's blood had been detected on Richard Tuite's clothing, he said he was unaware that Tuite had been arrested and charged with her murder in May 2002. The FBI had received no further request for assistance in the case, and he was not sure how they would proceed from here. After a thorough review of all the evidence, I filed my report in U.S. District Court on November 27, 2002. The FBI's position became clear less than four weeks later.

On December 19, 2002, Mary Ellen O'Toole filed an amended report, not in the criminal case pending in state court, but in the Crowes' civil case pending in U.S. District Court.[21] This was unusual, as her first report was

---

[21] *Crowe et al v. County of San Diego, City of Escondido*, United States District Court, Southern District of California, 99-CV-0241-R (RRB).

in the criminal case and the FBI rarely becomes involved in civil litigation unless they have some direct or substantial interest.

The opinions expressed in the first report were those of SSA O'Toole and her colleagues at the NCAVC. However, the opinions expressed in this second report were stated as being those of "the FBI." This change arguably implied increased "heft" as, technically, only the Director of the FBI approves "FBI opinions" and positions. The following are among the opinions expressed in the second report:

- Even though the best predictor of future behavior is past behavior, it was "unfairly prejudicial to Mr. Tuite" to consider him a suspect in the stab-bing/slashing attack of Stephanie Crowe simply because he had previ-ously perpetrated a stabbing/slashing attack against another stranger;[22]
- Tuite's presence near the Crowe residence did not elevate Stephanie Crowe's risk for becoming the victim of violence;[23] and
- When conducting a criminal investigative analysis, it is improper to consider such factors as coerced interviews, police procedures, and sta-tistical probabilities of adolescent violence (even though the case alleg-edly involved juvenile offenders).

For some reason, SSA O'Toole and her colleagues had also singled out a particular personality disorder (psychopathy) to be unworthy of consider-ation, although it had never been mentioned in this case.[24] While the Escondido authorities tried to explain away the DNA evidence by offering various sce-narios, the FBI decided the best way to handle this was to ignore it. Although SSA O'Toole and her colleagues were aware of that evidence when they wrote the second report, they studiously avoided any mention of it. To clarify those opinions and establish whose they were, the Director of the FBI and SSA O'Toole were subpoenaed to testify in deposition in the civil case pending in the U.S. District Court in San Diego. As might be expected, subpoenaing the Director of the FBI to testify brings increased scrutiny to a case.

By March 2003, FBI officials concluded that it was a mistake for the FBI to be involved in the civil case. They stated that SSA O'Toole's amended report "must be returned to the FBI." In a letter to the attorneys involved in the civil litigation, the FBI requested that "the parties return all copies of the report and agree not to further discuss its contents" and that "if the parties are unwilling to return the report voluntarily, the FBI will be required to move the Court for such an order." The FBI further stated that because SSA O'Toole "cannot appear as a designated expert witness, we assume that Plaintiff's

---

[22]Report on Mary Ellen O'Toole, December 19, 2002, p. 7.
[23]Ibid. p. 9.
[24]Ibid. p. 22, item No. 16.

motions for her video deposition and for a deposition of the Director of the FBI are moot and will be withdrawn."[25] However, SSA O'Toole's report had already been filed in U.S. District Court and was a matter of public record. There was no getting it back—that train had already left the station. Every interested party, including the media, had a copy. Richard Tuite's defense attorneys also had the report, and in it they saw an opportunity.

Their plan was to defend Tuite by putting the three boys on trial. That meant the state would have to prosecute Tuite and at the same time defend Crowe, Treadway, and Houser. By constructing a "trial within a trial," the defense hoped to create reasonable doubt in the minds of jurors as to Richard Tuite's guilt. The single most prominent obstacle in their path was the DNA evidence. It was difficult for the defense to come up with a credible explanation of how their client came to have the victim's blood spattered on his shirt and undershirt if he was truly innocent.

The prospect of having an FBI special agent take the stand and not only support their theory that the three boys were guilty, but also declare the DNA evidence to be irrelevant would be an amazing coup for the defense. After all, the FBI pioneered, developed, and refined much of the DNA technology in use by U.S. law enforcement today and trains many DNA analysts. The FBI has also established four regional labs around the United States to assist law enforcement agencies in analyzing DNA evidence and provides experts to testify in court as to DNA's relevance.

It seemed improbable the FBI would even consider, much less allow, an FBI special agent to take the stand and testify that the DNA evidence developed in this case was irrelevant. The defense attorneys also knew that state subpoenas were, in effect, nonbinding on FBI agents, and they could not compel SSA O'Toole to testify.[26] Still, it was worth a try, so they subpoenaed her. For some reason, the FBI approved her testimony. SSA O'Toole would take the stand and support the theory that the three boys were guilty, although a thorough investigation by the San Diego County Sheriff's Office and State of California had completely exonerated them. She would also testify that the DNA evidence that linked the defendant to the victim was irrelevant to her expert analysis of this case. SSA O'Toole's amended report, the one the FBI wanted returned and the contents of which they never wanted anyone to discuss again, was apparently back in play. It is my understanding that SSA O'Toole and her peers were attempting to justify excluding the

---

[25]Letter from K. Krasnow Waterman, FBI Headquarters, March 27, 2003.

[26]As a matter of policy, the FBI considers state subpoenas to be discretionary; otherwise, their agents would be spending most of their time in state court rather than fulfilling their primary federal obligations. The FBI considers two questions when deciding whether an agent should be allowed to testify in state court: (1) will the testimony serve the interests of justice; and (2) is the agent willing to testify? If the answer to both of these questions is yes, the agent is allowed to testify.

DNA evidence by declaring that their crime scene analysis was limited to the 1,800-square-foot house. Because the DNA was detected outside of that area, it was "irrelevant." A meaningful crime scene analysis can never be limited to a geographic area. This tortured reasoning, if taken to its illogical conclusion, would mean that DNA detected during an autopsy, from a rape kit, or any where outside of a designated geographic area would be deemed irrelevant to a crime scene analysis. This is ludicrous.

Not being directly involved in the criminal case, I contacted FBI Unit Chief Larry Ankrom and asked if this could really be true. Larry confirmed that SSA O'Toole was fully prepared to testify for the defense, stating: "We've been attacked and have to defend our position" (personal conversation with Larry Ankrom). I was stunned and told Larry that for an FBI agent to take the stand and even suggest to a jury that the DNA evidence in this case was irrelevant would not only be unconscionable, but would appear to be an attempt to obstruct justice and undermine the prosecution. Larry disagreed.

Up to this point I had been involved in the civil case only. Facing the proposed testimony of SSA O'Toole, the State of California needed a rebuttal witness, someone to tell the jury the importance of considering all the evidence when conducting a crime scene analysis. It was for this reason and this reason alone that the State of California subpoenaed me to testify in the criminal trial. I had no further contact with the FBI until after the trial. Prosecutors from the State of California Attorney General's Office appeared as shocked and confused as I was that the FBI was willing to put an agent on the stand and testify that, among others things, the DNA evidence at the heart of the prosecution's case was simply irrelevant to a meaningful crime scene analysis. The first question Detective Victor Caloca asked me was, "What the fuck is the FBI doing?" I had no idea.

The Trial

February 4, 2004, was the first day of jury selection. During the lunch break, Richard Tuite slipped away from the deputies guarding him and walked out of the courthouse. He was recaptured later that afternoon and returned to custody. Jury selection was completed and opening statements began on February 17, 2004. Over the next three months the jury heard testimony from 169 witnesses, including Ralph Claytor, who had since retired from the Escondido Police Department and moved out of state, and the FBI's Mary Ellen O'Toole. As anticipated, it was a trial within a trial. Tuite's attorneys attempted to prosecute the three teens while defending their client, and the prosecutors defended the three boys while prosecuting Tuite. Jurors saw Claytor's interrogation of the boys on videotape and heard his "misrepresentations" for themselves in the courtroom.

As the trial progressed, arguments were made over how the victim's blood came to be on Tuite's red sweatshirt and white undershirt. The defense argued that police mishandling of the evidence resulted in the accidental transfer of the victim's blood onto both shirts. They suggested that perhaps a camera tripod that had been at the bloodstained murder scene was later was used to photograph the red sweatshirt. Experts for the prosecution pointed out that the blood marks on the red sweatshirt were spatter stains, made by wet blood in motion, not transfer stains. The white undershirt had never even been photographed, so transfer stains from a camera tripod were impossible.

On April 7, 2004, the defense put SSA Mary Ellen O'Toole on the stand. She testified that Stephanie Crowe's murder was an *organized* crime scene, one that suggested "knowledge, familiarity and comfort." She defined "knowledge" as having information about the inside and outside of the house, and "familiarity" as having both "personal knowledge of the home" and the "habits of the occupants of the house." She defined comfort as "ease in being inside that home" and "being in a position to explain your presence if somebody comes out of their room and says, 'what are you doing here'?" She told the jury that "There was certainly knowledge, but beyond that there was familiarity beyond that, there was comfort with the layout of the home, the dynamics of the home, the people in the home, the pets in the home, and the people's habits and even the pets' habits."[27] She also testified that there was a "good possibility" multiple offenders had murdered Stephanie Crowe. She conceded that a single individual might have done it, but believed it was more likely multiple killers were involved because there were "a lot of things that have to be controlled."[28]

When asked if someone could "just be lucky and commit a crime successfully," she said no. SSA O'Toole stated she and her FBI colleagues were "very highly trained, specialized experienced analysts and luck has nothing to do with our analysis. ... luck is not a concept that we entertain at all in our assessments ... no, we don't consider luck."[29] She also testified that the NCAVC analysts consider "everything in forensic evidence; hairs, fibers, blood."[30] Here, however, she intentionally ignored the blood evidence when she wrote her second report. Although that evidence had not been detected when she wrote her first report, she testified that even if she had known about it then "it would not have made any difference to me."[31] How would the FBI react to criticism of SSA O'Toole's testimony? The answer came approximately two weeks later.

On April 22, 2004, Patrick Kelley, Deputy General Counsel for the FBI, wrote to William R. Fletcher, one of Richard Tuite's defense attorneys, that the

---

[27] Transcript of Mary Ellen O'Toole's testimony, pp. 4912–4915.
[28] Ibid. pp. 4928–4929.
[29] Ibid. p. 4929.
[30] Ibid. p. 4910, lines 18–19.
[31] Ibid. pp. 4997–4998.

FBI "views with dismay the conclusion which Mr. McCrary asserts and attributes as well to officials in the State of California, that SSA O'Toole's testimony 'obstructs justice' and 'undermines the prosecution.' At the conclusion of the Tuite trial, we intend to pursue appropriate action."[32] If this was an attempt to intimidate me, influence my testimony, or pressure the prosecutors, it failed. I took the stand on May 4 and testified to my analysis as outlined above.

On May 26, 2004, the jury found Richard Tuite guilty of the stabbing death of Stephanie Crowe. The jury publicly stated that they quickly determined the boys were innocent. After watching over 30 hours of interrogation tapes, they felt that detectives had abused them, and their "confessions" had been coerced. Jurors found that SSA O'Toole's testimony "defied common sense," and characterized former lead investigator Ralph Claytor as "a despicable rat" (Sauer, 2004).

How could the original investigation conducted by the Escondido Police Department, overseen by the San Diego County District Attorney's Office and supported by the FBI, have gotten so far off track? Why did these investigators and prosecutors try to convict good, hard-working, advanced placement ninth-graders for a murder they did not commit?

Comparison of Hypotheses

It is instructive to compare the two competing hypotheses in this case: (1) Michael Crowe, Joshua Treadway, and Aaron Houser planned and committed Stephanie's murder; versus (2) schizophrenic transient Richard Tuite broke into the Crowe residence looking for Tracy, saw Stephanie, and then killed her.

Let us first consider logistics. An unknown person entered the Crowes' house about the time Stephanie was killed. Tuite was seen near their residence around the same time. Likewise, Michael Crowe was close—right across the hall from his sister's bedroom. However, Treadway and Houser would have had to travel some distance on foot to get to the Crowes' neighborhood. The distance from Joshua's house to Aaron's house to Michael's house, and then back, was approximately 10 miles. Assuming he left just after 11:00 p.m., when he was known to still be at home, he would have had to walk about five miles in an hour and a half.

But there was another complicating issue, as Michael and Aaron's friendship had become strained. Would Michael enlist the help of a former friend to murder his sister? Would a former friend agree to become involved in such a brutal crime? Could Michael even trust Aaron with such a secret?

Richard Tuite was looking for a girl who resembled Stephanie and who once had lived in the area. He was belligerent that night, persistent, and

---

[32]Letter from Patrick W. Kelley to William R. Fletcher, April 22, 2004.

seemingly intent on going from house to house until he found her. He could have spotted Stephanie on the phone, as her room was the only lighted one in the house, believed she was Tracy, entered the home, attacked her with a knife, and fled. This scenario is possible and consistent with the facts.

Then there is the issue of the laundry room door. No one from the Crowe family had gone into the laundry room that night. Tuite had been seen next door and someone did enter the Crowe residence through that door when all of the family members were in their bedrooms. It could not have been Joshua Treadway as he would not have arrived by this time if traveling on foot.

When the police questioned Tuite, he had two plain matchbooks in his pockets that were identical to the type kept at the Crowe residence, on an outside ledge, three one-dollar bills, and some spare change. Since no analysis was done on these items, it cannot be determined if they came from the same stock of matches the Crowes used.

When we consider Stephanie's relationship with Michael, the hours prior to her murder are important. They watched television together, played, and generally enjoyed a family night at home. There were no reported episodes of anger or of Michael avoiding her. Their behavior was described as normal.

Occam's razor advises us to adopt the simplest theory (i.e., the one with the fewest assumptions) that adequately explains the facts. Even without the DNA evidence, the logic of the crime better fits Richard Tuite than Michael Crowe and his two friends.

Why would investigators make such serious errors? The problems began from the outset, with incomplete information gathering and a logically flawed hypothesis.

Investigative Errors

Three key problems with the initial investigation into Stephanie Crowe's murder snowballed into two more significant errors. The perpetuation of the wrong approach was ensured.

Incomplete Analysis

The issue of "no-forced-entry" is meaningful at a crime scene only if all access points to a premise were secure and could not have been breached without force. In this case the police knew that at 9:56 p.m. on the evening of the homicide, the laundry room door was unlocked. They subsequently learned that the sliding glass door in the master bedroom was also unlocked. Therefore, the lack of signs of forced entry meant nothing, as entry into the house could have been gained without the need to use force.

During the course of the investigation, however, this issue was repeatedly misrepresented. Detective Claytor testified in an affidavit he prepared for Michael Crowe's arrest that there was "a lack of evidence of forced entry and [there were] locked doors and windows,"[33] when in fact he knew that one or more doors were unlocked when he signed that affidavit. He stated that he later learned the motion detector was not working, and that the light that Officer Walters saw inside the house would have had to be turned on from a switch inside. He also indicated he considered the possibility of an intruder being in the house based on Cheryl Crowe's statements about her bedroom door opening and closing twice. However, Claytor testified that on the morning of the homicide he discussed this with Detective Sweeney and concluded someone inside the house had murdered Stephanie Crowe because there were no signs of forced entry. This indicates that Claytor was either not thinking carefully or else he just ignored the contradiction.

The investigators failed to do a full victimology, possibly due to their rush to judgment. Stephanie was a low-risk victim: there was no history of family violence, she had no association with delinquents, and the only thing that elevated her risk was the presence in the neighborhood of Richard Tuite. Stephanie resembled the girl, "Tracy," for whom Tuite was searching. Indeed, the time of death as estimated by the medical examiner was around the same time Officer Walters saw the door close at the Crowe house. Stephanie was on the phone with a friend at 10:00 p.m. and her light was still on. A prowler could have easily seen her alone in her bedroom through her ground floor window.

Errors in Logic

The statement that the laundry room door was locked is false. Officer Walters saw the laundry room door open shortly before 10:00 p.m. He also observed the laundry room door closed by someone from the inside. This was at a time when everyone inside the home had gone to bed except for Stephanie, who was in her bedroom talking on the telephone.

The statement "there is no evidence that a house was entered forcefully, so it wasn't" commits the fallacy known as the argument from ignorance. Lack of evidence does not automatically make the opposite state of affairs true. There may be other alternatives. No signs of forced entry could simply mean they were mistaken about all the doors being locked. Alternatively, someone could have entered by the screen door or in some other way that left no sign.

Prematurely closing off possibilities forces an investigation into directions too limited to allow for a full explanation of the facts. The only conclusion

---

[33]Deposition of Ralph Claytor, p. 640.

the Escondido detectives could see was that a family member was responsible. Their investigation became victim to tunnel vision.

Rush to Judgment and Tunnel Vision

By January 21, 1998, there was no physical or forensic evidence to reasonably support a conclusion as to whether the killer was a family member or an intruder, yet Detective Claytor testified that by 9:00 p.m. that evening he had concluded that someone inside the home was responsible for the murder. This myopic mindset by the lead detective jeopardized the integrity of the investigation and set the stage for the miscarriages of justice that followed.

Once investigators decided the murder was an inside job, they pinpointed Michael as the most likely culprit. Investigative notes written two days after the murder refer to Michael's room as the "suspect's room." Detectives compared Michael's shoe with an apparent shoe print found in blood, even though there were no similarities in class characteristics and Michael's shoe had no blood on it. Investigators failed to enhance the print or compare any other shoes to it. This makes some sense if there truly was no way for an intruder to enter the Crowe house. But this assumption was wrong. Investigators, trapped by their initial logical error, were now committed to the belief that Stephanie's murder was an inside job.

Tunnel vision is the narrow perceptual focus that unduly limits the consideration of the full range of alternatives. "Tunnel vision can result in the elimination of other suspects who should be investigated" (Rossmo, 2006, p. 4). It results in two critical problems: a narrowed focus too early on a single offender and the neglect of other possibilities.

Shortly after arriving at the scene, police concluded the murder was "an inside job." They then tried to prove their theory rather than test it, setting themselves up for future failure. Richard Tuite was dismissed as a suspect and released after a brief interview. Detectives failed to fingerprint or run a criminal background check on him, and they did not properly process his clothing for evidence, despite visible stains on his sweatshirt. Police photographed the items they found in Tuite's pockets, but returned them to Tuite afterward. These items included three crumpled one-dollar bills, 40 coins, a torn Snickers candy bar wrapper, two white matchbooks, and a Smith Brothers cough drop wrapper. Had the Escondido investigators kept these, they could have been compared with items found at or missing from the crime scene. A bag of individually wrapped Smith Brothers cough drops can be seen in police photographs of the Crowes' kitchen counter. Cheryl Crowe told investigators that she typically bought Snickers bars for the family, and that there were white matchbooks, similar to the ones Tuite had in his pockets, on an outside ledge near their barbecue. If the crime lab had examined these items and found fingerprints or DNA from any member of the Crowe family on them, their evidentiary value would be immense. But forensic analysis was not possible with only photographs, and the items found in Tuite's pockets were relegated to circumstantial evidence at best. Investigators lost potentially significant evidence because they believed Tuite was not a viable suspect.

Individuals suffering from tunnel vision can sometimes "find" evidence that does not exist. Detective Ralph Claytor testified before the grand jury that there was blood on a knife seized from the residence of Joshua Treadway. Yet a few weeks prior to this testimony, he had received a lab report stating there was no blood found on it. Claytor also testified there was blood in the sink at the Crowe home. That was also incorrect. The lack of blood in any sink or drain contradicted Joshua Treadway's claim the knife was washed off in the sink. This was one of several inconsistencies that should have alerted investigators and analysts to the unreliability of Treadway's "confession."

Anchor Traps

Anchor traps occur when "a person does not consider multiple possibilities, but quickly and firmly latches on to a single one, sure that he has thrown his anchor down just where he needs to be. You look at your map but your mind plays tricks on you—confirmation bias—because you see only the landmarks you expect to see and neglect those that should tell you that in fact you're still at sea. Your skewed reading of the map 'confirms' your mistaken assumption that you have reached your destination" (Goopman, 2007, p. 65). In this case the Escondido police, San Diego County prosecutor, and the FBI mistakenly dropped their anchors in what they believed to be a safe harbor, while ignoring the many indicators that they were actually still at sea.

Rigidity and Resistance

Closely related to tunnel vision is *belief perseverance*, the stubborn embrace of a belief in the face of disconfirming evidence. Despite Officer Scott Walters's report that he had seen a door close at the Crowe house at the time of the murder, Detective Claytor dismissed his report as irrelevant. He insisted Walters was mistaken.

Belief perseverance and tunnel vision are closely related to "confirmation bias," a type of selective thinking in which an individual is more likely to notice or search for evidence that confirms his or her hypothesis, while ignoring or refusing to search for contradicting evidence (Stelfox & Pease, 2005).

When professional colleagues suffer from the same cognitive biases, the potential exists for the development of "organizational momentum"—the inability of an investigation to change direction. It is difficult for a large investigative effort to redirect and shift its focus from an established hypothesis or a favored suspect. Change is disruptive and requires effort, energy, time, and money. This happened twice in the Crowe case—once at the local level and again with the FBI level.

Groupthink

Groupthink is a term coined by Yale scholar Irving L. Janis (1972) to describe the reluctance to think critically and challenge the dominant theory. It can appear in cohesive teams who are under significant pressure to make important decisions. When investigative decision making is corrupted by groupthink, the probability of a successful case outcome is reduced.

The symptoms of groupthink include overestimation of power and morality, close mindedness and rationalizations, and uniformity pressures to the extent of self-censorship. Information is selectively gathered to support the group's hypothesis, and contradictory opinions are rejected. More importantly, the dominant hypothesis is not challenged or critically assessed, so it becomes entrenched. Groupthink restricts information input and flexibility in decision making, so it must be avoided at all costs in complicated criminal investigations, particularly those that are "whodunits."

Ego

Both individual and institutional egos are evident in this case. The Escondido Police Department, the San Diego County District Attorney's Office, and the FBI had all been unwilling to admit that their analyses and conclusions were wrong. Even as disconfirming evidence accumulated, these agencies defended their positions. As Rossmo notes, "impressions remain even after the initial evidence they were based on is discounted" (2006, p. 7).

Conclusion

"Unfortunately, many murder cases first appear to be something other than what they are" (Rossmo, 2006, p. 4). Investigators must keep an open mind about how to interpret data until they have gathered as many facts as possible. At its inception, an investigation should be multidimensional. No single hypothesis should be either embraced or eliminated until all pertinent facts and evidence have been collected and thoroughly examined. In the Stephanie Crowe case, investigators quickly targeted three innocent teenagers while allowing a child killer to roam the streets for over a year. The initial Crowe investigation as conducted by the Escondido Police Department and supported by the FBI is a clear example of the dangers that can arise when investigators embrace a theory before they have a factual base to sustain it, and then refuse to adapt to new evidence when it is discovered.

Michael Crowe, Josh Treadway, and Aaron Houser were never viable suspects. Their preoffense and postoffense behaviors were consistent with innocence, not guilt. There were no incidences of violence in their backgrounds. Following the crime, Treadway and Houser behaved normally and attended school (Michael had been detained by the police). These were basically trusting and naive teenagers who were subjected to coercive interrogation techniques by veteran police officers more interested in validating their own hypothesis than in finding the truth. Their "confessions" were never thoroughly investigated for corroboration. Given the degree of initial resistance and the inconsistencies in their stories, effort should have been expended to reconcile their statements with the physical evidence. Had this been done, investigators would have discovered sufficient inconsistencies between the "confessions" and the facts to undermine the former's reliability. Zen teaches that it is impossible to add anything more to a cup that is already full. If you pour in more tea, it simply spills over and is wasted. The same is true of the mind. A closed attitude, an attitude that says "I already know," may cause one to miss important information. Zen teaches the concept of the beginner's mind, the mind that remains open and ready, despite years of training. "In the beginner's mind there are many possibilities," said Zen master Shunryu Suzuki. "In the expert's mind there are few" (Gonzales, 2003, pp. 91, 171; Suzuki, 2006, p. 65).

Thankfully, the ultimate miscarriage of justice was averted by the discovery of new forensic evidence through the efforts of Mary Ellen Attridge and an open-minded reinvestigation by the San Diego County Sheriff's Office. Lead Detective Victor Caloca and his colleagues developed probable cause to believe that Richard Tuite murdered Stephanie Crowe. Prosecutors for the State of California concurred and, led by David Druliner, Jim Dutton, and Gary Schons, they overcame a number of obstacles, including the false confessions and the baffling testimony of SSA Mary Ellen O'Toole. Also of great assistance in uncovering the chain of events and problems that led the investigation astray were the discovery depositions and background work by Milton Silverman and his associates in the civil case.

The jury convicted Richard Tuite. Because he suffered from schizophrenia, he was sentenced to 13 years imprisonment for involuntary manslaughter, in addition to four years and four months for escaping from custody and trying to bribe a deputy. In December 2006, Tuite's conviction was upheld by a San Diego appellate court, and in March 2007 the California Supreme Court declined to hear his appeal. The Crowe case influenced the California Commission on the Fair Administration of Justice to recommend legislation that "all statements made during custodial interrogation relating to a serious felony shall be electronically recorded." As of March 2008, the civil case brought by the families of the three teenagers against the Escondido Police Department and others is still pending.

References

Davis, S. E. (2005, April). Dangerous confessions: The psychology behind false confessions. *California Lawyer*, pp. 26–30.

Gonzales, L. (2003). *Deep survival: Who lives, who dies, and why.* New York: W. W. Norton.

Goopman, J. (2007). *How doctors think.* New York: Houghton Mifflin.

Gudjonsson, G. H. (1992). *The psychology of interrogations, confessions and testimony.* New York: Wiley.

Haunting questions: The Stephanie Crowe murder case, Part 1. *San Diego Union-Tribune,* 1999, May 11.

Janis, I. L. (1972). *Victims of groupthink: A psychological study of foreign-policy decisions and fiascoes.* Boston: Houghton Mifflin.

Kassin, S. M., & Gudjonsson, G. H. (2004). The psychology of confession evidence: A review of the literature and issues. *Psychological Science in the Public Interest, 5* (2).

Rossmo, D. K. (2006). Criminal investigative failures: Avoiding the pitfalls (part two). *FBI Law Enforcement Bulletin, 75*(9), 1–8.

Samenow, S. E. (1998). *Straight talk about criminals: Understanding and treating antisocial individuals.* Lanham, MD: Jason Aronson Publishers.

Sauer, M. (2004, May 28). Tuite trial jury's road to verdict revealed. *San Diego Union Tribune,* p. B1.

Stelfox, P., & Pease, K. (2005). Cognition and detection: Reluctant bedfellows? In M. J., Smith & N. Tilley (Eds.), *Crime science: New approaches to preventing and detecting crime* (pp. 191–207). Cullompton, Devon: Willan Publishing.

Suzuki, S. (2006). *Zen mind, beginner's mind.* Boston: Shambhala Publications.

Thorndike, E. L. (1920). A constant error on psychological rating. *Journal of Applied Psychology, 4,* 25–29.

U.S. Department of Justice. (1999). *Juvenile offenders and victims.* Washington, DC: U.S. Department of Justice.

Milgaard v. The Queen: Understanding a Wrongful Conviction for Sexual Homicide

9

NEIL BOYD AND
D. KIM ROSSMO

During the past three decades in North America, we have witnessed a considerable strengthening of both academic and public interest in the realities of wrongful criminal conviction (e.g., Denov & Campbell, 2005; Huff, Rattner, & Sagarin, 1986, 1996; Radelet, Bedau, & Putnam, 1992; Scheck & Neufeld, 2001). A number of high-profile cases in both the United States and Canada, most involving DNA evidence, have shone a critical light on the inevitability of human fallibility in the determination of guilt. That light has been particularly intense when culpable homicide is involved and when the nature of the homicide is especially repugnant, demanding a penalty of either life imprisonment or, in some parts of the United States, execution. The case that forms the backbone of this chapter, *Milgaard v. The Queen*,[1] falls into this category. Convicted in 1969 of the predatory sexual homicide of a young nursing aide, David Milgaard spent 23 years in federal prisons in Canada before securing his release (Milgaard & Edwards, 1999).

The narrative that follows is a recounting of the crime, investigation and arrest, his conviction, release, exoneration and compensation, and a subsequent government inquiry into the wrongful conviction. The authors of this chapter were both involved in an independent review of the case from 1991 to 1992 while Milgaard was still in prison; much of the information in this chapter originates from that study (Boyd & Rossmo, 1992, 1994).

The Crime

On the morning of January 31, 1969, visibility was poor in Saskatoon, Saskatchewan, because of ice crystals in the air; the temperature was 42 degrees Fahrenheit below zero. It was dark when Gail Miller left her rooming house at

[1] R. v. Milgaard, 2 Canadian Criminal Cases (2d) 206, 1970.

about 7:00 a.m., wearing her black winter coat. She was a 20-year-old nursing assistant on her way to work, walking to a bus stop a block and a half away, when she was either abducted or offered a ride by the person who killed her. She was stabbed repeatedly in the back and chest with a small paring knife and sexually assaulted. She died within 30 minutes of leaving her home.

Her body was found about an hour later, just after dawn, in the back alley between her rooming house and the bus stop. She was lying face down in a snow bank, her nurse's uniform pulled down to her waist, with her winter coat put back on. Her underwear was down around her ankles, as was her girdle and one of her stockings. Her brassiere strap had been broken and her half slip was around her waist.

She had been stabbed in the back four times near her right shoulder blade and seven times below and above her left breast. The four stab wounds in her back had penetrated her coat, but none of the total of 11 wounds had penetrated her nurse's uniform. The left side of her neck had also been badly slashed by a knife. Spermatozoa were recovered from her vagina. A paring knife blade was found underneath her body on the morning of the murder. Some weeks later the matching maroon handle was found a short distance away.

Four days later, a newspaper in a neighboring city, the *Regina Leader Post*, ran a story on a possible connection between the killing and three unsolved rapes, also involving a knife, which had occurred in the Riversdale neighborhood of Saskatoon in the fall of 1968. "Killer possible rapist," the headline read.

Investigation and Arrest

David Milgaard, a 16-year-old believer in "free love" and psychedelic drug use, had arrived in Saskatoon from Regina on the same morning that the murder occurred. He was traveling in a car with two like-minded companions, Nichol John and Ron Wilson; Wilson was driving. The three teenagers were looking for the home of their friend Albert "Shorty" Cadrain. They got lost upon entering Saskatoon and ended up stuck in the snow. Milgaard and Wilson walked off in different directions, looking for help. They eventually got the car moving and found Shorty's home. All four teenagers left the city shortly after noon.

Police interviewed many people after the Gail Miller murder, focusing on those who might have been in the vicinity at the time she was killed. But they made little headway until about a month after the crime. In early March 1969, "Shorty" Cadrain, who happened to live a block south of the crime scene, went to the Saskatoon police and told them he had seen blood on David Milgaard's clothes the morning of the murder. Cadrain said he first heard about Miller's murder in February when five Regina plainclothes officers questioned him. He later testified they had strip searched and rectally examined him. The officers then asked about the morning Gail Miller was murdered. Cadrain laughed at the suggestion that he, Milgaard, or Wilson had killed her. The Regina police charged him with vagrancy, and he was convicted and sentenced to a week in jail.[2]

To the Saskatoon police, initially suspicious of Cadrain's story, one startling fact must have leapt out. David Milgaard and his companions had been within a block of the crime scene on the morning of the murder. Furthermore, a trail of physical evidence led from Gail Miller's body to the Cadrain house (see Figure 9.1). When first contacted by police in March, both Ron Wilson and Nichol John consistently said they had no knowledge of Gail Miller's murder, and that neither they nor David Milgaard could be responsible. Ron Wilson, serving a jail sentence for theft at the time he was interviewed, was questioned on six occasions by police about the Gail Miller murder before his release. He repeatedly denied any involvement or knowledge of the crime. He was told that he was a suspect.

On May 24, 1969, the day after being driven back to Saskatoon by Saskatoon police, Ron Wilson made a statement implicating David Milgaard in the crime. He told the officers he had seen blood on Milgaard's clothing that morning, that Milgaard had a paring knife in the car, and that Milgaard had said "I fixed her" after returning to the car. On the same day, after spending a night in the Saskatoon jail cells, Nichol John made a statement implicating David Milgaard. She said that, while she had not seen any blood on his clothes or hands that morning, she had seen him stab a woman after trying to steal her purse. "The knife was in his right hand. ... All I recall seeing is him stabbing her with the knife," she told police, "The next I recall is him taking her around the corner of the alley."

"I think I ran in the direction Ron had gone," she continued, "I recall running down the street. I don't recall seeing anyone. The next thing I know I was sitting in the car again. I don't know how I got back to the car." Nichol John also indicated that when Milgaard returned to the car, "I remember moving over toward the driver's side because I didn't want to be near him."[3]

On May 30, 1969, police arrested 16-year-old David Milgaard and charged him with the first-degree murder of Gail Miller.

Trial and Conviction

The Case for the Crown at Trial

The theory put to the jury by the Crown prosecutor was that the crime probably began as a purse snatching incident and later turned into a rape and a murder. Crown counsel T. D. R. Caldwell called 45 witnesses in the nine-day

[2] Cross-examination of Albert Cadrain, Trial transcript, pp. 587–605.
[3] Witness Statement Form, Occurrence 641, 1969, May 24, Nichol John, pp. 4–5.

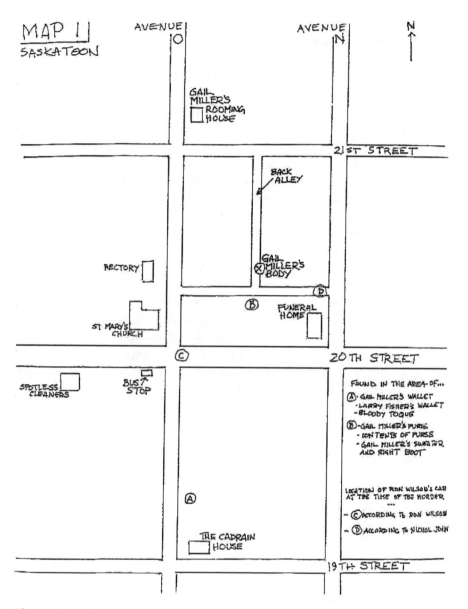

Figure 9.1 Map of Saskatoon showing Miller murder site and Fisher rape site. (From Boyd & Rossmo, 1992. With permission.)

trial, devoting about two-thirds of his time to the statements of witnesses and the remainder to the forensic evidence.[4] Counsel for Milgaard, Cal Tallis and Ian Disbery, did not call any witnesses for the defense.

---

[4] Trial transcript, Court of Queen's Bench, *Her Majesty the Queen against David Edgar Milgaard*, pp. 1–1266.

The Statements of Witnesses

Witnesses in Gail Miller's three-story rooming house indicated that at about a quarter to seven she was on the second floor of her building, dressed in her nurse's uniform, but had neither her boots nor her coat on. Adeline Nyczai, who lived on the third floor, testified that she heard someone leave the building from the second floor, presumably Gail Miller, at about seven.[5]

There were only two witnesses who were outdoors in the vicinity of the crime at about the time that it was occurring—church caretaker Henry Diewald and Maria Indyk, a parishioner of the church. Henry Diewald lived in the rectory of St. Mary's Church (see Figure 9.1), and every morning, at about 7:00 a.m., he would walk from the rectory to the church to open it for early parishioners. On the morning of January 31, he saw headlights in the icy mist, facing him from the alley across Avenue O. The headlights were about 50 feet from where Gail Miller's body was found. When he returned from the church and walked back to the rectory about ten minutes later, he noticed that the headlights were still there. At trial he indicated that he saw a person go from the driver's side in front of the headlights (toward the direction where the body was found), and back again. At the preliminary hearing, he indicated that this person was a little over five feet in height.[6]

Mrs. Indyk testified that she had gone to St. Mary's Church shortly after 7:00 a.m. and found it closed. She saw two women walking separately north on Avenue O, hurrying in the cold. She testified that she had not seen any headlights and that she did not know when the church eventually opened. She said that she spent about 10 minutes in the church, arriving at her work across the street at about 7:40 a.m.

The evidence established that Henry Diewald and Maria Indyk were in the vicinity of the crime at slightly different times, that a car may have been parked in the alley for about 10 minutes, and that two women were likely walking north on Avenue O sometime between 7:10 and 7:15 a.m.

David Milgaard's three companions gave evidence at trial that implicated him in the murder. Albert Cadrain said that he saw blood on Milgaard's clothes that morning. Ron Wilson said that he also saw blood on David Milgaard's clothes and that Milgaard was carrying a paring knife with a reddish brown handle in the car between Regina and Saskatoon. Nichol John told police prior to trial that she had seen Milgaard stabbing a woman. At trial she said that she could not recall such an incident, but the jury was made aware of her earlier statement. Just before the close of the trial, the Crown prosecutor introduced two witnesses—Craig Melnyk and George Lapchuk—who claimed Milgaard had reenacted the crime months later in a Regina motel room.

[5] Testimony of Adeline Nyczai, Trial transcript, pp. 631–644.
[6] Testimony of Henry Diewald, Trial transcript, pp. 654–662; testimony of Henry Diewald, Preliminary hearing transcript, pp. 201–217.

The critical witnesses in the conviction of David Milgaard were his two companions in the car on that cold morning in January, Ron Wilson and Nichol John; their testimony took almost three days of the nine-day trial. Ron Wilson testified that he, Nichol John, and David Milgaard drove into Saskatoon at about 6:30 a.m. Not long after their arrival they were driving south on what he later learned was either Avenue N or O, when they noticed a young woman in a black coat, also walking south along the sidewalk. They asked her for directions and continued to drive to the end of the block, where, in the process of turning, they became stuck in the ice in the middle of the intersection.

Initially, Ron Wilson tried to drive the car out of the snow, but his summer tires only spun on the ice. He testified at the preliminary hearing that he and David Milgaard then got out of the car and spent two to three minutes pushing the car both forward and backward, but without any luck.[7] They ultimately decided that they would look for help, and headed off in different directions.

At the preliminary hearing, Ron Wilson said that he was away from the car for about five minutes before returning to find Nichol John hysterical. David Milgaard was away from the car for no more than 10 minutes.[8] Wilson varied that testimony at trial, saying that he was away from the car for about 10 minutes, that he found Nichol John hysterical on his return, and that five more minutes passed before David Milgaard returned to the car, breathing heavily.

At trial Nichol John said that their car had been stuck in the ice, but not at the location claimed by Ron Wilson. She testified that they had been stuck in the alley behind a funeral home, within footsteps of the murder scene. She testified that both Wilson and Milgaard went for help and returned in "a few minutes." She could not remember who returned first, and did not say she was hysterical at the time.[9]

Nichol John was cross-examined at trial by the prosecution with respect to the statement she made to police on May 24, 1969. In that statement Nichol John indicated that when David Milgaard left the car, he tried to snatch the purse of a woman on the street and then stabbed her repeatedly, just in front of the car. At trial she said that she could not remember any stabbing or any purse snatching. Questioned by Chief Justice Alfred Bence, she responded in the following manner:

Q. Do you remember any part of it?
A. No.
Q. Are you saying you didn't tell Sergeant Mackie that?
A. I'm saying I don't remember if I did or didn't.

---

[7] Direct examination of Ronald Dale Wilson, Trial transcript, p. 195, Preliminary hearing transcript, p. 509.
[8] Cross-examination of Ronald Dale Wilson, Preliminary hearing transcript, pp. 507–515.
[9] Testimony of Nichol John, Trial transcript, pp. 390–400.

Q. Well, if you did see the accused grab the purse it's something you would have remembered, isn't it? Isn't it? Witness?

A. I don't know.

Q. Take a drink of water and stop crying.

A. If I could tell you what happened I'd tell you. I don't know. I can't remember.[10]

The evidence of Nichol John conflicted with that given by Ron Wilson; while she said that their car had been stuck in a back alley, he was very certain they had been stuck in the middle of a four-way intersection. He said that David Milgaard was away from the car between 10 and 15 minutes; Nichol John said it was only "a few minutes." Police did not find any tire tracks in the alley of the murder scene suggesting that a car had been stuck, spinning its wheels. And despite an extensive search, police did not find any blood other than in the immediate vicinity of Miller's body.

Both Nichol John and Ron Wilson agreed that shortly after 7:00 a.m., after getting unstuck, the three of them drove to the Trav-a-leer Motel (see Figure 9.2), about a mile from where Gail Miller's body was found. David Milgaard went into the motel and obtained directions and a map from the motel manager, Robert Rasmussen. Rasmussen testified that Milgaard spent about five minutes in the motel with him; he said that he had not noticed anything unusual about Milgaard or about his clothes, except that he was

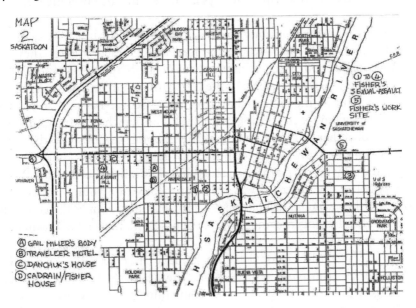

Figure 9.2 Map of area around Gail Miller Murder site. (From Boyd & Rossmo, 1992. With permission.)

[10]Testimony of Nichol John, Trial transcript, p. 471.

wearing only socks on his feet. He testified that David was polite, thanking him for the map.

Shortly before 7:30 a.m., the three teenagers left the motel and set out once more to find the home of their friend Albert Cadrain. A few minutes later they became stuck again, this time in a back alley about 10 blocks from the motel, behind a car that was also trapped in the ice. The couple that owned the car, the Danchuks, ultimately called a service station for assistance and invited Wilson, Milgaard, and John into their home to warm up.

The Danchuks testified that lighting had been good in their home, and that they had not noticed anything unusual about David Milgaard or seen anything on his clothes during the hour they spent together that morning. Walter Danchuk said that Milgaard was polite and soft spoken, and that he did most of the talking for the group—about selling magazines, and about trying to find their friend Albert Cadrain.[11]

Shortly after nine that morning, Milgaard, Wilson, and John arrived at the home of the Cadrains, located about a block and a half away from where Gail Miller's body was found. Albert Cadrain testified that he paid to have Ron Wilson's car, which had been suffering from starting problems, repaired at a local service station. The car was ready a little after noon and the four teenagers—Wilson, Cadrain, John, and Milgaard—then left Saskatoon and traveled west to Calgary and Edmonton, in search of illegal drugs. They returned from this trip a few days later, each ultimately going his or her separate way.

There were two last-minute witnesses at the Milgaard trial—Craig Melnyk and George Lapchuk—who came forward in January 1970. They told the court of a party in a Regina motel room in late May 1969. By then, David Milgaard knew he was a suspect in the Gail Miller murder, and when a news story about the killing appeared on television, George Lapchuk asked him what was happening. According to Melnyk and Lapchuk, Milgaard stated he had stabbed her 14 times; he then made stabbing motions into the pillow in the motel room, and laughed. Both Lapchuk and Melnyk told the court that, in their view, Milgaard was reenacting the Gail Miller murder. While this was going on, Milgaard was naked in bed with a young woman, Ute Frank; another woman, Debbie Hall, was also in the room.[12] The court also heard that David Milgaard and some of the others had taken LSD earlier that evening.

David Milgaard was convicted on January 31, 1970, after the jury had deliberated for approximately 11 hours. The headlines from the nine-day trial suggest that the statements of his companions were keys to his conviction. There were two headlines coming from Nichol John and Ron Wilson's

[11] Cross-examination of Walter J. Danchuk, Trial transcript, pp. 680–685.
[12] Testimony of Craig Melnyk and George Lapchuk, Trial transcript, pp. 1010–1067.

testimony: "Witness tells of knives in car with accused," and "Witness quoted at trial as saying she saw Milgaard stabbing woman." After the testimony of Albert Cadrain, the headline read, "Youth says blood on Milgaard clothing." And after Melnyk and Lapchuk had taken the stand, the headline read "Yes, I stabbed her, Milgaard quoted."

The Physical and Forensic Evidence: The Case for the Crown at Trial

Between January 20 and 31, 1970, the other headlines from the Saskatoon *Star-Phoenix* coverage of the trial were focused on the physical and forensic evidence: "No indication body moved," "Knife blade, handle linked at trial," "Court examines stabbing victim's purse," and "Crown completes case at Milgaard trial."

Hair samples and blood were taken from Gail Miller on autopsy, but for some unknown reason the semen found in her vagina was not subjected to any laboratory tests. Four days after the murder, however, two pale yellowish frozen clumps were found in the snow at the scene. They were tested, and one was said to contain both human seminal fluid and seven pubic hairs.

These clumps were of considerable importance at trial. In his almost two-hour introduction to the case against David Milgaard, prosecutor T. D. R. Caldwell spent more than 20 minutes on their significance.

The clumps were analyzed in March 1969 by serologist Bruce Paynter of the Royal Canadian Mounted Police (RCMP) Crime Detection Laboratory in Regina. He found the semen from the crime scene came from a type A secretor, a person with type A blood who secretes his blood type antigens into other bodily fluids, specifically, semen, urine, and saliva.

Hair and blood samples were taken from Albert Cadrain, Ron Wilson, and David Milgaard; a saliva sample was taken from David Milgaard in April 1969. David Milgaard, like about 40% of the population, was found to have type A blood; his saliva test indicated, however, that he was a nonsecretor. According to Staff Sergeant Bruce Paynter's testimony on direct examination, he did not find antigens in Milgaard's sample. "This would indicate that the person was a nonsecretor," he testified.[13]

In June 1969, the vial containing the clump of pubic hair and semen was sent back to the Crime Detection Laboratory and Staff Sergeant Paynter was asked to test for the possible presence of blood. He testified that he was not able to positively identify blood, but that one test led him to suspect that blood might well be present.

If there was type A blood in the sample, this would yield a positive antigen reading, regardless of whether the person was a secretor or a nonsecretor. The

---

[13]Direct examination of Staff Sergeant Bruce Paynter, Trial transcript, p. 961.

theory of the Crown was, then, that David Milgaard's blood had contaminated the sample found in the snow, thus rendering his nonsecretor status irrelevant. This was a vital and necessary element in the Crown's case. Without the presence of blood, the seminal stain excluded Milgaard.

Testimony from pathologist H. E. Emson supported the blood contamination theory. He indicated the blood in the sample could have come from the assailant, explaining this possibility to prosecutor T. D. R. Caldwell at trial:

> Q. Are there conditions under which human blood as such can get into seminal fluid or spermatozoa in the male person?
> A. Yes.
> Q. Could you tell the Court what they are please?
> A. One would be local injury to the male genitals. A second and quite common occurrence would be any inflammation, either internal or external, of the male genitals.
> Q. Are there any other causes?
> A. There are rarer conditions, but I think the injury and the inflammation are the most common ones.[14]

This was the extent of the forensic evidence that connected David Milgaard to Gail Miller. Chief Justice Bence, in charging the jury at the conclusion of the trial, did not mention this evidence, however, allowing them to draw their own conclusions as to its probative value.[15] In January 1971, the Saskatchewan Court of Appeal dismissed Milgaard's appeal against his conviction. In November of that year, leave to appeal to the Supreme Court of Canada was denied.[16]

Problems with the Case for the Crown at Trial

In many ways the case against David Milgaard must have seemed very strong. His three companions had all implicated him, albeit in different ways, and the seminal stain found at the scene of the crime appeared to have been connected to him. Lapchuk's and Melnyk's assertion of a reenactment provided the coup de grâce.

[14]Direct examination of Dr. H. E. Emson, Trial transcript, pp. 1157–1158.

[15]Dr. Emson's testimony that genital inflammation causing blood leakage is a "quite common occurrence" is an example of day-to-day language leading to a misunderstanding of probability (see Chapter 7). What exactly did he mean when he used the word "common"? We refer to the "common cold," but in reality the chances of having a cold at any one time are very low. Without some quantitative estimate, we really do not know how to interpret this evidence.

[16]R. v. Milgaard, 2 Canadian Criminal Cases (2d) 206.

But some important questions emerge from the trial transcript. As defense counsel noted, the timing necessary to allow David Milgaard to be the killer was extremely tight.[17] Within no more than 10 minutes of having stabbed and raped Gail Miller, Milgaard is seen by motel manager Rasmussen over a mile from the site of the murder, relaxed, polite, and wearing only socks on his feet. Within no more than 30 minutes of having killed Gail Miller, David Milgaard is seen by Walter and Olesia Danchuk; he is said to be chatty and polite.

None of these three disinterested observers noticed blood on his clothes or anything unusual about his demeanor. Nichol John also testified that she did not notice blood on Milgaard's clothes, despite being closest to him during this time.

More problematic was the testimony of Nichol John and Ron Wilson with respect to the few minutes in which the murder was said to have occurred. There was no physical evidence to suggest that a car had been stuck in the back alley where Gail Miller's body was found, despite what Nichol John said to police in May 1969. And it was impossible for Nichol John to witness a stabbing in that alley, in accordance with her statement, if she had been in the intersection of either Avenue N or O and 20th Street. Her evidence also did not explain how four of the 11 stab wounds penetrated Gail Miller's coat and none penetrated her white hospital uniform; Nichol John told police that Milgaard simply began to stab a woman in the alley after a failed purse snatching, but unless this woman had first been undressed, these cuts would have penetrated her nurse's uniform. Finally, despite what one would have expected from John's account, there was no trail of blood found, leading along the alley to the place where the body was found.

The validity of Albert Cadrain's testimony was also impugned during cross-examination. He had seen blood on David Milgaard's shirt, but not his sweater; Milgaard had been wearing his sweater from the time of the alleged attack to the time of his arrival at the Cadrain home. Cadrain also testified that when he was questioned in Regina by police about the Gail Miller murder, he initially had no recollection of seeing blood on David Milgaard:

Q. And I take it that you were being questioned about the Gail Miller murder?
A. Yes, I was questioned.
Q. And you were endeavouring to tell them the truth to the best of your recollection at that time?
A. Yes.

---

[17] As part of our independent review of this case, we conducted an exercise where actors played the roles of Miller, Milgaard, Wilson, and John. Using a television camera with a timer, we followed them around the scene of the crime, choreographing their movements according to the relevant witness statements so we could see how the four people interacted in space and time. It turned out that Miller would have been on the bus, well on her way to work, before there was any opportunity for Milgaard to leave his friends.

Q. And at that time you had no recollection of this blood that we are talking
about here today—isn't that correct?

A. I don't think so.

Q. You have no recollection of it at that time?

A. No.[18]

The forensic evidence was inconclusive, at its most optimistic (assuming blood contamination) tying David Milgaard to the 44% of the population who have type A or AB blood, and hence to the 44% of male Canadians who might have committed this crime (Jaffe, 1983). There is no evidence that the jury understood the limitations of these data. There was expert testimony that the stab wounds and the throat slashes found on the victim were most likely inflicted by a right-handed person; the police, however, noted that David Milgaard is left-handed.

David Milgaard was convicted on the basis of testimony from his three companions, Cadrain, Wilson, and John. During the police investigation, both Cadrain and Wilson had been told they were suspects, and both had given hair and blood samples to the police. Wilson indicated at trial that he was a regular user of LSD, and that he also injected heroin and LSD intravenously. The evidence at trial also revealed that all three had given inconsistent statements to police between February and May 1969.

Examination of the evidence at trial, even before subsequent recantations and the presentations of an alternative suspect, raises serious doubts about the validity of the conviction. Castelle and Loftus (2001) have pointed to a combination of individual and systemic factors contributing to wrongful convictions. In Milgaard we can see these factors emerging in his investigation, arrest, and trial: the compelling need to solve a horrendous crime, tunnel vision by police investigators, erroneous forensic science, the use of what arguably amounted to "jailhouse informants"—three young people, criminally involved, and motivated to lie in their own self-interest—and, finally, a late 1960s cultural opposition to the hippie lifestyle of David Milgaard and his companions.

The Other Suspect: Larry Fisher

A man by the name of Larry Fisher was living in the basement of the Cadrain house with his wife, Linda, at the time of Gail Miller's murder in January 1969. Larry Fisher grew up in Saskatchewan in a single-parent home, raised by his mother after his father left, apparently encouraged in this departure by the local RCMP. Fisher's father used to beat his mother and force her and

---

[18] Cross-examination of Albert Cadrain, Trial transcript, pp. 594–595.

the children out of the house when he brought a woman home for the night. What effect this had on Larry is unknown; his mother insists that he was too young to remember any of it. It is known he had problems with his mother, resenting her drinking and her drinking companions.

In December 1967 Larry and Linda Fisher were married in North Battleford, Saskatchewan. They moved to the working-class Riversdale area of Saskatoon a few months later. Linda was pregnant and their daughter Tammy was born in late April 1968. Six months later, the rapes began.[19]

In September 1970, 18 months after Gail Miller's murder, Larry Fisher confessed to Winnipeg police that he had raped and indecently assaulted four women in Saskatoon between the fall of 1968 and early 1970. His former wife, Linda, gave a statement in March 1990 to Joyce Milgaard, the mother of David, in which she said she recalled the day of Miller's murder. She swore that Larry did not go to work that morning. They were arguing—not an uncommon occurrence—when she heard news of the crime on the radio. Linda, half jokingly, accused Larry of killing Miller with their missing kitchen paring knife. His reaction was one of shock and fright. She initially reported her suspicions to Saskatoon police in 1980.[20]

Fisher's Sexual Assaults

The seven sexual assaults in Saskatoon, Winnipeg, and North Battleford that Larry Fisher confessed to are discussed in this section; the locations of his rapes in Saskatoon are shown in Figure 9.2.

Sexual Assault #1—Saskatoon, October 21, 1968

At about 7:30 p.m. Larry Fisher committed his first known rape on a woman in her early twenties, who was returning home from a local store. The victim used the same bus route as Fisher. He approached her in the 400 block of Avenue H South with a large bread knife, put his hand over her mouth, and threatened to kill her if she screamed. She was pulled into an alley and forced to remove her clothing; he then inserted the knife into her vagina. The attack was interrupted and Fisher fled.

Sexual Assault #2—Saskatoon, November 13, 1968

Larry Fisher attacked his second victim sometime between 6:30 and 8:00 p.m. while she was walking from her home to meet a friend. Fisher grabbed her

---

[19]The details of these sexual assaults were obtained from a report by Centurion Ministries, based on their investigation into the crimes of Larry Fisher. Unfortunately, as the official police reports for these cases are apparently missing, independent verification is lacking.

[20]Statement of Linda Fisher, March 10, 1990, Cando, Saskatchewan, pp. 1–4.

from behind, put his hand over her mouth, held a small paring knife to her throat, and said, "If you want to live, do as I say." After warning her not to scream, he dragged the victim into a lane off the 500 block of 18th Street East and raped her in a darkened yard. When he left he took several articles of her clothing, including her dress, bra, panty hose, and shoes. The victim was 16 years old.

Sexual Assault # 3—Saskatoon, November 29, 1968

A 19-year-old student, walking home from a University of Saskatchewan night class, was approached by Larry Fisher near Temperance Street and Wiggins Avenue.[21] He asked for directions, then grabbed her from behind, placed his hand over her mouth, and told her that he had a knife. When she screamed and struggled, he threatened to kill her if she was not quiet. While dragging her down an alley to a vehicle that he said he had nearby, Fisher was scared away by approaching headlights. On December 14, 1968, the Saskatoon *Star-Phoenix* published a police warning concerning the attacks of a serial rapist, active in the Riversdale area.

Sexual Assault #4—Saskatoon, February 21, 1970

Fifteen months after the Gail Miller murder, Larry Fisher attacked again.[22] The victim was an 18-year-old high school student working at the City Hospital canteen.[23] She returned home from work one evening on the 20th Street bus. Fisher was on the same bus. When the victim left the bus, Fisher followed, grabbing her from behind and pulling her into the yard of a house in the 200 block of Avenue V South. She resisted and bit him, but Fisher hit her several times in the face, threatening he could easily break her neck. He forced her to undress, raped her, and then fled. A Saskatoon police detective investigating the attack mentioned to the victim the similarities to the Gail Miller case.

Sexual Assault #5—Winnipeg, August 2, 1970

In the summer of 1970, Larry Fisher moved to Winnipeg to take a construction job. His fifth known victim was a nursing student at the Health Science Centre, not far from where Fisher was staying. At about midnight she caught the last bus to her house in the south end of Winnipeg. She walked from the transit stop and was almost home when Fisher approached her, asking for directions. He then grabbed her from behind, placed his hand over her

---

[21] This attack, unlike the three other assaults in Saskatoon, occurred outside the Riversdale area where Fisher lived. He was working nearby at the time, on a construction project at the University of Saskatchewan.

[22] Larry Fisher is not known to have committed any assaults between the time of Gail Miller's murder and the conviction of David Milgaard, a year later.

[23] City Hospital is where Gail Miller worked as a nurse's assistant.

mouth, and pressed a knife against her throat. When the woman screamed, he beat her beyond recognition, dragged her into a vacant lot, and ripped off her clothing. After the rape was finished, Fisher hogtied the victim with her own clothing and threatened to kill her if she called for help. He finished his attack by robbing the woman.

Sexual Assault #6—Winnipeg, September 19, 1970

Larry Fisher's second Winnipeg victim was a dental hygiene student who often wore a white lab coat to her classes downtown, near where Fisher lived. The victim caught a bus to her home in south Winnipeg just after midnight. In an echo of his last rape, Fisher grabbed the woman from behind on a residential street, within a block of her home. He put his hand over her nose and mouth, warned her that he had a knife, and pulled her between two buildings. While she struggled and screamed, he yanked her clothing aside and savagely bit her breasts.

Fisher then fled, only to be caught nearby by police. Detectives found a paring knife at the scene and located his pickup truck near the crime site. Fisher was arrested, jailed, and charged. He pled guilty to two charges of rape, robbery, and possession of a weapon dangerous to the public peace.[24] In May 1971, Fisher received a 13-year prison sentence for the Winnipeg attacks, and in December 1971, he received concurrent sentences from a Regina court for his confessions to the four sexual offences in Saskatoon. For reasons that have never been fully explained, the victims of the Saskatoon rapes were not notified of the clearance of their cases.

Sexual Assault #7—North Battleford, March 31, 1980

In January 1980, Larry Fisher was granted parole and moved to his mother's home in North Battleford. In late March he raped again, this time in a particularly savage attack. Sometime after 9:00 p.m. he sprung out from behind a hedge and grabbed a 56-year-old woman from behind. He pressed a knife against her neck and dragged her into the snowy backyard of a burnt-out house. He pushed her to the ground and pulled off her clothing. Fisher warned the victim not to scream and threatened to kill her, saying he had done it before.

After raping the woman, Fisher pulled his victim into the abandoned house, forced her to perform oral sex on him, and raped her again. He then bound her hands behind her back with her nylon stockings, tied her feet with her scarf, gagged her by stuffing her girdle into her mouth, and took her money from her purse. Then, despite the victim's lack of resistance, and with no explanation, Fisher slit her throat, stabbed her several times in the chest,

---

[24]Fisher also admitted to four or five additional indecent assaults in Winnipeg, but as the victims could not be located, no charges were filed.

and tried to suffocate her by holding his hand over her nose and mouth. The victim did not have a pulse when she arrived at the hospital, but ultimately recovered from her physical injuries.

Fisher was caught by police in the basement of his mother's house, washing blood from his work boots. In June 1980 he pled guilty to charges of attempted murder and rape and was sentenced to 14 years' imprisonment. Fisher was incarcerated in British Columbia's Mountain Institution and released after the full completion of his sentence in 1994 (he was denied parole because he refused any sex offender treatment). In 1997 he was arrested and charged with the murder of Gail Miller, and finally convicted of this crime in 1999.

Larry Fisher is best profiled as an "anger/retaliatory" or "punishment" rapist, an uncommon type, but one who may inflict serious harm or death upon his victim (Geberth, 2006). These sex offenders use a sudden, blitz style of attack, with excessive and unnecessary violence. Their purpose is to punish, debase, and degrade their female victims, for whom they have a great deal of anger. These victims are often symbolic, the rapist transferring his anger from some other woman he feels has hurt or wronged him. The attack usually occurs after he has suffered an imagined ego blow from another female.

The punishment rapist attacks anywhere, indoors or out, and anytime, with no temporal cycle or episodic pattern. He chooses victims of opportunity he perceives as vulnerable, and it is not unknown for him to attack more than one victim in a short time period. He may beat his victim before, during, and after the rape, which can involve multiple sexual attacks. His weapon is usually one of opportunity.

The punishment rapist typically is a male, usually more than 30 years of age, married or separated, his relationships stormy, characterized by much conflict and fighting. He is of normal intelligence, muscular and stocky in build, likes contact sports, and is probably involved in manual labor or an action-oriented job (Hazelwood, 2001).

This type of rapist is usually of low socioeconomic status, probably lives in cheap rental property, and may have a record for interpersonal violence or sexual assault. He is impulsive and self-centered, has an explosive temper, and may be a wife or a child beater. His rapes will usually take place in the immediate vicinity of his residence or place of work—his "comfort zone."

This sort of profile closely matches the crimes and the personal characteristics of Larry Fisher. Additionally, the modus operandi of his attacks has striking similarities: victims selected from his comfort zone, stalked and attacked on the street, sometimes with the presence of a car, victims grabbed from behind with the use or threat of a knife. They were violent rapes, with clothing manipulation as part of the anger. Many of his victims wore uniforms of some sort, perhaps suggesting some deep-rooted hatred of working females or women in uniforms; Fisher's mother wore a uniform to work, first while employed at a dry cleaners, and later, when employed by a hospital.

All of Fisher's Saskatoon rapes occurred in older, working-class, residential neighborhoods. The alleys that he pulled his victims down were like the alley in which Gail Miller's body was found: protected from observation by garages, fences, and vegetation. The police initially thought there might be a connection between Miller's murder and the Riversdale rapes; they had good reason: same immediate area, same type of alley, the use of a knife, and a brutal sexual assault. Today, all these crimes would be profiled as having been committed by the same type of offender, and, given the size and population of Saskatoon and the Riversdale area in 1969, they would likely be profiled as having been committed by the same offender.[25]

The Crown's theory that Gail Miller was murdered as the result of a purse snatching that went wrong was not realistic. We now know that she was murdered by Larry Fisher—a man who harbored an incredible amount of anger toward women. Her purse and some items of clothing were taken from the murder scene for psychological reasons, perhaps to mentally prolong the event, possibly to serve as a souvenir or trophy.

The Applications for Review

In December 1988 Winnipeg lawyer Hersh Wolch applied to Joe Clark, then Canada's Minister of Justice, for a judicial review in the case of David Milgaard. The application read, "The Applicant submits that this case is worthy of review by the Minister of Justice on the basis that advances in scientific technology have called into question the scientific evidence presented at the trial."

Counsel for Milgaard enclosed a seven-page report from Vancouver forensic pathologist, Dr. James Ferris. Ferris, a professor of pathology at the University of British Columbia and the head of forensic pathology at Vancouver General Hospital, concluded, "On the basis of the evidence that I have examined, I have no reasonable doubt that serological evidence presented at the trial failed to link David Milgaard with the offence and that in fact, could be reasonably considered to exclude him from being the perpetrator of the murder."[26]

The forensic evidence as tendered at trial did not totally exonerate Milgaard, but it was not neutral, neither in the way in which it was presented nor in the probabilities that it produced. The sequence with respect to the

---

[25]Statistics Canada data indicate that there were four rapes reported to police in the city of Saskatoon between October 1, 1968, and March 1, 1969 (*Number of Rape Offences for Saskatoon, 1968–69*. Ottawa: Statistics Canada). A man was charged with one of the rapes; the other three crimes were unsolved until Larry Fisher pleaded guilty to the attacks in Regina in 1971.

[26]Letter from James A. J. Ferris to Hersh Wolch, September 13, 1988, pp. 1–7.

assembly of the forensic evidence is critical. On February 4, 1969, four days after the murder, police found two pale yellowish clumps in the snow. They packaged them appropriately and sent them to the Crime Detection Laboratory in Regina. In one of the two vials nothing of value was found, but in the other, seminal fluid and seven pubic hairs were detected. When the semen was analyzed, it was found to come from a type A secretor.

On April 18, Saskatoon police Lieutenant Joe Penkala asked David Milgaard to provide two saliva samples to determine whether or not he was a secretor. When these were analyzed, no antigens were found, and it was accordingly presumed that Milgaard was a nonsecretor. The only way, then, to have reasonably connected Milgaard to the semen sample was through the possibility that his blood had contaminated the sample. Accordingly, the sample was sent back to the lab in June, with a request to check for blood. The RCMP serologist suspected that blood was present, but could not scientifically confirm this suspicion.

At trial, the theory of the Crown was that there was blood in the sample—blood from David Milgaard. This theory was bolstered by Dr. Emson's claims that blood within ejaculate would be "a quite common occurrence." In 1991, however, prior to the Supreme Court hearing, Dr. Emson indicated he would have to vary his testimony from what he had said at trial. He now knew that such shedding of blood into the urethra is not a common event (personal communication with Dr. H. E. Emson, September 1991).

Vancouver forensic pathologist James Ferris also addressed this issue in his 1988 report on the Milgaard case, calling the contamination of a seminal sample with the assailant's own blood unlikely. "I have also spoken to a number of personal contacts in other forensic science laboratories and on the basis of their experiences and my own experience, we are not familiar with a single case where seminal fluid or stains have been found to be contaminated by blood from the alleged assailant."[27]

There have been many concerns expressed about "the integrity and continuity" of the evidence.[28] The crime scene was subject to a good deal of trampling in the four days before the sample was recovered, and it cannot be proven conclusively that the semen found there was related to the murder of Gail Miller. It seems unlikely, however, that someone other than the assailant would have left a seminal stain at that location—outdoors in subzero temperatures—within the preceding few days.

Also enclosed with the application for judicial review was an affidavit from Deborah Hall. She was in the Regina motel room when David Milgaard "reenacted" the crime; she swore that she did not think it was a confession. "My interpretation of David Milgaard's response was that it was a completely

---

[27] Letter from James A. J. Ferris to Hersh Wolch, September 13, 1988.
[28] Letter from James A. J. Ferris to Hersh Wolch, September 13, 1988, note 24.

innocent and perhaps crudely comical comment. I know that if I had thought he was serious I would have left immediately. No one in the room thought anything of that particular conversation."[29]

Over the next two and a half years, counsel for David Milgaard brought a series of affidavits to the attention of the Minister of Justice, further questioning the validity of David Milgaard's conviction. None would ultimately be more telling than a letter in March 1990 from counsel David Asper to E. F. Williams of the federal Department of Justice, informing him of the existence of Larry Fisher, his history of brutal rape, and the alternative scenario for the morning of January 31, 1969.

In June 1990, private investigator Paul Henderson, working for Centurion Ministries, took a statement from Ron Wilson in which Wilson recanted most of his trial testimony. Wilson said that Milgaard did not have a paring knife, that he had never seen blood on his clothes, and that Milgaard had not said, "I fixed her." Wilson said that he and David had been away from the car once that morning, but for no more than three minutes. Wilson explained his statement at trial by saying that there had been a "sweat session" with police, and that he had been "manipulated."[30] Contacted at her home in Kelowna, British Columbia, Nichol John refused to speak with Paul Henderson about the Milgaard case.

Henderson also took statements from Albert Cadrain and his brother Dennis. Albert said that he was picked up by police and questioned 15 to 20 times, that there was "constant pressure, threats, and bullying," that he developed serious stomach ulcers and became "very paranoid." He was committed to the psychiatric ward at University Hospital in Saskatoon approximately a year after the trial.[31]

Dennis Cadrain said that his brother Albert would not lie about anything knowingly, but that he was prone to exaggeration and suggestion, and could be "manipulated" by police. "If ideas were planted in Albert's mind, it is quite possible that he would come to accept them as truth. Frankly, I would not consider my brother to be a reliable witness at that time, and for this reason."[32]

The recantation given by Ron Wilson to private investigator Paul Henderson in June 1990 was later confirmed before Department of Justice investigator Eugene Williams in July of that year.[33] Wilson had told Paul Henderson, an investigator working for David Milgaard, that he had been subjected to a six-hour "sweat session" by police, at the close of which he provided his

---

[29] Affidavit of Deborah Hall, sworn November 23, 1986, pp. 1–6.

[30] Statement of Ronald Dale Wilson, June 4, 1990, Nakusp, BC, pp. 1–6.

[31] Statement of Dennis Cadrain, May 26, 1990, Port Coquitlam, BC pp. 1–4; statement of Albert Cadrain, June 24, 1990, Port Coquitlam, BC, pp. 1–3.

[32] Statement of Dennis Cadrain, May 1990, Port Coquitlam, BC.

[33] Examination of Ronald Dale Wilson, July 20, 1990, Nakusp, BC, pp. 1–143.

statement of May 24, 1969. In fact, the session of polygraph testing and questioning lasted somewhere between three and a half and five hours.

Wilson's claims of manipulation and pressure by police are difficult to assess. The police were persistent in their pursuit of Wilson, John, and Cadrain, but this would not be unexpected, given their perception that David Milgaard was responsible for such a serious crime. On the other hand, Wilson, Cadrain, and John were also unsophisticated, socially and economically disadvantaged teenagers, and some of the tactics police employed may have inadvertently helped produce the inconsistency of the statements that these three witnesses provided between January and May 1969. Nichol John was kept in a police cell overnight before making her statement.

Ron Wilson indicated to Eugene Williams in 1990, and to us in 1991, that police treated him well. "They all treated me nice. What I tried to get across to Williams, which I never could, was that, like when you're watching TV ... you've got that bad cop who wants to beat this out of you and stuff—it doesn't happen that way. Later on in my dealings I had bad cops. But these guys were nice. I think, now that I look back on it, being nice gets them further ahead than being nasty to you."[34]

Ron Wilson's description of the morning of the murder had Milgaard away from the car for about two minutes, a length of time much more consistent with the extremely cold weather conditions that morning. He said that Nichol John was "fine" upon his return, and that it would have been "totally impossible" for David Milgaard to have killed anyone during such a short time period.

Of Nichol John's statement to police, Ron Wilson said, "If she would have seen that, she would have been gone so fucking fast it would make your head spin. There's no way she would have stuck around." He further states: "What she described couldn't have happened, period, because it never did happen."

Nichol John has continued to say that she cannot remember anything from the morning of the murder and has refused to discuss her testimony publicly. She attempted to avoid the subpoena requiring her to testify at the Supreme Court of Canada. During the inquiry, she simply reiterated her account of the event at trial—that she could not remember anything of what happened on that icy morning in Saskatoon.

According to Ron Wilson, he was simply interested in getting free from police questioning on May 24, 1969, going home, and "getting loaded." He was not forced to implicate David Milgaard, but implicating Milgaard was the easiest way to remove himself from a persistently stressful situation—two months of questioning by police. Wilson was a 17-year-old delinquent who usually placed his own interests first. He was involved in drugs and crime

[34]Interview with Ron Wilson, Kelowna, BC, October 7, 1991, p. 21.

until the early 1980s, using and selling heroin and LSD, and was for 10 years a member of the Regina motorcycle club, the Apollos.

Wilson also indicated that David Milgaard spent a night with Nichol John just before leaving on a trip to see his girlfriend, and Nichol retaliated by "hopping into bed with Shorty." David and Ron Wilson used Albert Cadrain for his money, taking his cash to pay for car repairs and to buy drugs in Alberta—drugs that Cadrain never saw. Ron Wilson and George Lapchuk passed bad checks, using David Milgaard's name without his knowledge. Ron Wilson sketches a picture of a disenfranchised street youth in 1969, on the fringes of the fledgling hippie culture and on the edge of a criminal lifestyle. They were all involved in using illegal drugs. "Friends" were passing acquaintances who you ran into in the park, spent a few days with, and who would then disappear for months. Loyalties and allegiances were nonexistent, and the primary concern was only to look out for yourself—survival, "better him than me." Police reliance on the statements of such individuals is one of the potential traps associated with wrongful convictions, a practice as problematic as the use of "jailhouse informant confessions."

In February 1991, A. Kim Campbell, the Minister of Justice, responded to the Milgaard application. She denied the application, writing that a review would be "inappropriate." She viewed the new evidence of Deborah Hall with skepticism: "[Hall] felt that David Milgaard was making a sick remark and was not serious. Whether her opinion of Milgaard's sincerity would have been shared by the jury is, at best, debatable." Of the forensic evidence, the Minister concluded, "The suggestion that the forensic evidence exonerates Milgaard misstates the value of that evidence. The forensic evidence tendered at trial, when elevated to its highest probative value, is neutral, establishing neither guilt nor innocence."[35]

She wrote of the recantation of Ron Wilson, "The current retraction by Mr. Wilson of much of his trial evidence is unconvincing." She called Wilson's claim that he was only separated from Milgaard for three minutes "simply not credible." She stated that Albert Cadrain had only experienced "personal and emotional difficulties" after the trial, not before. And of the alternative scenario of Larry Fisher, she wrote, "no guilt or suspicion of guilt can be attributed to Fisher in the absence of some form of evidence linking him to the crime."[36]

A second application, bolstered by additional detail, was made in a climate of emerging public opinion critical of the Minister of Justice. Canadian Prime Minister Brian Mulroney then intervened. All this eventually resulted in the holding of an inquiry in the Supreme Court of Canada. It was a most unusual move; the Supreme Court of Canada, exclusively a court of appeal, agreed to hear evidence in relation to the appropriateness of David Milgaard's conviction.

---

[35]Letter from A. Kim Campbell, Minister of Justice, to Hersh Wolch, February 27, 1991.
[36]Ibid.

The Supreme Court of Canada Inquiry

What did the Supreme Court of Canada conclude from all this evidence? Simply put, they decided that David Milgaard's innocence was no more likely than his guilt. It was a surprising conclusion to those with knowledge of the case. In a unanimous decision in April 1992, the five-member bench first set out guidelines for assessing wrongful convictions, or, more specifically, set out three different categories, each constituting a miscarriage of justice, but requiring different judicial responses. They argued that if Milgaard could satisfy the Court beyond a reasonable doubt of his innocence, he ought to be granted a free pardon. If, alternatively, he could satisfy the Court of the proposition that his innocence was more likely than his guilt, the Supreme Court would then consider "whether the conviction should be quashed and a verdict of acquittal entered." Finally, if there was simply new evidence before the Court that was "reasonably capable of belief" and "could reasonably be expected to have affected the verdict," this would also amount to a miscarriage of justice, requiring "the Minister of Justice to quash the conviction and to direct a new trial. … In this event it would be open to the Attorney General for Saskatchewan to enter a stay [of proceedings] if a stay were deemed appropriate, in view of all the circumstances, including the time served by David Milgaard."[37]

The Supreme Court of Canada opted for the latter option, writing of the evidence presented:

> While there is some evidence which implicates Milgaard in the murder of Gail Miller, the fresh evidence presented to us, particularly as to the locations and the pattern of the sexual assaults committed by Fisher, could well affect a jury's assessment of the guilt or innocence of Milgaard. The continued conviction of Milgaard would amount to a miscarriage of justice if an opportunity was not provided for a jury to consider the fresh evidence. It is therefore appropriate to recommend to the Minister of Justice that she set aside the conviction and direct that a new trial be held. It would be open to the Attorney General for Saskatchewan under the Criminal Code to enter a stay if that course were deemed appropriate in light of all the circumstances.

Shortly after this judgment, David Milgaard was released from federal penitentiary, and the Attorney General for Saskatchewan decided not to proceed to trial against him. Milgaard had already served 23 years in prison; the crime itself was now almost a quarter-century old. So Milgaard was in limbo. Although he was a free man, the Supreme Court had not said he was innocent and there was not going to be a new trial.

For David Milgaard and his family, his release from prison was bittersweet. He was finally free, but a cloud remained over his head. The Court

[37]Reference re Milgaard (Canada) [1992] 1 Supreme Court Reports 866, file no. 22732.

had, after all, said his innocence was not more likely than his guilt. There were many who maintained that he was properly convicted of the crime, and there was to be no compensation for his 23 years of confinement.

DNA Results

All of this changed on July 18, 1997, when DNA testing of Gail Miller's nursing uniform in the United Kingdom, monitored by both the Department of Justice and the RCMP, produced two findings: (1) there was no match between David Milgaard's DNA and the DNA from the sperm cells found on her uniform; but (2) there was a match between that DNA and Larry Fisher's DNA. Finally, science delivered to David Milgaard what a fallible human system of criminal justice could not—overwhelming evidence that he did not kill Gail Miller. And, of course, this DNA evidence led to the arrest and conviction of Fisher, now currently serving a sentence of life imprisonment in a Canadian penitentiary. DNA testing on Gail Miller's clothing had been tried twice before, in 1988 and 1992, but the existing science was not yet sufficiently developed to either link or exclude Milgaard. In 1999, James Ferris, a pathologist involved with the Milgaard case, told the Saskatoon *Star-Phoenix* that the 1988 and 1992 tests were too crude to obtain a profile; existing methods required very large and relatively fresh samples in order to obtain conclusive results (Perreaux, 1999).

In 2001, a forensic scientist involved in the 1997 testing told one of the authors of this chapter (Rossmo) that they had located a substantial amount of dried semen on Gail Miller's uniform that had never been tested or, apparently, even found. It seems that the original investigators failed to examine the lower inside back of her skirt. If the original RCMP forensic laboratory analysis had found this evidence, conventional serology techniques (isoenzyme testing) available in 1969 should have been sufficient to exonerate Milgaard. Thirty years later, in May 1999, David Milgaard was awarded compensation of $10 million by the Canadian and Saskatchewan governments, the largest such amount in Canadian criminal justice history. The Milgaard family was also promised a full inquiry into the wrongful conviction.

The Inquiry

In October 2004, after the criminal appeals of Larry Fisher had been exhausted, the province of Saskatchewan appointed a Commission of Inquiry into the wrongful conviction of David Milgaard. The Commission held public hearings in 2005 and 2006, posting transcripts of these hearings online.[38] The *Final Report of the Commission* is expected in 2008, after 119 days of public hearings and testimony from 133 witnesses, two of whom were the authors of this chapter. The mandate of the inquiry was set out at the time of its creation in 2004:

> The Commission has a mandate to inquire into and report on any and all aspects of the conduct of the investigation into the death of Gail Miller, and the subsequent criminal proceedings resulting in the wrongful conviction of David Milgaard on the charge that he murdered Gail Miller.
>
> The Commission also has the responsibility to seek to determine whether the investigation should have been re-opened based on information subsequently received by the police and the Department of Justice.
>
> The Commission will report its findings and make such recommendations as it considers advisable relating to the administration of criminal justice in the province of Saskatchewan.
>
> As provided in the *Public Inquiries Act*, the Commission shall perform its duties without expressing any conclusion or recommendation regarding the civil or criminal liability of any person or organization, and without interfering in any ongoing criminal or civil proceeding.
>
> The Commission will deliver its final report containing its findings, conclusions and recommendations to the Attorney General of Saskatchewan, who will make the report public.[39]

Conclusion

There are a number of key questions that have been asked about the wrongful conviction of David Milgaard, and it is hoped these questions will be addressed in some form in the Commission's Final Report. Why were Larry Fisher's rape victims in Saskatoon never told that their attacker had been arrested, convicted, and sentenced? Why did Larry Fisher plead guilty to his Saskatoon rapes in Regina, contrary to common practice in criminal cases? Why did Saskatoon Detective Eddie Karst indicate during the 1990s that he had never met Larry Fisher, when he actually went to Winnipeg to take a statement from him after he had been apprehended in that city? Did Karst simply forget his trip to Winnipeg, or was this part of a police cover-up that began after an awareness of Larry Fisher first surfaced in 1970—when David Milgaard was already in jail serving his life sentence? We await the release of the report, but in the interim a number of conclusions seem warranted.

It is best to await the conclusions of Commissioner Justice Edward Mac-Callum with regard to any allegations of possible police misconduct. What

---

[38] Available at http://www.milgaardinquiry.ca.
[39] See http://www.milgaard.inquiry.ca/terms/shtml.

we can conclude with certainty is that many of the hallmarks of wrongful convictions exist in the Milgaard case. A recent Canadian intergovernmental study, *Report of the Working Group on the Prevention of Miscarriages of Justice* (2004), cited six key areas: (1) tunnel vision; (2) eyewitness identification and testimony; (3) false confessions; (4) in-custody informers; (5) DNA evidence; and (6) erroneous forensic evidence and expert testimony. The report also noted a lack of education regarding the possibilities of wrongful conviction. In the Milgaard case, all but false confessions were relevant to the outcome. The police developed tunnel vision, despite a lack of physical evidence to support their theory of a purse-snatching-turned-rape/murder. The testimony by "eyewitnesses" Albert Cadrain, Nichol John, and Ron Wilson was contradicted by the available (and more reliable) physical evidence. Their evidence was a mixture of delusion and lies, an example of police reliance on untrustworthy and criminally involved informers. Erroneous forensic evidence was presented at trial, in what now must be seen as an incompetent attempt to force the data to fit the theory of the prosecution.

The lifestyle and characters of David Milgaard and his young companions must also be implicated in a full understanding of this wrongful conviction. Although he was most inappropriately the victim of a miscarriage of justice, his activities and those of his companions—theft and drug use—served to arouse suspicion on the part of police investigators. In the late 1960s, the attitude of the Saskatoon Police Department was decidedly antidrug and antihippie. Coincidentally, shortly before Milgaard's trial, Charles Manson and members of his "Family" were arrested for the Sharon Tate and LaBianca murders in California. It may be that Milgaard was viewed through this prism—a long-haired hippie capable of the most heinous acts of violence, a Canadian Manson, and drugged-up sex killer.

Finally, and generally speaking, neither the police nor the prosecution was sensitive enough to the possibility of error. Even in early 1997, before DNA testing made clear the truth of this crime, there were many in those communities who failed to recognize not only the several specific weaknesses in this case,[40] but also the inevitable fallibility of our justice system, even when it requires proof beyond a reasonable doubt. The burden of proof in criminal cases is not a standard of absolute certainty, and even a cursory knowledge of probability should introduce an element of humility into all criminal trials. In the final analysis, David Milgaard owes his freedom not to the "expert" judgment of human beings regarding his guilt or innocence, but to the advances of science, and the bright light that DNA testing shone on this case, freeing the innocent and convicting the guilty.

---

[40]Even after Larry Fisher's conviction, some police officers explained the DNA evidence by suggesting Milgaard first murdered Miller, and then Fisher happened to come along, found her body, and had sex with it.

References

Boyd, N., & Rossmo, D. K. (1992). *Milgaard v. The Queen: Finding justice—Problems and process*. Burnaby, BC: Criminology Research Centre, Simon Fraser University.

Boyd, N., & Rossmo, D. K. (1994, February). David Milgaard, the Supreme Court and Section 690: A wrongful conviction revisited. *Canadian Lawyer*, 28–29, 32.

Castelle, G., & Loftus, E. (2001). Misinformation. In S. Westervelt & J. Humphrey (Eds.), *Wrongly convicted: Perspectives on failed justice* (pp. 17–35). New Brunswick, NJ: Rutgers University Press.

Commission of Inquiry into the Wrongful Conviction of David Milgaard. (2004). Retrieved July 12, 2008, from http://www.milgaard.inquiry.ca.

Denov, M., & Campbell, K. (2005). Criminal injustice: Understanding the causes, effects, and responses to wrongful conviction in Canada. *Journal of Contemporary Criminal Justice, 21*, 224–249.

Geberth, V. J. (2006). *Practical homicide investigation: Tactics, procedures, and forensic techniques* (4th ed.). Boca Raton, FL: CRC Press.

Hazelwood, R. R. (2001). Analyzing the rape and profiling the offender. In R. R. Hazelwood & A. W. Burgess (Eds.), *Practical aspects of rape investigation: A multidisciplinary approach* (3rd ed., pp. 133–164). Boca Raton, FL: CRC Press.

Huff, C. R., Rattner, A., & Sagarin, E. (1986). Guilty until proven innocent: Wrongful conviction and public policy. *Crime and Delinquency, 32*, 518–544.

Huff, C. R., Rattner, A., & Sagarin, E. (1996). *Convicted but innocent: Wrongful conviction and public policy*. Thousand Oaks, CA: Sage.

Jaffe, F. A. (1983). *A guide to pathological evidence for lawyers and police officers* (2nd ed.). Toronto: Carswell.

Milgaard, J., & Edwards, P. (1999). *A mother's story: The fight to free my son David*. Toronto: Doubleday Canada.

Perreaux, L. (1999, October 22). Early DNA test failed to implicate Fisher—sampling considered too crude to obtain proper profile, court hears. Saskatoon *Star-Phoenix*.

Radelet, M., Bedau, H., & Putnam, C. (1992). *In spite of innocence: Erroneous convictions in capital cases*. Boston: Northeastern University Press.

Reference re: David Milgaard. (1992). 1 Supreme Court Reports (S.C.R.) 866.

Report of the Working Group on the Prevention of Miscarriages of Justice. (2004). Ottawa. Retrieved July 12, 2008, from http://www.justice.gc.ca/eng/dept-min/pub/pmj-pej/toc-tdm.html.

Scheck. B., & Neufeld, P. (2001). DNA and innocence scholarship. In S. Westervelt & J. Humphrey (Eds.), *Wrongly convicted: Perspectives on failed justice* (pp. 241–252). New Brunswick, NJ: Rutgers University Press.

A False Confession to Murder in Washington, D.C.

10

JAMES TRAINUM AND
DIANA M. HAVLIN

It is a capitol mistake to theorize before one has data. Insensibly one begins to twist facts to suit theories, instead of theories to suit facts. (Sherlock Holmes, *A Scandal in Bohemia*)

The Murder

On February 26, 1994, the cold and windy afternoon had not diminished the crowds at the open-air farmer's market in the parking lot of the Robert F. Kennedy Stadium in eastern Washington, D.C. While walking beside the lot around 1:00 p.m., John Evan's[1] normally well-trained Labrador retriever bolted toward the tree line by the icy Anacostia River. The dog had found something that captivated his interest. As Evans approached, the form began to take the shape of a body—a brutally beaten 34-year-old white male. The victim was later identified as Edward McMillan, a civil engineer with the U.S. Federal Government who had disappeared after leaving work the night before. Discovering what caused him to end up dead on the banks of the Anacostia was the responsibility of Detective Jim Trainum, a relativity new homicide investigator.

During his 11 years with the Washington, D.C., Metropolitan Police Department, Trainum had conducted numerous successful investigations of both violent and property crimes. He had learned the value of strict attention to detail, complete documentation, and methodical procedures. Unlike most homicide detectives at the Metropolitan Police Department, he had also been cross-trained as a Crime Scene Technician and was recognized for his multidisciplined approach to criminal investigations. In spite of this, his investigation into the murder of Edward McMillan fell victim to the numerous cognitive biases and organizational traps that continuously plague law enforcement. The McMillan case—although officially "closed" by arrest—remains unsolved.

---

[1] All names but those of the detectives have been changed.

205

Detective Trainum made mistakes and learned lessons during the McMillan murder investigation. And when he was called on to investigate the highly publicized and politically charged murder of three employees in an upscale Georgetown Starbucks, the results were different thanks in part to the lessons learned from the McMillan case. Awareness of the traps, however, does not make them disappear; law enforcement's obstinacy when it comes to examining and learning from mistakes only ensures that they will continue to occur.

One examination of racial bias concluded that unintentionally biased responses may occur in a given situation, even if the individual is aware of the bias and consciously attempts to prevent the response (Amodio et al., 2004). This phenomenon, absent the racial context, manifested itself in investigator attitudes throughout the McMillan homicide investigation.

Edward McMillan worked at a federal office building near the Smithsonian Institution and lived with his wife and child in suburban Virginia. By all outward appearances, McMillan resembled most federal government employees. His only contact with day-to-day Washington, D.C., was his commute to the federal office building where he worked. He disappeared on a Friday; after signing out of work around 4:00 p.m., McMillan walked to his car parked several blocks away in a townhouse complex where he had rented space. He never arrived home.

When Detective Trainum arrived at the scene of the crime, the area had already been sealed off from bystanders and the press, although neither was a problem because of the cold weather. McMillan was lying on his back, halfway inside the tree line. He was dressed in a business suit but his suit jacket and shoes were missing. His pant pockets were turned inside out and his wallet and Rolex watch were missing, although he still wore his wedding ring. His tie was looped around one wrist and a piece of telephone cord around the other, as if his arms had been secured separately to the arms of a chair. His belt was missing, and a torn belt loop led Detective Trainum to believe that it had been forcibly removed. Perhaps it was used as a binding, but then discarded when it proved unsatisfactory. Lying next to the body was a black bandanna.

Nearby on the tree line, at the mouth of a path leading down to the river, detectives found pens, a computer probe, a pocket protector, and pieces of cut telephone cord. At the end of the path was a large rock marked by blood spatter.

An autopsy later revealed that McMillan had defensive bruising on his forearms and lower legs and contusions to his face and upper body. The medical examiner concluded that McMillan's death was caused by a massive blow to the side of his head with an unknown blunt object. The estimated time of death was late Friday evening or early Saturday morning.

Over the next several days, detectives analyzed clues, created a time line, and responded to the increasing number of media inquiries. McMillan was not the typical murder victim, and the circumstances surrounding this crime were not those of the typical homicide. About 20 minutes after McMillan left work, a short white female subject wearing a baseball cap and glasses used McMillan's ATM card, with his correct personal identification number, at a nearby outside bank machine in an unsuccessful attempt to withdraw $300. Because McMillan had made a mistake during an ATM cash deposit of $300 earlier in the week, his account had been frozen by the bank until he could rectify the situation in person. The female subject continued to attempt to withdraw smaller and smaller amounts until she gave up without success.

Two hours later, an unknown subject used McMillan's American Express credit card to make purchases at a Maryland strip mall, 30 miles south of Washington, D.C. That person purchased three orders of carryout Chinese food and then walked next door to a drug store, where additional purchases were made.

An hour later, a short white female subject wearing a baseball cap and glasses entered a liquor store in the Capitol Hill neighborhood of Washington, D.C., and attempted to purchase several items with McMillan's American Express card. The female subject had just signed for the purchases when another store employee came in from a delivery and commented that the police were outside the store writing parking tickets. The female subject commented that she did not want to get a ticket and ran out of the store, leaving her purchases and the credit card behind. She did not return. According to the medical examiner's estimation, McMillan was alive during all of these transactions. Handwriting examiners concluded that the same person signed the credit card slips for all three transactions.

Investigators then found evidence suggesting McMillan's car, which was recovered by police in the townhouse lot, may have been used during the crime. A friend of his informed police that, on the day of the murder, McMillan's car was parked in the wrong space and was backed in rather than pulled in as was his usual habit. The rear license plate was also bent up at a right angle, perhaps to prevent it from being read.

Information surfaced about McMillan's private life. He had a heavy credit card debt and was described as unusually worried about something the week before his murder. The origin of the $300 cash deposit that had resulted in the freeze on his bank account was not known. Associates described McMillan as being loud and a name dropper and said that he would frequently disappear from work for hours at a time. Rumors surfaced of his involvement with prostitutes and in shady business deals. Deception seemed to surround him, even extending to his best friend, who had manufactured a fictitious military history for himself.

Detective Trainum analyzed the crime scene and began to develop his investigative theories. Some of these were based on fundamental assumptions (most murder victims know their killers), some on deductive logic (the three orders of Chinese food combined with the fact that McMillan's stomach was empty at the time of his death implied three suspects). Others were based on real or perceived (through the media, popular "profiling books," etc.) experiences of himself and his coworkers. Unfortunately, some of these theories eventually became etched in stone.

With evidence and witness statements now in hand, Trainum formulated the following theory. McMillan left work at approximately 4:00 p.m., and while en route to his car was confronted by the suspects, at least one of which was known to him. He apparently went voluntarily as there had been no report of a confrontation in an area with high volumes of both vehicular and pedestrian traffic. At least three individuals drove McMillan, in his own car, to an ATM machine, where they attempted to make a withdrawal (the short time from when McMillan left work to when his ATM card was used with the correct personal identification number supported the cooperation theory). The $300 amount was believed to be significant as it matched the mysterious deposit made earlier in the week. Trainum surmised McMillan owed these individuals money, or had perhaps cheated them, and now they wanted what was owed to them.

Frustrated, the abductors were now at a loss. Trainum found the crime perplexing in that it appeared poorly planned. He speculated on what happened next. Perhaps the abductors bound McMillan, either in the car or in a house—the use of telephone cord suggests that at some point McMillan was inside a residence—and then drove out to the strip mall in Maryland. Given that the credit card purchases were small, for personal use, and made only prior to McMillan's murder, detectives ruled out the possibility that this crime had been committed for purely financial gain.

The earlier "deal gone bad" theory was given further credence in Trainum's mind by the logical sequence of events. The three perpetrators drove McMillan to a secluded location by the Anacostia River and walked him down to the water's edge. They removed his shoes to prevent his escape. There, they sat him on the rock and began to beat and kick him to "teach him a lesson." McMillan attempted to escape, breaking loose and running back up the trail. They caught up to him at the mouth of the trail, and the subsequent struggle resulted in the loss of the pens and other items. The flight and fight continued until one of them finally kicked McMillan in the head, killing him.

This was Trainum's first experience with a media-driven case. He was fortunate in that, being new to homicide investigations, his caseload was manageable and he was not greatly distracted during those first crucial days. His partner picked up a new case the next day, a street shooting witnessed by police officers who made an arrest on the scene. For Trainum, however, the constant need to brief police management, who were desperate to announce to the media that an arrest had been made, began to influence his thought processes.

By sidetracking investigations, organizational traps waste precious time. Detectives know that every homicide has a period during which the likelihood of an arrest is maximized.[2] When that time has past, not only do memories fade, but other cases move to the forefront. Once this happens, detectives typically will not have another opportunity to return to the investigation.

Trainum methodically combed through McMillan's papers, computer records, telephone records, and credit card receipts to develop an accurate picture of his life and associates. He knew that he needed a database to keep track of the voluminous information, but, with none being available within the department, he relied on his memory and index cards. A grainy surveillance camera photo of the white female at the ATM (with most of her face obstructed by a baseball cap), as well as a composite drawing made from descriptions obtained from employees of the Capitol Hill liquor store, were broadcast by the media, bringing a flood of "sightings," all of which required follow-up. Trainum rapidly became overloaded with information and had no support staff available to help him sort through and prioritize leads. More importantly, tip prioritization was based on the specific "profile" developed by Trainum and his coworkers from what few characteristics they could determine from their evaluation of the crime scene.

Although profiles are an important tool in the prioritization of leads and the dedication of resources, several tips were dismissed because they did not fit one aspect or another of the "profile." The investigation shifted away from a methodical review of the facts to a "tip-driven" case, with detectives investigating the lead du jour.

The Suspect

Finally, Detective Trainum received what appeared to be a credible lead from a telephone call in reference to another employee of McMillan's federal agency, identified as Richard Thomas. Thomas lived in a high-rise apartment building near McMillan's parking space. He was slight in build and considered strange by his coworkers. Thomas had several relationships with Russian women. He would bring them from overseas as "brides" and try to help them build careers as models, but eventually they would abandon him to work as escorts in local massage parlors. More to the point, the anonymous caller said that Thomas had a daughter, Susan, who somewhat resembled the girl in the composite.

According to the caller, Susan Thomas was a very disturbed young woman. She was addicted to drugs and had violent tendencies. She had physically attacked her father in the past, and the police had been called on several occasions. Susan was believed to be a prostitute, frequenting the area where

---

[2] The well-known "48-hour rule" is valid; those cases with significant solution potential (e.g., multiple eyewitness and domestic violence murders) tend to be quickly solved.

McMillan parked his car. According to the caller, Susan had several children by different men, but was currently associating with a man with a criminal background known as Buck.

Among the numerous leads and tips collected by detectives, this call stood out as it had detailed information that fit the investigative profile. Here was a woman with a history of prostitution, drug abuse, and violence, who had a connection to the victim. Her physical description roughly matched both the woman in the ATM photograph and the composite drawing. A query of police databases confirmed that Susan and her father had a violent past, and that police had been called to their house several times. Susan had been investigated by a neighboring law enforcement agency for child abuse, and was currently living in a homeless shelter for families with the two children of whom she had custody. Trainum postulated that McMillan's frequent absences from work and his mounting credit card debit were the result of a connection to Richard and Susan Thomas and the Russian models.

There was little else to go on. Although they tried, investigators failed to establish a direct connection between the two men beyond their common employer and the proximity of Thomas's residence to McMillan's parking space. But they intuitively believed they were on the right track. There were a couple of other tips, none with any substance. Pressure from police officials and the media to close the case continued to mount.

The Investigation

The laboratory reports came back on the credit card slips and the American Express card; no fingerprints were found on any of the documents. Despite this news, Detective Trainum knew there was another forensic tool that could potentially link a specific suspect to this crime—handwriting analysis. The same person had signed all three slips. Trainum felt safe in assuming the white female with the baseball cap and glasses seen by the Capitol Hill liquor store employees and the white female in the ATM surveillance photo were the same person. The next step was to collect handwriting samples.

The Metropolitan Police Department does not have an in-house handwriting analysis expert, so Trainum turned to an examiner from another local law enforcement agency, a person previously used by the prosecutor's office. The examiner suggested as many handwriting samples as possible be collected from all known suspects. He assured Trainum that he could help narrow the suspect field through elimination.

Trainum searched for handwriting samples in court and police files for the three suspects. The majority of Susan's samples came from a handwritten statement she had given police in the neighboring jurisdiction concerning the child abuse allegations.

Trainum delivered these samples along with the forged credit card slips to the handwriting examiner. When the examiner finished his analysis, he placed the written material from the first two suspects down on the table, saying they could safely be eliminated. Dramatically, he then put Susan's sample on the table and stated he was almost positive she was the person who had signed the credit card slips. If he had more handwriting samples, taken under controlled conditions, he was confident he could be 100% certain. This was the break Trainum was looking for.

Despite the seemingly definitive results given by the handwriting analysis expert, proving in court that the person who forged McMillan's name was the actual murderer was a different story. So instead of an arrest warrant for murder, prosecutors authorized one for credit card fraud and forgery. They did, however, authorize the issuance of a search warrant for the apartment in the homeless shelter where Susan lived with her two children. The warrant allowed detectives to seize evidence of both credit card fraud and murder. The plan was to arrest Susan and question her about both crimes. Although they did not have a warrant for his arrest, detectives also wanted to bring in her boyfriend, Buck, for questioning. It was believed that by playing them against each other, at least one would break and confess.

The execution of the warrants left Susan shocked and disoriented. She was taken into custody and driven to the homicide office, where she was placed in a monitored interview room to await the arrival of detectives. Her children were removed from the homeless shelter and placed in protective custody. Back at her apartment, detectives seized several items of clothing and personal papers, but nothing was found directly linking Susan to McMillan or his murder.

The Interview

Detective Trainum started off slow and gentle, explaining to Susan that she had been arrested for credit card fraud, summarized the interview process and her rights, and assured her that the police wanted to hear her side of the story and "straighten things out." Meanwhile, Susan protested her innocence and waived her rights. Trainum told Susan about the handwriting expert and how he had identified her as the signer of McMillan's credit card. Susan maintained her innocence, inquired about her children, and asked about the status of her boyfriend Buck, who was being interviewed simultaneously.

The interview then moved on to the murder. Trainum bolstered the strength of the case against her by using the handwriting expert's findings. Susan's claims of innocence reached the point of hysteria. He then showed her the grainy ATM photograph. Susan denied it was her, but admitted the person in the picture looked like she could be her twin sister. When asked to provide additional handwriting samples, Susan first agreed and then quickly became uncooperative, saying, "They are just going to be used against me." Although encouraged by these developments, Trainum ultimately realized he was at an impasse.

As a "tie breaker," Susan agreed to take a voice stress test. The test is similar to a polygraph, but instead of monitoring heart rate, respiration, and other physiological factors, it measures the level of stress in the voice during responses to key questions. The detective who gave the test reported the findings did not indicate Susan was lying, but some abnormality in the results was present. The detective's lieutenant, also a voice stress examiner, disagreed. He stated that the test results indicated deception in her denials of involvement in the credit card use and the murder. It was with this interpretation that investigators decided to confront Susan.

At this point in the interview, due to the results of the handwriting analysis and their own expectations, detectives fell into a confirmation bias by ignoring evidence that failed to fit their theory, and placed undue emphasis on information that did support their theory (Begley, 2005). Furthermore, investigators were inclined to agree with their superior, the lieutenant, who also represented a voice of authority as a certified voice stress examiner. This unwillingness to be the odd voice out in the group is a significant aspect of paramilitary culture—the pressure to conform to group standards and submit to the authority of superiors.

Reenergized by the new evaluation of Susan's voice stress test, detectives conducted a second round of interviews. The new strategy was to first obtain a confession to the credit card forgery. They emphasized the pettiness of the crime and reminded Susan that her voice stress test had indicated deception. Faced with this onslaught, Susan finally confessed to the credit card fraud, but not to the murder. To formalize the proceedings, Susan agreed to have her confession videotaped.

But her confession made little sense. Susan said she used the credit cards after finding them hours before the abduction took place. She incorrectly named the credit cards she was supposed to have used, as well as the stores they were used in. To further impress on her the strength of the evidence, Susan was shown the forged credit card slips to help "refresh" her memory. Later, she was able to tell detectives the names of the stores she "visited," the name of the street they were on, and the approximate amounts of the purchases—but not the specific items she purchased. The detectives failed to notice these inconsistencies as they unintentionally fed her information supporting their theory.

The detectives moved on to the murder. Again, Susan's denials were emphatic. Detectives began to give her "excuses" by vilifying the victim and minimizing her involvement. Susan eventually began to waver, and she admitted to having seen the victim earlier the day of the murder. She said that, although she was seven months pregnant,[3] McMillan had approached her near his office building to solicit her for sex. She said he was persistent to the point that she had to strike him with a stick to get him to leave her alone. Afterward, Susan claimed she was approached by some men who were offended by McMillan's behavior and wanted to teach him a lesson.

This story was full of holes, but detectives continued the interrogation. Susan was shown crime scene photographs and inadvertently provided with other important facts. Although her story became more plausible as the interview progressed, she was still unable to provide simple but key details. Finally, the detectives had enough, and Susan was charged with first-degree murder.

Police culture does not encourage self-examination. Detectives tend to be very protective of their cases, and for one detective to work on or review another's case without specifically being asked constitutes a severe breach of an informal code. Often, a case will stall for years before the lead detective will open it for review by a colleague.

With the benefit of hindsight, investigators who later reviewed the interview transcript have found clear indications that Susan's answers were oriented to what she though the detectives wanted to hear. Furthermore, when Susan was vague, detectives tended to lead her to a specific answer using body language or facial expressions. Her answers were largely guesses, and the interviewing detectives chose to focus on those that matched their theory and ignore those that did not. This is a chilling example of how a person, even when he or she are aware of a cognitive bias, may still be unable to stop the process, mitigate the consequences, or prevent future influences (Amodio et al., 2004).

The Investigation Continues

More handwriting samples were obtained from Susan by court order and sent to the original handwriting expert. He knew Susan had confessed and been charged with McMillan's murder. After comparing the new samples to the forged credit card slips, he stated he was 100% positive Susan Thomas had committed the forgery.

Meanwhile, based on Susan's information, detectives identified a third suspect in the crime, known only as Boo. For days, a surveillance team watched Boo peddle music cassettes on the streets in his neighborhood, while Buck was interviewed again and again. He insisted he could tell the detectives nothing about the murder, but his history of lying and making grandiose statements about his life made the detectives question his truthfulness. Susan continued to vacillate between denial and cooperation. A subsequent

---

[3] None of the witnesses had described the short white female who used the credit cards as pregnant, or even overweight.

polygraph indicated she was deceptive. Susan then reverted to admitting her involvement in McMillan's murder, but she was still unable to provide any of the crucial details that should have been easy to recall.

It was time to move to the next step. During their background check of Boo, investigators learned he had an outstanding warrant for failure to pay child support. As his surveillance was not productive, Detective Trainum decided to arrest Boo on the warrant, and then interrogate him about his and Susan's role in the murder. As he set out to make his sales rounds on the street one morning, Boo was picked up and brought to the homicide office for questioning.

When Trainum entered the room, Boo was obviously distraught, sitting with his face in his hands. Trainum eased into the conversation, talking about how people sometimes get caught up in events and things happen that are not intentional or planned. Boo listened intently, nodding in agreement with everything Trainum said. When the line of questioning finally came around to McMillan's murder, Boo paused and looked at Trainum quizzically. As the meaning of Trainum's words sank in, Boo became visibly distraught, at one point leaping out of his chair, yelling, "What do you mean, what do you mean?!" He maintained he knew nothing of the murder or Susan's arrest. Boo agreed to a polygraph examination and unequivocally passed.

Trainum was now stuck. Susan was now refusing to cooperate, again insisting on her innocence. But, Trainum reminded himself, she had confessed, something that police officers in general believe that innocent people do not do. He reviewed his notes and the interview video again and again, always concentrating on the points that supported her guilt. If she was not involved, how did she know those things?

If Trainum was going to convince his superiors—and himself—that Susan was the murderer, her confession had to be corroborated and any alibi refuted. Trainum prioritized a list of leads to pursue; the first task was to obtain the records from the shelter where she had been living. Maybe these would provide a lead to any unknown associates, or at least corroboration that she was out on the night of the murder.

The shelter was very cooperative, and, armed with a subpoena, Trainum obtained a copy of Susan's entire file. More importantly, he learned that there was a sign-in/sign-out log maintained by the guard at the front desk of the shelter. All residents had to sign the log when they left or entered the building. According to staff, the guards were conscientious about enforcing this rule.

This seemed like an encouraging first step. Trainum was convinced the log book would show Susan was not in the shelter the night of McMillan's murder. As he drove back to his office, he began to glance through the log, getting a feel for how the entries were made. Then he turned to the page corresponding to the date of the murder. As Trainum read the entries, he almost ran the car off the road. In shock, he pulled over so he could confirm what he had just seen.

While Susan had been in and out of the shelter repeatedly that night, she had only been gone for short periods. If the entries were correct, there was no way she could have participated in the murder. Trainum went back over the book again and again. Could any of the signatures have been forgeries? Maybe the logs had somehow been manipulated? After examining them carefully, he concluded they were genuine.

Trainum went straight to the prosecutor's office and showed him his discovery. They both agreed this was a serious problem. Others were brought in to discuss and brainstorm the issue. A time line of Susan's activities in the log was developed, and Trainum attempted to determine the likelihood Susan could have been in and out of the shelter as recorded, yet still have been the woman at the ATM machine, at the Chinese restaurant, and at the Capitol Hill liquor store the night of the murder. Without success he tried to figure out how Susan could have committed the murder during the short time periods she was away from the shelter. As a last effort, the log book was submitted to the original handwriting analyst to determine if Susan's signatures might have been forged that night.

The analyst concluded the signatures were hers. The case against Susan Thomas was in serious trouble.

The Corroboration

Investigative meeting after meeting was held. Experienced detectives and prosecutors were consulted. Efforts to establish Susan's guilt became more and more complex. No one suggested she might actually be innocent. The handwriting expert had confirmed Susan signed the credit card slips and, most important, she had confessed. The axiom that innocent people do not confess was reiterated. Finally, Detective Trainum and the prosecutor agreed that the core of the investigation came down to the accuracy of the original handwriting examination.

Federal law enforcement handwriting experts do not like to review the work of other law enforcement agencies, but when the situation was explained, a handwriting analyst from the Secret Service agreed to look at the case. Trainum took the forged credit card slips and the original samples taken after Susan's arrest to the Secret Service office in Washington, D.C. When the examination was complete, the findings were definitive—Susan Thomas was not the forger of McMillan's signature on the night of his murder.

That was enough for Trainum. The foundation of his case had collapsed. Other members of the department, however, were not so easily convinced. Not only had Susan confessed, but she had provided details that could only have been known by someone involved in the murder. It took another analysis by a handwriting expert from the FBI, who confirmed the findings of the

Secret Service, to convince them that the charges against Susan should be dropped. But many still believed she was guilty.

Several days later, the case of *United States v. Susan Thomas* was dismissed. There was no public explanation as to why, except the government was not willing to go forward with the prosecution at that time. The case had lost momentum. During the months spent on pursuing Susan as a suspect, other leads had gone uninvestigated. And since an arrest had been made, the case was officially "closed" on the books of the Metropolitan Police Department.

Conclusion

For years, the case languished on a shelf. Considered closed by departmental standards, there was no incentive for anyone to continue investigating; reclosing a closed case does not increase a police agency's homicide clearance rate. And in the culture of policing, reviews of such cases to see what may have gone wrong are not encouraged. The case remained assigned to Detective Trainum, who believed Susan did not participate in the actual murder. But somehow she had inside knowledge, perhaps through knowing the actual killers. How else could she have provided the details she did? The shadow of Susan Thomas continued to block the investigation's progress.

More years passed, and DNA exonerations of death penalty inmates brought the issue of false confessions into public light. Homicide cold case reviews became more common, and Detective Trainum himself initiated a program to systematically review the Metropolitan Police Department's cold homicide cases. Such reviews can result in police departments identifying various investigative and procedural shortcomings that were difficult to pinpoint during the case itself. In the McMillan case, this review resulted in Trainum identifying his own mistakes. When fresh eyes reviewed the case, the untrustworthiness of Susan's confession and the problems leading up to it became apparent.

In discussing the case with others, both inside and outside of law enforcement, Trainum is constantly reminded of the power of a confession. Most express sincere disbelief that an innocent person would confess to a crime he or she did not commit. The McMillan homicide investigation highlighted many of the traps awaiting unwary detectives. But it also highlighted the fact that these traps can befall well-meaning investigators who, without malice, believe they were on the right track. Although some might blame the original handwriting examiner for throwing off the investigation,[4] it was the detectives who continued to ignore the exculpatory evidence that was present.

---

[4] In a study of wrongful convictions involving 86 DNA exonerations, forensic science testing errors were found in 63% of the cases and false/misleading testimony by forensic scientists in 27% (Saks & Koehler, 2005).

The individual and institutional biases and pitfalls that can cause an investigation to flounder will always exist. The key is to recognize and acknowledge them. This is the first, but not the last, step toward their prevention. Education, critical case reviews by persons outside the immediate investigation, and videotaping of entire interrogations for review are steps that will mitigate the impact of the cognitive biases that befell the McMillan investigation. But what is perhaps more important is for police agencies to embrace a cultural shift in which personal and institutional egos are suspended, and scientific and logical principles of testing and theory challenging are accepted. Adopting an attitude of open-mindedness in which detectives work as hard to exonerate as to convict will help ensure that investigations are conducted in a professional manner that best leads to the truth.

References

Amodio, D. M., Harmon-Jones, E., Devine, P. G., Curtin, J. J., Hartley, S. L., & Covert, A. E. (2004). Neural signals for the detection of unintentional race bias. *Psychological Science, 15*, 88–93.

Begley, S. (2005, February 4). People believe a 'fact' that fits their views even if it's clearly false. *Science Journal*, p. B1.

Saks, M. J., & Koehler, J. J. (2005). The coming paradigm shift in forensic idendification science. *Science, 309*, 892–895.

What Happened to Theresa Allore?

11

JOHN ALLORE AND
PATRICIA PEARSON

My sister, Theresa Allore (Figure 11.1), disappeared from the campus of a small liberal arts college in the southeastern region of Québec on Friday, November 3, 1978. Five months later, her body was found by the side of the road, less than a mile from the student residence where she lived. Although a medical-legal cause of death was never determined, it is most probable Theresa was strangled.

In the November 3, 1978, issue of the student newspaper, someone published a poem titled "Grace" containing the following lines:

> At evening someone will take a stick
> and destroy all life;
> someone will take a scarf
> to strangle all sound.

Who was the writer? Theresa wore a scarf the night of her disappearance. Was this a message from the murderer?

The questions—tantalizing and once possibly knowable—are now unanswerable. The poem was discovered and brought to my attention in 2006 by an observant librarian and archivist working now at the Champlain College library, the same school Theresa attended 30 years ago. The poem is a curiosity. I suspect it is only a coincidence and has nothing to do with Theresa, but we will never know for sure. What might have been easy to investigate in 1978 (who wrote it and why) is now lost to time. Try finding a former student editor who even remembers their college experience, let alone who submitted a single poem for publication three decades in the past.

The police who originally investigated Theresa's death missed this detail. There were no detectives scouring the pages of newspapers. There was no one exploring creative avenues and possibilities of the criminal mind. You are left dumbfounded and frustrated by the loss of opportunity. If this detail was overlooked, what else was missed?

As it turns out, quite a lot. In the past five years since I began reinvestigating Theresa's death, I have often been left frustrated and angry at the

Figure 11.1 My father, mother, me, my brother, and Theresa, shortly before her death.

amount of information that was overlooked by the original investigators and continues to be ignored by the Sûreté du Québec (Québec's provincial police force), the current investigating agency. After she was found by that roadside, face down in a small creek, investigators led my family to believe that, although the definitive manner of her death was unknown, Theresa probably died from her own negligence. She got drunk and wondered off into the night. Or she had a reaction to the drugs she must have taken and fearful students covered up the overdose. Maybe she came to that place by the side of the road and committed suicide. That Theresa was an adventurous teenager known for taking risks only preyed on my parents' vulnerabilities. Shamed, and coerced into blaming themselves, and with my brother then 18 and myself 14 and still needing their attention, my mother and father accepted the police's suggestions and closed the book on Theresa's death.

So what really happened to Theresa? This was a question that I never really thought about until after I was married and my wife and I celebrated the birth of our first child. Suddenly, the subject of young girls and women, and their place in the world, and how they are perceived and treated in that world began to resonate with me. Central questions in reframing my expectations of society became how exactly did Theresa die, and what conclusions did investigators finally reach at concerning her death?

In 2001 I began to take steps to access Theresa's police file. At that time, I wasn't even sure if the information still existed. If it did exist, I was fairly optimistic the answers to my questions would lie in the file, and I was modest in my expectations of what those answers would reveal. I believed that getting the file from current law enforcement authorities would be a simple task. Overall, I thought the process would take a month at most.

It has now been five years. During that time, with the assistance of some very special and dedicated individuals, we discovered that Theresa did not die of a drug overdose. She was most likely the victim of a serial sexual predator. In the 19-month period surrounding Theresa's murder, two other young women also disappeared and were discovered in a similar manner. Their deaths remain unsolved. In all, we have collected just under 20 incidents of intimidation, harassment, and sexual assault against young women in the area during the same period. Some of these cases are undoubtedly related and intertwined. All of these events occurred within a 100-square-mile area in and around the town of Sherbrooke and the village of Lennoxville, in the Eastern Townships of Québec about 90 miles east of Montréal, between 1977 and 1981.

Our investigative persistence and the efforts of my colleagues have been the subject of much praise. Yet I find nothing really remarkable about the attempts we made to find the truth of Theresa's death. I am not a police officer. I have no formal experience in investigating crimes, let alone violent crimes. Instead, I did what seemed logical. I tried to think like a police officer. Or rather I tried to think according to my idea of how I thought police officers think. It seemed logical to me to analyze the most basic aspects of the crime; reviewing source documents, reinterviewing original witnesses when they could be found, and most important, having a geographic understanding of the places and events that concluded with Theresa lying facedown in a creek in rural Québec. Investigating was handicapped by the fact that I no longer lived in Canada, but now reside 1,000 miles away in Chapel Hill, North Carolina. No matter. It's an electronic age so I used the tools I assumed police officers used—Google, MapQuest, and Internet telephone directories—to pursue the truth.

I enlisted the assistance of an old friend and journalist, Patricia Pearson. Patricia had authored a book on female criminality and had covered the high-profile trials of Paul Bernardo and Karla Homolka, responsible for on the horrific rapes and murders of two teenage girls in St. Catharines, Ontario. I asked Patricia to write an article about Theresa's death. At that time, I still believed in the folklore that Theresa overdosed on drugs and was taken from her dorm room to a creek by the side of the road by panicked friends. As far as the Sûreté du Québec and now my family were concerned, Theresa had been pulled under by the riptide of 1970s party culture. I was hoping publicity would encourage those panicked friends to break their conspiracy of silence and come forward with an account of Theresa's last night.

Patricia and I met in Sherbrooke in March 2002. Our plan was to review Theresa's police file, stored away and gathering dust in the Sherbrooke police office. On the morning of March 15th, I met with Corporal Robert Theoret of the Sûreté du Québec who was cordial and watchful as I pored over sections of Theresa's crime file for seven hours. We later found out that Theoret had removed from the file a list of evidence, photographs of the crime scene, certain witness statements, the final report from Corporal Roch Gaudreault the lead investigating officer in 1979, and all notations about suspects, which remained confidential under Canada's privacy laws.

When I had first written to the Sûreté in the early summer of 2001, they offered me broader access to the file, but this had changed by March 2002 and what I could see was restricted. Perhaps this was just standard procedure or maybe the police were feeling defensive. They certainly weren't worried about compromising their investigation. When asked about potential DNA evidence and a forensic review of the bra and underwear that Theresa was wearing, Theoret informed me the Sûreté du Québec disposed of this evidence five years after her death. I persisted in trying to determine to know the chain of command, authorization procedure, or on whose authority the evidence was destroyed, but to this day the Sûreté du Québec, has never offered a reasonable explanation for why they disposed of evidence in an unsolved crime. By way of apology, Theoret offered the following explanation:

"In cases such as these, we cannot keep things forever—we have limited storage capacity."
"Can you tell me currently what is the status of my sister's case?"
"Currently the file is open—we never close a file; it is an unsolved crime."
I would hear this cop-speak refrain all too often over the coming years.
"Then why not try to solve it?"
"Monsieur Allore, I have a lot of unsolved crimes. Unfortunately, my staff is too busy to work on the case."

I asked Theoret what had been the final conclusion in Corporal Gaudreault's report. Theoret shrugged his shoulders. I asked him if any students or teachers had been suspects in the case. Again a shrug. I asked if he had read the file. He said yes. I asked him what he thought happened. "She was probably picked up, and never made it back to her home. It's a mystery. It's a crime that will never be solved. It happens a lot."

Apart from this excruciating indifference, we had a quandary. While the Sûreté was not inclined to investigate Theresa's death, they still wouldn't divulge their findings from 23 years ago. Without access to key parts of her file, I didn't know where to begin. I was just a guy—an accountant—who lived hundreds of miles away. Patricia was a former crime journalist. We both had small children, jobs, lives.

The following morning Patricia and I drove out to the place where Theresa's body was found. Although the college Theresa attended was in the village of Lennoxville, because of overcrowding many of the students were housed at King's Hall, a residence facility eight miles from the main campus in the tiny rural village of Compton. The creek where she was found is about a mile outside the village, down what was then a gravel road into

Figure 11.2 Chemin de la Station, where Theresa's body was found.

a valley and countryside farming fields. While driving there, it quickly became apparent that Theresa did not walk to this location. The spot is in the middle of nowhere. There is nothing around, just the empty foreboding of bare cornfields and overflowing creek beds made muddy from winter run off (see Figure 11.2).

Patricia asked me why the police believed Theresa had not been sexually assaulted even though she was found wearing only her underwear. I explained that Corporal Gaudreault had told my father there were no visible signs of rape on her body. Also, her underwear had not been ripped or torn and no indications of a struggle were evident. There was an off-ramp next to the road where a farm tractor could enter to plow the field. It was a good spot for a vehicle to stop. If you turned the car lights off, no one would know you were there, no one would know what you were doing. This was the point when I first realized what had really happened. This was the place where I shed 20 years of vague, uninformed speculation and saw for the first time that my sister was murdered. Patricia echoed my thoughts when she took one look at the surroundings and said, "This was a sex crime."

Champlain College is located on the outskirts of Lennoxville beside the older and much statelier Bishop's University from which it rents some of its facilities. Amid the hills of the Eastern Townships and the lush surrounding farmland, the Cégep, founded in 1967, would have been a lovely place to attend one's final years of high school—unless, like my sister, you arrived at the tail end of the 1970s. Over the previous decade, Champlain College's enrollment had risen to over 1,000 students, and officials faced a housing crisis. Plans were under way to build another dormitory, but in the meantime, as a stop-gap measure, two buildings had been hastily leased in the tiny farming village of Compton, eight miles from the school.

The distance of the dorms from the college had already sparked controversy among the students, something I learned from reading *The Touchstone*, Champlain's student newspaper from that period. Students were complaining about the shuttle buses that were their only means of transportation to and from the dorms. If they missed the bus from Lennoxville, they had to pay for an expensive taxicab ride or else hitchhike. The student handbook provided a brief list of hitchhiking "dos and don'ts."

A new residence being built close to campus fell behind schedule, however, and Champlain staff announced in the spring of 1978 that they would have to "run Compton again." Editors at *The Touchstone* were aghast. "I was enraged," one wrote, "by the smug way in which the fates of two hundred more new students were so easily dispatched."

Over half of the students quartered in Compton were under the age of 18. They had two staff members on site, a 25-year-old, Jeanne Eddisford, and a former elementary school principal, Stewart Peacock. Both slept in King's Hall, a rambling Victorian mansion that had once served as a girl's boarding school (see Figure 11.3). Neither inhabited Gillard House, the squat, co-ed brick dormitory next door. No one conducted room checks. The students were encouraged to make their own meals and to be as independent as possible.

It was an optimistic experiment in free living, but what it meant, in essence, was that 240 teenagers were living in an isolated, poorly lit area without adequate transportation or effective supervision. "There is definitely something wrong at Compton," *The Touchstone* editorialized. "Stewart Peacock is very seldom seen at Gillard House, of which he is the newly appointed director."

The result was wholly predictable. "For most boys and girls, it's their first time away from home," one Compton resident told *The Touchstone*. "There are no restrictions, no curfews, and especially no parents. They go wild." Co-ed parties featuring beer, pot, and LSD were so common that the night watchman

Figure 11.3 King's Hall, one of the student residences at Compton.

for the Compton dorms grew fed up. After confronting Peacock about "the drug problem" to no avail, he quit in disgust, according to a statement he later gave to the Sûreté du Québec. Two school officials, Doug MacAuley, director of student services, and Joe Gallagher, assistant director of student services and counseling, abruptly resigned from Champlain around this time. Gallagher said only that his position had become "structurally unsound," making it impossible for him to "accomplish his goals." Gallagher further told *The Touchstone* he hoped the problems he saw on the campus would be solved, and that those in position to act upon them knew what they were.

In addition to the chaos on the college campus, the village of Lennoxville was experiencing its own troubles, troubles that started long before Theresa's death. As early as January 1978, student newspapers reported three separate incidents of sexual and verbal assaults on women. The Lennoxville police force failed to take the situation seriously. When then police chief, Kasimir Kryslak, justified police inaction by arguing that in the five years since he had been police chief there had been only one reported incident of sexual assault, student writers countered that at least eight rapes had occurred in Lennoxville during 1977. Many of the attacks had been quite severe. One female student was dragged to the ground and beaten over the head with a board.

In February 1978, *The Touchstone* continued the story. Women were being molested by a short man in jeans and a green parka. Others described a different short man, one with black hair and a beard. Complaints had been made to police and officials at both Champlain College and Bishop's University. The girls were scared to walk home at night. Many classes didn't end until after dark. Lights that were supposed to illuminate the campus had burnt out. Female students were scared and anxious. The police and the schools did nothing. "Will someone have to get raped," one girl wrote, "before the police stop shrugging off the problem?" Eventually the town of Lennoxville fired Kryslak. His replacement, Leo Hamel, did nothing to improve the situation. He told *The Touchstone*, "everyone [was] making a mountain out of a molehill."

For the remainder of the year, the hysteria quieted down on the college campus. Then, in the fall of 1978, reports of a sexual predator reemerged. In early October 1978, a short man in a ski mask harassed a female student in an empty campus hallway. Two weeks later, on October 30, a student walking to Champlain College at night was confronted by a naked man standing by a tree. "I'm certainly not going to walk after dark anymore. I was scared half to death," she said. Chief Hamel brushed off the incident, commenting that such things were to be expected at a university where so many women congregated. In an editorial dated November 3, 1978—the last day Theresa was seen alive—student writers protested because authorities were not taking the situation seriously.

Friday, November 3, 1978, was gloriously mild for late autumn in the Eastern Townships. Theresa left her room on the second floor of Gillard House early that morning and walked across the lawn in a long, beige sweater-coat, wearing Chinese slippers, no socks and a flowing green scarf that my mother had given her for her 19th birthday (Figure 11.4).

Figure 11.4 Theresa in her dorm room shortly before her death.

She joined her girlfriends, Jo-Anne Laurie and Caroline Greenwood, in the pleasant dining room at King's Hall, where sun streamed through the French doors. Over breakfast, they chatted about their weekend plans. Then the three women boarded the shuttle bus; after reaching the main campus, they parted ways to attend classes.

Theresa was an excellent student, curious, creative, and sharp, making straight As in humanities and statistics. She was not inclined to "go wild." She had already lived away from home for a year, working in a ski factory while she shared an apartment with girlfriends in Pointe Claire, Québec. It was true that Theresa took risks—she hitchhiked. I remember one occasion when Theresa and I took the train to downtown Montréal for a day of shopping. On the way back, Theresa decided to hitchhike. She told me to stand in the bushes while she stood by the expressway with her thumb out. Soon a transport truck stopped. After a moment of talking to the driver, she waved at me to come out of the bushes. But the trucker took one look at me and drove off.

Theresa planned to spend the weekend of November 3rd working on a book report about Zen Buddhism for her psychology class. She declined an invitation to go to her friend Caroline Greenwood's family farm. At supper time, an acquaintance ran into her in the dining hall on the Champlain campus. Theresa borrowed a cigarette, and the girls agreed to meet up later in Gillard House to listen to records.

Theresa missed the 6:15 p.m. shuttle bus. The next one was not due until 11:00 p.m. We don't know what she did next. Did she position herself on the graveled edge of Highway 143, the route back to Compton, and stick out her thumb? Theresa was fearless about hitchhiking, something that always caused my parents much concern.

The last time anyone saw Theresa was 6:15 p.m. Or was it? A friend named Sharon Buzzee gave a statement and swears to this day she saw Theresa on the stairs in King's Hall around 9:00 p.m. the night of November 3, shortly before she planned to head to Gillard House and listen to records. Buzzee's account, although corroborated by others, was never taken seriously by police.

It appears Champlain College faculty failed to notice one of its students missing for close to a week. Theresa's friends began to worry much sooner. When they returned from their respective weekend adventures, they knocked on her door to visit, only to find her absent. None of them were confident enough to raise an alarm. "Theresa didn't need anyone to worry about her," Greenwood later stated. "She always told us not to be her parents," Laurie said. Her friends didn't want to seem nosy or neurotic.

On Friday, November 10th, my brother—who was also a student at the college—overcame his own fear of "checking up on Theresa" and called home. My parents immediately notified the Lennoxville Police, and jumped into their car to drive to the college from their home in St. John, New Brunswick.

The cold month that followed was a scene from any parent's worst nightmare. Offers of help were few. Their experience was similar to far too many other families whose missing children are neither famous nor young enough to generate wide sympathetic attention. During the winter, no one organized a search of the farmland and woods surrounding Compton where Theresa's body lay through the winter, a mile and a half from Gillard House. My father knocked on doors, a desperate, frantic man, asking everyone everywhere, in shops and houses and farms and rectories throughout the Eastern Townships, if they had seen his daughter. People merely shook their heads and shrugged.

The police were reluctant to expend much effort looking for what they thought was a teenage runaway who had hitchhiked from Lennoxville to points unknown. Lennoxville Police Chief Leo Hamel did show a picture of Theresa to U.S. immigration officers in Vermont. He also checked with her old roommates in Montréal and took statements from students in Compton. But he didn't search the college grounds.

My mother recalls that he was compassionate, but thought he might be somewhat out of his depth. Corporal Roch Gaudreault of the Sûreté told my father there was little they could do now, and that Theresa's body would probably turn up when the snow melted. The comment, my father said later, was like "a nail between the eyes."

Figure 11.5 Private Detective Robert Beullac.

Campus Director Dr. Bill Matson suggested to my family that Theresa may have had problems. "Dr. Matson," my father wrote in notes he made at the time, "gave me the theory that Theresa may have had lesbian tendencies." He said Theresa, if found, would need psychiatric treatment, by court order if necessary. He asked us if Theresa was an adopted child. Leo Hamel asked the same question. He said he'd received information that Theresa may have gone somewhere where disturbed people go and advised us to return to New Brunswick and wait for something to happen. Instead, my parents hired a private detective.

Robert Beullac of the Bureau D'Investigation Metropol arrived at Champlain in late November and immediately searched for physical evidence at Gillard and King's Hall (Figure 11.5). He noted that Theresa's purse was still in her room, as were her hiking boots, which she invariably took with her when she left the village overnight. He uncovered the fact that Sharon Buzzee had seen Theresa at King's Hall, thus unraveling Dr. Matson's theory that she had hitchhiked off into the wild-blue yonder to pursue her lesbian tendencies with disturbed people.

Both Dr. Matson and Chief Hamel suggested Buzzee's statement wasn't credible, something she told me in 2002. Hamel had already speculated in the local press that Theresa may have headed off to Vermont, and in December, one month after she disappeared, he began to speculate that she had been involved in drugs. Sherbrooke was rife with drug dealers at that time. But it took a gargantuan leap in logic to conclude that a studious girl who'd arrived in the area just six weeks earlier had been killed by a drug associate.

Why were police thinking this way? Was it a function of the times to implicate a young woman in her own disappearance? Or were other factors at play?

Interestingly, earlier in the year of Theresa's disappearance, a young man was found dead on a golf course, having apparently been there for several months after wandering off drunk from the Bishop's University pub. Corporal Gaudreault and his partner Real Chateauneuf concluded it was impossible to determine the cause of death, and decided he must have died of exposure. But stories persist to this day that young Jacques Turcotte was murdered.

Private investigator Beullac determined that on November 3, 1978, two Gillard House students were taken to the hospital after imbibing an intoxicating blend of LSD and alcohol. One was found face down on the lawn after midnight and ferried to Sherbrooke by the disgruntled night watchman.

Student alcohol and drug use, the series of sexual assaults, the shuttle controversy, a housing crisis, rumored affairs between teachers and students—one would be naive to think that Champlain was not concerned about its reputation. In the summer of 2002, the Director General of Champlain College, Gerald Cutting, who was head of student services in 1978, wrote me claiming the college had done all it could in the search for my sister.

Perhaps it had, but Suzanne DeRome, who was on the College Board, recalls the disappearance and death of Theresa Allore was not discussed during board meetings, and a subsequent review of the minutes bears this out. Sharon Buzzee remained unaware that Theresa was dead until someone mentioned it to her in the 1990s. And a man who taught at Champlain was shocked to learn only in 2002 that a student had died during his years there.

No one from Champlain sent my parents a note of condolence. There were no candlelight vigils and no posters. It was almost as though Theresa had never existed.

Police knew that on the night Theresa disappeared some students at Gillard House had taken LSD. What if they'd invited Theresa to join them? What if she suffered from an allergic reaction or the acid had been laced with a toxin? What if she had overdosed? Would the students have panicked and hidden her body, terrified of being caught?

But it was all speculation. Theresa liked testing her limits. But she wasn't the type to get drunk or party hard. In a statement to the Sûreté du Québec, her friend Jo-Anne Laurie said that Theresa occasionally smoked marijuana, but wasn't into drugs. Other students echoed this view. The students who had done LSD insisted they hadn't even seen her the night she disappeared.

Still, you never know about these things. What if Theresa had yielded to a sudden impulse and dropped acid that night? The possibility wormed its way into my parents' minds.

Parents who had grown up in the 1940s and 1950s were faced with an alien landscape of sex and drugs and rock 'n' roll. My parent's fears were reinforced by things the Champlain College officials suggested: "Kids today. Deviant. Lesbian. Into drugs. You never knew." Or did you?

Christmas came and went with no news of Theresa. Officials at the college, it appeared, had a hard time coping with the disappearance. In January, Stewart Peacock, the director of residence where Theresa lived, quietly resigned, citing personal reasons. Peacock promptly disappeared. He has never been interviewed by police in this matter. His replacement, Jeanne Eddisford, later told me she felt overwhelmed and alone in her job that winter, responsible for 240 anxious adolescents worried about the missing student. In January, she called in the Lennoxville Police and a number of students were arrested for possession of marijuana. At the same time, King's Hall was shut down and all the students, including my brother Andre, were herded over to the dorm where Theresa had lived. Rumors ran wild.

On Valentine's Day 1979, my parents and I were having dinner around our dining table in our house in St. John, New Brunswick. My parents had bought a big Victorian home for large family gatherings. Now it felt empty and silent. Then a piece of plaster suddenly loosened itself from the ceiling. It fell to the side of the table in the shape of a heart. I remember at that moment how I knew Theresa wasn't missing. She was dead.

My sister's body was found at 10:00 a.m. on Friday, April 13, 1979—Good Friday—by a muskrat trapper named Robert Ride. Ride parked his pickup truck along a steep embankment just outside the village of Compton. He was setting his wire traps in the mud along the edge of a pond when he saw something tangled in the underbrush that he later described as looking like a mannequin. As he got closer, he realized it was the body of a woman, face down in the water at the pond's edge (Figure 11.6). The skin was gray, the hair matted. She was naked except for a bra and panties.

Roch Gaudreault and Jacques Lessard arrived at the scene just after 11:00 a.m. The coroner, Michel Durand, and a mobile crime unit were there soon after. By noon the area was crowded with investigators and news photographers. Detectives broke into teams and began to search the area. In a green garbage bag, by the ditch at the entrance to a farmhouse, they discovered some women's clothing, including a pink sweater (see Figure 11.7). In the cornfield they found two pieces of a green scarf, the same scarf given to Theresa by my mother. It had been torn in two pieces, separated by a distance of approximately 50 feet.

Corporal Gaudreault examined the body. It was lying face down in 8 to 10 inches of water. There was a watch on the left wrist, a ring on the left

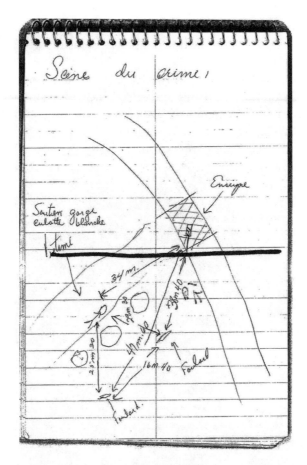

Figure 11.6 Police sketch of the Allore body recovery site.

forefinger, and earrings on both ears. Gaudreault observed what appeared to be strangulation marks around the neck. This observation is documented in the coroner's report, but was later omitted from the police case file.

On Saturday, April 14, 1979, my sister's body was taken to the chief coroner's office, the Laboratoire de medicine legale, in Montréal. Theresa's former roommate from Point Claire, Joey Nice, was brought to the lab to see if she could make a positive identification of the body. She was unable to determine whether or not the body was Theresa's. Later, Corporal Gaudreault showed Nice the green garbage bag of clothing that was found at the crime scene, but she stated the women's clothing did not belong to Theresa.

My family arrived at the medical lab at 11:30 a.m. My father was taken into the medical lab where Theresa's body lay on a stainless steel table. He noticed a scar on the forehead, similar to one where he accidentally struck Theresa with a snow shovel when she was a little girl. My father was not able

Figure 11.7 Investigators Roch Gaudreault and Jacques Quirion search through the bag of clothing found at the crime scene. (Photograph courtesy of Allo Police/Photo Police [1979]. With permission.)

to identify Theresa. He was then asked to authorize a dental analysis, a procedure that requires the removal of the lower jaw by cutting away the entire oral cavity. My father authorized the request. He was never the same man again.

Later that afternoon Corporal Gaudreault, Coroner Durand, and my father met to discuss the case. Gaudreault assured my father that, despite the decomposition, the autopsy would determine what happened to Theresa. But Gaudreault was already leaning toward a possible suicide, perhaps a drowning, or a drug overdose. Durand mentioned the bruises under the armpits. What had caused those? While Gaudreault gave no explanation, he doubted

Theresa was the victim of a sexual predator. Neither Gaudreault nor Durand ever mentioned the strangulation marks observed on Theresa. The first time my father heard of them was when I showed him the coroner's report in 2002. The police officers concluded the matter could be quickly resolved if intoxicating levels of alcohol or drugs were found in her system. Gaudreault told my father the worst was over.

Twenty-three years later, I was living in North Carolina and employed as treasury manager for the city of Durham. I was communicating with Patricia Pearson in Toronto; we were both working to get to the bottom of Theresa's death. Patricia contacted Dr. Kim Rossmo, who was then Director of Research for the Police Foundation, a nonprofit think tank in Washington, D.C. Originally a beat cop from the Vancouver Police Department in British Columbia, Rossmo earned his doctorate in criminology from Simon Fraser University by pioneering a technique called geographic profiling. This is a criminal investigative technique that analyzes crime locations to determine where a serial offender most likely lives. Geographic profiling, and the associated *Rigel* software Rossmo helped develop are now used by the Royal Canadian Mounted Police, Scotland Yard, the Bureau of Alcohol, Tobacco, Firearms and Explosives, and dozens of other law enforcement agencies around the world.

Rossmo became famous in Canada for arguing in 1998 that a serial killer was behind the disappearances of dozens of prostitutes from Vancouver's Skid Row long before his superiors conceded those vanishings were linked. This eventually became known as the Pig Farm case, for which Robert "Willie" Pickton was convicted in 2007. Maybe Rossmo could provide some insight into Theresa's death. So Patricia described to Rossmo what had happened to my sister, how she had been found, and the police theory of her death—a drug overdose followed by her body disposal by panicked friends.

Rossmo responded flatly, "That theory doesn't make sense."

"Why not?"

"Because she was left with only her bra and panties."

"But the pathologist didn't find any evidence of rape."

"That doesn't necessarily mean anything. The absence of such evidence is not uncommon with a decomposed body.[1] The killer also might have used a condom. Or maybe he had a sexual dysfunction and couldn't engage in normal intercourse."

If Theresa Allore was murdered, a key question is "Where?" How could Theresa have overdosed or been killed in her student residence without anybody noticing? How could someone have carried her body to a car without being seen? There were students milling about everywhere that evening, and a night watchman was outside.

---

[1] The loss of soft body tissue and fluids through decomposition or animal activity can make it difficult to determine if a sexual assault has taken place.

Around this time I received a package from my father. I had asked him to send any newspaper clippings he had collected from 1978. The package contained several yellowed news accounts of Theresa's disappearance and death. The stories were in English and French. Many of the English accounts I'd already read, but I had ignored the French ones because my command of the language was limited. But gradually that changed. My many dealings with Québec officials had forced me to learn French. In an article published April 14, 1978, in the French language newspaper, *La Tribune*, I read the following paragraph:

> With the discovery of the body of the young girl on Good Friday yesterday, this marks the second consecutive experience that SQ agents have had to deal with. On March 24, 1979—Good Friday—Children found the body of Manon Dubé of Sherbrooke. The cause of her death is still unknown, and the case is still open. Another coincidence; both victims, as it is evident with Theresa Allore, went missing on a Friday night, and they were both found partially submerged in water.

Armed with this information, I called Bob Beullac, the detective my father hired in 1978 to help find Theresa. Bob was still in the business of sleuthing, although now only working part time. I wanted to see if he recalled anything about a young girl being found in the Sherbrooke area just seven months before Theresa disappeared.

I asked Bob for his recollection of how Theresa died. He stated that there were two theories: the first was she had been killed by a sexual predator, and the second was she had died of a drug overdose while partying and her body was then dumped off campus by other students. He said the second theory gradually became more compelling, in part because the autopsy revealed small amounts of vomit in her throat. However, because he was not the investigating officer, he was never given all the information. Most of what he learned came from my father or police contacts. In retrospect, he believed the second theory implausible because of the amount of effort needed to remove a body from a residence. If she had died in a room, the simplest thing to do would have been to just leave and close the door.

I next asked Bob if he recalled the case of Manon Dubé, a girl who died around the same time and under similar circumstances as Theresa:

"Oh, you mean Camirand."

"No, I mean Dubé."

"No, her name was Camirand. I'm looking at the article right here. Do you want me to send it to you?"

Minutes later I received his fax. The article was from a French tabloid, *Allo Police,* and it discussed the discovery of my sister's body. Then in the final paragraph: "For SQ agents of Sherbrooke, this recalls the violent death of another young girl, Louise Camirand, 20 years old, found dead on March

25th, 1977 in Austin near Magog. Everything indicates that Theresa Allore was also the victim of a sadistic murder."

So now there were three possible murders: (1) Louise Camirand, found on March 25, 1977; (2) Manon Dubé, found on Good Friday, March 24, 1978; and (3) my sister, also found on a Good Friday—but also a Friday the 13th—in April 1979. According to newspaper accounts, all three women died under similar circumstances, and all three were found in the Eastern Townships in less than a two-year span.

Who were Manon Dubé and Louise Camirand and had their deaths ever been solved? These questions turned out to be perplexing mysteries. I found that people from the area simply had never heard of the two young women. This was not surprising—most residents of the Eastern Townships had also forgotten about Theresa Allore. Both newspaper stories referenced one of the other two deaths—La Tribune, the similarities between Allore and Dubé, and Allo Police, the connections between Allore and Camirand. The articles also stated detectives were investigating the similarities. If the connections had panned out, surely police would have said something. Everyone would have remembered the existence of a serial killer. But serial killers were the product of overripe imaginations. They did not roam the tranquil landscape of rural Québec.

Manon Dubé

During the evening of Friday, January 27, 1978, 10-year-old Manon Dubé was playing with her friends (Figure 11.8). They decided to go sledding on the snow banks behind the parking lot of the local Caisse Populaire Bank. This was close to Manon's home, only three blocks from where her mother was waiting for her in their first-floor apartment on rue Bienville in the southeast end of Sherbrooke. Around 7:30 p.m., as it got dark, the children decided to head home. From the Caisse Populaire on the corner of Belvedere and Union, the young girls crossed the street and proceeded to walk east on rue Union, passing in front of St. Joseph's Elementary School. At the corner of Union and Craig, one block from Manon's home, they stopped. Manon's younger sister, Chantel, decided it was too cold to walk and ran ahead. This corner is the last place Manon was seen alive. She never arrived home; she simply disappeared.

When Manon Dubé was reported missing by her mother, police acted swiftly. They immediately put out a bulletin on the wire with her picture. Police hit the streets with a 16-officer search team and combed a nearby wooded area with two tracking dogs. An additional 13-officer party conducted a house-to-house search along rue Bienville. They failed to find anyone who saw the missing girl. Manon's sister, Chantel, told police someone in a dark Buick had been following her and her cousin during the prior week. Other

Figure 11.8 Manon Dubé.

parents mentioned that strangers had approached their children on the street in recent months.

Less than a week into the disappearance, investigators got what appeared to be a break. Manon's mother received a telephone call demanding $25,000 for the safe return of her daughter. Mrs. Dubé told police that on three separate occasions since Manon went missing, her telephone rang, but when she answered it, the person on the other end hung up. Mrs. Dubé was a recent widow who, upon the death of her husband, received approximately $20,000 from his insurance. Perhaps someone was aware of this money and kidnapped Manon in order to collect it.

The following day police announced the ransom call was most likely a hoax. The Dubé's telephone number had been broadcast on a local radio station. Someone probably called up Mrs. Dubé as a sick joke. Hope turned to despair. Mrs. Dubé prepared for the worst: "I can't help but think she has been abducted, attacked, or raped. I pray to God this hasn't happened."

The police widened their search parameters and began to look in the surrounding Eastern Townships countryside. Locals on snowmobiles volunteered to search the area farmlands. Clairvoyants from the region were consulted in hopes of locating Manon. Finally, on the evening of Friday, March 24th, two young boys found Manon's partially frozen body face down

Figure 11.9 Location where Manon Dubé's body was found. (Photograph courtesy of Allo Police/Photo Police [2001]. With permission.)

in a brook near Ayer's Cliff, 30 miles south of her Sherbrooke home (see Figure 11.9).

Investigators from both the Sherbrooke Municipal Police and the Sûreté du Québec's Coaticook Detachment, including Corporal Roch Gaudreault, arrived on the scene shortly after dark. Dubé's body was locked in two inches of ice and had to be carefully removed with a hatchet. On first view, there were no signs of violence or molestation. She was found, as she was last seen, wearing her snowsuit and boots. The only thing missing was one red mitten. There was a small gash on her forehead but this was initially thought to have been caused by the effects of the frozen ice. Because of the condition of the body, investigators speculated that Manon was moved to this location shortly after her disappearance.

An autopsy was performed, but the pathologist was unable to determine the exact cause of death. Some investigators speculated that perhaps Manon was the victim of a hit-and-run accident and the cut on her head was caused by an automobile fender. Still others wondered if she had simply frozen to death. Most agreed that sexual molestation—although possible—was unlikely. She was found with her clothes on; the assumption was made that if she had been raped, she would have been found undressed.

For 23 years the case remained dormant. Then, in 2001, the sister of Manon, Chantel Dubé, asked Sherbrooke police to look at it one more time. They agreed and a new investigation was launched, subjecting the 23-year-old case to the scrutiny of modern forensic techniques. Many members of the original investigation team were still alive and willing to assist. Unfortunately—and inexplicably—most of the evidence from the case had been destroyed. The team had a modern crime lab at their disposal, but they had nothing to analyze. All that remained were some particles taken from the gash on Manon's head. It turned out that whatever caused the cut was metallic, either a car bumper or a blunt instrument. The sample was tested, but the results were inconclusive, and the source could not be determined.

With little new evidence, the investigation team shifted their focus from "how Manon died" to "why Manon died." The possibility that a relative accidentally killed the girl was considered. It turned out that the brook where Manon was found is on land owned by the Dubé family in 1978. The property is a small lot, and back then had a one-story cottage situated about 100 feet from the brook. Detectives speculated that maybe Manon was accidentally hit by someone she knew, and that the grieving relative panicked and brought her body to the brook. Another theory was that she was, in fact, kidnapped—a relative who was aware of the insurance money abducted Manon in hopes of collecting a ransom. Somewhere along the way the kidnapping went wrong, and the young girl died.

In all of their conjecturing, investigators from both 1978 and 2001 never seriously considered the possibility that Manon Dubé had been abducted for the purposes of sexual molestation. In 1978, *Allo Police* ran the headline: "Manon 10 ans, a-t-elle ete Victime d'un Maniaque?" In 2001, their by-line read: "Victime D'un Pedophile?" Despite accusations of sensationalism both then and now, *Allo Police* was being more than salacious. The paper offered a serious theory worthy of consideration given the circumstances under which the young girl disappeared and how and where her body was found.

The official police position, however, was that this was the least probable motive. When I spoke to Patrick Vuillemin, a member of the new investigative team looking at Dubé's death, he said he seriously doubted Manon had been the victim of a sexual predator; there were no overt signs of a struggle he believed would be associated with sexual violence. Shortly thereafter, Vuillemin, faced with mounting pressures and responsibilities, was forced to close the 2001 investigation into the 1978 case. The determination was, again, inconclusive. But investigators would eventually pay a price for their shortsightedness.

Louise Camirand

If the cause of death of Theresa Allore and Manon Dubé was inconclusive, there was never any doubt about the murder of Louise Camirand. Camirand was found on a back road with a ligature around her neck (see Figure 11.10). She had been raped and mutilated. It was one of the worst acts of violence the Eastern Townships had ever experienced. Unlike Dubé and Allore—whose bodies were found months after they had disappeared—Camirand was found within two days of her murder, and the pathologist had no difficulty in determining her cause of death.

Friday, March 25, 1977, was a cold but clear morning. Friends Robert Curtis and Florent Henri were intending to spend the day chopping firewood.

Figure 11.10 Louise Camirand's body in the snow. (Photograph courtesy of Allo Police/Photo Police [1977]. With permission.)

The two men drove their tractor along R.R. 2, also known as chemin des Peres, which overlooks the shores of beautiful Lake Memphremagog, just under 18 miles from Sherbrooke, Québec. The friends turned their tractor onto chemin Giguere and headed into the backcountry. At chemin McDonald they turned again and headed even farther into the forest. About 135 feet into the woods they noticed something lying in the snow to the side of the road. Curtis descended from the tractor and moved in to take a closer look. There he found a body lying frozen in the snow bank. When he removed the jacket covering the body, he saw a young nude woman lying face down in the snow.

Investigators from the Sûreté du Québec arrived soon thereafter. The victim had a bootlace wrapped around her neck, a black leather glove on her left hand, and an engagement ring on her right hand. Nearby they found a pile of clothing—a pair of dark pants, a winter coat with a fur collar, a pair of light blue stockings, and a scarf. The woman's boots and underpants were not recovered.

On the evening news that night, Mr. and Mrs. Gilles Camirand of Sherbrooke, Québec, saw a news bulletin about the body of a young girl found near Austin, Québec. Immediately they knew it was their 20-year-old daughter, Louise, missing since Wednesday evening, March 23rd. On Saturday afternoon Mr. Camirand traveled to Montréal and positively identified the body as that of his daughter. This was a horrendous shock. Louise was a good girl. She lived on her own, but stayed in close contact with her family. She was engaged to be married in the spring.

Louise Camirand was independent. After dropping out of school, she worked as a dentist's secretary, a lawyer's assistant, and finally as a part-time archivist at the local hospital. This hospital was located three blocks from the apartment she kept on Bryant Street in Sherbrooke. Louise was also a military cadet. Most evenings were spent at the downtown armory on King Street and Belvedere, home to the Sherbrooke Hussars. On Wednesday, March 23, 1977, Louise planned to meet her fiancé, Daniel Braun, at the armory (see Figure 11.11). Around 9:30 p.m., Louise left her apartment to buy cigarettes. She walked south on Bryant to King Street and proceeded two blocks west to the Provi-Soir on the corner of Jacques Cartier. The storekeeper remembered that, after she purchased some cigarettes and milk, Louise lingered at the newspaper rack flipping through magazines. It appeared she was waiting for someone. Suddenly, she left the store, crossed the street, and stood at the corner for a short time. The storekeeper was the last person to see Louise Camirand alive.

When Camirand failed to show up at the armory, Daniel Braum became worried. He immediately called her apartment, first at 10:30 p.m. and again at 1:15 a.m., but there was no answer. Shortly thereafter, Braun had a friend drive him to Louise's apartment where he found the place much as he had left it that afternoon, except that now there was a pack of cigarettes on the counter. Braun also noticed that Louise's purse and boots were missing. Her glasses were left on the kitchen counter.

The next day Braun told Louise's parents she was missing. He and her father filed a missing persons report with the Sherbrooke Police Department. Tragically, at the same time they filed the report, investigators were looking at Camirand's body in the woods.

The results of the autopsy report were gruesome. Camirand had been violently raped. After the sexual assault, the assailant—or assailants—strangled her to death using a 35-inch lace that appeared to be from a military boot. But that wasn't all. Camirand had suffered massive internal hemorrhaging. Someone had inserted an object into her vagina and mutilated her reproductive

Figure 11.11 Louise Camirand and her fiancé.

tract, liver, and intestines—they literally gutted her internal organs. Speculation was that a car jack was used. Investigators and medical experts believed Louise suffered these indignities before she was dumped 20 miles from Sherbrooke in the woods off chemin Guigere.

Once again, the police investigation was under the direction of Corporal Roch Gaudreault. But in this instance, because of the severity of the crime, the Montréal Bureau des Enquette Criminelles provided assistance. Over a six-month period, detectives interviewed 250 people that may have been associated with the crime. They found nothing. From tracks in the snow, investigators determined the type of vehicle that transported Camirand to the body dump location. Police searched in vain for a vehicle with a 44-inch wheel track, such as a Renault 5, Austin Mini, or Toyota Celica. Gradually, the case lost momentum; by the end of 1977, Louise Camirand became a statistic, one of 52 unsolved murders in the province that year and still unsolved to this day.

Louise Camirand. Manon Dubé. Theresa Allore. One brutal murder and two suspicious deaths. All three frequented the town of Sherbrooke and its southern suburbs. All three were dumped within a 20-mile radius south of Sherbrooke. A cluster of three unresolved female deaths in a region of 90,000 people[2] in just over 19 months was highly unusual.

The idea of linking Camirand, Dubé, and Allore had begun as a process of exclusion. But in trying to find reasons that would prove there was *not* a connection between the three young women, it was becoming increasingly difficult to eliminate any of them from the picture. The fact that Camirand was so brutally murdered, while Allore and Dubé showed little signs of violence, was reason enough for most Québec investigators to dismiss a link between the three deaths.

But Patricia Pearson and I had the assistance of the criminologist Kim Rossmo. It was Rossmo who introduced us to a behavioral theory called "the least-effort principle." The theory suggests that—contrary to the popular opinion that serial killers are lone drifters, floating randomly from crime to crime—offenders, in reality, tend to commit crimes within a comfort zone located near, but not too close, to their residence. Geoprofiling involves the use of mathematical equations to locate serial offenders. Rossmo theory's offered law enforcement a proposition; if detectives could provide at least five incidents linked to the same perpetrator, the algorithm could reduce the search area for the criminal's residence by more than 90%.

When Rossmo was informed about the two additional cases, his answer was immediate. Yes, Dubé could have been sexually assaulted. Her snowsuit didn't

---

[2] This was only 1.5% of the Québec population at the time. As there were fewer than 10 unsolved female homicides in the province outside of the major urban areas of Montréal and Québec City, this region had 10 times the female homicide risk rate as the rest of the province (if you accept that Allore and Dubé were murdered).

need to be removed for someone to have committed a sex act. Or her body could have been redressed. Rossmo also had a response to the police theory that Dubé was the victim of a hit-and-run. While good investigators followed the least-effort principle, what Québec police seemed to be using was the most-effort principle. "The operative word in a hit-and-run is *run*," said Rossmo. "You do not stop, gather up a body, put it in your vehicle where it will leave trace evidence, drive 20 miles, drag it through the snow, and dump it into a brook." Rossmo wanted more information. He asked for a map detailing the residences, workplaces, places last seen, and body dump sites for all victims. With this information—assuming the crimes were connected—he hoped to produce a geographic profile showing where the offender lived during the late 1970s.

Like the rest of us, Louise Camirand, Manon Dubé, and Theresa Allore had their habits and routine activities. They tended to regularly frequent the same places. Camirand's apartment and workplace were within three blocks of each other in Sherbrooke. The armory where she attended cadet meetings was on the main boulevard, a straight shot, a mile-and-a-half bus ride from her apartment.

Manon Dubé may have only been 10 years old, but at four feet nine inches, she was quite tall for her age. She might have looked like a teenager to a passing motorist in the dark. Dubé's circle of activity was even smaller than that of Camirand's. Dubé rarely traveled outside a three-block radius from her home, an area that encompassed her school and the parking lot of the Caisse Populaire Bank on rue Belvedere where she last played. This lot was less than a mile south of the armory visited by Camirand.

Theresa Allore frequented the 12-mile corridor between Compton, where she lived, and Lennoxville, where she attended school. Where she was last seen—King's Hall or the College dining room—depends on whose story you believe. But whatever story you accept, this much is certain: Theresa Allore missed the bus the night she disappeared. Under either scenario, she would have been forced to hitchhike back to her residence.

Students who hitchhiked from Lennoxville to Compton in 1978 usually stood at the corner of chemin Bel-Horizon[3] and route 143, where the Lion Pub, a popular student watering hole, stood (see Figure 11.12). Chemin Bel-Horizon runs east-west. Traveling east on Bel-Horizon takes you back into Sherbrooke. In fact, traveling less than two miles east on Bel-Horizon takes you back to rue Belvedere. From there it is a little over a mile to the Caisse Populaire Bank, and just under a mile from there to the Sherbrooke armory. The Lion Pub to the Caisse Populaire Bank to the armory; Allore to Dubé to Camirand—all within a four-mile stretch with only one turn.

---

[3] Bel-Horizon is more commonly known as Belvedere; there are actually two streets in Sherbrooke named Belvedere, and they intersect. To avoid confusion, I refer to the east-west Belvedere as Bel-Horizon.

Figure 11.12 The Lion Pub, at the corner of rue Belvedere and route 143.

There was a further point of reference. My sister's red wallet was found discarded by the side of the road on the outskirts of Sherbrooke on chemin MacDonald (see Figure 11.13). But chemin MacDonald is actually an extension of rue Belvedere. If you follow Belvedere south for a mile from the downtown armory you reach the Caisse Populaire Bank. One more mile and you are at Bel-Horizon where a left turn takes you to route 143 and the Lion Pub. If you carry on straight, heading south, Belvedere becomes MacDonald. A little further and you arrive at the location where Theresa's wallet was found.

If you follow chemin Macdonald to its end, you run into route 143. Turn left (north) and within two miles you are back at the corner of rue Bel-Horizon and route 143—the location where Theresa Allore hitchhiked by the Lion Pub.

While checking the geography of the crimes, I contacted the man who found Theresa's wallet in the spring of 1979. He told me that on October 3, 1978—one month prior to Theresa's disappearance—his daughter had also been attacked. She was an 18-year-old student at the local French-language Cégep, a petite brunette with dark eyes like the other victims. She was walking her dog along chemin MacDonald when a man suddenly stopped his car across the road and just behind her. He jumped out and began running toward her on a diagonal across the two-lane black-top.

Instantly, she understood she was in danger. She had been heckled before by cruising men: "Baby, baby. Wanna party?" But this was something else. She was terrified and ran into the family apple orchard, thinking, "I can outwit him, I know the area better, I've got my dog." The man followed, chasing her through the shadows. She felt as if she'd fallen out of her life and into a horror movie.

In a remarkable stroke of good fortune, a police car came down the steep hilly road. The officers from the Coaticook Detachment of the Sûreté

Figure 11.13 Guardrail near where Theresa's wallet was found.

du Québec saw the man and grasped at once that his behavior was alarming, even though they didn't see his intended victim. They leapt out of their cruiser and stopped him. His intended victim was so terrified she remained hidden in the orchard.

The next morning, her mother coaxed her into phoning the police to describe what had happened. The officers told her they had run a check on the man. He had convictions for sex offences in Manitoba. As no crime had taken place, they had let him go. All she can remember about him now is that he was small—a small man with a prior sex conviction and an appetite for predation.

So now there were five geographic points of reference.

Heading into Sherbrooke from rue McDonald, first the red wallet—thrown out the window on the left shoulder—then past the site of the attack in by the apple orchard. Travel a mile to Bel-Horizon (turn right and you come to the Lion). Go another mile and you are at the Caisse Populaire. Finally, proceed just under a mile to the armory. Five locations, all within three miles of each other, and all located on the main artery of rue Belvedere.

Where the young women's bodies were discovered is as equally telling as the locations from which they had disappeared. The three dump sites ranged 10 to 20 miles south of the area frequented by the victims in Sherbrooke.

Theresa Allore's body was found on chemin de la Station, only a mile from the village of Compton and 10 miles from Lennoxville/Sherbrooke. The easiest way to get to this location from Lennoxville is to follow the route that the Champlain bus service would have traveled: take route 143 from the corner of Bel-Horizon, go south one mile, and then turn left on route 147 and head out to Compton.

Manon Dubé was found off chemin Brook. The road is located outside the tiny village of Massawippi, approximately 13 miles south of Sherbrooke. To get to chemin Brook from the Caisse Populaire, you follow Belvedere (which turns into chemin MacDonald) until it intersects with route 143. If you turn right on 143 and head south for 10 miles you reach Massawippi.

Allore's body was dumped off of route 147, Dubé's off of route 143. The two sites are separated east-west by a distance of five miles. And there is a connecter; outside Massawippi you can get on route 208, which takes you directly to Compton.

Camirand's body was dumped outside the village of Austin, 20 miles southeast of Sherbrooke. This was the longest distance in the three cases. The path from where Camirand disappeared to where her body was found is direct. King Street heading east out of Sherbrooke from the armory and the bus stop turns into route 112. This route eventually bends southeast, and after 15 miles crosses chemin des Peres, the same road along which Robert Curtis and Florent Henri had been driving their tractor the morning they found Camirand's body.

All three dump sites spread out to the south from the central area of Sherbrooke/Lennoxville. Moving left to right (west to east), first there is the Camirand body dump site near Austin, then five miles farther (although not directly) there is the Dubé body dump site near Massawippi, and finally, after another five miles (this time directly), the Allore body dump site near Compton.

Eighteen months after Camirand's murder, and two days after Theresa Allore disappeared, two hunters walking through a forest near Memphremagog came across a pair of woman's slacks and a shirt, resting on a log. When Theresa was reported missing some days later, the men called Detective Leo Hamel, who investigated. The clothes were no longer there.

The area where the hunters had seen the women's slacks and shirt was just off Rue Giguare, within a quarter mile from Camirand's dump site. If this was Theresa's clothing, the proximity to Camirand's body dump site strongly suggests a link between the two murders. When confronted with this information, Leo Hamel explained that at the time of Theresa's disappearance he was looking for a runaway. He did not make a connection with the Camirand murder; he did not even know that a young girl's body was found in the same area.

Corporal Roch Gaudreault's actions—or inactions—are hard to understand. When he took over the investigation of Theresa Allore's death in the spring of 1979, he had Hamel's report about the clothing. Furthermore, Gaudreault had been to the Memphremagog forest himself; when Camirand's body was found in the winter of 1977 he was the police officer assigned to the case. The location where the clothing was seen and the location where Camirand's body was recovered were within a quarter mile of each other. Why did Gaudreault not explore the possibility of a connection?

Figures 11.14 and 11.15 show maps of Sherbrooke and Lennoxville and the Eastern Townships in Québec, respectively, along with the following locations related to the Allore, Dubé, and Camirand cases:

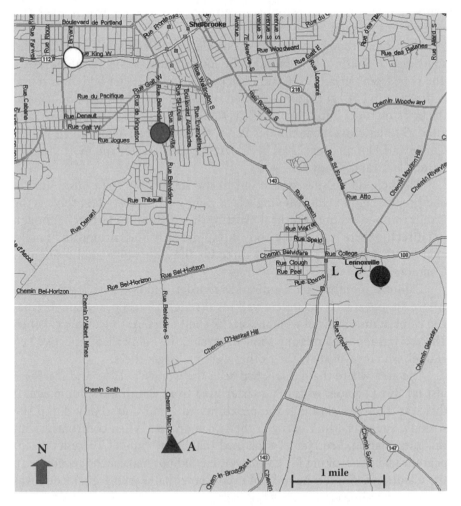

Figure 11.14 Sherbrooke and Lennoxville, Québec.

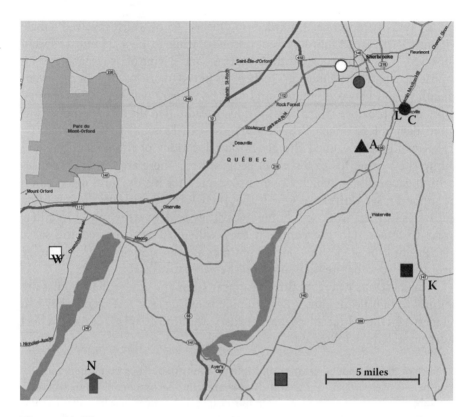

Figure 11.15 Eastern Townships, Québec.

- Louise Camirand last seen (white circle);
- Manon Dubé last seen (gray circle);
- Theresa Allore last seen (black circle);
- Louise Camirand's body found (white square);
- Manon Dubé's body found (gray square);
- Theresa Allore's body found (black square);
- Theresa Allore's wallet found (black triangle);
- Lion Pub (L);
- Champlain College (C);
- Apple orchard (A);
- King's Hall (K); and
- women's clothing seen (W).

It needs to be said that the police investigating my sister's death worked within a complicated and rivalry-stricken law enforcement system. As one former officer suggested, "Back then, it was terre de chasseur. Hunter's turf. We didn't talk, we didn't share files. We were the greens and they were the blues. We were making the rules of investigation up as we went along."

In 1977 there were 179 murders in Québec, 63 of which involved female victims. That year 52 murders went unsolved, while in 1978, 23 murders went unsolved. In 1979, provoked by the brutal rape and slaying of two teenagers at an amusement park, the Sûreté du Québec was forced to disclose that in the seven-month period between January and July 1979, there had been 228 reported rapes in the province. The Minister of Justice admitted the actual number was more likely at least double this because most sexual assaults go unreported.

Kim Rossmo studied the geographic locations of the abductions and dump sites, using his expertise in geoprofiling. There are several premises behind geoprofiling, which Rossmo pioneered for his doctoral dissertation at Simon Fraser University. One is that predators will operate along routine pathways in their work and home lives. They seldom stray into unfamiliar areas to attack. On the contrary, they will often have passed the same victim—or type of victim—dozens of times at a bus stop or a parking garage near their work, before they summon the nerve to attack.

The locations where victims disappear from and where their bodies are found are significant clues in geographic profiling. For one thing, they can suggest whether three disparate murders are linked. In his formal report Rossmo stated the following:

> Each of these incidents involve multiple locations that, when combined, form a persuasive pattern. Camirand disappeared in Sherbrooke, close to where Dubé went missing. She was later found in Magog, nearby what may have been Allore's clothes. Dubé, in turn, was found a few miles from Allore's body outside Compton, just off a route linking Compton to Magog. Allore's wallet was found just south of the area where both Camirand and Dubé disappeared, very near an attack on a fourth woman. ... The locations associated with these deaths are intertwined, woven together in the landscape south of Sherbrooke, Québec. Three murders in a 19-month period, in such a tight geographic cluster, is highly suspicious. All were young, low risk women. They were most probably attacked on the street, transported, and their bodies then dumped at a different location. The similarities are not likely the result of chance. These cases should be fed into ViCLAS (Violent Crime Linkage Analysis System), and reexamined as a group of potentially linked sex murders.[4] Serial murderers

---

[4] Crimes are linked through some combination of physical evidence, offender description, or crime scene behavior (Rossmo, D. K. [2000]. *Geographic profiling*. Boca Raton, FL: CRC Press). In a murder without witnesses and decaying physical evidence, crime scene behavior may be the only option. But to the degree that the scene is old or destroyed, important information regarding what exactly happened may be lost. Even at the best of times, crime scene comparisons are always probabilistic; in other words, we can only talk about the likelihood that two crimes are connected. Linking crimes behaviorally requires comparing similarities versus differences for both related and unrelated crimes. Like crimes should show more similarities than differences, and unlike crimes, more differences than similarities. These comparisons are usually assessed in terms of proximity in time and space between offenses, comparable modus operandi, and the presence of "signature" (fantasy-based rituals that go beyond what is necessary to commit the crime).

typically live closer to the victim encounter sites than body disposal locations. This offender was most likely based in Lennoxville or South Sherbrooke during the period from 1977 to 1978.

In late summer 2002, Patricia published her series of articles in Canada's *National Post* newspaper.[5] Titled *Who Killed Theresa?*, the story detailed our findings and included Kim Rossmo's analysis of the crimes.

In conclusion, we asked that Theresa's case be reopened, and hoped that homicide investigators in the Eastern Townships had improved their techniques during the past 20 years. The friends and family of a murder victim should not have to investigate the crime on their own.

In the five years since those articles appeared, I can, unfortunately, say only this: Québec homicide investigators are no better prepared today than they were 30 years ago. A warning to anyone who suffers the experience that my family went through—you will be on your own.

First things first—did the case files for the deaths of Theresa, Louise, and Manon get entered into ViCLAS? The answer is, eventually, yes. But this routine investigational procedure did not happen easily. There was ongoing media coverage and pressure to reopen the investigations after Patricia's articles were published. Stories appeared in local and national English and French print, radio, and television media, asking police to look into the matter. After initially insisting justification was lacking, the Sûreté du Québec agreed in November 2002 to assign one officer, on a part-time basis, to my sister's case, but only my sister's case. They refused to look at her murder as part of a potential series. In January 2003, after the media attention and the recommendation of an expert in behavioral science, the Sûreté du Québec reluctantly capitulated and entered Theresa's data into the ViCLAS system. Inexplicably, the data on Louise Camirand was not entered until 2006, and then only after I heard from a colleague that it still wasn't in the system. Fortunately, Manon Dubé's information did not have to wait. In 2001, a sharp Sherbrooke investigator, regarded as bit of a rogue by his peers, saw the value in ViCLAS and entered the information on his own initiative.

In late fall of 2002, I started a web log. *Who killed Theresa?* was set up to funnel incoming information that might help solve the crime. In the wake of the Patricia's articles, women slowly began to contact the website with personal accounts of attacks in the Sherbrooke area during the late 1970s. One of the first people to contact me was Caroline Rowell. Rowell had been a writer with the Bishop's college paper, *The Campus*, in 1978. At that time, there had been a series of sexual assaults on campus, and Rowell had covered these stories. She had been one of the only journalists in the area to repeatedly warn that there was a growing problem of sexual violence against women.

[5] Pearson, P. (2002, August 10). Who killed Theresa? *National Post*.

For the most part, the mainstream papers like the French *La Tribune* and the English *Sherbrooke Record* ignored the situation.

A single person was not responsible for all of the attacks that occurred in the Sherbrooke area in the late 1970s. Nevertheless, some of them are likely connected. One of the more comprehensive studies of paraphiliacs found that 70% of their total offenses were committed by only 5% of the offenders; this indicates a high degree of serial sex offending.[6] The challenge is determining which crimes are linked. And there were undoubtedly many more unreported attacks.

Where were the police during all this? An unsolved file is never closed—or at least that is the official line. The Sûreté du Québec say they have assigned a part-time investigator to follow up any new leads. The reality is less impressive. Many people are afraid to contact the police. I have generated more leads than they have. A case may be open, but that doesn't mean the police are actively working it. For 30 years my family has heard, "The file's right here on my desk." Just because my running shoes are on my feet doesn't mean I've taken up jogging.

Until very recently, Québec, the second largest province in Canada, did not have an official cold case squad. British Columbia and Ontario, the other major provinces, have such units, the former's created back in 1996. I have lobbied for the establishment of a cold case squad since 2002. The Québec's Minister of Public Security, which oversees police services in the province, wrote in a 2006 letter that the Sûreté du Québec had been operating such a unit for the last few years. This claim was later retracted by the police, however, who denied establishing a full-time cold case squad. In October 2007, the Deputy Minister told me that a cold case squad does in fact exist, but its mandate only went back 25 years. This bureaucratic limit left Allore, Dubé, and Camirand, indeed, out in the cold. Appeals to extend this timeline fell on deaf ears until very recently. Finally, in August 2008, the Sûreté confirmed the cold case bureau's mandate had been extended to all Québec murders, including the deaths of Allore, Dubé, and Camirand. This reform was a long time coming. Now that these cases are no longer in limbo, we hope they will be actively investigated.

In June 2005, I received the first official acknowledgment from the Québec government that Theresa was murdered. As part of an appeal to the provincial victims fund, IVAC (Indemnisation des victims d'actes criminels, or Crime Victims Compensation Act), they determined the following:

> The Bureau de la révision administrative cannot accept the drug overdose theory held by the police to explain Theresa Allore's death, on the grounds

---

[6] Abel, G. G., Mittelman, M. S., & Becker, J. V. (1985). Sexual offenders: Results of assessment and recommendations for treatment. In M. H. Ben-Aron, S. J. Hucker, & C. D. Webster (Eds.), *Clinical criminology: The assessment and treatment of criminal behaviour* (pp. 191–205). Toronto: M & M Graphics.

of the toxicity analysis conducted in 1979. In our view a theory of accident or accidental death is inconsistent with the discovery of a body face down, in an arm of a river, far from the road, clothed only in underwear. Considering that the victim disappeared in November and the body was found in April, the clothing is inconsistent with death without incident. The discovery of her scarf and purse far from her body also militates in favour of unnatural circumstances of death.

Given these facts, the Bureau de la révision administrative finds that Theresa Allore did not die a natural death and that the circumstances of her death were criminal in nature.

In the spring of 2006, frustrated yet again by the lack of police initiative, a group of supporters and I returned to the woods of Memphremagog to search for evidence. The task was simple; in 1978 hunters found clothing matching the description of Theresa's. Also, Louise Camirand's body had been discovered nearby. Although it seemed logical to search the area, the police had failed to do so for three decades.

What we found was quite interesting: an old woman's purse; the soles from a pair of women's shoes; and a few large bones (see Figure 11.16). These items were analyzed by a forensics laboratory in Vancouver, British Columbia. Unfortunately, they were too deteriorated to provide any useful evidence and the bones were from an animal. But even if these items were not my sister's, just imagine what police might have discovered had they done their job properly in 1978.

I have become very frustrated. I still miss my sister. I wish I could see her again. I wish I could do something positive that would make her loss less hard on my family. I have now gone back to graduate school to study justice administration and public policy. Today I am less involved with the details of Theresa's investigation; I've become more interested in the big picture of what makes the justice system work—or not work (Figure 11.17).

Figure 11.16 Purse found during a search of the Memphremagog woods.

Figure 11.17 Me and Theresa.

I was recently looking at my sister's college report card from just before she died; she had straight As in psychology, chemistry, and statistics. I could never figure out why she was taking such an odd assortment of courses. Then a friend told me Theresa had confided to her that she wanted to be a criminologist. It is so like my sister to have the last laugh.

Wrongful Innocence Claims: Roger Coleman and Benjamin LaGuer

12

D. KIM ROSSMO

A wrongful conviction is the worst possible outcome of a criminal investigative failure. Not only is an innocent person incarcerated for a crime he or she did not commit, but the guilty party remains undetected and at liberty, an ever present risk to the community. Developments in DNA testing have resulted in the discovery of many such cases, some more egregious and irresponsible than others, and various organizations, including the Innocence Project and Centurion Ministries, have been formed to assist the convicted innocent.

There is another side to this coin, however—that of the imprisoned criminal who makes loud and persistent claims of innocence, but who is in fact truly guilty. Such cases typically involve a coordinated campaign, including lawyers, reporters, politicians, and academics crusading for the release of the "wronged" party. It turns out crusaders are no more immune to psychological biases, group dynamics, and probability misunderstandings than police investigators and prosecutors.

Roger Coleman

One of the better known of these cases is that of Roger Keith Coleman, convicted and executed for the sexual murder of his sister-in-law in Grundy, southwest Virginia (Frankel, 2006; Tucker, 1997). On March 10, 1981, 19-year-old Wanda Faye Thompson was found raped and murdered, lying in blood on her bedroom floor. She had been stabbed twice in the chest and was nearly decapitated by a vicious throat slash. Police quickly focused on 22-year-old Roger Coleman, who was married to the victim's 16-year-old sister. Coleman had been previously convicted of an attempted rape in 1977, in which he entered the home of a local teacher and threatened her at gunpoint, forcing her to tie up her terrified six-year-old daughter. After his release from prison, and just two months before the murder, he exposed himself and masturbated in front of a town librarian. He also had a history of making obscene telephone calls as a teenager.

Coleman was soon arrested by police and charged with Thompson's murder. He pled innocent although the evidence at his 1982 trial was persuasive:

- Three blood spots on his pants matched the victim's blood type.
- Two pubic hairs found on the victim had similar characteristics to his.
- Semen found at the crime scene contained type B antigens, the same as Coleman's blood type and only found in 9% of the overall U.S. population.
- The bottom 10 inches of both his pant legs were wet (there was a creek close to the victim's house).
- Coleman's cell mate claimed he had confessed to him.

The jury quickly found Coleman guilty and decided upon the death penalty. He maintained his innocence throughout his imprisonment. "For what it's worth, I didn't do it," he wrote one pen pal from prison. Just before his execution, his last words began: "An innocent man is going to be murdered tonight."

Coleman was a model prisoner who, while on death row, founded a program to counsel young men in trouble. He was described as bright, personable, "honest and open," charming, solicitous, thoughtful, sympathetic, and vulnerable (Frankel, 2006). He soon developed a following that included a death row counselor, a sophomore student pen pal (who ended up falling in love with Coleman), Kathleen ("Kitty") Behan, a lawyer with the high-powered Washington, D.C., law firm Arnold and Porter, and eventually, Jim McCloskey, Executive Director of Centurion Ministries.

Centurion Ministries is a secular nonprofit organization that has been successful in establishing the innocence of at least 40 convicted offenders.[1] "The primary mission of Centurion Ministries is to vindicate and free from prison those who are completely innocent of the crimes for which they have been unjustly convicted and imprisoned for life or death."[2] Factual innocence is an important part of their focus; they are not concerned with legal issues such as whether or not the individual received a fair trial (Centurion Ministries has dropped four cases in which the prisoner was proven guilty).

When Coleman contacted McCloskey, the unordained Presbyterian minister read the trial transcript, interviewed Coleman in prison, and then drove to Grundy where he spent a month investigating the murder. Finding gaps in the police investigation and problems with the time line of the crime, he became convinced of Coleman's innocence. Unfortunately, he focused on only one side of the equation and failed to interview Coleman's surviving victims.

---

[1] One of these was David Milgaard, who spent 23 years in prison for a sex murder he did not commit (see Chapter 9).

[2] Centurion Ministries. Retrieved January 18, 2008, from http://www.centurionministries.org.

McCloskey realized it would take physical evidence to get Coleman off death row. But when the possibility of DNA testing (which was not available in 1982) was suggested to Coleman, surprisingly—and telling in retrospect—he was not interested. "He told McCloskey that after his arrest he had had sex in jail with a female guard, and he feared the authorities had planted his semen from that encounter as evidence. McCloskey dismissed Coleman's fears as classic jailhouse paranoia, 'but I also felt a certain amount of discomfort in my mind as to why he wasn't eager for DNA testing'" (Frankel, 2006, p. 21). This bizarre, and sexually egocentric, story says much about Coleman.

A judge eventually agreed to have the evidence—a limited sample of semen recovered from the victim—reexamined. But the findings actually added to the probability of Coleman's guilt. The DNA test narrowed the donor to only 2% of the population. When this result is combined with the B blood grouping, the match probability drops to 0.2%. In a community the size of Gundy, this practically singled out Coleman.

There should have been loud warning bells ringing in the "Coleman is innocent" camp. Instead, they either ignored or explained away these problems and attacked their own forensic expert. They also developed an alternative suspect. Arnold and Porter went so far as to issue a press statement claiming they had found the real killer, a local man with a history of trouble with the law. But it turned out that he had type A blood. The "suspect" eventually filed a libel suit against Behan and her firm for $5 million. The suit was settled for an undisclosed but substantial amount of money.

Coleman's final appeal was unsuccessful. It was rejected by the Virginia Supreme Court, and the decision was later upheld by the U.S. Supreme Court. A federal judge stated, "'this court finds the case against Coleman as strong as or stronger than the evidence adduced at trial'" (Frankel, 2006, p.23). In an attempt to delay the execution, Coleman's lawyers appealed to Virginia Governor L. Douglas Wilder, and his supporters began a high-profile media campaign that included *Good Morning America*, the *Today* show, *The Phil Donahue Show*, *Larry King Live*, *Newsweek*, and the *Washington Post*. They made appeals to dozens of celebrities. Coleman's picture appeared on the front cover of *Time* magazine, with the headline "This Man Might Be Innocent. This Man Is Due to Die."

But some of Coleman's supporters felt uncomfortable by all this "spin." And while the media were convinced, the campaign had little effect on Wilder. The Governor did, however, offer Coleman an opportunity to take a last-minute polygraph examination. He failed. Roger Coleman was executed in Virginia's electric chair on May 20, 1992.

McCloskey had promised Coleman he would prove his innocence, even if only posthumously. Eventually, advancements in DNA technology made another attempt at analyzing the evidence feasible. Virginia Governor Mark R. Warner authorized the testing. This was the first time a DNA test had been approved in a case where the convicted party had already been executed. Warner's decision, therefore, carried some political risk, and he is to be commended for his willingness to seek the truth.

The testing was done by Ontario's Centre of Forensic Sciences in January 2006. McCloskey agreed to let ABC *Nightline* film him while he heard the outcome. The results conclusively established Coleman's guilt, with a random match probability (profile frequency) between his DNA and semen from the murder scene of 1 in 19 million. McCloskey was shocked and dismayed. "'I keep asking myself: Where did I go wrong? What did I miss?'" (Frankel, 2006, p. 12). He held a press conference and admitted his mistake to reporters, answering all their questions and calling the DNA results a "victory for the truth." By contrast, Arnold and Porter ended all public comment. Kitty Behan, now a partner in the firm, abandoned her fact-driven reputation. "Behan has told friends that she still believes Coleman was innocent and that she doesn't accept the test findings" (Frankel, 2006, p. 24). And one of Coleman's advocates conjectured that Coleman had no memory of the murder (although his memory seemed to be working perfectly well when he expressed reluctance to take the first DNA test).

Ironically, Behan and McCloskey became victim to many of the same traps that have snared police detectives involved in wrongful conviction cases. Among other problems, these included: tunnel vision (e.g., rationalizing Coleman's lack of interest in DNA testing); groupthink (e.g., believing that the morality of what they were doing justified cutting ethical corners); and errors in understanding probabilities (e.g., ignoring the initial DNA and serology evidence). And, as can be seen from the case examples in this book, Behan's stubborn response is also typical. All too often personal beliefs outweigh hard evidence.

Although Jim McCloskey initially erased Coleman from the website of Centurion Ministries (Frankel, 2006), he later replaced the case. There he now says: "We all make mistakes, and I made a whopper that was magnified a million times over, especially since the whole world seemed to be watching."[3] McCloskey has to be admired for both his work to release the innocent and his refreshing lack of ego. Like the rest of us, he is fallible. Unlike many of us, however, he is willing to publicly admit it. It is encouraging to see someone so genuinely interested in the truth.

Benjamin LaGuer

The Benjamin LaGuer case appears to be a similar false alarm. In January 1984, LaGuer was charged with rape, assault, robbery, and burglary in relationship

---

[3] Centurion Ministries/Cases/Roger Keith Coleman—Grundy, VA. (2006, January 17). Retrieved January 18, 2008, from http://www.centurionministries.org/cases.html.

to a brutal sexual assault of a 59-year-old woman. He was arrested and convicted for the crime and given a life sentence. LaGuer has always claimed to be innocent, and his efforts for release have been supported by a significant number of scholars, politicians, and journalists. In 2005, I was requested to do an analysis of the LaGuer case by a Massachusetts state representative who was considering holding public hearings into possible police and prosecutorial misconduct during the investigation.

For the most part, the facts in this matter are less in dispute than their interpretation. Around 9:00 p.m., on July 12, 1983, a man wearing jogging shorts and mismatched striped gym socks broke into the victim's apartment in Leominster, Massachusetts. He beat and robbed her, taking her money, jewelry, and pocketbook. Then, over an eight-hour time period, he vaginally, orally, and anally raped her. The offender placed a plastic bag over the victim's head, causing her to pass out, but not before she struggled with him, scratching and drawing blood. He threatened to kill her if she identified him. Police discovered the victim the next day, bound by the cords from her telephone and hair dryer. She had suffered serious physical injuries in the attack and was taken to the hospital.

The victim identified LaGuer as her assailant. He was living in his father's apartment next door to the victim (his father was visiting Puerto Rico and was not home at the time of the crime). The victim had seen him before, once when he rang her doorbell to ask to be let into the apartment building, another time when she saw him enter his father's apartment.

The morning following the rape, LaGuer visited Fitchburg State College (at one point, the victim's assailant had told her he was from Fitchburg), then stayed at his sister's home. Police picked him up when he returned to the apartment on July 15. LaGuer was wearing jogging shorts, tube socks, and no shirt, and there were mismatched socks rolled into pairs in his apartment. Police noticed and photographed a deep scratch on his back. LaGuer first explained that the scratch came from a nail at a bar, then changed his story and said it was from splinters or nails from a picnic table. After the victim picked him out from a photo line-up, he was arrested and charged with aggravated rape, assault and battery, robbery, and break and entry.

LaGuer did not have a criminal record, but was mentioned in police files as a "possible suspect" in a burglary when he was 17 years old. He had been in the military, but while stationed in Germany was caught in possession of hashish during a drug sting; he claimed he was just "in the wrong place at the wrong time." After being sent back to basic training as punishment, he was allowed to leave the Army with a general discharge. He then returned to Leominster.

LaGuer pled not guilty. The court ordered LaGuer to provide a saliva sample for testing in order to compare his blood type against evidence found at the crime scene. But LaGuer swallowed another inmate's saliva, which he then spat out for investigators when asked to provide the sample. The crime laboratory found the test results "inconclusive" as to blood type. LaGuer's evidence tampering only became known years later. In a recurring theme, rather than take responsibility for his actions, LaGuer implied he did it on the advice of his lawyer. During his trial, the defense argued that a particular Hispanic male who lived in the same apartment complex was the offender. But the court believed the victim and found LaGuer guilty. He was sentenced to life imprisonment.

Benjamin LaGuer has maintained his innocence. While in prison, he set up a detailed website about his case.[4] Over the years, he has had a illustrious group supporting his claims of innocence, including the president of Boston University, a former U.S. Justice Department Chief for Civil Rights, MIT's luminary linguist and activist Noam Chomsky, a Harvard Law School professor, the associate provost for John Jay College, the dean of the School of Law at Boston University, a gubernatorial candidate, senators, state representatives, and journalists—"a legion of prominent members of academia, law, finance and clergy."[5] His supporters contributed thousands of dollars to his legal defense fund. Northeastern University even established a collection of LaGuer's papers.

In 1999, Boston University's president asked his Office of General Counsel to develop a legal strategy for Benjamin LaGuer. This plan involved new counsel and an effort to analyze crime scene evidence for DNA. Eventually, after court approval, Dr. Edward T. Blake of Forensic Science Associates, was asked to do the testing. On March 22, 2002, the results revealed that LaGuer's DNA had a random match probability to the crime scene samples of 1 in 100 million.

In a remarkable 180-degree turnabout, LaGuer claimed the police had tampered with the crime scene evidence. But this theory was an excuse too far for many of his supporters:

> Dr. Blake, calling Mr. LaGuer "a master manipulator and a flimflam artist," said the [tampering] theory defies credibility, not only in its feasibility, but in its timing. "The time to make those claims is not now … . If this is some concocted thing, why did we spend all this time and effort on concocted evidence? It's only concocted because Mr. LaGuer didn't like the results of the testing." (Bruun, 2002)

> To believe Mr. LaGuer's ludicrous theory that someone stole his underwear and sperm 20 years ago, you'd have to believe that a resourceful cop anticipated the

[4] BenLaGuer.com (http://www.benlaguer.com).
[5] Retrieved January 29, 2008, from http://www.benlaguer.com/index.html.

advent of DNA testing two decades before its use. ... [LaGuer] manipulated the system and preyed on the goodwill of people troubled by the idea that an innocent man may have been wrongly convicted." (Williamson, 2002)

We will not again believe in Ben the social abstraction—the public cause, the traveling medicine show—nor will we abet him in its creation." (Fletcher, 2002)

LaGuer is nothing if not resilient. Predictably, he and his remaining supporters began to attack Dr. Blake and the reliability of DNA testing (Goldscheider & Kessis, 2006). Even his lawyer David Siegel morphed in the LaGuer worldview from championing hero to self-serving opportunist.

Three years after the DNA test results, I received an official letter from Representative Ellen Story, Third Hampshire District, the Commonwealth of Massachusetts, asking for a review of the LaGuer case:

> I am writing on behalf of both the people of the Third Hampshire District and a group of my colleagues. ... We are seeking a case analysis involving the conviction of a state prisoner named Benjamin LaGuer, who has served 22 years of a life sentence. ... If the claims raised by these records are true, a determination we hope you can help make, we may be facing a gross injustice and a judicial scandal. ... We believe this case holds special significance. We have already begun a fact-finding process and, if warranted, will hold public hearings. Before we proceed further, we would like you to review this material and prepare a brief advisory letter indicating whether you believe these claims of tainted DNA due to evidence mishandling and possibly criminal misconduct by police and prosecutors meets a preponderance standard. Your expertise in this matter will greatly aid the legislature in carrying out its duty. (E. Story, personal communication; May 26, 2005)

I wrote back to Representative Story, asking to speak to her or one of her staff members for clarification of the request. I was contacted by Eric Goldscheider, "a constituent of Re. Story's," who had studied the LaGuer case for some time and was the person who first brought it to her attention. He provided the answers to a number of my questions. The main issues of interest were the possibility of DNA contamination, the mental state of the victim,[6] and the presence of unidentified fingerprints found on the base of the victim's telephone. My report, completed on July 12, 2005, follows in full (the footnotes are from the original report, but their *numbering* has been adjusted for consistency with the rest of this chapter).

---

[6] While I am responsible for any errors in the interpretation of their comment, I wish to acknowledge the helpful expertise on this point of Dr. Kris Mohandie, Dr. Joel A. Dvoskin, Dr. Peter Collins, and Dr. David Stubbins, members of the International Criminal Investigative Analysis Fellowship (ICIAF).

Advisory Opinion re Conviction of Benjamin LaGuer

This advisory report discusses various issues brought to my attention regarding the conviction of Benjamin LaGuer for a 1983 rape in Leominster, Massachusetts. The information I was provided with came from Rep. Ellen Story, House of Representatives, the Commonwealth of Massachusetts. This material included:

- *Errors in the Ben LaGuer DNA Analysis* (Benjamin LaGuer, April 28, 2005);
- A letter from Lawrence Kobilinsky to James C. Rehnquist (May 28, 2004);
- E-mails from Dr. Bruce Jackson (June 28, 2004);
- *DNA testing links convicted rapist to scene* (March 23, 2002; Associated Press);
- *Dr. Edward T. Blake refers to "a tale of two cases"* (Matthew Brunn, March 31, 2002, *Worcester Telegram & Gazette*, p. B1);
- Copies of police reports and evidence documents, with commentary, prepared by Eric Goldscheider;
- Emails from Eric Goldscheider, answering specific questions I had; and
- A time line and additional material, located at http://www.benlaguer. com/index.html.

I have not read the original police reports or trial transcripts, visited the crime scene, interviewed any parties, or reviewed any response or rebuttal from the district attorney's office, law enforcement agencies, or the state crime laboratory. My advisory opinion is offered within the context and limitations of the information provided.

There are only three ways to prove criminal guilt: (1) witness; (2) confession; or (3) physical evidence. From the provided information, it appears the primary evidence contributing to LaGuer's conviction was the testimony of the rape victim. There is some debate over the physical evidence, though it is unclear what role such evidence played at trial. Benjamin LaGuer has not confessed to this crime.

A follow-up police report records that the victim, in addition to describing her assailant, stated she had "seen this man several times and has seen him going in and out of the apt next to her the Laguer apt ... once he rang her buzzer ... he said hello to her" (Det. Ronald N. Carignan, July 14, 1983).

It appears the victim saw and knew of LaGuer prior to her attack. Her prior knowledge, and the time she was held by her assailant during the rape (eight hours), indicates misidentification is not the issue. This leaves the possibility of false witness testimony.[7] LaGuer questions the victim's credibility by noting she was institutionalized in the 1950s with a diagnosis of schizophrenia

---

[7] According to the Innocence Project, however, false witness testimony is only one-fourth as common as mistaken identifications in wrongful convictions (http://www.innocence project.org/causes/index.php).

and had a history of domestic abuse. At one point, he also calls into question whether or not she had actually been sexually assaulted.

The credibility of any witness suffering from mental illness is related to their cognitive and functional status at the time of the alleged offense, and not their diagnosis per se. The latter is often more prejudicial than probative. There is little reliable evidence that schizophrenia has a predictable effect on testimony accuracy, which is highly specific to the situation and person. Was there any prima facie evidence the alleged victim suffered from psychotic symptoms around the time of the alleged crime? If so, would the symptoms appear likely to cause the person's testimony to be inaccurate? Testimony competence is a matter of judicial decision, usually based on psychological or psychiatric expert opinion. These experts look for relevant hallucinations or delusions; the fact that the victim was in the "habit of losing her keys" falls far short of demonstrating mental incompetence. The judge in the LaGuer case, the person in the best position to make such a decision, ruled the victim's mental health inadmissible at trial.

LaGuer explains the results of the incriminating DNA test by contamination. He asserts Massachusetts State Police assistant chemist Mark T. Grant handled LaGuer's underwear at the same time as he was handling the rest of the evidence from the case. "DNA from LaGuer's illegally seized underwear was initially run together [*sic*] the rape kit. Such improper handling and history of shabby testing." "LaGuer's illegally seized underwear had been tested together with rape the kit" [*sic*]. But there is no specific information regarding laboratory testing procedures that supports these allegations.

If the DNA testing was not contaminated, the results prove LaGuer's guilt beyond any doubt. If contamination occurred, the test results have no probative value. The impact of the test, therefore, can be determined by assessing the probability of contamination. A valid DNA match would dramatically raise the prior odds of guilt (to a probability of near certainty). An invalid DNA match (through contamination) would not change the prior odds of guilt. The posterior probability of guilt, then, is equal to the probability of a contaminated DNA test multiplied by the prior probability of guilt, added to the probability of an uncontaminated DNA test multiplied by the DNA posterior probability of guilt:

$$P(G) = p(G)\, p(C) + p'(G)\, [1 - p(C)],$$

where $P(G)$ = posterior probability of guilt; $p(C)$ = probability of a contaminated DNA test; $p(G)$ = prior probability of guilt; and $p'(G) \approx 1$ = DNA posterior probability of guilt. For example, if the prior probability of guilt was 95%, and the probability of a contaminated DNA test was 25%,[8] then the posterior

---

[8] The DNA contamination would actually have had to occur with two samples—the spermatozoa recovered from the victim's pubic hair and unknown cellular source material present on "Tissue D."

probability of guilt would be 98.75%. In summary, the DNA test results increase the probability of LaGuer's guilt. Even if contamination was shown to be a certainty, the results still fail to exonerate him as no other male DNA was identified from the spermatozoa recovered from the victim's pubic hair.

The most likely explanation for why LaGuer's underwear was not listed in the exhibits taken from his father's apartment is that they were seized from his person at the time of his arrest, two days after the crime. This is standard investigative procedure in sexual assault investigations because of the possibility of evidence transfer from the victim.

LaGuer's fingerprints did not match a set of four prints found on the base of a Trimline telephone from the victim's apartment. The wire of this telephone was used, along with the cord from a hairdryer, to bind the victim's wrists. No information is available regarding what other comparisons, if any, were done with these prints. The fact that police found fingerprints on the base of a Trimline phone is hardly surprising considering the design of a Trimline telephone. They could have come from the victim or a visitor to her apartment. It is unfortunate, however, that the prints were apparently never identified and have now been lost. It is not uncommon for police agencies to destroy evidence in solved cases after the end of the appeal process. The failure to inform LaGuer's defense counsel of the existence of this evidence at the time of the original trial may or may not have been contrary to disclosure laws in Massachusetts in 1984. Given the totality of circumstances, however, they are not evidence of his innocence.

It has been estimated that 0.5% of all felony cases are wrongful convictions.[9] Most of these are the result of mistaken identifications and other errors; police and prosecutorial misconduct are less common causes. Actual conspiracies are rare, and multi-agency conspiracies (e.g., police, crime lab, and district attorney's office) more the work of fiction writers. It should be remembered that police errors occur in every major crime investigation; this is particularly so in older cases because standards for physical evidence handling were lower.

LaGuer's writings are often biased and misleading (e.g., *Errors in the Ben LaGuer DNA Analysis*). These range from factual incorrect conclusions and assertions ("The absence of male DNA ... contradicts any possibility of an eight-hour sexual assault;" "How could LaGuer have raped a fungal infected woman for eight unremitting hours and not become infected?" "Contrary to all forensic reports ... Judge Hillman ruled that LaGuer's DNA 'matched the male profile'"), to ad hominem attacks on those whose findings, opinions, or actions he disagrees with ("Detective Ronald N. Carignan was a liar" "Wysocki's secret search could not be legitimate" "Why is Conte lying" "Siegel's ... display of cowardice" "source was a hoax" "It was a fraud"), to media hype ("'David Siegel looked in my eyes and saw the truth of my innocence' LaGuer says"). While this propaganda does not influence the likelihood of his

---

[9] Huff, C. R., Rattner, A., & Sagarin, E. (1996). *Convicted but innocent: Wrongful conviction and public policy.* Thousand Oaks, CA: Sage.

guilt, anyone wishing to independently review the case should be wary of the veracity of LaGuer's writings.

More critical is LaGuer's actions in mixing another inmate's salvia with his own. In my opinion, this action demonstrates his tendency to manipulate, and weakens his credibility. His explanation is unconvincing.

I have provided my opinion on certain key areas in the debate over LaGuer's guilt. As an early response was requested, only limited information was reviewed. There may be additional facts that could alter these findings. This document is restricted to issues of LaGuer's "actual innocence," as opposed to his "legal innocence." It is not a legal opinion, and there may be issues in law supporting his appeals. There are some unanswered questions that Mr. LaGuer's defense counsel likely wishes to pursue, and the relevant authorities should do their best to cooperate in the interests of transparency of justice. Presently, however, I do not see any credible and convincing evidence supporting the suggestion that LaGuer was wrongfully convicted.

Dr. D. Kim Rossmo

Research Professor and Director
Center for Geospatial Intelligence and Investigation
Department of Criminal Justice
Texas State University

Representative Story never acknowledged or responded to my report. But four months later, I received a letter, stamped: "This correspondence is forwarded from a Massachusetts Correctional Institution." It was from Benjamin LaGuer. He was responding to my report, a copy of which someone had provided him.

Over the next six months, he sent me seven letters. At one point, he asked me to consider drafting a new report, admonishing: "am I going to let you be a fool?" (B. LaGuer, personal communication, April 22, 2006).

I did not revise my report. But I became curious as to how it ended up in LaGuer's hands. I also wondered if the report had been shared with the prosecution. So I contacted Worcester Assistant District Attorney Sandra Hautanen, who was currently preparing to respond to LaGuer's appeal on the issue of the fingerprints found on the victim's telephone. She had never seen or heard of my report. It turned out that Eric Goldscheider was a reporter and advocate of LaGuer's who had written several stories about the case and was currently working on a book. Needless to say, the viability of the book project depended much on LaGuer actually being innocent.[10] So much for Representative Story's request being "on behalf of the people."

---

[10] As of August 2008, the book has not been published.

LaGuer lost his appeal. The Massachusetts Supreme Judicial Court rendered their decision on March 2, 2006. While cautioning that the prosecution should have shared the report with the defense, they ruled: "nothing in the [fingerprint] report demonstrates, or even suggests, that the defendant had not been at the scene or had not committed the crimes charged." (The court did not find it necessary to consider the DNA evidence.)

Did Benjamin LaGuer receive a fair trial? I cannot answer that question. Is he factually guilty? Conjectures and theories aside, the actual evidence supports the conclusion, beyond any reasonable doubt, that he brutally raped his neighbor in 1983.

LaGuer continues to refuse to accept responsibility for his actions. His supporters have only enabled him. The victim in this case is deceased. But one wonders, if she were still alive, what she would think of the intelligentsia who became part of the LaGuer "medicine show," people who, despite years and miles of distance from her apartment that horrible night of the crime, "knew" more about what had happened to her than she did.

Well Intentioned but Misdirected

LaGuer and Coleman fooled some very bright people. But their cases are not isolated incidents. Jack Abbott, who wrote *In the Belly of the Beast*, conned Norman Mailer into supporting his parole bid. After his release from prison, it took Abbott only six weeks before he killed again, stabbing a waiter in a trivial argument (McCrary & Ramsland, 2003). Less well known is the story of Austrian Johann "Jack" Unterweger, convicted in 1976 of strangling a teenage prostitute and given a life sentence. While in prison, he wrote several plays, poems, short stories, and a best-selling autobiography. The Viennese elite, admiring his literary talents, successfully petitioned for his freedom. Paroled in 1990, Jack became a celebrity, in demand as a talk show speaker and a guest at trendy gatherings. He was a charming example of how art could rehabilitate criminals. But within a year of his release he had brutally murdered six prostitutes. After a spree of at least 11 homicides in three countries, he was finally arrested and brought to trial. Jack continued to be a media darling; he sold his story to a magazine, claiming police had set him up because of his past. With public opinion on his side, he fully expected to be found not guilty. But the evidence was strong and he was convicted in 1994. He hanged himself in his jail cell using an intricate knot identical to that found on his victims' ligatures (McCrary & Ramsland, 2003). Jack Unterweger, author, bon vivant, reporter—and serial killer.

The supporters of these criminals suffered from the halo effect, a cognitive bias whereby one positive trait (e.g., intelligence, talent, charm, etc.)

influences the perception of other traits (e.g., moral rehabilitation, lack of dangerousness, etc.) or of the overall character of the person (inherent goodness). Often, the physical attractiveness stereotype (physically attractive people are also socially attractive) plays a role. But a charming and talented psychopath is still a psychopath. Charisma, intelligence, and communication skills are trademarks of criminals successful in convincing others of their "innocence." Unfortunately, these characteristics are not related to actual innocence. In fact, the opposite traits—dislikable personalities, low intelligence, and poor communication skills—are more likely to be correlated with wrongful convictions.

Often, well-intentioned people eager to help do not question the validity of their mission. While I was a doctoral student at Simon Fraser University, someone posted a petition on the bulletin board asking for the release of two Canadians imprisoned in Brazil for kidnapping. Several professors and graduate students signed the petition until someone scrawled next to it: "How do you know these people are innocent? Have you thought about the kidnapping victim?" There were no more signatures after that.

Wrongful convictions do occur, and innocent people are imprisoned. But most claims of innocence are bogus. Dr. Blake notes that 60% of the convicts seeking DNA tests are further implicated by the results (Bruun, 2002). It is not surprising that guilty prisoners claim to be innocent and want a DNA test. There is always the possibility of an error in the testing. As faint as this hope may be, from the offender's perspective, they have nothing to lose. They can also surround themselves with an aura of innocence during the appeal and testing process. Blake suggests this is particularly important for inmates convicted of sex crimes because of their low position in the prison hierarchy.

In any criminal investigation—especially a long and complicated one—mistakes and errors will occur. But these do not automatically translate into the innocence of the accused party. The best approach is to seek the truth—an objective, careful truth based on evidence, facts, logic, and skepticism; not a subjective dogmatic opinion, entangled by personal and organizational egos.

References

Bruun, M. (2002, March 31). DNA findings difficult to rebut—Doctor rejects LaGuer claims. *Worcester Telegram & Gazette*, p. B1.

Fletcher, A. (2002, April 4). Slants and rants. *Worcester Magazine*.

Frankel, G. (2006, May 14). Burden of proof. *Washington Post Magazine*, pp. 8–13, 19–24.

Goldscheider, E., & Kessis, T. (2006, August 17). Quest for certainty: Is forensic DNA foolproof? *Northampton Valley Advocate*.

Huff, C. R., Rattner, A., & Sagarin, E. (1996). *Convicted but innocent: Wrongful conviction and public policy*. Thousand Oaks, CA: Sage.

McCrary, G. O., & Ramsland, K. M. (2003). *The unknown darkness: Profiling the predators among us.* New York: HarperCollins.

Tucker, J. C. (1997). *May God have mercy: A true story of crime and punishment.* New York: Dell.

Williamson, D. (2002, April 2). Media fell for tactics of LaGuer. *Worcester Telegram and Gazette.*

Recommendations IV

How Police Departments Can Reduce the Risk of Wrongful Convictions*

13

DOUG A. LEPARD AND
ELIZABETH CAMPBELL

In recent history, convictions of the innocent and other miscarriages of justice in Western democracies have been more prevalent than commonly thought.[1] The notion of a balanced criminal justice system capable of weeding out false testimony, mistaken identifications, poorly collected or processed scientific evidence, and other errors is, in practice, far less successful than it should be. In Great Britain, fabricated or coerced confessions and other falsified evidence have been responsible for notorious wrongful convictions such as those involving the Guildford Four[2] and the Birmingham Six,[3] who were accused of several murderous bombings attributed to the Irish Republican Army. In the United States, the Innocence Project[4] has exonerated through DNA testing 197 people convicted of serious crimes,[5] some of whom were on Death Row. In the State of Illinois, Governor George Ryan, a death penalty supporter, imposed in January 2000 a moratorium on executions after 13 men on Illinois Death Row were exonerated by DNA.[6] And in Canada, a small but increasing number of convictions have been overturned where the accused were factually innocent of the crimes of which they were convicted.

---

* An earlier version of this chapter was presented by the authors at the International Society for the Reform of Criminal Law, June 2007, Vancouver, BC.

1 It is estimated that one in 200 felony convictions in the United States is a wrongful conviction (Huff, Rattner, & Sagarin, 1996).

2 For a media chronology of the Guildford Four wrongful conviction story, see http://news.bbc.co.uk/onthisday/hi/dates/stories/october/19/newsid_2490000/2490039.stm.

3 For a media chronology of the Birmingham Six wrongful conviction story, see http://news.bbc.co.uk/onthisday/hi/dates/stories/march/14/newsid_2543000/2543613.stm.

4 According to its website (http://www.innocenceproject.org), "the Innocence Project is a national litigation and public policy organization dedicated to exonerating wrongfully convicted people through DNA testing and reforming the criminal justice system to prevent future injustice."

5 As of March 27, 2007; http://www.innocenceproject.org.

6 See http://archives.cnn.com/2000/US/01/31/illinois.executions.02/.

The issue is taking on a higher public profile because of the work of the Innocence Project, various commissions and inquiries, and popular books about
wrongful convictions such as John Grisham's *The Innocent Man: Murder and
Injustice in a Small Town* (2006).

Some of the more notorious wrongful convictions in Canada are those of
Donald Marshall, who spent 11 years in prison for the 1971 murder of Sandy
Seale in Sidney, Nova Scotia;[7] David Milgaard, who spent 23 years in prison for
the 1969 Saskatoon murder of nursing aide Gail Miller (see Chapter 9);[8] Guy Paul
Morin, who endured a 10-year legal ordeal for the 1984 Queensville, Ontario,
murder of nine-year-old Christine Jessop;[9] and Thomas Sophonow, who spent
almost four years in prison and was tried three times before being acquitted
in 1985 on a second appeal, and finally exonerated 15 years later of the 1981
murder of 16-year-old doughnut shop employee Barbara Stoppel.[10] It is notable
that without the availability of advanced DNA testing, Milgaard, Morin, and
Sophonow were extremely unlikely to have been proved innocent.[11]

The problem of wrongful convictions in Canada has resulted in a series
of inquiries, Royal commissions, and other analyses. The resulting recommendations were well synthesized in the 2004 *Report on the Prevention of
Miscarriages of Justice* (hereinafter referred to as "the Heads of Prosecution
Report").[12] To simplify discussion, this section will provide an overview of the
police-relevant recommendations from Canadian commissions or inquiries
into wrongful convictions. These recommendations are directed at improving
investigations by addressing both the problems associated with mishandled
investigations generally, and specific problems such as mistaken identifications, false confessions, in-custody informants, those aspects of police culture
that contribute to wrongful convictions, and ideas for ongoing education to
ensure police stay current on issues with respect to wrongful convictions.

[7] See http://www.canadianencyclopedia.ca/index.cfm?PgNm=TCE&Params=A1ARTA000
    5123.
[8] See http://www.milgaardinquiry.ca.
[9] *The Commission on Proceedings Involving Guy Paul Morin*, The Honourable Fred
    Kaufman, Commissioner, 1998. See http://www.attorneygeneral.jus.gov.on.ca/english/
    about/pubs/morin.
[10] *The Inquiry Regarding Thomas Sophonow*, The Honourable Peter Cory, Commissioner,
    2001. See http://www.gov.mb.ca/justice/publications/sophonow/intro/index.html.
[11] Milgaard won the right to a new trial based on the availability of new evidence, but the
    Crown elected not to proceed, leaving him "not guilty." His exoneration only occurred
    several years later through DNA analysis. Morin was exonerated only because post-
    conviction DNA analysis proved he was not the donor of the semen found on victim
    Christine Jessop's underwear. Sophonow was acquitted in 1985 after multiple trials and
    appeals, but was only exonerated in 2000 by DNA evidence.
[12] The report was a product of a Federal/Provincial/Territorial group of "Heads of Prosecu-
    tion," and was authored by D. A. Bellemare, Q.C. of the Federal Prosecution Service, and
    Rob Finlayson of the Manitoba Justice Prosecutions Service. It can be located online at
    http://www.justice.gc.ca/en/dept/pub/hop/.

Recommendations for Police

For each major issue identified in the literature, a description of the issue will be provided, followed by the relevant recommendation(s). Then, the response of a major Canadian urban police force, the Vancouver Police Department (hereinafter the VPD),[13] will be examined in terms of how it has responded to the issues in order to reduce the risk of a wrongful conviction. For simplification, the VPD response will refer to the recommendations of the Heads of Prosecution Report, as they are representative of those from other commissions and inquiries into wrongful convictions.

Eyewitness Identifications

The misidentification of suspects by eyewitnesses to the crime has been identified as one of the leading causes of wrongful convictions. This cause was looked at in detail in the Sophonow inquiry and was examined again in the Heads of Prosecution Report. They reviewed three types of line-ups shown by police to eyewitnesses for offender identification purposes: photograph line-ups, live line-ups, and "show-ups."

A photo line-up is the most common of the three and had traditionally been conducted with 6 to 10 photos arranged together on a single piece of paper. The line-up was shown to a witness by the investigating officer, and the number of the photo the witness selected, if any, was recorded on a form. The officer typically read a series of instructions from the form before the photos were shown. The process was not usually recorded by audio- or videotape.

Based on research into the causes of a mistaken identification, the Sophonow report recommended a new procedure:

- The "photo pack" should contain at least 10 subjects.
- The photos should resemble as closely as possible the eyewitnesses' description or, if that is not possible, then they should be as close as possible in appearance to the suspect's photo.
- Everything should be recorded on video or audio from the time the officer meets the witness through showing the photos to the end of the interview.
- The officer showing the photo pack should not know who the suspect is and should not be involved in the investigation.
- The officer should tell the witness that he does not know who the suspect is or whether his or her photo is contained in the line-up, and the

[13] The Vancouver Police Department (http://www.vpd.ca) has an authorized sworn strength of 1,237 officers and serves an official population of almost 600,000 in the core city of a metropolitan region of over two million residents. Vancouver is the largest urban area in British Columbia, and the third largest in Canada.

officer should advise the witness that it is just as important to clear the innocent as it is to identify the suspect.

- The photo pack should be presented to each witness separately.
- Photo packs must be presented sequentially and not as a package.
- There should be a form for signatures setting out in writing the comments of the officer and the witness; all comments of the witness must be recorded verbatim and signed by the witness.
- Officers should not speak to witnesses after the line-up regarding their identification or their inability to identify anyone.

The Heads of Prosecution Report adopted the findings of the Sophonow report and made six recommendations regarding the methodology employed for photo line-ups, summarizing the process described above.

Photo line-ups are by far the most common tool used in the VPD (and other Canadian police agencies) for identification of unknown suspects by witnesses. The key change recommended by the Heads of Prosecution Report was switching from a line-up where photos are presented side-by-side to a photo pack or sequential presentation of photos. The VPD responded by creating a "task team" to ensure the necessary policies, procedures, and training were developed for effective and efficient implementation of the photo-pack process. This work was completed by July 2005. (The full policy/procedure and associated forms can be obtained from the Vancouver Police Department.)

Live line-ups were also dealt with in the Sophonow report, and recommendations for an appropriate procedure were similar to those with respect to photo line-ups. Specifically, the recommendations were:

- The line-up should contain a minimum of 10 persons.
- The fillers in the line-up should match as closely as possible the description given by the witness or, if that is not possible, they should resemble the suspect.
- An officer who does not know the case or the suspect should be in the room with the witness.
- Everything should be recorded, preferably on videotape.
- The witness should be advised that the officer does not know who the suspect is and that the suspect may not be in the line-up.
- All statements made by the witness should be recorded verbatim and signed by the witness.
- The officer should escort the witness from the premises after the line-up.
- If there has been an identification, the witness should be asked as to the degree of certainty of identification—that question and answer should be recorded verbatim and signed by the witness.

Although the VPD historically conducted live line-ups in a specially designed facility, it abandoned this investigative strategy as a result of a Supreme Court of Canada decision in 1989, making this recommendation moot.[14]

In the Heads of Prosecutions Report, "show-ups" were also considered. "Show-ups" involve the physical presentation of a single suspect to a witness during an investigation. This may happen by the police arranging for an "accidental" encounter on the street or through attending a court appearance of the suspect. The recommendation in that report was that "show-ups" should be used only in rare circumstances, such as when the suspect is apprehended near the crime scene shortly after the event.

The VPD had used a variation of the "show-up" known as an "impromptu line-up." Generally, this involves placing a suspect with a group of people (typically in a bar or similar location), securing any exits, and then walking the witness through the premises to see if the suspect can be identified. However, for a variety of reasons—not the least of which being the right of a suspect to refuse to participate—impromptu line-ups are very rarely employed. The VPD is now in compliance with the related recommendation.

Criminal Informants

The concerns related to jailhouse informants were discussed in detail in both the Morin and the Sophonow reports, but the Driskell report[15] demonstrates that there are risks with any criminal informants, whether the alleged confession is said to have taken place in jail or when the suspect was not in custody.

In Sophonow, it was suggested that jailhouse informants be prohibited from testifying as a general rule, and only in rare cases should their testimony be permitted. It was recommended in the Morin and the Heads of Prosecutions reports that special protocols be established for dealing with in-custody informants and investigating their reliability. Those reports also suggested that provinces establish an in-custody informer registry and the police contribute relevant information to that registry such as any instances of an individual disclosing an alleged confession by another inmate.

The reports in Morin, Sophonow, and Driskell all set out similar procedures that should be followed when dealing with any criminal informant. The informant's report of an alleged confession should be videotaped and taken under oath using nonleading questions. At the outset, the informant should be advised of the consequences of untruthful statements and false testimony. All

---

[14] In *R. v. Ross*, [1989] 1 S.C.R. 3, the Supreme Court of Canada held that a suspect could not be compelled to cooperate with a live line-up.

[15] *Report of the Commission of Inquiry into Certain Aspects of the Trial and Conviction of James Driskell*, The Honourable Patrick J. LeSage, Commissioner, January 2007. See http://www.driskellinquiry.ca/index.html. James Driskell spent over 13 years in prison after being wrongfully convicted of the murder of Perry Dean Harder in 1990.

contacts with the informant should be videotaped from beginning to end or, if videotaping is not possible, audiotaped. Any discussion of benefits offered or provided by the police or Crown, or any benefits sought by the informant, should be recorded and disclosed. The police operational manual should also reflect the continuing obligation to disclose potentially exculpatory material to the Crown postconviction, whether or not an appeal is pending.

The statement made by the informant must be thoroughly investigated. A review of the statement should be conducted to determine whether the information could have been obtained from media reports or evidence at a preliminary inquiry or trial if the trial is under way or there was a previous trial. The statement should also be assessed for material that could only be known by the person who committed the crime, for disclosed evidence that is detailed and significant as to the manner in which the crime was committed, and for evidence that has been confirmed by police investigators as correct and accurate. The police should also investigate whether the informant has any prior experiences testifying as an informer or as a witness generally.

Informants are important in solving crimes, but use of their testimony requires great caution, particularly if they are in custody. The VPD considers the use of jailhouse informants a rare but "necessary evil" in police work. It is an area fraught with risk because of the skill demonstrated by jailhouse informants in gathering compelling information that appears could only be known to the offender, and the role such informants have played in wrongful convictions. For example, in the Sophonow case, multiple in-custody informants came forward with purported confessions, and the Crown adduced testimony at trial from three of them. In-custody informants were described by Commissioner Peter Cory in the Sophonow report as:

> the most deceitful and deceptive group of witnesses known to frequent the courts. … They rush to testify like vultures to rotting flesh or sharks to blood. They are smooth and convincing liars. Whether they seek favours from the authorities, attention or notoriety they are in every instance completely unreliable. It will be seen how frequently they have been a major factor in the conviction of innocent people and how much they tend to corrupt the administration of justice. Usually, their presence as witnesses signals the end of any hope of providing a fair trial.

The Heads of Prosecution Report makes several recommendations designed to minimize the risks posed by in-custody informants. Improved training was a key recommendation. The VPD sends investigators to several courses at the Canadian Police College in Ottawa and the Justice Institute of British Columbia (JIBC) during which the problems associated with in-custody informants are covered. In addition, one of the authors (LePard) developed and regularly delivers to new investigators a three-hour training session on avoiding wrongful convictions, during which the problems of in-custody informants are reviewed.

A significant challenge with in-custody informants is the need for corroboration of their claims, a necessary step because of their inherent lack of credibility. So it is somewhat surprising that no one has recommended capturing these confessions by "wiring" the suspect's cell and attempting to have the jailhouse informant reengage the suspect in the conversation that allegedly took place. A repetition of the confession would provide reliable and generally incontrovertible evidence. In addition, when dealing with an in-custody informant, a polygraph test should be utilized. But it is far preferable that a police cell mate be utilized in a covertly video- and audiotaped cell so that all aspects of the operation can be controlled.[16] In fact, the use of an in-custody informant by the VPD is exceedingly rare, and police undercover cell plants are typically relied upon for obtaining "cell mate" statements from suspects.

The Heads of Prosecution Report also recommends that appropriate policy guidelines be developed regarding the use of in-custody informants. The VPD has a specialized Source Handling Unit overseen by a sergeant with considerable expertise in this area who has oversight responsibility for all informant-handling issues. In addition, the VPD has recently extensively amended several areas of its *Regulations and Procedures Manual* to reflect both the recommendations of the Heads of Prosecution Report and best practices in the field of informant handling. The new procedures pay particular attention to the risks of using information from in-custody informants, recognizing specifically their role in previous wrongful convictions. Approval from both a police supervisor (sergeant) and manager (inspector) are required before information from an in-custody informant may be utilized. Further, the procedure sets out a series of factors that investigators must consider in attempting to determine the informant's credibility.[17]

Mishandling of Investigations

The investigations analyzed in the various wrongful conviction reports were found to have been mishandled in a variety of ways. Tunnel vision, one of the major concerns, will be discussed separately below. Here we will look at recommendations relating to specific investigative problems such as searches, note taking, and interviews.

Notwithstanding these specific issues, the overall management of serious crime investigations is key to ensuring that the "mishandling" found in various

---

[16] A notable recent example was the evidence given in the 2007 Robert Pickton murder trial involving the use of an audio- and videotaped cell plant operation that occurred shortly after Pickton's arrest in February 2002.

[17] The nature of the procedure is such that it must remain confidential, on advice of the VPD's Freedom of Information and Privacy Unit Coordinator.

wrongful conviction cases is avoided. Investigations into serious offenses are often stressful and complex and require strong leadership, teamwork, and a variety of skill sets. Although it is important to address specific problems, as outlined above, the importance of implementing a systematic approach to investigations cannot be overemphasized; it is noteworthy that a systematic approach to investigations was typically absent in cases resulting in wrongful convictions. This is not surprising, considering that most known wrongful convictions in Canada resulted from investigations that took place prior to the development of a systematic approach to handling serious cases in the mid-1990s.

In Canada, the Canadian Police College's major case management (MCM) model, developed in 1994 and refined since then, is the accepted "best practice" for managing serious investigations and is followed by the VPD. MCM is a methodology for managing major cases that provides for accountability, clear goals and objectives, planning, efficient utilization of resources, and control over the speed, flow, and direction of the investigation. One of its nine key principles is the importance of ethical investigations. Justice Archie Campbell cited the MCM model in his review of the Paul Bernardo investigation as "a well-thought out approach to the problems of major serial predator investigations, solidly grounded in Canadian investigative experience and the lessons learned from failures and successes."[18] He went on to say:

> The Canadian Police College Course deals in a highly organized and systematic manner with issues such as the accountability of the senior officer in charge, the organization of the major investigative functions such as liaison with victims and their families, team building, financial administration, file organization, scene examination, profiling of victims and suspects, computerized investigative techniques, preparing for Crown disclosure, processing tips, planning the arrest and the interview, handling inter-jurisdictional issues, public appeals and planning for the deluge of information that results from them, dealing with the inevitable stress inflicted on the investigators and the victims and their families, establishment and management of the command post, and dozens of other issues faced daily by the officer in charge of a major serial predator investigation.[19]

The MCM model training prepares candidates to assume and retain effective command of coordinated investigation teams by providing the wherewithal to recognize, understand, and deal with a variety of critical management issues inherent to such investigations. The MCM model repackages the cumulative skills, knowledge, and experience derived from the successes and failures of Canadian law enforcement and organizes them in a manageable format, which makes them more effective and readily applied.

---

[18]Justice Archie Campbell, Bernardo Investigation Review, Government of Ontario, 1996, p. 271.
[19]Ibid. p. 324.

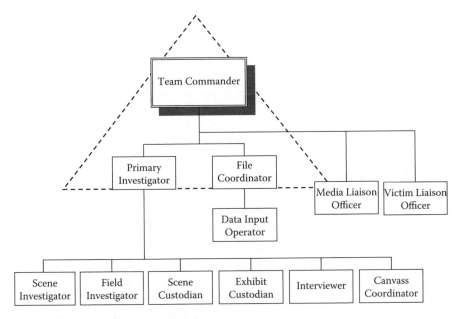

Figure 13.1 Major case management command triangle.

Fundamental to the MCM model is the "command triangle," as shown in Figure 13.1. The Team Commander is at the top of the triangle, and the File Coordinator and Primary Investigator report to him or her. Data entry staff report to the file coordinator, and all field investigators report to the Primary Investigator. It is the responsibility of the Team Commander to decide the speed, direction, and flow of the investigation and to ensure it proceeds in a lawful and ethical manner, following established best practices that, among other benefits, minimize the chances of a wrongful conviction.[20]

The VPD sends its investigators and investigative supervisors on MCM training and also participates in a provincial MCM accreditation program for managers of serious and complex investigations. Aspects of MCM training regarding wrongful convictions are also delivered at the earliest opportunity for new investigators. For example, in the VPD training described earlier regarding avoiding wrongful convictions, the importance of offering suspects an opportunity to provide a response to allegations is stressed with the explanation (including examples) of the reality of false and mistaken allegations. It is also stressed that it is the responsibility of every investigator in every investigation, not just serious and complex investigations, to guard against those factors that lead to wrongful convictions.

---

[20]The Canadian Police College's *Major Case Management Manual* has a much fuller description of the selection criteria and duties of the various positions in the MCM model.

Implementation of the MCM model and training on effective case management help ensure that investigations are not mishandled generally and the problems arising from the specific issues set out below are minimized.

Missing Persons Investigations and Searches

One of the investigative problems identified in the Morin report resulted from the situation in which police were initially dealing with a missing person report that later turned into a murder investigation. A number of witnesses had already been interviewed without their statements being properly recorded. In addition, the initial searches had been conducted in a manner that did not meet the standards for a murder investigation. As a result, it was recommended that officers conducting a missing persons investigation be mindful that the case could escalate into a murder case. Therefore, they must keep an accurate and complete record of statements from relevant persons, and must protect potential evidence from removal or contamination. In addition, it was recommended that searches in missing persons investigations be supervised by a trained search coordinator and conducted in accordance with standardized search procedures.

The Morin report also addressed proper search procedures upon the discovery of a body and recommended that a search of a body site include a grid search; preservation of the scene against inclement weather; adequate lighting; coordinated search parties with documented search areas; a search plan and search coordinator; full documentation of items found and retained, together with their precise location and continuity; adequate videotaping and photographing of the scene; adequate indexing of exhibits and photographs; adequate facilities and methods for transportation of human remains; decontamination suits if necessary; and sufficient resources to avoid cross-contamination of different sites.

The VPD has had a specialized Missing Persons Unit for many years; however, its performance was inconsistent, and a major review of the Vancouver's Missing Women investigation identified systemic problems in the Unit. As a result, in 2004 the VPD contracted a consultant with relevant policing experience to conduct a comprehensive audit of the Missing Persons Unit, resulting in extensive changes. Since then, the VPD's Missing Persons Unit has made great strides; it is now considered the leader in Canadian policing with respect to missing persons investigations and is looked to by police agencies across Canada for best practices because of its extraordinary success (Brethour, 2007).

Part of the Unit's success can be attributed to its incorporation within the Major Crime Section, along with the Homicide and Robbery/Assault Squads, which are all managed by the same inspector. This structure helps to ensure that investigations are handled in a coordinated fashion with recognition of the potential for a missing persons investigation to evolve into a homicide file. The Missing Persons Unit is responsible for the coordination and oversight of any search for a missing person, and the police officers involved are guided by detailed procedures that address the recommendations discussed earlier.

In addition, in 2005 the VPD created its Search and Canvass Team. This group of over 60 deploys squads of at least eight officers specially trained by police experts from the United Kingdom and the VPD to conduct searches for missing persons and criminal evidence. They also canvass for witnesses and take their statements.

The four-day course required to join the team is adapted from a joint British Army and Police Antiterrorist Squad search course in the United Kingdom. Also included is a second element of detailed canvasses and reenactment canvassing from combined UK and VPD experiences, utilizing existing UK standards and practices, including a structured paperwork system.

The course includes theory; practical application of personnel; fingertip, line, vehicle, and route searches at crime scenes; venue searches (defensive and/or existing threats); use of specialized equipment; canvasses and reenactment canvasses; and the incorporation of canine and boat team searches.

The team has been very successful since its creation, recovering evidence in robberies and homicides, and locating missing persons. For example, in April 2006 the team was called out 13 times during the intensive investigation into the gunpoint kidnapping of Graham McMynn.[21] The team was used for canvassing, video canvassing, searching, arrest teams, media strategy, and public reassurance. The searches included line searches of rural and urban areas, fingertip searches of the crime scenes, and coordination of the river and shoreline searches. The team also searched one of the crime houses and approximately 30 bags of garbage, separating DNA materials for forensic identification. The team recovered important evidence and also located several witnesses. And in May 2006, when a child went missing in Vancouver's notorious Downtown Eastside, the Search Team Coordinator organized an extensive search involving over 100 officers that resulted in finding the child. In 2006 the team was deployed 44 times.

The Search and Canvass Team initiative has significantly improved the VPD's ability to respond to serious incidents and has identified and implemented a number of best practices, including:

- A systematic reporting process that details the activities of search and canvass members.
- Creation of relationships with outside agencies that can supply specialized support such as the Royal Canadian Mounted Police (RCMP) Dive

---

[21] For a detailed newspaper article on the McMynn kidnapping, see Mulgrew, Bolan, Skelton, and Bridge (2006).

Team and Air Support, the Canadian Military, and civilian search and rescue teams.

- Improved evidence-gathering standards in regard to physical evidence as well as interviews and written statements.
- An improved method for lead investigators to communicate their expectations for a search and/or canvass via a search contract or agreement document.
- Identification of the requirement for further training and education in relation to crime scene management, including DNA issues, exhibit control, and scene contamination, thus improving the skills and abilities of officers in both patrol and investigative positions to appropriately manage a crime scene.

The search training developed in the VPD, including the antiterrorist aspect, is now being studied for use at the Zole Winter Olympics and beyond, and is expected to be adopted as a national standard.

Note Taking

Documenting statements and other evidence through written notes was discussed in the Morin report. It was recommended that police have policies for note taking and note-keeping practices. Such policies better regulate the contents of police notebooks and reports in order to reinforce the need for a complete and accurate record of interviews, police observations, and police activities.

As was noted in the Driskell report, the police do not take notes solely to assist their own recollection in the future. They are recording information that may have great significance to the accused and to the Crown, although that significance may not be known for some time. In the Driskell report, it was recommended that complete, detailed notes be taken by police of all information and that all notes be passed on to the Crown.

The importance of good notes is stressed at the recruit training level at the Justice Institute of British Columbia and in every investigator's course delivered internally in the VPD. In addition, the VPD has policies and procedures regarding note taking that range from the issue of content to retention of notebooks. In 2005, the VPD, in an effort to improve primary investigations, initiated additional training on various issues from note taking to giving evidence in court. For example, in 2005 a training bulletin was distributed that set out the VPD's expectations for note taking, and the issue is also covered in a variety of training courses. It is standard practice in the VPD that every involved officer submits a copy of all notes with the Report to Crown Counsel.

Interviewing

The proper recording of police interviews was addressed in both the Sophonow and Morin reports. All interviews of suspects must be videotaped or at least audiotaped in their entirety. The Lamer report[22] recommended that in major crime investigations, all police station interviews be videotaped and field interviews be audiotaped. If an oral statement is not recorded on tape, it should be reread to the suspect at the police station on videotape and his or her comments recorded or, alternatively, the statement should be put in writing and the suspect permitted to read and sign it, if it is regarded as accurate by the suspect (Morin). In the Morin report it was also recommended that all significant witnesses in serious crime cases be interviewed in a similar fashion.

Coincidentally, and for a variety of reasons, since the 1990s there has been a move in Canadian policing to videotape interviews of suspects whenever practicable. Canadian courts have "raised the bar" in a number of respects regarding suspect interviews, recognizing that only a taped statement is a truly reliable reflection of what the suspect and interviewer said in the interview room. A videotaped interview eliminates, or at least greatly reduces, the problems caused by "misunderstandings" or inaccurate note taking. This provides a benefit to police investigations, in that it is much more difficult for a defense lawyer to allege interview improprieties that might result in a statement being ruled inadmissible.

In addition, a videotaped statement provides the Court an opportunity to judge the tenor of the conversation and the condition of the suspect, allowing a more informed decision as to the voluntariness of the statement. Further, while confessions that are not videotaped are not necessarily inadmissible, where facilities are available and the police failed to use them, the confession will be inherently suspect and may be ruled inadmissible.[23] Finally, with recent research into the phenomenon of false confessions (Kassin & Gudjonsson, 2004) and wrongful convictions, resulting in part from inappropriate suspect interviews, videotaping suspect interviews protects the rights of those wrongly accused.

In consideration of various issues of prosecutorial effectiveness, the Heads of Prosecution Committee (composed of the senior Crown Counsel from each province and territory in Canada) has produced draft guidelines recommending that all statements made by an accused party be either audio- or videotaped if at all feasible.

---

[22] *The Lamer Commission of Inquiry Pertaining to the Cases of: Ronald Dalton, Gregory Parsons, Randy Druken*, The Right Honourable Antonio Lamer, 2006. See http://www.justice.gov.nl.ca/just/lamer. Dalton, Parsons, and Druken were each wrongfully convicted of murder in three different cases.

[23] *R. v. Moore-McFarlane* (2001), 160 C.C.C. (3d) 493 (Ont. C.A.). See also *R. v. Menezes* (2001), 48 C.R. (5th) 163 (Ont. S.C.J.).

Ideally, then, both to ensure that inculpatory statements have the best chance of being found admissible and to minimize the chance of misinterpretation, the best practice is to use a tape recorder at the scene of arrest for early conversations, and to tape all interactions with the suspect during transport, including during movement from cells to the interview room. However, it is recognized that, excepting a planned arrest, it is impracticable for frontline officers to audiotape suspect interviews because of the cost of equipment, transcriptions, and associated issues.

Although the VPD is committed to taking all reasonable steps to implement best practices regarding the interviewing of suspects, at the field interview stage in an urban area such as Vancouver, it would be virtually impossible—and counterproductive—to require that all statements be audiotaped.

Notwithstanding the challenges of interviews at the point of arrest, in the interview room, all suspect conversations can and should be videotaped, or at the very least, audiotaped. Like many police services in Canada, the VPD has multiple interview rooms fully equipped with digital audio/video recording devices. In addition to other benefits, use of this equipment reduces the likelihood of factors that could lead to a wrongful conviction, and it is the practice for all planned interviews of suspects to be audio- and videotaped.

Video recording protects police investigators from false allegations of interviewing improprieties and protects suspects from the potentially serious consequences of inaccurate note taking,[24] fabricated evidence, or interview strategies that render a confession untrustworthy.[25] Videotaping of suspect interviews wherever possible is best practice, serves the interests of justice, and is now reflected in the policies and practices of the VPD.

Alibi Witnesses

The Morin and Sophonow reports made recommendations regarding interviews of alibi witnesses. It was recommended that any alibi be investigated by officers other than those directly involved in investigating the crime or the accused. Interviews with alibi witnesses should be videotaped or at least audiotaped in their entirety. When interviewing alibi witnesses, they should not be cross-examined, it should not be suggested to them that they are mistaken, and they should not be influenced to change their position, although it

---

[24]For example, in the wrongful conviction of Thomas Sophonow, investigators' notes of an interview with Sophonow suggested he provided information only the killer could have known. This was highly unlikely as Sophonow was not the killer!

[25]In the United Kingdom and other Western nations, there have been several infamous cases where it was determined that police officers fabricated or coerced false confessions. One of those is the Guildford Four, where the suspects signed a false confession after being beaten by police.

is appropriate for police to instruct them that it is essential they tell the truth and the consequences of failing to do so (Sophonow).

One important aspect of the MCM model employed by the VPD is the assignment of a "contrarian" role in serious investigations. The investigator assigned to this position is expected to be skeptical when a suspect is identified, and to attempt to "disprove" evidence pointing in the suspect's direction. Carefully gathering and recording of alibi evidence is part of this role. This accomplishes two purposes. First, if the suspect is innocent, he or she can then be eliminated as early as possible, freeing up investigative resources and removing the aura of suspicion surrounding that person. Second, if the suspect is actually guilty, then the role of contrarian will assist in eliminating potential defenses such as false alibis.

Retention of Evidence

Missing evidence is one of the problems that can arise when looking at older cases, either to assess whether there was a wrongful conviction or determine the possibility of prosecution. The Sophonow report recommends police forces keep police notebooks and that they should be kept for at least 20 years, but preferably 25 years, from the date that the officer leaves the force or retires. Notebooks can be preserved on microfiche to minimize storage issues.

The storage of original evidence was addressed in both the Morin and the Sophonow reports. It was recommended in the Sophonow report that exhibits, whether filed in court or gathered in the course of the investigation, should be stored for at least 20 years from the date of the last appeal or the expiry of the time to undertake that appeal.

Since 2001, the VPD has had a policy requiring that police members who leave the VPD turn their notebooks in to VPD archives. The retention policy requires they be kept permanently. The VPD also has a detailed evidence retention policy that sets out the number of years reports and evidence are retained, depending on the nature of the incident involved. For example, the reports on murders and sex offenses are kept permanently, and for robberies, they are kept for 10 years. In the case of physical evidence, for homicides and sex offenses, the evidence is kept permanently, and evidence in less serious cases is disposed of after varying lengths of time, after consultation with the investigator.

False Confessions

The Heads of Prosecution and other reports have discussed the problem of false confessions and the psychology that underlies them, and made recommendations to minimize their occurrence. These include requiring the entire suspect interview to be videotaped (not just the final statement); reviewing investigation standards on interviewing to ensure they enhance reliability and accurately preserve the contents of the interview; training about the existence, causes, and psychology of police-induced confessions, including why some people confess to crimes they did not committed;[26] and training on the use of proper interview techniques.

An important practice in reducing the possibility of a wrongful conviction based on statements attributed to the accused is to videotape the entire interview; the VPD is committed to this practice, not only with respect to preventing wrongful convictions, but also to ensure inculpatory statements have the best chance of being ruled admissible.

The problem of police-induced false confessions is also covered in a variety of training programs, beginning with a cursory examination in recruit training at the JIBC, and more extensively in advanced investigators courses at the JIBC and Canadian Police College. In addition, the issue is specifically covered in the aforementioned VPD training on avoiding wrongful convictions. Investigators are taught not only to videotape interrogations in their entirety, but also to understand the psychology of police-induced false confessions and how psychological strategies can cause both guilty and innocent people to confess. They are also taught the importance of testing statements against known facts.

Finally, the MCM model imposes the investigative standards recommended in the Heads of Prosecution Report. This investigative methodology is now used in all significant criminal cases. As a national and best practice standard, application of the MCM model ensures that major investigations proceed in an orderly, coordinated, and defensible manner. It is noteworthy that a key role of the Team Commander in the MCM model is to ensure that the highest technical and ethical standards are maintained so that investigations are not compromised by "short cuts," poor practice, and inappropriate investigative practices.

False Allegations

The issue of false allegations is not specifically covered in the literature around wrongful convictions. However, it is a problem in practice and one that police investigators must be aware of, so it is discussed in somewhat more depth than other issues in this chapter. False allegations arise in two broad sets of circumstances. The first is when a crime *has* occurred, but allegations are made against an innocent party. The second is when allegations are made

---

[26]False confessions usually result from a combination of factors, including the suspect's psychological vulnerability, wish to protect someone else, desire to escape custody, and/or lack of ability to cope with interrogative pressure.

against an innocent party about crimes that have *not* occurred. Motivations for false allegations include maliciousness; revenge; hope to gain advantage (such as with in-custody informants); emotional and/or mental instability; to use as a weapon in custody disputes;[27] as a result of improper and/or coercive police questioning, particularly where children are concerned; and finally as a tool to extricate oneself from a difficult situation, such as a female who had "a sexual encounter with someone other than their boyfriend or husband, or a young person acting against the wishes of their parent" (Light & Ruebsaat, 2006, p. 77). Often, a combination of these factors is involved, as seen in the examples below.

Some false allegations are a product of emotional instability on the part of the complainant and may result from a need for attention. In a VPD case (investigated by LePard) that generated considerable publicity, the complainant made repeated allegations of stalking she produced compelling "evidence" in the form of phone traces, a recording purported to be the suspect making an obscene call, a witness who reported seeing the suspect at the victim's home, and an allegation that the suspect had tried to kill the victim in his car. Although charges were originally recommended against the "suspect," additional investigation requested by Crown to further corroborate the allegations revealed that, in fact, all the evidence had been engineered or fabricated. The complainant, who had a long history of attention-seeking behavior, was convicted of public mischief. Key to avoiding a miscarriage of justice was a careful examination of the complainant's background and thorough analysis of the evidence.

In three cases involving Lower Mainland teachers all investigated by the same police officer, mentally ill women made bizarre allegations of sexual assaults that were initially deemed credible. Overzealous and incompetent investigations had a devastating impact on the teachers, and one case of a "recovered repressed memory" resulted in charges and multiple trials before the teacher was exonerated.[28] A second teacher successfully sued for damages after being wrongfully accused of raping the complainant in the classroom. "It was obvious, the judge said, that the girl was experiencing the onset of schizophrenia" (Ouston, 1998). In the third case, the victim alleged her father, mother, and 50 others had "abused her as part of satanic cult activities" (Ouston, 1998), yet she was still considered a credible witness by the investigator. An internal police review of the case concluded that there "is an

---

[27]One recent study found that where a custody or access dispute has occurred, 12% of child maltreatment allegations were false, three times the rate where no custody or access dispute was involved (see Nico Trocme, University of Toronto, Faculty of Social Work & Nick Bala, Queen's University Law School, 2004, *False Allegations of Abuse and Neglect When Parents Separate*, available on-line at http://www.leadershipcouncil.org/docs/trocme.pdf).

[28]*R. v. Kliman*, [1994] B.C.W.L.D. No. 587.

onus on the investigator to judge the credibility of the victim in conducting an unbiased investigation … [the investigator] clearly made a biased assessment … without any consideration of the bizarre and unbelievable comments" (Ouston, 1998).

Flawed and leading interviews of children can result in false allegations and miscarriages of justice. For example, by the 1990s, allegations of satanic and ritual abuse of children had become common, resulting in part from improper investigative and interviewing techniques that created "group hysteria."[29] The most notorious Canadian case was in Martensville, Saskatchewan, where tunnel vision and improper police interviews of suggestible children in day care by an inexperienced officer led to numerous bizarre allegations.[30] Eventually, nine people were charged, including five police officers.[31] Even after an independent review by a joint RCMP/Saskatoon Police Department task force raised serious doubts about the allegations, the Crown continued the prosecutions. But only the teenage son of the caregivers was found guilty of fondling two of the children; there never was a satanic conspiracy of pedophiles.

One of the officers who was eventually exonerated, John Popowich, never returned to police work and lost an eye when attacked in a restaurant after his charges had been stayed. He was subsequently awarded $1.3 million by the Saskatchewan government for malicious prosecution and received a written apology from Saskatchewan's Minister of Justice affirming Popowich was "fully innocent." Separate reviews conducted by the Crown[32] and the RCMP[33] found the investigation seriously flawed, particularly in the interviews of the children.

False allegations of sexual offenses by complainants seeking to extricate themselves from a difficult situation are a troubling reality for police investigators. Statistics Canada reports that in 2002, 16% of sexual offenses were "unfounded," more than twice the rate of other violent offenses (Kong, Johnson, Beattie, & Cardillo, 2003, p. 9). In an extraordinary case, the first exoneration by DNA in the State of Illinois was of Gary Dotson, who was wrongfully convicted of the 1977 rape of a 16-year-old girl and sentenced to 25 to 50 years in prison.[34] The key evidence against him was the girl's identification and flawed forensic science, particularly around tests done on semen found in the girl's underpants. In 1985 the victim recanted her

---

[29] See http://members.shaw.ca/imaginarycrimes/timeline.htm for one timeline of ritual abuse cases.

[30] The case was explored in the CBC series *The Fifth Estate* in an episode titled "Hell to Pay" (2003, February 12); http://www.cbc.ca/fifth/martin/scandal.html.

[31] For a timeline of the case, see http://www.cbc.ca/fifth/martin/timeline.html.

[32] See http://www.cbc.ca/fifth/martin/docs/mar_orl.pdf.

[33] See http://www.cbc.ca/fifth/martin/docs/mar_rcmpl.pdf.

[34] See http://www.law.northwestern.edu/news/fall02/dotson.html.

allegations, stating that the semen in her underpants was from sex with her boyfriend the day prior to her allegation, and that she had wanted a cover story in case she was pregnant. A court hearing was ordered, but the judge decided the complainant's original evidence was more credible than her recantation, saying the latter was "implausible."[35] It was not until 1989 that advanced DNA analysis positively excluded Dotson as the donor of semen found in the complainant's underpants, and proved that it was in fact from her boyfriend.[36]

Coercive police questioning of witnesses, particularly those who are psychologically vulnerable, can lead to false allegations, either because the witnesses come to believe the allegation or they wish to avoid further police questioning. For example, in the Milgaard case, repeated and coercive questioning by police of the three youths who were with Milgaard at the time of the murder led them to make false and highly damaging allegations against him and were the basis of his conviction (Boyd & Rossmo, 1992, p. 18). Likewise, in the much more recent case of the murder of Breann Voth by Derek Post,[37] improper police interviewing of a drug addicted "witness" led her to allege that she had seen two men—the original suspects—commit the crime. The trial judge said the following about the interview:

> I am disturbed that [the witness] is asked to close her eyes and imagine she's watching a movie. The interrogation encourages her to engage in speculation and imagine herself in various places. I find the nature of the questions and the circumstances under which they were made, shocking ... [the investigator] encourages her to imagine a story. It is an atmosphere ideal for implanting false memories. (Bellett, 2005)

Each of the examples above provides lessons for police investigators and was used in VPD training regarding wrongful convictions, the content of which is summarized below. First and foremost, investigators are taught that, while they must demonstrate professionalism and compassion toward complainants, their role is to determine the facts, not to act as an advocate. An investigator's responsibility to an accused person is the same as it is to a complainant—conduct a fair and ethical investigation, following best practices, motivated only by a search for the truth. As described elsewhere in this section, tunnel vision is frequently implicated in wrongful convictions. Therefore, it is extremely important to keep an open mind, not jump to con-

---

[35]National Desk. (1985, August 22). "Rape case judge calls recantation 'implausible'," *New York Times*, p. A13.

[36]See http://www.law.northwestern.edu/wrongfulconvictions/exonerations/iDotsonSummary.html.

[37]*R. v. Post*, 2005 BCSC 1522.

clusions, and to follow the other best police practices set out in this chapter to avoid wrongful convictions.

Carefully conducted interviews and follow-up investigation are key to determining if an allegation is false. Allegations must be compared against known facts, and efforts should always be made to find corroboration, and to question why it cannot be found if that is the case. Investigative tools such as statement analysis can be invaluable for determining if a statement is deceptive.[38] It is entirely appropriate and necessary to check a complainant's background to see if there is a history of suspicious complaints. Where children are involved, it is crucial that only an investigator properly trained in conducting nonleading and age-appropriate interviews be utilized. The background to the disclosure and any previous interviews must be carefully examined for the possibility that the allegation has already been tainted by leading questions.

Although bizarre allegations can be true—keeping an open mind means this possibility must be considered—generally speaking, the more bizarre the allegation, the less likely it is to be true, no matter how credible and articulate the complainant appears. And while a mental illness does not necessarily mean a complaint is not credible, if the illness is one involving psychosis and delusional thinking, then this should be a major red flag for the investigator. In addition, great care must be taken in interviewing those who are emotionally or mentally frail, including those with substance abuse problems, as they may be more susceptible to leading or suggestive questioning. Complainants may make false allegations for the same reasons discussed earlier regarding false confessions, including coercion, and investigators must guard against unduly influencing a witness or complainant's statement.

Finally, with respect to suspects, it is crucially important that they be given an opportunity to provide a response to allegations against them, and that any denials or alibi evidence proffered be fully investigated with an open mind as to their truthfulness.

Police Culture

There is a recognized need for police to foster professional ethics and a culture that guards against tunnel vision and noble cause corruption. Commissioner Fred Kaufman in the Morin report defined tunnel vision as "the single-minded and overly narrow focus on a particular investigative or prosecutorial theory, so as to unreasonably color the evaluation of information received and one's conduct in response to that information." One of the suggestions in the Morin

[38] Statement analysis training has been common for police investigators since the 1990s; the best-known system originated with a former Israeli police investigator, Avinoam Sapir (http://www.lsiscan.com/).

report was that investigators should not attain an elevated standing in an investigation through acquiring or pursuing the "best" suspect or lead. This produces competition that can isolate investigative teams from each other.

Bruce MacFarlane, QC (2006) noted that tunnel vision often occurs when there is substantial public or media pressure on police to solve a crime. This increases the need to quickly identify a viable suspect and can cause a premature focus on a person against whom there is only some evidence. Tunnel vision results when other potential leads or lines of inquiry are ignored. Even when a prime suspect has been identified, police should continue to pursue all reasonable investigative avenues, no matter in what direction they lead.

Noble cause corruption was described by MacFarlane as a phenomenon where police think it is justifiable to fabricate or artificially improve evidence, or in some other fashion bend the rules to secure the conviction of a person they believe is guilty. Nobel cause corruption can manifest itself in false testimony, excessive force, illegal searches or surveillance, or other questionable police strategies. It is conduct that masks itself as legitimate on the basis that the guilty must be brought to justice, despite evidentiary, substantive, or constitutional considerations that might "get in the way."

Predisposing or environmental circumstances often set the stage for investigative failures. These factors include public pressure for an arrest in high-profile cases, an unpopular suspect, an investigative environment where the pursuit of the truth is surrendered to a desire to "win" at virtually any cost, and the mindset that the end justifies the means because of the belief the suspect is guilty.

To address these concerns, it was recommended in the Morin report that police agencies endeavor to foster within their ranks a culture of policing that values honest and fair investigation of crime and the protection of the rights of all suspects and accused parties. Management must recognize it is their responsibility to foster this culture. Police need to develop and maintain a culture that guards against early investigative bias, one that emphasizes the importance of constant and continuous fact verification.

A key role of the Team Commander in the MCM model employed by the VPD and other police agencies is to ensure investigations proceed in a lawful and ethical manner. The role of contrarian is important to guard against tunnel vision and premature investigative conclusions. Implementation of the MCM model with police officers properly trained in their roles is the best defense against tunnel vision, bad police practice, overzealousness, bias, noble cause corruption, and incompetent investigations. To this end, the VPD requires that all sergeants and inspectors in charge of investigative units receive MCM training. In addition, the VPD is committed to the RCMP's provincial MCM Accreditation process and has an accredited Team Commander who sits on the evaluation committee. Finally, part of the philosophy of MCM is to encourage independent reviews of investigations. The VPD supports this philosophy and has entrenched a system of conducting facilitated debriefings of major cases as a learning exercise. A detailed report is prepared setting out the challenges of the investigation, what went well, what did not, and lessons and recommendations for the future. These reports are available to all VPD members on the VPD's "knowledge base" (see below for further information).

The value of integrity is incorporated into all VPD investigator training, particularly the session on avoiding wrongful convictions, where the role of the contrarian, the importance of ethical conduct, and the need to challenge inappropriate actions are all stressed.

It should also be noted that the hiring process for VPD recruits is highly comprehensive and includes a polygraph examination. A key "show-stopper" is any issue with integrity, the first of VPD's four IPAR values (along with professionalism, accountability, and respect), and members are expected to live these values in every aspect of their work. For example, officers are repeatedly advised that if they have to choose between letting an alleged criminal go free or compromising their values, then they are expected to let the criminal go free. In 2006, VPD created an ethics officer position to specifically ensure ethical issues are constantly reviewed and reinforced. The VPD values are imbued in a variety of ways, including being incorporated into every promotional process.

Education

It was recommended in the Morin and other reports that police officers should receive regular training on the known or suspected causes of wrongful convictions and on how police can help prevent these injustices. Recommendations were also made regarding specific areas of training, including:

- The identification and avoidance of tunnel vision (Morin); annual tunnel vision training with examples and discussion (Sophonow, Heads of Prosecutions).
- Ethical training (Morin).
- A wide range of investigative skills, on a continuing basis (Morin).
- The appropriate use and limitations of criminal profiling; while this technique may have value for generating investigative ideas, the creation of a profile once a suspect is identified can be misleading and dangerous (Morin).
- The limitations of forensic fiber comparisons (Morin).
- Police protocols regarding in-custody informants and appropriate methods of dealing with them and investigating their reliability (Morin).

- The perils of eyewitness misidentifications (Heads of Prosecutions).
- The appropriate use and limitations of polygraph results (Morin).
- How to address and evaluate "late breaking evidence" (evidence that could reasonably be expected to have been brought forward earlier), including the need to explore the information available to the witness, the reason or motivation for the untimely disclosure, the necessity to try to confirm such evidence, and the requirement to view such evidence with caution (Morin).

In the Morin report, a number of specific topics were identified for police training with respect to conducting witness interviews:

- Interviewing techniques that enhance the reliability of witness statements and the techniques that detract from their reliability.
- The dangers of unnecessarily communicating information to a witness that might color their account of events.
- The dangers of communicating an investigator's assessment of the strength of the case or his or her opinion of the accused person's character.
- Interviewing techniques for young witnesses, including the requirement to have a disinterested adult present.

The Heads of Prosecutions Report recommended police training on the existence, causes, and psychology of police-induced false confessions, including why some people confess to crimes they have not committed and techniques to enhance reliability when interviewing suspects or witnesses.

The VPD fully supports the recommendations discussed above. They are incorporated into the MCM training delivered by the Canadian Police College, the JIBC, and internal investigator training courses. They are also covered in a specific training session on wrongful convictions delivered in the Level II Investigators Program to all VPD members within their first five years of service, irrespective of their assignment. At a minimum, all officers will be introduced to these issues during their basic training, and again in greater depth during their first five years on the job. Any officer who moves into an investigative squad will then receive considerably more training, including the Level I and Level II Investigator Programs (formerly known as the Major Crime Course), the Sexual Offense Investigator Program, various interviewing and interrogation courses, and major case management training. Finally, the VPD Investigation Division has created a "Knowledge Base," a searchable intranet-based electronic library of literature promoting investigative excellence. It includes a section on wrongful convictions containing the reports of relevant commissions and inquiries, as well as other appropriate literature. Its creator, the Division's Deputy Chief, promotes the use of, and encourages new contributions to, this resource.[39]

Conclusion

There can be no greater failure of the criminal justice system than to convict an innocent person. Yet we know it happens, and with greater frequency than once believed. If one extrapolates from the 197 convicted persons exonerated of serious crimes by DNA in the United States, and the small but growing number in Canada, it is only reasonable to assume that the real number is far higher, as in many cases DNA evidence is not available. This is unacceptable.

Fortunately, it is possible to reduce greatly the potential for wrongful convictions. In every Canadian case discussed earlier, serious, avoidable errors were made in the police investigations, as well as by other players, in the criminal justice system. There is now considerable research on why investigative failures leading to wrongful convictions occur, which provides a map for preventing them. Proper recruiting and training, implementation of the major case management model, fostering a culture of excellence in ethical investigations, and ongoing education into the causes of wrongful convictions and proper investigative techniques are necessary to create an environment in which only the guilty are convicted. A wrongful conviction not only hurts the individual convicted, it hurts society, both in terms of the true guilty party being allowed to remain free, and in terms of the public's confidence in the criminal justice system. The police play a pivotal part in this system and must therefore have a significant role in preventing wrongful convictions.

References

Bellett, G. (2005, October 6). "Judge rules out other men in Voth killing: Justice Harvey Groberman also slams police interrogation for 'manipulating' addict into implicating 2 men." *Vancouver Sun*, p. B5.

Boyd, N., & Rossmo, D. K. (1992). *Milgaard v. the Queen: Finding justice—Problems and process*. Burnaby, British Columbia: School of Criminology Research Centre, Simon Fraser University.

---

[39]One example from the "Knowledge Base" is a superb and detailed article on the most common reasons for failed investigations by Rossmo (2005).

Brethour, P. (2007, January 13). Streetwise: B.C.'s finest finders—Missing persons unit of Vancouver police had a perfect record in 2006: 4,004 found. *Globe and Mail*, p. S1.

Grisham, J. (2006). *The innocent man: Murder and injustice in a small town*. New York: Doubleday.

Huff, C. R., Rattner, A., & Sagarin, E. (1996). *Convicted but innocent: Wrongful conviction and public policy*. Thousand Oaks, CA: Sage.

Kassin, S. M., & Gudjonsson, G. H. (2004). The psychology of confessions. A review of the literature and issues. *Psychological Science in the Public Interest, 5* (2), 33–67.

Kong, R., Johnson, H., Beattie, S., & Cardillo, A. (2003). *Sexual offences in Canada*. Juristat, Canadian Centre for Justice Statistics, *23*(6), 9.

Light, L., & Ruebsaat, G. (2006, March). *Police classification of sexual assault cases as unfounded: An exploratory study*. Centre for Leadership and Community Learning, Justice Institute of British Columbia.

MacFarlane, B. A. (2006) *Convicting the innocent—A triple failure of the justice system*, p. 52. See http://www.canadiancriminallaw.com.

Mulgrew, I., Bolan, K., Skelton, C., & Bridge, M. (2006, April 13). Daring raid by combined forces frees McMynn. *Vancouver Sun*, p. A1.

Ouston, R. (1998, February 27). Three discredited sex cases linked. *Vancouver Sun*, pp. A1–A2, B5.

Rossmo, D. K. (2005). *Criminal investigative failures*. Unpublished manuscript, Texas State University, Department of Criminal Justice, San Marcos, TX. [Edited version appears in two parts (September and October 2006), in the *FBI Law Enforcement Bulletin 75*(9 & 10).]

Reducing Investigative Failures through Effective Major Case Leadership*

14

JOHN C. HOUSE,
JOSEPH EASTWOOD, AND
BRENT SNOOK

Criminal investigative failures in Canada have raised questions about the competence of individuals who manage major cases (see, for example, FPT Heads of Prosecutions Committee Working Group, 2004; Kaufman, 1998). Major cases are those investigations, such as homicide or serial sexual assault requiring a response that falls outside the parameters of standard services provided by police agencies (Canadian Police College, 2002). Managers of such cases are typically senior officers who are responsible for the organization and behavior of all personnel involved. Although this is arguably one of the most consequential areas of policing, little is known about the knowledge, skills, and abilities (KSAs) of effective major case managers. Beyond a couple of studies on effective detectives (Maguire, Noaks, Hobbs, & Brearley, 1993; Smith & Flanagan, 2000), it seems that judicial inquiries and police training programs are the primary sources of knowledge regarding the competencies that major case managers should possess and exhibit. Given the lack of empirical research in this area, we urge readers to embark on the challenge of determining the characteristics of effective major case managers.

This chapter is divided into six sections. In the first section, we put the current chapter into context by reviewing six Canadian criminal investigative failures. In the second section, we summarize both the problems raised in Canadian judicial inquires about major case management and major case management training available in Canada. In the third section, we review the empirical research on the KSAs required for effective major case management. In the fourth section, we discuss the literature on leadership and

* This research was sponsored by the Canadian Police College Police Research Scholarship Program. We thank Richard M. Cullen for his contribution to an earlier version of this chapter. We also thank Craig Bennell, Paul Taylor, and Mike Luke for their comments on earlier drafts of this chapter.

draw upon that research as a potential source of guidance for research and training in this area. In section five, we report the results of a study that aimed to identify the competencies associated with effective major case managers in Canada. In the sixth section, we conclude with a call for future research on major case management.

Canadian Criminal Investigative Failures

Although the current chapter does not focus on investigative failures, it is nevertheless useful to reflect on a few such cases to learn about their common errors. Six Canadian investigative failures are reviewed briefly below to highlight some of the central contributing factors.

Donald Marshall, Jr.

On May 28, 1971, 17-year-old Sandy Seale was stabbed in Wentworth Park in Sydney, Nova Scotia. He later died in hospital. Within a couple of pressure-filled days, detectives decided that 17-year-old Donald Marshall, Jr., was their primary suspect for a variety of reasons—he was an eyewitness to the murder, he sustained an injury from the incident, he was seen running from the park, and he was known to the police as a troublemaker. These reasons led to a quickly developed theory that Marshall killed Seale after an argument. Marshall was eventually arrested, charged, and convicted for Seale's murder and sentenced to life imprisonment. He spent 11 years in prison before being acquitted in 1983. A second investigation revealed that Marshall and Seale had encountered Roy Ebsary and James MacNeil while walking through the park. The interaction between the four men ended with Ebsary stabbing Seale in the stomach and slashing Marshall's arm. Ebsary was later convicted of manslaughter.

The *Royal Commission on the Donald Marshall, Jr., Prosecution* was convened to examine what went wrong with the investigation. The Commissioners' report was released in 1989 (Hickman, Poitras, & Evans, 1989). Among other issues (e.g., poor legal assistance), the report was critical of the premature focus on Marshall. Much of the problem was attributed to tunnel vision (defined as the single-minded and overly narrow focus of an investigation or prosecutorial theory so as to unreasonably color the evaluation of information received and investigators' conduct in response to the information). The report was critical of police conduct in the investigation and was particularly damning of oppressive interviewing methods that contributed to false statements from witnesses. It was concluded that, even when witnesses recanted their statements, they were threatened with perjury. Senior police officers were found to be negligent in failing to challenge or recognize deficiencies in the investigation. Overall, the Commissioners' report was blunt in stating that the police response was "incompetent to the point of negligence. Had proper and thorough investigation techniques been followed, it is highly unlikely that later events would have unfolded as they did" (Hickman et al., 1989, p. 36).

David Milgaard

On January 31, 1969, the body of Gail Miller was discovered in an alley in a working-class district of Saskatoon, Saskatchewan (see Chapter 9). It was determined that the 20-year-old nursing assistant had been raped and stabbed to death. Police offered a $2,000 reward to anyone who could provide information that would lead to the conviction of the perpetrator. In March, Albert Cadrain heard about the reward money (which he later collected) and went to the police with a story about David Milgaard. He told them Milgaard had shown up on the day of the murder at his home with blood on his clothes and in a hurry to leave town. Cadrain left for Alberta with Milgaard and his two friends, Ron Wilson and Nichol John. He also informed police that Milgaard tossed a woman's cosmetic case out of the car and threatened he would have to get rid of Wilson and John because they knew too much. Based on this information, corroborated by statements from Wilson and John, Milgaard was arrested for the murder. Milgaard served 23 years in prison before being released in 1992.

A serial rapist, later identified as Larry Fisher, had been operating in the same area, and at the same time, where Miller's murder took place. After initially considering a link between the rapes and the murder, police then ignored the crimes. Supporters of Milgaard suggested Fisher should be considered a viable suspect for Miller's murder. Unfortunately, officials would not reopen the investigation until a DNA test implicated Fisher as Miller's murderer in 1997. Milgaard was exonerated and eventually received $10 million in compensation from the government. Fisher was convicted of Miller's murder and has now lost all his appeals.

On January 17, 2005, a *Commission of Inquiry into the Wrongful Conviction of David Milgaard* began hearings in Saskatoon. Upon the writing of this chapter, all of the evidence has been heard but the Commissioners' report is pending. Evidence heard at the inquiry supports published criticisms of the police investigation, including a premature focus on Milgaard and coercive interviewing of witnesses by detectives (Karp & Rosner, 1991; Milgaard & Edwards, 1999).

The Scarborough Rapist/Green Ribbon Task Force

Between 1987 and 1990 Paul Bernardo, known as the Scarborough Rapist, terrorized the Greater Toronto Area by committing 14 sexual assaults in

Scarborough and one in Mississauga. The Metropolitan Toronto Police recognized links between the crimes early in the investigation and began accumulating a large volume of information. Although the significance of Paul Bernardo's name was not fully realized when it first surfaced, he was interviewed in due course and asked to provide biological samples. Shortly thereafter, Bernardo relocated to the Niagara region near the home of his then fiancée Karla Homolka where he continued his attacks on women. In December 1990, with Karla's help, he murdered Tammy Homolka, her sister. In June 1991, he abducted and murdered Leslie Mahaffy, also with Karla's help. Over the following months, Bernardo stalked more young women; in April 1992, again with Karla's assistance, he abducted and murdered Kristen French.

The Green Ribbon Task Force (GRTF), established following the French murder, began as a joint-forces team between the Niagara Regional Police and the Halton Regional Police. Although Bernardo and Homolka were eventually arrested and prosecuted, there was much criticism of police conduct that compromised investigative procedures in this case. The joint investigation between the GRTF and the Metropolitan Toronto Police was specifically condemned because the two organizations functioned as separate entities, driven by competing interests. In 1996, Justice Archie Campbell released the *Bernardo Investigation Review* (Campbell, 1996). Among other problems, Campbell concluded that there had been systematic failures in the joint investigation that related to a lack of cooperation and communication between the Toronto police and the GRTF. Justice Campbell attributed this investigative failure to poor management and lack of leadership. He was especially critical of the fact that no single individual was in charge of the joint investigative effort.

Guy Paul Morin

On October 3, 1984, nine-year-old Christine Jessop was reported missing in Queensville, Ontario. Her whereabouts remained unknown until December 31, 1984, when her decomposed remains were discovered approximately 23 miles from her home in a rural area of Durham region. During the course of interviewing people in the town, one of the lead detectives noted that one of Jessop's next door neighbors had a 24-year-old son who was a "clarinet player, weird type guy" (Makin, 1992, p. 98). During an interview with Morin, the detectives claimed (this part of the interview was not recorded) he said: "All little girls are sweet and beautiful, but grow up to be corrupt" (Kaufman, 1998). Despite a lack of physical evidence, this interview was enough to make Morin their primary suspect. On April 22, 1985, Guy Paul Morin was arrested and charged with Jessop's murder.

Morin remained in custody until his acquittal at trial on February 7, 1986. The Crown appealed and the Ontario Court of Appeal ordered a new trial in

June 1987, which commenced in the fall of 1991. In 1992, Guy Paul Morin was convicted of the first-degree murder of Christine Jessop and was incarcerated. In February 1993 he was granted bail pending an appeal. In January 1995 DNA analysis determined that Morin was not the source of semen found on the victim's undergarment. Later that year, Morin's conviction was set aside by the Ontario Court of Appeal and a verdict of acquittal was entered. The case remains unsolved.

The Commission on Proceedings Involving Guy Paul Morin was convened to explore what went wrong with this case. Justice Fred Kaufman released his report in 1998. He was particularly critical of the police investigation, specifically stating that the premature focus on Morin was a central issue in the investigative failure, especially as there were other good suspects. The uncritical use of jailhouse informants, pressure by police to influence a witness's time estimation, failure to preserve the crime site, and the misinterpretation of evidence (e.g., drawing conclusions from ambiguous information) were also identified as major problems (see also Makin, 1992).

The Thomas Sophonow Case

On December 23, 1981, 16-year-old Barbara Stoppel was murdered while she worked in the Ideal Donut Shop in Winnipeg, Manitoba. She was found in the women's washroom with a nylon cord around her neck and died in the hospital five days later. Several witnesses told police they had seen a tall man wearing a cowboy hat lock the door from the inside and proceed to walk toward the back of the store. Nearly a month passed without any primary suspects being identified. At the end of January 1982, investigators received a phone call from a police officer in British Columbia who remembered an incident where a man named Thomas Sophonow contacted them about giving a ride to a hitchhiker who went missing and was never found. The police officer did a background check and discovered that Sophonow had a police record. Moreover, the police sketch of Stoppel's killer resembled a photo of Sophonow in the police files. Vancouver police interviewed Sophonow and determined he had stopped for coffee at a Tim Hortons doughnut shop on the same street where Stoppel was killed, and that he was aware of her murder. Based primarily on eyewitness accounts and inadequate physical evidence, Sophonow was arrested and charged with her homicide on March 12, 1982. A jailhouse informant testified Sophonow had confessed to him.

In late 1982 Sophonow's first trial ended in a mistrial when the jury failed to reach a verdict. But following a second trial in early 1983, Sophonow was convicted. He appealed the ruling, the conviction was set aside, and a new trial was ordered. In 1985 he was again tried and convicted. He once again appealed, and the Court of Appeal set aside the guilty verdict and ordered an acquittal. Although the Crown appealed that ruling, the Supreme Court of Canada dismissed the Crown's appeal. In 1998 the Winnipeg Police Service commenced a reinvestigation of the murder and, in June 2000, publicly announced Sophonow was not responsible for the murder and that another suspect had been identified.

The Inquiry Regarding Thomas Sophonow was convened in Winnipeg, Manitoba, to examine the circumstances of this investigative failure. In 2001 Justice Peter Cory (2001) concluded that significant police errors had contributed to the conviction. He criticized the use of jailhouse informants and expressed concerns over the manner in which certain interviews were conducted. Moreover, police were criticized for the manipulation of eyewitness accounts so that Sophonow could be more readily identified. Tunnel vision was also considered a contributing factor to the wrongful conviction.

Gregory Parsons

On January 2, 1991, the body of Catherine Carroll was discovered in her St. John's, Newfoundland, home by her 19-year-old son Gregory Parsons. It was determined that Carroll had been stabbed to death in the upstairs bathroom of her home. Members of the Royal Newfoundland Constabulary (RNC) responded to the scene after Parsons called 9-1-1. Parsons told police that he had been attempting to contact his mother for a couple of days prior to the murder and became concerned, thus prompting him to force entry into the house. Investigators did not accept his story. Following a brief investigation, which included the consideration of hearsay statements that Parsons had intended to harm his mother and other circumstantial evidence, he was arrested and charged with murder. On February 15, 1994, he was convicted and sentenced to life in prison.

On March 23, 1994, Parsons was released pending the outcome of his appeal. Exhibits were resubmitted to a crime laboratory in 1997. It was anticipated that advances in DNA analysis procedures might bolster the prosecution's case. Surprisingly, the results revealed that Parsons's DNA did not match the crime scene DNA. On November 5, 1998, Parsons was formally acquitted of the murder. A second RNC investigation eventually identified, charged, and convicted Brian Doyle of the second-degree murder of Carroll.

In June 2006 retired Chief Justice of Canada Antonio Lamer (2006) released his report, The Lamer Commission of Inquiry Pertaining to the Cases of: Gregory Parsons, Randy Druken, Ronald Dalton. Evidence in the Carroll investigation suggested that some of the main problems included a premature focus on Parsons, overreliance on hearsay statements, misinterpretation of evidence, lack of coordination, and poor leadership.

A Take-Home-Message: Improve Major Case Management!

The judicial inquiries into the aforementioned high-profile criminal investigative failures have identified a variety of common problems that should be corrected to avert future failures. Of relevance to the current chapter, the inquiries provide recommendations about the types of competencies that effective case managers should possess (e.g., Campbell, 1996; Hickman et al., 1989; Kaufman, 1998), such as: (1) the ability to identify and deal with noble cause corruption and maliciousness by any member of an investigative team (e.g., threatening witnesses with perjury); (2) knowledge about best policing practices (e.g., avoiding coercive interrogations); and (3) awareness of the errors that result from information processing (e.g., misinterpretation of evidence).

Justice Campbell's (1996) inquiry, in particular, made specific recommendations regarding the improvement of major case management. Campbell recommended that a single individual should be in charge of the case, and that this individual should have proven investigative ability and experience working complex major cases, as well as strong administrative, leadership, and team building skills. Justice Kaufman (1998) supported Campbell's recommendations in his inquiry into the wrongful conviction of Guy Paul Morin. The recommendations made in such inquiries reflect the belief that criminal investigative failures can be reduced through the employment of competent major case managers.

What Is the Role of a Major Case Manager?

LePard and Campbell (see Chapter 13) provide a diagram of the major case management model that is advocated by the Canadian Police College (CPC). The coordinated investigation team commander (referred to as the major case manager throughout this chapter) is situated at the pinnacle of the command triangle. This individual is the person upon whom the ultimate authority and responsibility for the coordinated investigation team (CIT), all of its resources, and its mandate are conferred (Canadian Police College, 2002). A major case manager is typically a senior police officer who is responsible for the organization and behavior of all personnel involved in a major investigation. The CPC's major case management training manual provides guidance on the characteristics of individuals who are suitable for the position, along with their specific roles and responsibilities.

This manual dictates that major case managers should be experienced police officers who have a substantive background in criminal investigations. Specifically, the CPC manual suggests that a major case manager should be a senior police supervisor and, when and where possible, a seasoned member with extensive experience in the type of crime under investigation. For example, if the team is investigating a serial murder, the major case manager should have experience in homicide investigations. According to this manual, the appointment of experienced personnel should be the main consideration.

Like the inquiry commissioners, authors of this manual have made seemingly logical recommendations regarding the qualities required of effective major case managers. For example, the manual states clearly that major case managers need to drive the investigation and not be driven by it or influenced by outside forces (e.g., the media, politics). The major case manager should also be able to communicate effectively with all participants of the CIT on their own level. It is through this communication that all members of the investigation will remain well informed. The major case manager should be an experienced investigator with a proven ability to delegate, coordinate, organize, and control a complex, multifaceted investigation. Furthermore, he or she must be a capable and decisive leader, able to evaluate large quantities of information and to deploy resources as needed. Finally, a major case manager needs to possess above average leadership and team-building skills that facilitate harmonious work relationships with subordinates over prolonged periods of time and under adverse conditions. Such leadership helps ensure that all members of the investigative team maintain a confident and constructive perspective in spite of the magnitude and duration of the work.

A similar major case management training manual was created for police agencies in Ontario. The *Ontario Major Case Management Manual* also nominated crime-specific experience as an important factor in selecting a major case manager (Ministry of Community Safety and Correctional Services, 2004). Superior communication skills, knowledge of the *Canadian Charter of Rights and Freedoms*, and demonstrated leadership qualities were all deemed critical for major case managers to possess.

What is common to both of these manuals is the focus on "getting the job done," making sure major case managers have the skills to direct and complete a range of investigative tasks, and developing the procedural skills associated with major case management. Unfortunately, although both manuals highlight leadership skills as crucial for a major case manager, they do not provide direction on how to train leaders. This omission is troubling since "lack of leadership" was a main source of criticism from commissions of inquiry. Furthermore, although the manuals do present some of the other general characteristics of effective case managers, they do not highlight a systematic process for assessing or identifying those individuals.

The authors of the major case management manuals suggest that one of the most important steps in conducting a successful major investigation is to have a single competent major case manager overseeing all aspects of the investigation. Indeed, as the aforementioned examples of criminal investigative failures suggest, the lack of a competent individual leading the investigation can lead to serious consequences. Because the number of experienced major case managers is expected to decline over the next few years due to retirement, more and more inexperienced and junior officers will begin to occupy these positions. This lack of experience needs to be countered by research identifying the KSAs necessary to be a successful major case manager. Findings from such research will facilitate better training of current major case managers and earlier identification of new managers, leading to fewer investigative failures.

What Do We Know About Effective Major Case Management?

As far as we are aware, no research has been published on major case police managers in Canada or the United States. Some research, however, has examined the competencies required for a variety of police roles in the United Kingdom (Home Office, 1991; McGurk, Gibson, & Platton, 1992; Maguire et al., 1993; Wigfield, 1996). The competencies required for effective policing can generally be classified into those important for completing investigative tasks (e.g., communication, decision making, investigative competencies) and those dealing with colleagues and the public (e.g., motivating, supporting, assisting).

In one comprehensive study, Smith and Flanagan (2000) attempted to identify the competencies of an effective senior investigating officer (SIO), the British equivalent of a major case manager. They defined an SIO as the lead detective who makes the principal decisions within a serious crime investigation and takes responsibility for its outcome. Smith and Flanagan interviewed 40 SIOs from 10 British police agencies and identified 22 competencies that an SIO should exhibit to perform effectively in the role. These competencies were grouped into three clusters:

1. *Investigative ability*, which includes the competencies associated with the assimilation and assessment of incoming information into an investigation, and the processes by which lines of investigation are generated and prioritized.
2. *Knowledge levels*, which relate to the different types of underpinning knowledge that an SIO should possess, such as knowledge of investigative procedures, the legal and court processes, how to deal with informants, and what resources are available to the SIO.
3. *Management levels*, which encompass a broad range of competency types that were further subdivided into *people management* (e.g., team building, staff support, staff development, and interpersonal competencies), *general management* (i.e., routine management competencies

that would be associated with any management role), and *investigative management* (e.g., planning the investigation, consulting with advisors, and handling expert advice).

Smith and Flanagan argued an ideal SIO should be highly competent in all three categories and that there is an increased risk of an investigative failure when these conditions are not met. They also noted it is not always possible to have an individual in charge who possesses all the required abilities, often because of the lack of formal identification and training of SIOs. They suggested improvements for recruitment and training, including identifying potential SIOs early in their career so they can be properly trained and developed; establishing a formal mentoring program for future SIOs; ensuring a balance between training and experience; encouraging self-development of SIOs so they remain up to date on investigative procedures; and conducting open and constructive debriefing sessions to identify and correct mistakes.

Running a Major Case: Management or Leadership?

There has been considerable debate regarding whether management and leadership are the same concept (Yukl & Van Fleet, 1992). Clearly defining the two terms might assist in bridging the somewhat incongruent message between major case management manuals that focus on the development of procedural skills and commissions of inquiry that focus on the need for leadership.

Definitions of Management and Leadership

Managers are typically regarded as those individuals who carry out position responsibilities and exercise authority (Burn, 2004; Northouse, 1997; Yukl & Van Fleet, 1992). Kotter (1990) has argued that management is best understood in terms of functions such as (1) planning and budgeting (e.g., setting future targets, allocating resources); (2) organizing and staffing (e.g., establishing an organizational structure, staffing jobs with qualified individuals, delegating responsibility); and (3) problem solving (e.g., monitoring results). Leaders, on the other hand, inspire, shape ideas, and change the way people think about what is possible. Yukl and Van Fleet (1992), for instance, define leadership as "a process that includes influencing the task objectives and strategies of a group or organization, influencing people in the organization to implement the strategies and achieve the objectives, influencing group maintenance and identification, and influencing the culture of the organization" (p. 148). Of course, the distinction between management and leadership is not always clear, and there are times when leaders manage and managers lead (Yukl, 1989). Furthermore, both roles involve deciding what needs to be done, creating networks of people and relationships to accomplish an agenda, and ensuring that people accomplish set goals. Some people also argue that leadership is simply a part of good management, as the success or failure of managers can often be judged on their leadership qualities (Hannaghan, 1998). Although some researchers use the terms "manager" and "leader" interchangeably, research suggests these should be understood as different, albeit related, activities (Cooper, 2003; Kotter, 1990).

Despite the term major case manager, a closer examination of the competencies identified from judicial inquiries, research on effective police officers, and training manuals suggests they are all constituents of *leadership* (see DuBrin, 2004). We believe existing leadership research is an area that should provide valuable insights into the sorts of competencies effective major case managers ought to possess.

Two Components of Leadership

Researchers often classify leadership into two primary categories: (1) task-oriented and (2) socioemotional. Task-oriented skills focus on organizing followers toward task accomplishment, while socioemotional skills focus on reducing tension and enhancing morale. Although these categories are sometimes assigned different names, this two-factor model of leadership has been observed by a number of researchers (e.g., Bales & Slater, 1955; Halpin & Winer, 1957; Kahn & Katz, 1953). For instance, in what is known as the Ohio State Leadership Studies, the two factors were labeled (1) *initiating structure*, where the focus is on achieving the group's goal; and (2) *consideration*, where the focus is on maintaining harmonious group relations (Fleishman, 1973; Fleishman, Harris, & Burtt, 1955; Stogdill, 1974). Similarly, Bales and Slater (1955) described (1) *task-specialists*, who are good at organizing, summarizing, and directing task behavior; and (2) *socioemotional specialists*, who are good at reducing tension, raising morale, and encouraging participation. Researchers at the University of Michigan have reported a similar division, labeling their dimensions *production oriented* and *employee oriented* (Kahn & Katz, 1953). Last, the widely referenced Managerial Grid Model (Blake & Mouton, 1985) is also based on a similar two-dimensional division in leadership style between *concern for people* and *concern for production*. There are obvious consistencies between the various studies, with all describing a similar dichotomy of leadership skills.

Of particular relevance to the current chapter is research showing that the most effective leaders are those who score high on both dimensions simultaneously (e.g., Blake & Mouton, 1985). This dual style of leadership allows for the integration of both production and people concerns. According to Blake and Mouton, "it is a goal-centered, team approach that seeks to gain optimum results through participation, involvement, commitment, and conflict solving" (1985, p. 13). Despite the equal importance of both types of leadership skills, it appears to us that the competencies for successful major case management currently being recommended by judicial inquiries and training manuals are skewed toward task-oriented competencies (see also Geberth, 1990), thereby failing to give equal weight to the socioemotional component of leadership. The extent to which our hunch is supported is examined in the study reported below.

Examining Effective Major Case Manager Narratives

Here we report the results of an examination of the competencies of Canadian major case managers who have managed successful investigations. We hope this preliminary examination will encourage future research that leads to improved training and selection procedures.

Method

Participants

Participants were 51 police officers (from municipal, provincial, and federal agencies) across Canada who were nominated by senior police officers and lawyers as *effective* major case managers. There were 48 men and 3 women, between 36 and 57 years of age ($M = 47.7$ years, $SD = 4.7$). They had an average of 26.3 years ($SD = 5.0$) experience working as a police officer, 8.3 years ($SD = 5.9$) experience as a major case manager, and 11.5 years ($SD = 6.4$) experience within a major crime unit. At the time of the interviews, the sample consisted of two deputy chiefs, 6 superintendents, 20 inspectors, 1 lieutenant, 17 staff and detective sergeants, and 5 sergeants. Ninety-four percent of the officers reported that they had received formal supervisory or management training; of these, 67% reported receiving major case management training from the Canadian Police College, 47% from the Ontario Police College, 14% from their home agency, and a further 8% from other organizations. In terms of their highest level of education achieved, 28% of the officers indicated they had some college or university education, 26% had a Bachelor's degree, 24% had a college diploma, 12% had a high school diploma, 6% had a Master's degree, 4% had a university certificate, and 2% had other sorts of education. Seventy-six percent of the officers were assigned to major crime/homicide units, and 67% were working as major case managers.

Procedure

The interviews were divided into two parts and completed in a single session within the police officer's local jurisdiction. Officers first read instructions that defined a case manager as the individual who has overall command and responsibility for an investigative team. They were asked to provide a verbal account of what they considered to be the most successful major case they had managed. Specifically, participants were asked to talk about their thoughts, decisions, and actions from the beginning of the investigation through to its conclusion in court. They were asked not to refer to the thoughts, decisions, or actions of other members of the investigative team. In part two, participants were instructed to read the definitions of 21 case manager competencies (adapted from Smith & Flanagan, 2000; see Appendix A for definitions) and rank them from most (1) to least (21) important for effective major case management. The competency *leadership* was removed from the ranking task because it was felt that this competency encompasses all of the other 21 competencies (DuBrin, 2004). Each interview lasted approximately two hours, after which participants were debriefed about the purpose of the research.

Narrative Coding and Inter-Rater Reliability

The narratives were transcribed verbatim from an audiotape and were proofread. The transcripts were coded by the first author. Competencies were derived through a grounded approach to categorizing written text, which involved iterative refinement and modification of the content dictionary until it reflected the content of narratives across all participants' data (Glaser & Strauss, 1967; Holsti, 1969; Krippendorff, 1980). A total of 52 competencies were identified from the narratives. Each of the competencies was carefully defined (see Appendix B for content dictionary) to avoid discrepancies in category assignment. All competencies were coded as dichotomous variables.

An example of an excerpt of one major case manager's narrative is shown in Box 1. The italicized parts of the text refer to information that was used to infer a competency (located inside the square brackets). For instance, the italicized text "slow things down" would have been coded as "preparation and planning." Similarly, "give me updates" would have been coded as "debriefing."

Box 1. Case Narrative Example.[1]

MCM Interview # 23: And so I arrived on the scene and immediately the first thing I do when I arrive on scenes is I *slow things down* [preparation/planning]. Everybody has a tendency in my opinion to get a little excited by the fact that there is a potential homicide and they're thinking, they're doing a good job of thinking ahead and planning, but sometimes there's too many people thinking and planning; and what we have to do is slow things down for a more manageable investigation. So when I usually arrive at the scene I take the opportunity to sit in my vehicle and get my notes caught up and I *ask for the Detective Sergeant to give me any updates* [debriefing], any things changed since I was en route, just in case of a communications gap and he couldn't get

[1] The excerpt is verbatim except for identifying information.

---

a hold of me. And then I asked to speak to the first officer at the scene and I usually *get a description from the first officer* [debriefing] at the scene as towhat they observed upon their arrival at the scene; how were they dispatched, who was present when they arrived, who did they speak to, who helped them gain entry to the residence, what did they observe, what did they touch, what did they do, how did they leave and secure it; just so *I have an idea of the level of contamination* [forensic knowledge] if any and how many civilians may have observed the crime scene; that you know how the potential holdback evidence may be affected. After I did that I met again with the Detective Sergeant and got an *update as to what detectives we had on the case; what roles he had assigned them* [debriefing], and if they were detectives I didn't know I asked a little bit of background on who these folks were; if I hadn't worked with them before, what their strengths and weaknesses were *so I could ascertain just what kind of team I would be looking at* [position matching]. Once I got that information *we discussed then who the search warrant writer would be* [position matching]; *we identified who the Lead was from* [position matching] the local crime unit and *we set up our command triangle* [responsibility delegation] in Major Case Management. And I also *asked what resources were in back up from neighboring detachments* [resource acquisition/management] if needed, *or any special units that could be called to assist* [resource acquisition/management]. We had sufficient people on the ground at that point in time. *I was satisfied that having any more than that would complicate the matter* [forecasting], make it more difficult for me to manage the case. And I asked that people doing the *canvassing* cease and come back where *I'd brief them, I briefed them* [briefing] on the importance of the canvass. In my humble opinion the canvass is one of the most important tools investigatively we have at major crimes that is often overlooked or ignored or not given the credence that it deserves. And I like to bring the team together, the people who are doing the canvass and *go over the importance of filling out the canvass form completely* [briefing], taking the time to do a proper canvass at each residence, making notes in their notebook that somebody wasn't home, or when they spoke to the people in a residence, who were visitors that had to get back to; whether or not there was information obtained that would require follow up by an investigator, etc. And *I praise them for the importance of canvass work* [prioritization of activities] and that; you know that would give us a solid start on our investigation. Deploy them back out for the canvassing and then I want to *meet with the investigators* [briefing], I'm a firm believer, although most if not all of our detectives are usually skilled in witness statements and taking statements, writing statements out, through years I learned that when I was a detective, from Detective Inspectors and Staff Sergeants at the time, they came up through the ranks, that no matter how much we train or prepare people for statements, sometimes we get a little lazy and we slide back to bad habits and I like to sit down with the investigators that are going to be doing a lot of the key statements and just *identify to them how I like to see statements* [briefing].

Reliability of the coding was assessed by having the third author independently code five of the narratives. The reliability of coding, measured using Cohen's Kappa (Cohen, 1960), was 0.80 in relation to the competencies coded in the narrative, suggesting a high level of agreement between the coders (Fleiss, 1981). Disagreements between the coders were resolved through discussion and mutual agreement prior to analysis.

Smallest Space Analysis

Smallest Space Analysis (SSA) was conducted on an association matrix of Jaccard coefficients using SSA-I (see Borg & Shye, 1995; Guttman, 1968; Lingoes, 1973, for a detailed description of SSA). SSA is a nonmetric multidimensional scaling procedure that is based on the assumption that any domain can best be understood by examining the relationship between every variable and every other variable in that domain. The SSA program was chosen because the examination of correlations between large numbers of variables is often difficult to interpret. The SSA program visually depicts correlations between competencies. It accomplishes this by computing correlation coefficients between all competencies, rank ordering these correlations, and plotting each competency as a data point in geometric space. A spatial representation is formed such that the rank order of the distances between the points is inversely related to the rank order of the correlations (see, for example, Canter & Heritage, 1990). In other words, the closer any two competencies, the higher the correlation between them (i.e., the more likely it is that they cooccurred in the case managers' narratives). The SSA program calculates the degree to which the correlations between the competencies are adequately represented by the spatial distances between them. This produces a value known as the coefficient of alienation (Borg & Lingoes, 1987); the smaller the coefficient of alienation, the better the fit (i.e., the match of the visual plot to the calculated correlations). The SSA program runs multiple iterations, adjusting the spatial representation of the data to produce the smallest possible coefficient of alienation. The final geometric space is then examined for any potential interpretable structure.

Results

Smallest Space Analysis

A total of 52 competencies were identified in the narratives. The 50 competencies used in the analysis are shown in Figure 14.1.[2] The two-dimensional solution of the 50 competencies produced a Guttman-Lingoes coefficient

---

[2] The competencies *focus maintenance* (3.9% occurrence) and *scheduling* (3.9% occurrence) were removed from the analysis because their distance from the other competencies made the SSA plot very difficult to visualize and interpret.

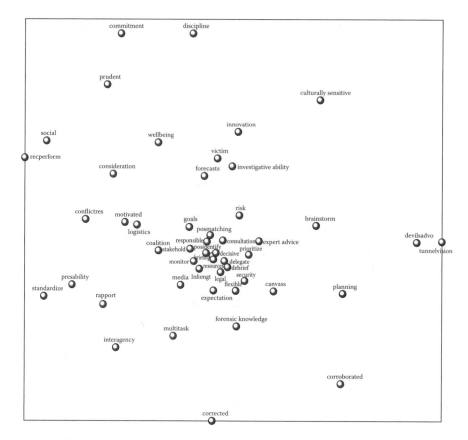

Figure 14.1 SSA of major case management competencies (complete competency labels and definitions appear in Appendix B).

of alienation of 0.28 in 12 iterations, indicating a reasonable degree of fit between the spatial representation of points and the actual cooccurrence of competencies (Lingoes, 1973). As shown in Figure 14.1, the group of competencies clustered in the center of the plot illustrates those variables that define features of major case management. For instance, *decisiveness, resource acquisition/management, briefing,* and *position identification* are plotted very close to one another, indicating high intercorrelations among these four competencies. Conversely, those variables less central to major case management are more dispersed toward the edge of the plot. The variables *cultural sensitivity, commitment,* and *rapport building* are spatially distant, thus none are highly correlated with one another nor are they highly correlated with competencies clustered in the center of the geometric space.

The percentages of narratives that contained a particular competency are listed in Table 14.1. We divided the competencies into those that occurred in more than 70%, between 30% and 70%, and in less than 30% of the case managers' narratives. The most frequent group was comprised of six competencies:

Table 14.1   Frequency Categorization of Major Case Management Competencies

Competency Type	Frequency Bands		
	> 70%	30% to 70%	< 30%
Task-Oriented	Briefing	Position Matching	Investigative Ability
	Resource Acquisition/ Management	Debriefing	Logistics Handling
	Responsibility Delegation	Consultation	Multi-tasking
	Position Identification	Taking Responsibility	Correction
	Decisiveness	Flexibility	Innovation
	Legal Awareness	Information Management	Inter-Agency Sensitivity
		Informing Stakeholders	Preparation/Planning
		Security/Evidence Integrity	Corroboration
		Expectations	Presentation Ability
		Monitoring/Overseeing	Standardization
		Goal/Objective Setting	Commitment
		Prioritization of Activities	Prudence
		Forensic Knowledge	Disciplining
		Brainstorming	Devil's Advocate Technique
		Canvassing	Tunnel Vision Awareness
		Managing Expert Advice	Cultural Sensitivity
		Media Management	Victim/Family Attention
		Risk Analysis/ Management	
		Forecasting	
		Building Coalitions	
Socioemotional			Conflict Resolution
			Recognized Outstanding Performance
			Individualized Consideration
			Team Motivation
			Rapport Building
			Well-Being Considered
			Socializing

briefing (discussed by 82% of the case managers); *resource acquisition/ management* (82%); *responsibility delegation* (78%); *position identification* (78%); *decisiveness* (71%); and *legal awareness* (71%). The middle group was comprised of 20 competencies, including *position matching* (69%); *debriefing* (67%); *taking responsibility* (61%); *goal/objective setting* (51%); *canvassing* (43%); and *forecasting* (33%). Many of the competencies in this band, as well as the six in the high-frequency band, are oriented toward accomplishing tasks and organizing and initiating structure within the investigative team. The least frequent group was comprised of 24 competencies, including *investigative ability* (29%); *conflict resolution* (20%); *logistics handling* (29%); *presentation ability* (20%); and *recognizing outstanding performance* (10%).

A partitioning of the SSA geometric space according to *task-oriented* and *socioemotional* competencies is shown in Figure 14.2. Before analysis, we determined that 43 of the competencies were task-oriented and 7 were socioemotional. The task-oriented region contains 34 competencies (79% of the task-oriented variables), which largely reflect accomplishing tasks and organizing and initiating a structure within the investigative team. For example, clear task-oriented competencies pertain to conducting door-to-door inquiries (canvassing), setting goals for the investigation (goals), or delegating a particular job, duty, or right to appropriate member(s) of the investigative team (delegate).

The socioemotional region consists of 16 competencies (including all seven socioemotional and nine task-oriented), which are largely oriented toward reducing tension, raising morale, and encouraging participation. As can be seen, some of the socioemotional competencies include expressing concern about the basic health and the quality of primary and family relationships of members of the investigative team (well-being), taking steps to exert a positive influence, enthusiasm, and commitment to team (motivated), and giving personal attention to members, acting as an advisor and coach, providing personal feedback, and stimulating personal and professional development (consideration).

Competencies that overlap both types include bringing together people from multiple police agencies to tackle a particular problem (building coalitions) and identifying inadequate work performance or taking steps to correct a personnel problem (corrected). Interestingly, the most frequently mentioned competencies are all located in the task-oriented region, indicating this component of leadership is more salient in the minds of effective major case managers.

To gauge the internal reliability (how much the competencies are related to one another) of the task-oriented and socioemotional regions, we calculated Kuder-Richardson 20 (K-R 20) coefficients. The K-R 20 values are 0.75 for the socioemotional region ($n = 16$) and 0.64 for the task-oriented region ($n = 34$). In other words, the competencies in each region are moderately related to one another.

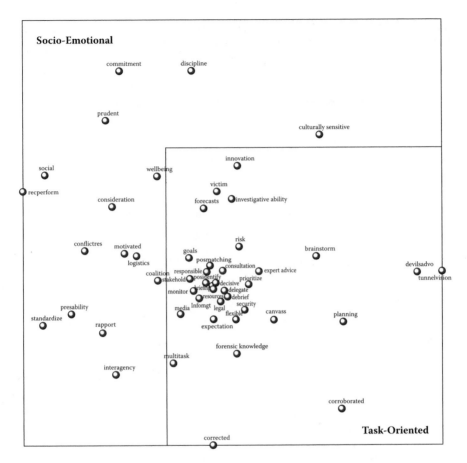

Figure 14.2 SSA interpretation showing the partition of task-oriented and socio-emotional competencies (complete competency labels and definitions appear in Appendix B).

Rank Order of Competencies

A summary of the results from the rank ordering of the 21 competencies identified from previous research on effective SIOs (Smith & Flanagan, 2000) is contained in Table 14.2 (two officers did not complete this part of the procedure). The police officers, on average, ranked *communication* (M = 4.55, SD = 3.37) and *decision making* (M = 5.65, SD = 4.06) as the most important competencies for effective case management. *Professional integrity* was identified as the most important competency most frequently (ranked first by 20% of the police officers), followed by *communication* (16%) and *interpersonal skills* (14%). The majority of officers ranked *communication* (69%), *decision making* (57%), and *investigative competence* (51%) as three of the five most important competencies. Other competencies that were frequently

Table 14.2   Summary of Rank-Ordering of Major Case Management Competencies (Complete Competancy Lables and Definitions Appear in Appendix A)

| | Descriptive Statistics | | | | | | | | | |
| | Mean Rank | | Ranked First | | Ranked Last | | Top Five | | Bottom Five | |
Competency	Mean	SD	n	%	n	%	n	%	n	%
Communication	4.55	3.37	8	16	0	0	34	69	0	0
Decision-Making	5.65	4.06	6	12	0	0	28	57	1	2
Investigative Competence	6.73	5.01	5	10	0	0	25	51	2	4
Interpersonal Skills	6.76	4.59	7	14	0	0	23	47	1	2
Team Building*	7.71	5.20	5	10	0	0	19	39	3	6
Professional Integrity	8.06	6.00	10	20	0	0	20	42	6	12
Appropriate Delegation	9.12	4.79	1	2	0	0	17	35	4	8
Organization	9.16	5.41	1	2	1	2	14	29	6	12
Planning	9.94	4.66	0	0	1	2	10	20	3	6
Adaptation	10.55	4.55	0	0	1	2	7	14	4	8
Consultation*	10.96	5.40	0	0	0	0	12	24	11	22
Information Appraisal	11.59	5.14	0	0	1	2	8	16	10	22
Foresight	12.02	5.64	1	2	3	6	6	12	12	24
Information Management	12.84	5.48	0	0	3	6	5	10	16	33
Underpinning Knowledge	13.27	6.06	3	6	6	12	5	10	18	37
Innovation	13.31	4.57	0	0	1	2	3	6	13	27
Resources	13.71	4.86	1	2	2	4	2	4	19	39
Staff Support*	14.61	4.35	1	2	1	2	1	2	19	39
Strategic Awareness	15.37	5.60	0	0	10	20	5	10	25	51
Staff Development*	16.92	3.74	0	0	6	12	0	0	32	65
Managing Expert Advice	17.92	3.68	0	0	13	27	1	2	39	80

Note: * = socioemotional competency.

ranked in the top five were *investigative competence* (51%), *interpersonal skills* (47%), *professional integrity* (42%), and *team building* (39%).

Twenty-seven percent of the case managers ranked *managing expert advice* as the least important competency, while the next least important competencies were *strategic awareness* (20%), *staff development* (12%), and *underpinning knowledge* (12%). The majority of officers ranked *managing expert advice* (80%), *staff development* (65%), and *strategic awareness* (51%) as three of the five least important competencies. Other competencies that were frequently ranked in the bottom five were *staff support* (39%) and *managing resources* (39%).

Discussion

The results reported here suggest that exemplary major case managers in Canada behave in a predominantly task-oriented manner. Although the multivariate analysis revealed two distinct components of major case management, most major case managers described thoughts, decisions, and actions that reflected task-oriented competencies to a greater extent than socioemotional competencies. Although there were few socioemotional competencies, the major case managers also indicated that task-oriented competencies were most important for effective case management on the rank-order task. These combined results suggest that major case managers typically consider socioemotional competencies to be less essential than task-oriented competencies for managing a successful investigation.

The fact that the SSA plot (Figure 14.2) could be partitioned into task-oriented and socioemotional competencies is consistent with previous leadership research (e.g., Vroom, 1991). The finding that the task-oriented competencies were discussed frequently and the socioemotional competencies less frequently supports the anticipated overemphasis on task-oriented competencies. This is potentially explained by the fact that the training these major case managers received (e.g., from the Canadian Police College or the Ontario Police College) is primarily oriented toward acquiring task-oriented competencies. Such training could have a dual effect on the results: (1) the officers might actually follow a more task-oriented approach because of their training; and (2) the officers might have felt they should not discuss socioemotional thoughts, decisions, and actions because, according to their training, task-oriented competencies are considered most important for effective major case management. A second potential explanation is that leadership styles are contingent on the situation (e.g., Fiedler, 1967; Strube & Garcia, 1981). Because major cases normally fall outside of the parameters of standard policing services, major case managers might have been working with individuals who were relatively inexperienced with major cases, and therefore had to spend more time "getting the job done" than paying attention to such team considerations as enhancing morale (Hersey & Blanchard, 1988). Future research should examine whether major case managers are able to identify a particular investigative situation and employ a leadership style that meets the demands of that situation. A third explanation may be that socioemotional competencies are simply less important than task-oriented ones in managing major cases.

In accordance with the results of the multivariate analysis, the competencies that were deemed most important by the major case managers on the rank order task also tended to be task oriented. In particular, communication, investigative competence, decision making, and interpersonal skills were considered the four most important competencies required to successfully lead major criminal investigations. On the surface, some of these terms (e.g., interpersonal skills) might appear to refer to socioemotional competencies, but given the definitions that were provided to the managers, we consider them to be task oriented (see Appendix A for definitions). However, 17 of the 21 competencies were task oriented according to our classification; hence, the apparent overemphasis on task-oriented competencies is not entirely surprising. Future research might benefit from an examination of the face validity of these competencies. In other words, how would major case managers classify each of the 21 competencies into task-oriented and socioemotional categories? Furthermore, it must be remembered that the competencies were ranked relative to one another; therefore, a low rank indicates a less important, but not necessarily an unimportant, competency.

These preliminary findings may have implications for the training and selection of major case managers. Although the Canadian police community has introduced systematic procedures through major case management training programs, the next step may be to integrate task-oriented and socioemotional competencies into their training. Given the uncertainty that is associated with the investigative environment, major case managers should have the ability to adopt a leadership style that meets the demands of a particular investigative situation. For instance, a major case manager may find him- or herself in an investigative context that requires either socioemotional competencies (e.g., the ability to motivate task-proficient officers who are conducting protracted investigative tasks), task-oriented competencies (e.g., the ability to direct an inexperienced investigative team), or some combination of the two. In terms of selecting officers to lead major criminal investigations, senior police officials should bear in mind the importance of the core competencies that were identified in this study, as well as the finding that socioemotional competencies were identified less frequently from the major case manager narratives. Given that balanced leadership approaches have been found to lead to increased group satisfaction and performance (Blake & Mouton, 1985), future police training and selection may wish to focus equally on task-oriented and socioemotional competencies. Having said that, the major case management competencies reported in this chapter (and a balance of the two broad types) must be validated in the policing context before they can be adopted with confidence.

The fact that the major case managers who participated in this study were nominated by peers in the criminal justice system because they were deemed to be exemplary could lead one to argue that the underemphasis on the socioemotional component indicates that such competencies are not essential for effective major case management. However, leadership research (e.g., Bales & Slater, 1955; Blake & Mouton, 1985; Halpin &Winer, 1957; Kahn & Katz, 1953) suggests that even these exemplary managers might be more effective if they more heavily utilized socioemotional competencies. Indeed, some of the managers recognized the need to enhance morale and reduce stress during an investigation (otherwise, socioemotional competencies would not have been identified during content analysis of the narratives). Future research should seek to measure directly the relationship between leadership ability and major case manager effectiveness. The use of leadership inventories, for example the Least Preferred Co-Worker Scale (Fiedler & Chemers, 1974), is one way to accomplish this.

This research has three potential limitations. First, generalizing from the major case managers' narratives to training and selection issues may be somewhat problematic because simply describing a particular thought, decision, or action does not necessarily mean the officer has that competency. Moreover, because the major case managers' narratives did not include a particular competency does not necessarily mean they do not have that competency in their investigative repertoire. For instance, the nature of the task might have prompted the major case managers to detail their task-oriented competencies and possibly neglect to mention socioemotional aspects of managing the case. Second, the nature of a particular investigation (e.g., type of crime and team dynamics) may dictate whether certain competencies are utilized, thus influencing whether or not they were mentioned in subsequent discussions of that investigation. Third, it was assumed that the major case managers participating in this study were actually "effective" major case managers and not just officers that managed successful cases. Although it was not possible to be absolutely certain that the managers themselves were "effective," steps were taken to try to ensure this was the case (e.g., multiple nominations of the same individuals from disparate nominators).

Bearing in mind the aforementioned caveats, the findings from this research suggest there is a set of core competencies associated with successful major case management. In particular, the task-oriented competencies of holding briefings with team members, being decisive, managing resources, identifying team positions, delegating responsibilities, and being aware of current legal issues appear to be the defining features of effective major case management. In addition, effective major case managers considered communication to be the most important competency, followed first by decision making and then investigative ability. These findings suggest that major case managers believe that task-oriented competencies are the most important components of effective case management. Given the diversity of criminal investigations, we believe the training and selection of major case managers will be enhanced by emphasizing both components of leadership.

Conclusion

Primarily through the use of forensic techniques such as DNA testing, a number of high-profile criminal investigative failures have come to light in Canada over the past several years. Subsequent judicial inquiries into these miscarriages of justice have identified several concerns, including questions about police conduct in major cases. In particular, the lack of a single competent individual overseeing the investigation was highlighted as a central contributing factor to several of these investigative failures. In an attempt to improve criminal investigations in Canada, both the Canadian Police College and the Province of Ontario's Ministry of Community Safety and Correctional Services produced major case management training manuals that state major case managers should be decisive leaders, with extensive criminal investigation experience, capable of controlling complex, multi-faceted investigations. Although these manuals identify leadership skills as crucial for a major case manager, they do not include instructions on how to train leaders. Furthermore, the manuals do not highlight a process for identifying or assessing those individuals who possess the general characteristics of an effective case manager.

Previous research on the competencies required for effective policing has classified them according to whether they relate to (1) completing investigative tasks, or (2) dealing with colleagues and the public. Along with this research, findings from the leadership literature are relevant to the major case management field. Competencies identified from judicial inquiries, research on effective police officers, and training manuals suggest they are all constituents of *leadership*. Researchers in this field often divide leadership competencies according to whether they are (1) task oriented, or (2) socioemotional. Evidence from both effective policing and leadership research suggests that major case managers should possess both types of competencies in order to be successful (i.e., team satisfaction and performance). Results from an analysis of detailed narratives provided by effective Canadian major case managers, however, suggest that there is an overemphasis on task-oriented competencies and an underemphasis on socioemotional competencies.

Given that the number of inexperienced major case managers is expected to rise over the next several years, there is a need for research to identify the knowledge, skills, and abilities required for successful major case management. We urge readers to pursue such research. Increased knowledge in this area will result in better training of current major case managers and early identification of potentially successful major case managers, ultimately helping avoid future investigative failures.

Appendix A: Competencies and Their Definitions Used for the Rank Order Task

Adaptation: Adapting to the changing needs of an investigation.

Appropriate Delegation: Delegating roles and responsibilities to appropriately qualified individuals while maintaining control of the case.

Communication: Clearly and effectively communicating when presenting information.

Consultation: Enabling team members to contribute their ideas and opinions in an open and constructive atmosphere.

Decision Making: Methodical decision making based on objective assessment of information.

Foresight: Keeping current with legislation, technology, and forensic science.

Information Appraisal: Assimilating, evaluating, and reviewing incoming information, and generating options and alternatives.

Information Management: Managing information and understanding information management systems.

Innovation: Employing a creative approach, ideas, techniques, and technology, and thinking "outside the box."

Interpersonal Skills: Relating to people across all levels, inside and outside the investigation.

Investigative Competence: Understanding the investigative process and demonstrating sound judgment.

Managing Expert Advice: Engaging outside specialists appropriately and managing their input.

Organization: Establishing an efficient structure of the investigation and investigative team.

Planning: Setting performance goals, and developing, assessing, and prioritizing lines of inquiry.

Professional Integrity: Taking an ethical approach.

Resources: Managing staff and finances; ability to negotiate resources; prioritizing resource deployment.

Staff Development: Providing opportunities for staff to develop skills.

Staff Support: Ability to motivate; concern for welfare of supporting staff.

Strategic Awareness: Awareness of how investigation relates to, and impacts, overall organizational objectives.

Team Building: Dealing with staff in an equitable manner; recognizing the strengths and weaknesses of team members and building on them.

Underpinning Knowledge: Possessing a basic level of investigative and legal knowledge.

Appendix B: Coding Dictionary for Competencies Derived from the Content Analysis of the Major Case Management Narratives

Note: The abbreviations in parentheses are used to represent each competency in Figures 14.1 and 14.2.

Brainstorming (brainstorm):   Encouraging members of the investigative team to suggest ideas and discuss them as a group before making a decision (typically occurring in the context of a team meeting).

Briefing (briefing):   Organizing team meetings where participants are provided with information.

Building Coalitions (coalition):   Bringing different groups/agencies together for a particular purpose or to address a particular problem (e.g., bringing together multiple police agencies to tackle a particular problem).

Canvassing (canvass):   Ensuring that door-to-door inquiries are conducted.

Commitment (commitment):   Committing time and energy beyond what is routine or normally expected (e.g., spending long hours working on the case, coming in early and leaving late).

Conflict Resolution (conflictres):   Resolving conflict between two (or more) opposing parties who have interests or goals that appear to be incompatible.

Consultation (consultation):   Discussing or consulting with team member(s) or some other appropriate individual(s) prior to making a decision.

Correction (corrected):   Identifying inadequate work performance or ability and implementing steps to correct the problem (e.g., observing inadequacies in statement content and instructing subordinates on the correct methods for taking statements).

Corroboration (corroborated):   Seeking to find proof or confirmation of an account or statement that provided new information or evidence (e.g., compared physical evidence to statements to assist in substantiating evidence).

Cultural Sensitivity (culturally sensitive):   Demonstrating sensitivity and/or awareness of the habits, traditions, and beliefs of a society, or culture, as it may apply to the investigation.

Debriefing (debrief):   Questioning or querying personnel to acquire information about work they have done in relation to the investigation (e.g., debriefed investigators who have returned from canvassing residences in the area of the crime scene).

Decisiveness (decisive):   Making decisions quickly and confidently.

Devil's Advocate Technique (devilsadvo):   Encouraging team members to argue a contrary point of view in discussions of evidence or an investigative approach.

Disciplining (discipline):   Punishing or penalizing an individual for unacceptable performance or behavior during the course of the investigation.

Expectations (expectation):   Articulating clear expectations to each team member.

Flexibility (flexible):   Assessing a situation and changing the direction of the investigation as appropriate (e.g., reframing the problem in light of new information).

Focus Maintenance (focus maintained):   Ensuring the investigation does not become sidetracked on other issues (e.g., does not permit the investigative team to follow targets unrelated to the primary investigation).

Forecasting (forecasts):   Planning or making estimates and projections about future demands and requirements on the investigation (e.g., thinking ahead to the need for resources required to address disclosure demands at the conclusion of the investigative phase).

Forensic Knowledge (forensic knowledge):   Possessing knowledge of current forensic science techniques.

Goal/Objective Setting (goals):   Settting or establishing goals (aim or purpose) and objectives for the investigation.

Individualized Consideration (consideration):   Giving personal attention to members, acting as an advisor and coach, providing personal feedback, and stimulating personal and professional development.

Information Management (infomgt):   Recognizing the need to organize and manage information coming into the investigation.

Informing Stakeholders (stakehold): Imparting timely information to appropriate individuals or groups with a vested interest in being kept informed on the work of the investigative team (e.g., regularly advising police executive officers on the progress of the investigation).

Innovation (innovation): Describing the use of a new or novel idea or technique in the investigation.

Inter-Agency Sensitivity (interagency): Sensitivity to potential inter-agency issues or conflicts in multijurisdictional investigations.

Investigative Ability (investigative ability): Understanding of appropriate investigative protocols and knowledge of investigative techniques.

Legal Awareness (legal): Considering potential legal implications of investigative activities (e.g., seeking legal advice on an issue, or considering how the actions of the investigative team may be impacted by the Canadian Charter of Rights and Freedoms).

Logistics Handling (logistics): Describing the complex facilitation of logistical issues in getting the investigation organized (e.g., pulling together the combination of resources, personnel, staging the investigation, getting resources on scene, accommodations, and so on).

Managing Expert Advice (expert advice): Engaging outside specialists appropriately and managing their input.

Media Management (media): Taking steps to deal with issues relating to the media and their contact with the investigation (e.g., the assignment of a media relations person).

Monitoring/Overseeing (monitor): Monitoring (watching and carefully evaluating) and overseeing (watching to make certain that a job or activity is being done correctly) the investigation, rather than taking on an active participatory role in executing tasks.

Multi-Tasking (multitask): Managing multiple responsibilities and issues simultaneously (e.g., dealing with multiple problems and issues that are arising at around the same time).

Position Identification (posidentify): Identifying specific roles and positions (not specific persons) required to staff the investigative team, taking into consideration required attributes of human resources (e.g., creating an organization chart indicating the various positions within the investigative team).

Position Matching (posmatching): Matching individuals to roles and positions based on the candidate's recognition of strengths, skills, and abilities (or lack thereof) of prospective team members.

Preparation/Planning (planning):   Taking steps to ensure that appropriate preparation and planning preceded some action (e.g., preparing in advance of conducting a critical interview).

Presentation Ability (presability):   Effectively conducting formal, structured presentations to stakeholder group(s).

Prioritization of Activities (prioritize):   Prioritized activities in the investigation (e.g., instructing the team that a certain task was important and was to be done prior to any other task).

Prudence (prudent):   Considering and making decisions based on the potential effect that the investigation might have on other areas of the organization (e.g., returning human resources borrowed from another area of the organization when feasible).

Rapport Building (rapport):   Creating a state of harmony and good interpersonal relations within the investigative team.

Recognizing Outstanding Performance (recperform):   Acknowledging outstanding performance by members of the investigative team (e.g., providing documented assessments/commendations to be maintained on the team member's personnel file).

Resource Acquisition/Management (resources):   Obtaining and managing appropriate financial/physical resources required for the investigation. In addition to funds, resources may include assets such as computers, vehicles, appropriate facilities, or any other equipment required to undertake the investigation.

Responsibility Delegation (delegate):   Delegating a particular job, duty, or right to appropriate member(s) of the investigative team.

Risk Analysis/Management (risk):   Considering risk factors that may impact the safety of police personnel or members of the public (e.g., utilizing the services of a tactical unit to execute a search for a potentially armed individual).

Scheduling (scheduled):   Organizing or developing working schedules for members of the investigative team.

Security/Evidence Integrity (security):   Ensuring that appropriate continuity, security, and scene retention procedures are in place (e.g., addressing issues relating to the continuity of exhibits, or correct procedures regarding the separation of witnesses).

Socializing (social):   Ensuring that members of the investigative team are encouraged or provided opportunities to socialize in a setting outside the investigation.

Standardization (standardize):   Establishing a common or standardized approach to the conduct of the investigation (e.g., recognizing that different agencies use different procedures and settling on a common procedure to be followed by all personnel assigned to the case).

Team Motivation (motivated):   Taking steps to create a positive influence, enthusiasm, and a commitment to the team.

Taking Responsibility (responsible):   Accepting personal responsibility for the conduct and outcome of the investigation.

Tunnel Vision Awareness (tunnel vision):   Indicating an awareness of potential problems associated with selective thinking or tunnel vision.

Victim/Family Attention (victim):   Ensuring that victims, and/or family members of crime victims, are provided with appropriate attention and assistance from police.

Well-being Considered (well-being):   Demonstrating concern with the basic health and the quality of primary and family relationships of members of the investigative team (e.g., making sure that the team members receive meals and/or can deal with family responsibilities).

References

Bales, R. F., & Slater, P. E. (1955). Role differentiation in small decision-making groups. In T. Parsons, R. F. Bales, J. Olds, M. Zelditch, Jr., & P. E. Slater (Eds.), *Family socialization and interaction process*, (pp. 259–306). Glencoe, IL: Free Press.

Blake, R., & Mouton, J. (1985). *The managerial grid III*. London, UK: Gulf Publishing.

Borg, I., & Lingoes, J. (1987). *Multidimensional similarity structure analysis*. New York: Springer.

Borg, I., & Shye, S. (1995). *Facet theory: Form and content*. London: Sage.

Burn, S. (2004). *Groups: Theory and practice*. Belmont, CA: Thompson Wadsworth.

Campbell, A. (1996). *Bernardo investigation review: Report of Mr. Justice Archie Campbell*. Toronto: Queen's Printer for Ontario.

Canadian Police College. (2002). *Canadian Police College major case management manual* (6th ed.). Ottawa: Canadian Police College.

Canter, D. V., & Heritage, R. (1990). A multivariate model of sexual offence behaviour: Developments in 'offender profiling.' *Journal of Forensic Psychiatry, 1*, 185–212.

Cohen, J. (1960). A coefficient of agreement for nominal scales. *Educational and Psychological Experiment, 20*, 37–46.

Cooper, D. (2003). *Leadership for follower commitment*. London: Butterworth Heinemann.

Cory, P. (2001). *The inquiry regarding Thomas Sophonow*. Winnipeg: Government of Manitoba.

DuBrin, A. (2004). *Leadership: Research findings, practice, and skills.* New York: Houghton Mifflin.

Fiedler, F. E. (1967). *A theory of leadership effectiveness.* New York: McGraw Hill.

Fiedler, F. E., & Chemers, M. M. (1974). *Leadership and effective management.* Glenview, IL: Scott, Foresman.

Fleishman, E. (1973). Twenty years of consideration and structure. In E. Fleishman & J. Hunt (Eds.), *Current development in the study of leadership* (pp. 1–40). Carbondale: Southern Illinois University Press.

Fleishman, E., Harris, E., & Burtt, H. (1955). *Leadership and supervision in industry.* Columbus: Ohio State University, Bureau of Educational Research.

Fleiss, J. (1981). *Statistical methods for rates and proportions* (2nd ed.). New York: Wiley.

FPT Heads of Prosecutions Committee Working Group. (2004). *Report on the prevention of miscarriages of justice.* Ottawa: Department of Justice, Canada.

Geberth, V. J. (1990). *Practical homicide investigations: Tactics, procedures, and forensic techniques* (2nd ed.). New York: Elsevier.

Glaser, B., & Strauss, A. (1967). *The discovery of grounded theory: Strategies for qualitative research.* New York: Aldine.

Guttman, L. (1968). A general nonmetric technique for finding the smallest coordinate space for a configuration of points. *Psychometrika, 33,* 469–506.

Halpin, A., & Winer, B. (1957). A factoral study of the leader behavior descriptions. In R. Stogdill & A. Coons (Eds.), *Leader behavior: Its description and measurement* (pp. 39–51). Columbus: Ohio State University, Bureau of Business Research.

Hannaghan, T. (1998). *Management: Concepts and practice* (2nd ed.). London: Pitman.

Hersey, P., & Blanchard, K. (1988). *Management of organizational behavior: Utilizing human resources* (5th ed.). Englewood Cliffs, NJ: Prentice-Hall.

Hickman, T., Poitras, L., & Evans, G. (1989). *The Royal Commission on the Donald Marshall, Jr., Prosecution.* Halifax: Government of Nova Scotia.

Holsti, O. (1969). *Content analysis for the social sciences and humanities.* Reading, MA: Addison-Wesley.

Home Office. (1991). *Career development of police officers in England and Wales: Guidance to forces on good practice.* Home Office Circular No. 104/1991.

Kahn, R., & Katz, D. (1953). Leadership practices in relation to productivity and morale. In D. Cartwright & A. Zander (Eds.), *Group dynamics* (pp. 554–571). New York: Harper and Row.

Karp, C., & Rosner, C. (1991). *When justice fails: The David Milgaard story.* Toronto: McClelland and Stewart.

Kaufman, F. (1998). *The Commission on proceedings involving Guy Paul Morin.* Toronto: Queen's Printer for Ontario.

Kotter, J. (1990). *A force for change: How leadership differs from management.* New York: Free Press.

Krippendorff, K. (1980). *Content analysis: An introduction to its methodology.* Newbury Park, CA: Sage.

Lamer, A. (2006). *The Lamer Commission of inquiry pertaining to the Cases of: Gregory Parsons, Randy Druken, Ronald Dalton.* St. John's, NL: Office of the Queen's Printer.

Lingoes, J. (1973). *The Guttman-Lingoes nonmetric program series.* Ann Arbor, MI: Mathesis.

Maguire, M., Noaks, L., Hobbs, R., & Brearley, N. (1993). *Assessing investigative performance.* Cardiff: Cardiff University Press.

Makin, K. (1992). *Redrum the innocent.* Toronto: Viking Canada.

McGurk, B., Gibson, R. L., & Platton, T. (1992). *Detectives: A job and training needs analysis.* London: Home Office Central Planning Unit.

Milgaard, J., & Edwards, P. (1999). *A mother's story: My battle to free David Milgaard.* Scarborough, ON: Doubleday Canada.

Ministry of Community Safety and Correctional Services. (2004). *Ontario major case management manual.* Toronto, ON: Government of Ontario.

Northouse, P. (1997). *Leadership: Theory and practice.* Thousand Oaks, CA: Sage.

Smith, N., & Flanagan, C. (2000). *The effective detective: Identifying the skills of an effective SIO.* Police Research Series Paper 122. London: Home Office Policing and Reducing Crime Unit.

Stogdill, R. (1974). *Handbook of leadership.* New York: Free Press.

Strube, M. J., & Garcia, J. E. (1981). A meta-analytic investigation of Fiedler's contingency model of leadership effectiveness. *Psychological Bulletin, 90,* 307–321.

Vroom, V. H. (1991). Leadership revisited. In B. M. Staw (Ed.), *Psychological dimensions of organizational behaviour* (pp. 413–423). New York: Macmillan.

Wigfield, D. (1996). Competent leadership in the police. *Police Journal, 69,* 99–107.

Yukl, G. (1989). *Leadership in organizations* (2nd ed.). Englewood Cliffs, NJ: Prentice-Hall.

Yukl, G., & Van Fleet, D. (1992). Theory and research on leadership in organizations. In M. D. Dunette & L. M. Hough (Eds.), *Handbook of industrial and organizational psychology Volume 3* (2nd ed.) (pp. 147–197). Palo Alto, CA: Consulting Psychologists Press.

Necropsies and the Cold Case

15

JASON ROACH AND
KEN PEASE

Everything that can be invented has been invented.

Charles H. Duell, Commissioner, U.S. Office of Patents, 1899

Rossmo (2006a, 2006b) has supplied a masterful account of the cognitive and organizational pitfalls that characterize criminal investigative failures. In the United Kingdom at least, this perspective is largely absent from official manuals for senior investigating officers, with the exception of somewhat unspecific advice to keep an open mind (e.g., Centrex, 2005). Rather than attempt a modest update of the Rossmo work, in this chapter we seek to do two things:

1. Briefly discuss the notion of framing and the implications of this for the investigative enterprise generally.
2. Take one example of how framing works, drawing a parallel with postmortems/autopsies—here termed necropsies[1]—and advocate the systematic use of cold case reviews to fuel investigative improvement.

Framing concerns the perception of a range within which options are considered (see Kahneman & Tversky, 2000). For example, in one experiment, people were asked if they would buy a theater ticket after losing a ticket they had already bought for an equivalent amount of money. It turns out they are less likely to decide to buy the replacement ticket. It all depends on how the loss is "framed." A lost ticket is generally framed within "theater going," so its replacement is seen as aversive.

---

[1] The term necropsy is preferred over postmortem and autopsy because the latter terms are used in the United States and the United Kingdom, respectively. Necropsy is more culturally neutral. It also includes postdeath examinations of other species, where the same elements apply, which make the comparison with cold case detections appealing.

A more profound example derives from the Wright brothers' struggle toward powered flight. Their rivals had "framed" propeller design within a marine engineering context. The Wright brothers framed it otherwise:

> A propeller moves a ship by displacing a volume of water. It bites into the water like a corkscrew moving into a cork as it rotates. And many of the Wrights' predecessors (and successors) supposed that an airplane's propellers should be a flat blade that could cut into the air. But, unlike water, air is highly compressible. Perhaps a propeller should not be flat. The brothers drew a brilliant analogy. A propeller is a wing travelling in a spiral course. The analogy depends upon envisaging a model of a wing, carrying out a mental rotation, and observing that it corresponds to half of a rotating propeller. As the wing rotates, it generates not lift but thrust. A flat blade ... does not generate much thrust. The blade should instead be cambered like a wing, and the principles for lift apply to the thrust of propellers, too. (Johnson-Laird, 2005, pp. 16–17)

Other elements in the success of the Wrights include a read-across from bicycle riding—riders have to lean into corners. Aircraft, likewise, should tilt while turning or they risk plummeting. When propeller design was framed as analogous to ship screws, progress was limited. This problem is not uncommon. In numerous design contexts, new products are often framed in terms of preceding technologies. Early motor cars, designated "horseless carriages," looked exactly like that. Duell's quotation at the start of this chapter, along with many (better known) concerning the impossibility of flight, rocket power, the dismissal of the motor car as a fad, the projected world market for only five computers,[2] and the military requirement for a mechanical horse rather than a tank (Dixon, 1994), all attest to the power of inappropriate framing, ridiculous only with hindsight. Indeed, there is a case for arguing that most of the examples of military incompetence in the Dixon book may be thought of as inappropriate framing.

What is the evidence that framing has served to hobble the detective process? One such instance concerns the framing of the use of DNA and fingerprints as tools for the unique identification of offenders. When so used, the techniques are powerless to find those who have had no previous contact with the criminal justice system, as their fingerprints or DNA profile will not be on record. Pease (2006) estimates that, because of the churn rate of active offending, no more than two-thirds of active offenders will be found in a database, and no more than two-thirds of those who are found in a database will be active offenders. Forensic traces can, however, be used to make statements about likely characteristics of the person leaving the traces. These

---

[2] See http://www.cochrane.org.uk/inside/quotes.php#others (accessed June 9, 2007).

include eye and hair color (McDonald & Foy, 2004), tooth defects, and short-ness of stature (Mullis et al., 1991) from DNA analysis, and age, recent drug or alcohol intake, and cosmetic use from fingerprints (Leggett, Lee-Smith, Jickells, & Russell, 2007). Just as was the case in vehicle design, the frame slips as time and experience suggests, and in major crime investigations ancestral DNA and similar techniques can serve a suspect pool reduction purpose (see Wilson, Weale, & Balding, 2003). Nonetheless, the frame has yet to cross discipline boundaries. The relevant developments in fingerprint testing are too recent to comment fairly on the failure of integration with the DNA markers. However, this is not the case when one considers the work of Farrington and Lambert (2000), who took a novel and pragmatic approach to offender profiling. They identified those aspects of phenotype about which observers were least often mistaken and showed that combinations of such markers yielded small suspect pools. The Farrington and Lambert approach could be used to complement the DNA and fingerprint approaches outlined above. Discipline boundaries seem to get in the way, and forensic and witness evidence are not readily seen together except in a substitutive way.

Cremation is an excellent means of covering up medical mistakes. The postmortem is an equally fine, often indispensable, means of revealing them, and of instilling confidence in a correct diagnosis. In the 1912 pioneering study of the relationship between diagnosis in life and cause of death revealed by necropsy, Richard Cabot showed that in nearly half of 3,000 studied, diagnosis and necropsy judgments were at odds. Matters seem to have moved on. Shojania, Burton, McDonald, and Goldman (2003) analyzed 53 studies published over four decades covering some 13,000 necropsies. The rate of major discrepancies between diagnosis and necropsy (thankfully) fell by around one-third per decade. There remain 4% of U.S. hospital deaths where a correct diagnosis could have led to survival. The rate is higher in Europe and Australia. The results of Shojania et al. came as a surprise because case series from individual centers showed no decline in discrepancies. The likely reason for this is the decrease in the use of nonforensic necropsies, from 30 to 40% in the 1960s, to 6% today. Autopsies are restricted to ever more diagnostically challenging cases, in particular, those cases in which there is most likely to be a diagnosis-necropsy discrepancy. Correction for the decline in the use of necropsies is needed before the improvement in diagnosis becomes visible. That said, physician accuracy in identifying cases that yield diagnostic surprises is far from perfect (Britton, 1974; Heasman & Lipworth, 1996).

The U.S. decline in necropsies is shared by the United Kingdom and continental Europe (LePage, 2006), with UK hospital necropsy rates at 4%.[3] The reasons mooted are depressing. They include fear of litigation in the United

---

[3] Ibid.

Kingdom, following the scandal at Alder Hey Children's Hospital in which organs were harvested at autopsy for research purposes without parental consent.[4] This resulted in the current unwieldy consent process. More generally, if a necropsy shows a "Class I" error, namely one where the prognosis might have changed had the diagnosis been accurate, the inducement to sue would certainly increase. Whether as cause or consequence of the decline, there is now a shortage of trained histopathologists (Reilly, 2006). The decline in necropsies is a matter of concern to informed parties, not least because diagnoses made with confidence can nonetheless be in error. Although necropsies are carried out primarily in challenging cases, there is little pressure to reduce deaths occasioned by confident but incorrect diagnoses. Substantial science underpins medicine. This is less obviously the case with respect to criminal detection (see Newburn, 2007).

Detection is a form of diagnosis. By what means can detectives find out if they are right or wrong? Feedback from miscarriage of justice cases is interesting but inadequate because cases contending for this label reflect putative errors in one direction only—besides, deeming a conviction unsafe scarcely amounts to exculpation. The more precise equivalents to necropsies are DNA detections years after the event (termed long-lapse detections [LLDs] in what follows). The same potential for refining future practice exists by comparison of the LLD offender with the original suspect, without the major disadvantage of legal threat, unless there was a clear wrongful conviction. In this event, the case would not have been the subject of cold case review. What would happen if cases were selected for review from among those where a conviction had been secured is a question of no little interest. This is the central recommendation of this chapter, namely that cold case reviews be carried out for a sample of crimes in which conviction was secured. In the United States, the Innocence Project has exonerated 203 prisoners by DNA testing, including 15 who served time on death row. These people served an average of 12 years in prison before exoneration and release.[5]

Necropsies and LLDs are equivalent in the following respects:

1. The provisional decision (diagnosis or suspect identification) is taken under conditions of uncertainty and—typically—time pressure.
2. The subsequent outcome (necropsy/LLD) is as close to definitive as the human condition allows.
3. The necropsy/LLD permits improvement of the quality of provisional decision making only if studied systematically.

---

[4] See http://news.bbc.co.uk/2/hi/in_depth/health/2001/bma_conference/1421350.stm (accessed January 21, 2007).

[5] See http://www.innocenceproject.org/about/Mission-Statement.php (accessed June 9, 2007).

The major point of possible difference confers a sense of urgency on the research proposed. LLDs depend overwhelmingly on forensic improvements, recently, most notably in the processing of smaller and otherwise more problematic DNA samples. Because the newer practices have now been largely incorporated routinely in the investigation of serious cases, the number of LLD detections is likely to fall. Although there will certainly be progress in DNA forensics to yield a trickle of such cases, the dramatic changes producing significant numbers of LLDs are probably now in the past. This means that there is a window of opportunity in which to analyze LLDs in a wider range of cases, including cases where convictions are considered unproblematic, while case files and the recollections of investigating officers remain available. In contrast, death is always with us, and the continuing supply of cases for necropsy is thus ensured!

If the necropsy parallel is accepted, the case files and circumstances surrounding every crime investigation eventually resolved by LLD should be minutely examined. Involved police participants should be interviewed and their experiences used to better inform subsequent detective practice and training. It is not much of an exaggeration to say that currently LLD outcomes are more the occasion for celebration than for analysis. For example, the *Daily Mail* reported:

> A killer who got away with the murder of a grandmother for 12 years was behind bars last night after finally being trapped by his DNA. ... advances in DNA profiling meant samples stored from the investigation could be matched to the one provided by O'Callaghan in February this year. [A senior police officer added] "The message that needs to go out to people who think they've got away with horrendous crimes is that the Cold Case Review Unit is here and it isn't going away." (December 1, 2006, p. 35)

This case is chosen for the irony that the cold case review team was never involved. It was the happy circumstance of another offense leading to the taking of a criminal justice DNA sample that brought O'Callaghan to justice.

At the risk of apparent naiveté, we should distinguish five circumstances in which the LLD case may be informative (see Table 15.1). To clarify, a case can be resolved by confession or inculpation by witnesses rather than by detective work. In such situations, the phrase "offender flagged" is used. If the person inculpated by LLD is not the person flagged or detected, the phrase "nonoffender" detected or flagged is used.

This simple breakdown suggests that there is something to be gained from cold case review in *all* circumstances. Policing does not share the reputation of medicine, and confirmation of judgment, even in settled cases, is not to be derided. The point is that settled cases are not revisited by cold case review, and information about true positives is thereby forgone. The notion

Table 15.1   LLD Case Circumstances

Case Status	Conviction	No Conviction
Offender arrested	Police process vindicated by LLD	Case preparation called into question by LLD
Innocent person arrested	Miscarriage of justice identified by LLD	Court vindicated by LLD
Offender suspected	Witness/confession; case vindicated by LLD	Case preparation called into question by LLD
Innocent person suspected	Witness/confession-based miscarriage of justice identified by LLD	Court vindicated by LLD
Case unsolved	Impossible	Review of detective process indicated

of the cold case review has been framed in an inappropriately narrow way to exclude such cases. Of course forensic evidence is minutely reconsidered in appealed cases, but that is not relevant to the point made here, namely that LLD should be framed as a routine quality assurance process rather than as an aid to belated detection in serious cases.

A Superficial Scrutiny of LLD Cases

The remainder of this chapter provides narratives of a number of LLD cases to illustrate what appear to be common points for consideration, and they are followed by the outline of a research program to take advantage of the time-limited opportunity that LLDs confer. We have no illusions about the superficiality and lack of detail in the cases presented. That is why a proper research program is needed. The choice that we faced was whether to include the inadequately documented case examples as providing pointers and thereby invite ridicule, or to omit them and forgo the opportunity of persuading the reader that there is something worth investigating. We chose to invite ridicule.

Clues from Necropsy-Revealed Errors

Are there any clues from necropsy analysis as to the kinds of circumstances that lead to error? Graber, Franklin, and Gordon (2005) identify several overlapping putative causes for error. These include:

1. *System failure*—for example, lost x-rays or lack of qualified staff on duty.
2. *Incompetence*—for example, failure to detect a gangrenous leg.
3. *Premature closure*—arrival at a diagnosis that seems to fit the facts, with subsequent failure to recognize other emerging possibilities.

The third reason in particular resonates with those familiar with the criminal investigation process and is covered in the Centrex (2005) document. The notion of intolerance of ambiguity as an individual trait, with subsequent reluctance to change a judgment, has a venerable history in personality psychology (see Adorno, Frenkel-Brunswick, & Levinson, 1950), and its relevance to the practice of medicine has also been recognized (DeForge & Sobal, 1989). The observation that the rate of increase in confidence outpaces the rate of increase in accuracy in decision making generally is of almost equal age (Oskamp, 1965). Work by Lindsey McLoughlin (2007) and others at the Jill Dando Institute for Crime Science, University College London, provides particularly dramatic evidence. She demonstrates that the accuracy of police officer anticipations of where crime will occur during the next week is wholly unrelated to the confidence with which such predictions are advanced. It will emerge that this phenomenon is a candidate as a central factor in cases where LLD comes into play.

Before presenting necropsies of the following LLD cases, to which we have had privileged access, a further word of caution is prudent. Case information has been collected from "cold case" review files and interviews with the cold case officers involved, all of which information stems from the original investigations. Our caution is twofold. First, some cases stretch back some 25 years, to a time when UK police recording standards and procedures were very different from those now demanded—where surviving investigation records were found to be at best scant and at worst untraceable. The second alludes to the phenomenon of hindsight bias, where cold case officers have reviewed original investigations safe in the knowledge that DNA evidence has served to unmask previously unknown offenders. We acknowledge the possible effect of such bias in the necropsy process and a need to minimize the effect by searching as widely as possible for information on the cases, incorporating the exploration of media representations, publicly accessible information (e.g., Internet sites), the case review process, and personal recollections of the investigation of selected cases. The problems dutifully acknowledged, a selection of LLD necropsies is presented. It should be noted that, in the research program outlined at the end of the chapter, hindsight bias would not be a consideration in that investigating officers could be interviewed before the cold case review yielded a result.

Long-Lapse Detection Case 1: Mary Gregson
In August 1977,[6] Mary Gregson, 38 years old, was murdered as she walked the short distance along the canal from her house to work. She was sexually

---

[6] Mary Gregson lived in Shipley, a small town in West Yorkshire in the north of England.

assaulted and strangled before her body was dumped in the River Aire.[7] When Mary failed to return home, she was reported missing. Her body was found the following day.

At the time of the murder, the Yorkshire Ripper (Peter Sutcliffe) had reached the height of his notoriety but had not been identified, and the initial local opinion was he had claimed Mary as his latest victim (Sutcliffe lived and offended nearby).[8] West Yorkshire detectives soon discounted the Gregson murder from the Ripper investigation, on differentiating modus operandi and victim selection grounds. The Ripper inquiry was consuming a significant amount of local police resources, but detectives still interviewed some 9,000 people in the investigation of her homicide. Semen stains were found on Mary's clothing and were subjected to blood grouping tests. A prime suspect was never identified.

In 1999, a 47-year-old local man, Ian Lowther, was arrested and charged with the sexual assault and murder of Mary Gregson. Forensic scientists had by then extracted sufficient DNA evidence from warehoused crime scene evidence. Lowther was matched after a new sweep of local males. He was sample number 53. He had not moved since the murder, 22 years earlier.

The original inquiry focused initially on builders in the area. Lowther was among 830 construction workers interviewed by police in the early stages—all were employed on the new Inland Revenue building, close to Mary Gregson's house, on the opposite side of the canal. Lowther lived only a few hundred yards from the spot where Mary's body was found. When interviewed, he admitted walking along the canal on the day of the murder after an afternoon's drinking at a local pub. He was the only person who admitted being near the crime scene on that day. Lowther was questioned again several weeks later as part of a police house-to-house sweep of the area.

The case files state that a local woman, originally from Italy, volunteered information to the original investigation. She told police, with the aid of an Italian-speaking priest, that she was walking along the canal on the afternoon in question where she heard noises coming from behind some bushes. Surmising that it was probably an amorous couple, she asked, in broken English, if everything was okay. A man replied that they were fine. She then inquired as to his name. He replied, "Ian." The Italian woman later told police that he was called "Jan." The description she gave was vague. The police had no success tracing the man, not noting the phonetic similarity between Ian and Jan for a native Italian speaker.

---

[7] See http://www.forensic.gov.uk/forensic_t/inside/news/list_casefiles.php?case=4 (accessed January 29, 2007).

[8] Peter Sutcliffe, the Yorkshire Ripper, killed 13 women (he is believed to have attacked at least 23) between 1975 and 1980. His crimes were predominantly perpetrated in red-light areas across Yorkshire, in the north of England. At the time of Mary Gregson's murder, the nation was gripped with fear and would continue to be until 1980 when Sutcliffe was finally apprehended.

Hindsight is truly a wonderful thing. Our aim here is not to criticize the original police investigation for not finding Mary Gregson's killer, but to learn from that which hindsight affords:

- Lowther was a local resident and remained so—a common phenomenon among murderers (e.g., see Rossmo, 1998, 2000; Canter, 2003), so the investigation was focused in the right place.
- Lowther had no offenses on record either before or after the killing of Mary Gregson. In fact, one police officer involved referred to Lowther's one and only known crime as "His 10 minutes of madness" (Owens & Ellis, 2004).
- The Italian woman's testimony, coupled with Lowther's admission that he had walked along the canal on the afternoon of the murder, might have gone a long way to elevating him to the status of serious suspect.
- The cold case officers believe the Italian witness had stumbled upon the murder in progress. In that case, it is (with the seductive benefit of hindsight) surprising they did not ask more about "Jan's" voice. More pertinently, the number of men with phonetically similar names to Jan (Ian, John, and Jack) would account for a maximum of approximately 5% of the 830 construction workers who made up the original suspect pool.[9]

The recording and collation of information practices prevalent at the time of the original investigation probably played a significant role here (Petherick, 2005). The failure to collect, collate, and interpret information adequately has long been identified as a critical cognitive problem common to ill-fated police investigations. This particular problem was identified in the Yorkshire Ripper investigations by the Byford Inquiry (1981).

This short reconsideration of the Mary Gregson murder shows, therefore, that the original "investigative diagnosis"—the killer was a local man linked to the construction site near the victim's home—was correct. This was where the original murder inquiry might have found the killer. Cold case review officers also followed this theory, despite a psychological profiler's advice to the contrary, and they began a DNA sweep of this group. It is possible a Bayesian approach to evidence elements might have made Lowther stand out even more from the other suspects in the pool (see Taroni, Aitken, Garboline, Biedermann, 2006).

---

[9] This rough estimate was reached through an examination of popular names from Lowther's generation on the "Friends Reunited" website.

Long-Lapse Detection Case 2: Lesley Molseed

Lesley Molseed was 11 when she was sexually assaulted and murdered in October 1975. She had been abducted while walking to a local shop in Rochdale, Greater Manchester. Her body was found clothed, on open moorland, three days later. Her killer had ejaculated on her underwear. She had been stabbed 12 times.[10]

Within three months of Lesley Molseed's murder, police had spoken to more than 12,000 people, taking nearly 5,000 statements.[11] As with the Gregson case, the shadow of the Yorkshire Ripper was felt because of both the timing and the geography; it was only in 2000 that DNA evidence excluded Sutcliffe from consideration. Case documents from the original police inquiry record no contact with or mention of the man who more than 30 years later was to be identified as Lesley's murderer. He lived a few miles outside the search area. This case was destined to represent one of the saddest miscarriages of justice in recent British legal history.

In December 1975, 22-year-old Stefan Ivan Kiszko, a local tax clerk, had been arrested for Lesley Molseed's sexual murder. He was a loner with no social life beyond his mother and aunt. He evoked unfriendly attention because of his large, ungainly appearance and arguably obsessive behavior, such as writing down the license plate numbers of vehicles he thought were driven recklessly. Kiszko had never been in trouble with the law and had never met Molseed. Three 13-year-old girls claimed Kiszko had "exposed" himself to them just before the estimated time of Molseed's murder. At Kiszko's trial, the judge, Justice Park, commended the girls for their bravery and honesty.[12] Sixteen years later, in 1991, during the inquiry into Kiszko's conviction, all three admitted what they had said in 1975 was untrue. They did it "for a laugh."[13] Kiszko confessed to murdering Molseed within two days of his arrest. Police seized on perceived inconsistencies between his several accounts of the days in question. During the 1991 investigation it was found that Kiszko was not informed of his right to legal representation, he was not permitted to have his mother present despite his request for her, and he was not interviewed under caution until police decided he was their prime (and only) suspect.[14] Kiszko maintained from the beginning that, not only was he innocent, but that his confession had been given under duress.

Kiszko was later identified as having an XYY karyotype. Males with this condition tend to be poorly coordinated, of below average intelligence, and

---

[10] See http://en.wikipedia.org/wiki/Stefan_Kiszko.
[11] See http://news.bbc.co.uk/1/hi/england/6123053.stm (accessed February 20, 2007).
[12] Ibid.
[13] See http://en.wikipedia.org/wiki/Stefan_Kiszko.
[14] Ibid.

large in stature. In the 1960s and 1970s, the XYY chromosome complement came to be associated with violent criminality. The "logic" was that men commit more crimes than women, and doubling the number of the chromosomes that identified the male as such would be likely to increase the male-linked propensity to violence. Police, prosecution, and Kiszko's legal defense chose to present his XYY condition and the medication he took for it as mitigating factors. There was case law precedent for this (Fox, 1971). In actuality, while XYY males are indeed overrepresented in the populations of special hospitals, they are actually less violent than the average patient (Shah & Roth, 1974).

Jones (2000) suggested that such violence as XYY males do exhibit may be a consequence of a social reaction to their size (being perceived as thugs and bullies). Nonetheless, at the time of the Molseed murder, a letter from a professor of genetics opined that "The probability factor makes the criminal XYY a predictable dangerous person and the standards of duty of care should accordingly be raised" (Fox, 1971, p. 6). "Duty of care" in this case is a euphemism meaning indefinite detention. The professor's letter went so far as to suggest future victims of undiagnosed XYY males should be able to sue the state for negligence.

Kiszko had jotted down the license plate number of a car seen near the murder scene. Instead of this being taken as symptomatic of Kiszko's obsessional nature, which was well known by many who knew him, it was seen by police as evidence of him being in the right place at the right time, even though he did not time or date these notes. There was medical evidence that Kiszko had broken his ankle several months before the murder. When coupled with his obesity, it might be argued he would have found it very difficult to climb the steep slope to the scene of the murder from the location where he had recorded the license number.[15] The defense failed to explore this.

In July 1976, Kiszko was sentenced to life imprisonment for sexual assault and murder. Those responsible for Kiszko's incarceration took his continued protestations of innocence as merely symptomatic of his illness. He was denied parole because he refused to admit guilt or engage in sex offender treatment programs. Had he confessed, he would probably have been released on parole in the early 1980s. He remained in prison for 15 years, before finally being pardoned in February 1992. He died of a heart attack in 1993 at the age of 41, just before Christmas. Stefan Kiszko's mother directed her anger not at police but at David Waddington, who had conducted her son's defense, suggesting that it was he who should be "strung up."[16] Among other issues, he had entered a manslaughter plea against his client's wishes. Waddington eventually rose to be British Home Secretary.

[15]Ibid.
[16]Ibid.

As they said in Casablanca, "Round up the usual suspects." More usually associated with banana-republic police, it has long been the fallback position for
idle and desperate detectives. The friendless, the mentally disabled, and the
weird are vulnerable when police are under pressure.[17]

In November 2006 Ronald Castree was arrested for the sexual assault
and murder of Lesley Molseed. He had been identified by a DNA profile.
Castree had been arrested nine months earlier for assaulting a prostitute.
He had been taken to a local police station and interviewed, along with the
victim, but charges were dropped when she was judged to have mental health
problems. Castree voluntarily gave a DNA sample, which was submitted to
the UK National DNA Database (NDNAD). This sample was soon linked to
scene evidence from Molseed's murder. Why did the police fail to find Castree during their initial inquiry?

The investigation was characterized by numerous manifestations of
confirmation bias—the premature movement from information generation to case building (Stelfox & Pease, 2005). This might have mattered less
had not the defense been so compliant and indifferent to the prosecution's
theory and its problems. It is something of a pyrrhic victory that Kiszko
was pardoned before Castree was identified. Sherlock Holmes claimed that
"When you have eliminated the impossible, whatever remains, however
improbable, must be the truth" (*The Sign of Four*). But it is difficult to eliminate all the impossibles, and improbables can too easily lead to miscarriages
of justice. Accusations of indecent exposure (later revealed as untrue), a
reputation for weirdness, the untimed record of a vehicle license number,
and the confession of a suggestible man were improbables converted into
Kiszko's conviction. The historic context of the case—an embattled police
force preoccupied with the Ripper investigation—perhaps pressured detectives to get results. Itiel Dror and his colleagues have convincingly and
repeatedly shown the fragility of expert forensic judgments when placed
under pressure (Dror, Busemeyer, & Basola, 1999; Dror & Charlton, 2006:
Dror, Charlton, & Peron, 2006).

After the exoneration of Kiszko, police began to generate new suspects
from the original inquiry. A convicted pedophile who was identified as
the prime suspect by the author of a 1997 book (a local reporter convinced
of Kiszko's innocence) was investigated along with some 300 other men,
including Peter Sutcliffe, the Yorkshire Ripper, and child killer Robert Black.
All were excluded by DNA evidence. Lesley's killer, Ronald Castree, never
emerged during the police investigation. The Kiszko case is a strong example
of the need for data verification of cold case reviews, as advocated here.

---

[17]See http://www.thefirstpost.co.uk/index.php?menuID=2&subID=1074 (accessed February 20, 2007).

Long-Lapse Detection Case 3: John Humble

On October 20, 2005, John Humble, a 49-year-old from Sunderland in northeast England was charged with perverting the course of justice. The charge against him was:

> You sent a series of communications, namely three letters and an audio tape, to West Yorkshire police and press claiming to be the perpetrator of a series of murders that at the time were the subject of police investigation.[18]

The reader may be forgiven for wondering why this case may be important, but the murderer in question was Britain's most notorious serial killer of the twentieth century. The activities of Humble (known as "Wearside Jack," because of his strong regional accent that identified him as a native of Sunderland at the mouth of the River Wear) were blamed for leading police away from Peter Sutcliffe, the real Yorkshire Ripper. This diversion allowed the real killer to claim three more victims before his arrest in January 1981. The arrest of Humble as Wearside Jack, almost 30 years after his sabotage of the Ripper investigation and 25 years after the arrest of Sutcliffe, represents one of the longest of LLDs. Humble was identified via DNA from saliva found on preserved envelopes sent to police by Wearside Jack. He was arrested for being drunk and disorderly several years before and had voluntary given a buccal swab, which was entered into the NDNAD. Our focus is not on the Ripper investigation, for this has been well documented elsewhere (e.g., see Byford, 1981), but rather on the Wearside Jack case. We are interested in why police failed to identify Humble for a quarter of a century.

On September 13, 1979, a "Special Notice" was issued by West Yorkshire Police to all forces in England, giving details of 16 murders and attempted murders linked to the Yorkshire Ripper. The crimes were connected by various sources of information, including tire tracks and details from what was termed the "Sunderland" letters and tape. No mention was made of descriptions and photofit impressions provided by surviving victims. With regards to suspects, the "Special Notice" stated (Byford, 1981, p. 17):

> A person can be eliminated from these enquiries if:
>
> A. He was not born between 1924 and 1959
> B. He is an obvious coloured person
> C. His shoe size is 9 or above
> D. His blood group is other than B
> E. His accent is dissimilar to a North Eastern (Geordie) accent.

---

[18] See http://www.execulink.com/~kbrannen/wearside.htm (accessed October 28, 2005).

The last two criteria related specifically to a series of 1978 letters and one audiotape believed at the time to have been sent by the Ripper to senior officers in charge of the investigation. Based on the above elimination criteria, the real Ripper (who spoke with a West Yorkshire accent) would have been eliminated as a suspect. Indeed, Peter Sutcliffe was interviewed in this period for a fifth time and discounted by detectives due to his accent. The Ripper investigation had been ongoing since 1975 and continued until Sutcliffe's arrest in January 1981.

When the first two letters were received in 1978, they were routinely checked, considered of little significance, and dismissed as the work of a crank along with many other similar communications. As the desperation to catch the Ripper intensified, another letter and an audiotape arrived. Perceptions of their authenticity grew as confirmation bias and premature closure set in (Stelfox & Pease, 2005). Wearside Jack was elevated from a possible to a prime suspect when the decision was made to go public with the tape in the hope that a member of the public might recognize his voice. Lord Byford describes the effect the letters and tape had on both police and public: "they were conditioned to believe that they came from the killer who was a native of Sunderland; the letters and tape were used to eliminate suspects" (1981, p. 148). The public response to the publicity given the letters and the tape had an overwhelming impact on the Major Incident Room and its limited resources. In his summary, Byford concluded:

> This stopped the processing of actions from the Incident Room for a period and eventually the additional burdens imposed on the staff employed there proved an important contributory factor in the specific mistakes which allowed Sutcliffe to remain free. ... Sutcliffe might have still been arrested, however, despite the problems arising from the failure of the Major Incident Room had the letters and the tape not been used as factors for elimination of suspects. (1981, p. 148)

Once elimination criteria had been set and a huge publicity campaign mounted accordingly, then "the die had been well and truly cast" (Byford, 1981, p. 148).

Sutcliffe was arrested and identified as the "Yorkshire Ripper" on January 2, 1981. Eighteen months of the five-year inquiry had been in exclusive pursuit of a suspect with a Wearside accent. At a press conference immediately following Sutcliffe's arrest, the first question asked was whether he spoke with a Wearside accent. The Chief Constable of West Yorkshire police replied that he had no idea, as he had not yet spoken to Sutcliffe.[19] In fact,

[19]Press interview shown in the UK ITV documentary, *The Ripper Hoaxer: Wearside Jack* (2006). ITV Productions.

Sutcliffe did not. Furthermore, his handwriting did not resemble that in the letters. Wearside Jack had been a major investigative distraction and nothing more.

With the Ripper arrested, the search began for Wearside Jack, now known to be the perpetrator of a hoax that likely cost three lives. Voice, handwriting, and type B blood were the only identifying characteristics that could be relied on. This led to an increase in the size of the suspect pool as age, shoe size, and other criteria were now unknown. All the police had were a few letters and a tape. At best, all they could charge a suspect with was "perverting the course of justice." But if Wearside Jack was responsible for killing Joan Harrison, as suggested in the letters, then police were still chasing a murderer. The availability bias is a common trap in these types of circumstances. If a primary hypothesis (e.g., Wearside Jack and the Yorkshire Ripper are the same person) is disproved, then an alternative hypothesis is selected, but without first reviewing all the available evidence.

That happened here. If Wearside Jack was not the Ripper, then he must be the killer of Joan Harrison. This belief was compounded when Sutcliffe confessed to numerous attacks but denied killing Harrison. Why would he admit to some murders but not others? It was later determined that Harrison was murdered by someone else entirely. Police persisted with the hypothesis that Wearside Jack knew information that only the killer would know. However, the details about Harrison's murder known to Jack had been made public.

West Yorkshire police, even if they thought Wearside Jack was a killer, did little to track him down after the arrest of Sutcliffe. The inquiry was scaled down in 1981, although the case remained open until first considered closed in 1993. Senior officers retired (both enforced and of their own volition). Some were demoted.[20] The "post-Ripper" period was seen as a time to bury past ghosts and restore public confidence in the police force. The West Yorkshire Constabulary had taken a battering, and it was now time to recover and move on. Arguably, this was only possible if it distanced itself from the Ripper inquiry and any related investigations such as the search for Wearside Jack. If Wearside Jack was the murderer of Joan Harrison, the responsibility for the investigation fell on the Lancashire Police.

Various conspiracy theories have been offered to explain the West Yorkshire police's apparent lack of interest in finding Wearside Jack. The urban legend that he was a disgruntled police officer surfaced several times over the next decade and can be seen as an extension of the preceding "Ripper is a police officer" legend. Both were fueled by the interpretation of lack of investigative progress as indicative of a police "cover-up." Detective Superintendent Dick

---

[20]Detective Superintendent Dick Holland returned to uniform and was assigned to "rural policing" for the remainder of his career. He was seen by many as a scapegoat for the problems of the Ripper inquiry.

Holland fanned the flames somewhat by acknowledging that the police officer-as-Wearside Jack theory had been investigated during the Ripper inquiries, but perhaps not to the extent to which it should have been.[21] A perceived lack of interest from West Yorkshire police, coupled with the lack of progress in identifying Wearside Jack, therefore continued to fuel this speculation. The simpler and less interesting explanation—that police felt every clue had been investigated—was ignored. Such was the situation for many years. It did not stop numerous television documentaries and books from offering new "insights" and "probable" Wearside Jack suspects (e.g., see Lavelle, 1999, 2003).

On September 17, 2003, a West Yorkshire police spokesperson announced that they had officially ended their hunt for Wearside Jack as the hoax was perpetrated over 25 years earlier, and, as such, they could no longer realistically charge the individual concerned with "wasting police time."[22] The offense carried a maximum custodial sentence of six months and a £2,500 fine. Media interest, however, did not stop and journalists continued to propose suspects whom the police investigated but to no avail.

Advances in low copy number DNA (e.g., see Roach & Pease, 2006) allowed police to test saliva samples extracted from the envelope seals. This ultimately proved to be successful. On October 18, 2005, police arrested John Humble. He had not been identified in any of the previous investigations. Humble was on the UK NDNAD as a result of being arrested for drunk and disorderly conduct. His DNA provided the vital match that unmasked him as Wearside Jack. At the time of the first letter in 1978, Humble was only 22. He was arrested in the early 1970s for attacking a police officer and thought his punishment too severe. Humble was aggrieved because the officer was off duty at the time and, therefore, in his eyes, a civilian. The letters and tape may have been a way of addressing his perceived grievance by making the police "pay" for the way he was treated. Humble was also obsessed at the time with the Yorkshire Ripper and confessed to a certain jealousy of his notoriety and a desire to be part of the media frenzy.[23] Humble carefully followed the media reports (he even kept a scrapbook) and knew much about the Ripper case. The tone and content of the letters were found to closely match the published letters supposedly sent by Jack the Ripper in the previous century.

Although he was not implicated in the Yorkshire Ripper murders, there was still a belief that Wearside Jack had murdered Joan Harrison. Forensic examinations of the envelopes in which the letters arrived identified the person who licked them (presumably the author) as a secretor with type B blood—the same as found from the analysis of semen found on Joan

---

[21] See http://www.execulink.com/~kbrannen/wearside.htm (accessed October 26, 2005).
[22] Ibid.
[23] Press interview shown in the UK ITV documentary, *The Ripper Hoaxer: Wearside Jack* (2006). ITV Productions.

Harrison. The connection between Wearside Jack, the Ripper, and Harrison's killer seemed strong as only 6% of the UK population have that particular blood type. However, it must be remembered that this still represents 1.5 million males. When John Humble was identified as Wearside Jack, investigators determined he was innocent of Harrison's homicide.[24]

How a necropsy of this longest of long lapse detections can serve as a lesson for future investigative practice has been discussed throughout this section. Several tentative conclusions can be made. A high-ranking officer recently suggested to the first author (Roach) that he considered sending several of his detectives on investigative journalism courses on the understanding that they often find suspects quicker than police. He added the proviso that police are bound to conduct such investigations "by the book," while journalists are not.[25] Case-sensitive information often finds its way to the media as illustrated by the Joan Harrison murder case. Humble read of the suggested link between the 1975 Harrison killing and the Ripper crimes in an article in one of Britain's popular national newspapers. Police failed to consider this and saw such knowledge as evidence that the letter came from the Yorkshire Ripper.

In summary, investigators might learn something from Sherlock Holmes, England's foremost detective:

> Then, with your permission, we will leave it at that, Mr Mac. The temptation to form premature theories upon insufficient data is the bane of our profession. I can only see two things for certain at present: a great brain in London and a dead man in Sussex. It's the chain between that we are going to trace. (*The Valley of Fear.*)

Long-Lapse Detection Case 4: The Dearne Valley Shoe Rapist

Between 1983 and 1986, six women were sexually assaulted (four were raped) by the same man in South Yorkshire. He had terrorized women, dragging them off the street in the early hours of the morning while they made their way home alone from local night clubs—tying them up before violently sexually assaulting them. In each case he lay in wait with a stocking over his head. He dragged his victims to a secluded area and tied their hands and feet with stockings. After attacking them he took their shoes (hence his signature title). He also stole other items including

---

[24]The first author (Roach) was with detectives in Preston (Lancashire, England) when West Yorkshire detectives contacted them and said, in their opinion, Humble was not a killer. Therefore, there would not be any worth in Preston CID officers interviewing him about the murder.

[25]The majority of that "book" was written as a result of the Byford Report on the failings of the Yorkshire Ripper inquiries.

perfume and jewelry, although this was not made public by police during the investigation.

The original investigation yielded little, so police appealed to the public through the BBC *Crimewatch* program, which produced three thousand possible suspects.[26] Those leading the investigation also chose to enlist the help of a psychological profiler who suggested that the likely offender would be in his late twenties, unemployed or of "unskilled" labor, and probably single. With no arrest, the case eventually grew cold.

In April 2006, cold case review investigators arrested James Desmond Lloyd, 49 years of age. He was charged with three counts of rape and two attempted rapes in the 1980s, to which he pleaded guilty. DNA evidence had linked him to the crimes. He had no criminal record and was not on the NDNAD. Lloyd was trapped by the technique of familial searching. DNA evidence identified over 40 possible matches in the local area, and police painstakingly investigated every suspect and their immediate families. Lloyd's sister was on record for involvement in a previous drunk driving offense for which her DNA had been obtained. She had, despite his seemingly blameless life, led them to Lloyd. When officers searched his work premises they found hundreds of pairs of women's shoes, some new, some worn, and—crucially— some that had belonged to the sexual assault victims.[27] Lloyd twice attempted suicide. He had told his father he was about to be arrested for crimes he had committed over 20 years ago.

The cold case review had exposed Lloyd as the Dearne Valley Rapist and devastated the lives of many of those around him. He was described by family, friends, and neighbors as a family man, a workaholic, and a man with few outside interests.[28] Lloyd had risen from an apprentice at the print works where he began as a teenager to the position of manager with a salary of £42,000. It was his respectable career and stable home life—he had been married for over 20 years to the same woman and had two children—which led those around him to utter disbelief at his arrest for rape.

Lloyd was organized in the commission of his attacks on his victims and left few clues as to his identity. At the time of his rapes, Lloyd was in his late 20s and still single. In summary, the review of this case appears to offer little other than underlining the fact that some crimes are just difficult to solve.

---

[26]BBC *Crimewatch* is a public appeal-based program aired monthly on national television. It affords police the facility of appealing to the public directly with regard to cases where the offender has not been identified. The program often contains case updates and reconstructions in the hope of jogging the memories of crucial witnesses. It can overwhelm police with information from a concerned public wishing to help.

[27]See http://www.yorkshiretoday.co.uk/ViewArticle2.aspx?SectionID=55&ArticleID=1634 (accessed February 13, 2007).

[28]See http://news.bbc.co.uk/1/hi/england/south_yorkshire/5187634.stm (accessed February 13, 2007).

Long-Lapse Detection Case 5: Geraldine Palk

Forensic Science Service (FSS) scientists used an "intuitive approach" to obtain a murderer's DNA profile after all evidence from the crime had seemingly gone. The FSS's specialist DNA unit used DNA Low Copy Number to obtain the profile of Geraldine Palk's suspected killer from a plastic tube used to store the medical swabs taken from her body a decade earlier. All other evidence in the case was apparently used up in previous tests undertaken in 1991, so scientists decided in 2001 to try and examine the plastic "sleeve" that the swab had been kept in. They hoped material from the cotton wool swab had been left on the inside of the tube when the swab was placed inside. The tip of the wooden swab stick was also tested in case genetic material from the original cotton wool swab had soaked through. Remarkably, a full DNA profile was obtained and, when it was searched against the National DNA Database®, it matched with Mark Hampson, whose profile had been put on the database after his arrest for another crime. Hampson was found guilty of murder at Bristol Crown Court in November 2002 and jailed for life.[29]

We have no additional information on this case, so the reader may wonder why we included it. We did so for two reasons. First, like all the individual cases described in the FSS website case file, this one refers to a case where no conviction had occurred. Second, it illustrates the DNA practice ingenuity that can now be regarded as standard. This underlines the time-limited nature of the opportunity for the systematic analysis of cold case reviews. Unless there is another leap equivalent to Low Copy Number analysis, almost all the cases of interest for clarifying successes and failures of the detective process are already in the system.

Your Point Being?

We wish to see cold case reviews of all murder, manslaughter, and rape investigations over the past decade involving:

1. Cases where no conviction has occurred
2. Cases where a not guilty plea was entered
3. A systematic sample of cases otherwise cleared

By thus extending the frame within which the cold case review is considered, we can gain the widest possible benefits in understanding the process of detection, and, not insignificantly, reach a position where greater trust is properly placed in the machinery of justice. Some of those convicted will be

---

[29]This account was taken from the Forensic Science Service website: http://www.forensic. gov.uk/forensic_t/inside/news/list_casefiles.php?case=16 (accessed June 13, 2007).

acquitted, without having appealed. Some detective tactics will have their credibility enhanced, others diminished. Detective hubris will be challenged and detective competence lauded and hopefully rewarded.

It must be acknowledged that the wider a frame is set, the more challenging becomes the task of combining probabilities. But that is to set too wide a frame for this chapter.

References

Adorno, T. W., Frenkel-Brunswick, E., & Levinson, D. J. (1950). *The authoritarian personality*. New York: Harper.

Britton, M. (1974). Diagnostic errors discovered at autopsy. *Acta Medica Scandinavica, 196*, 203–210.

Byford, L. (1981). Sir Lawrence Byford report into the police handling of the Yorkshire Ripper case. Retrieved July 5, 2008, from http://www.homeoffice.gov.uk/about-us/freedom-of-information/released-information/foi-archive-crime/1941-Byford-report/.

Cabot, R. C. (1912). Diagnostic pitfalls identified during a study of three thousand autopsies. *Journal of the American Medical Association, 59*, 2295–2298.

Canter, D. (2003). *Mapping murder: Walking in killers' footsteps*. London: Virgin.

Centrex. (2005). *Practice advice on core investigative doctrine*. Cambourne: ACPO.

DeForge, B. R., & Sobal, J. (1989). Intolerance of ambiguity in students entering medical School. *Social Science Medicine, 28*, 869–874.

Dixon, N. R. F. (1994). *On the psychology of military incompetence*. London: Pimlico.

Dror, I. E., Busemeyer, J. R., & Basola, B. (1999). Decision making under time pressure: An independent test of sequential sampling models. *Memory and Cognition, 27*, 713–725.

Dror, I. E., & Charlton, D. (2006). Why experts make errors. *Journal of Forensic Identification, 56*, 600–616.

Dror, I. E., Charlton, D., & Peron, A. E. (2006). Contextual information renders experts vulnerable to making erroneous identifications. *Forensic Science International, 156*, 74–78.

Farrington, D. P., & Lambert, S. (2000). Statistical approaches to offender profiling. In D. V. Canter & L. J. Alison (Eds.), *Profiling property crimes* (pp. 235–273). Aldershot, Hants: Ashgate.

Fox, R. G. (1971). The XYY offender: A modern myth? *Journal of Criminal Law, Criminology and Police Science, 62*, 59–73.

Graber, M. L., Franklin, N., & Gordon, R. (2005). Diagnostic error in internal medicine. *Archives of Internal Medicine, 165*, 1493–1499.

Heasman, M. A., & Lipworth, L. (1996). *Accuracy of certification of cause of death*. London: HMSO.

Johnson-Laird, P. N. (2005). Flying bicycles: How the Wright brothers invented the aeroplane. *Mind and Society, 1*, 1–22.

Jones, S. (2000). *Understanding violent crime*. Buckingham: Open University Press.

Kahneman, D., & Tversky, A. (2000). *Choices, values and frames*. Cambridge: Cambridge University Press.

Lavelle, P. (1999). *Wearside Jack: The hunt for the hoaxer of the century*. Durham, NC: Northeast Press.

Lavelle, P. (2003). *Shadow of the Ripper: The secret story of the man who helped the Yorkshire Ripper to kill and kill again*. London: John Blake Publishing.

Leggett, R., Lee-Smith, E. E., Jickells, S. M., & Russell, D. A. (2007). Intelligent finger-printing: Simultaneous identification of drug metabolites and individuals by using antibody-functionalised nanoparticles. *Angewandte Chemie, 46*, 4100–4103.

LePage, M. (2006, November 13). Death of the autopsy. *New Scientist*, pp. 28–31.

McDonald, P., & Foy, C. (2004). *Potential genetic markers for the identification of forensically useful morphological traits*. London: Police Foundation.

McLaughlin, L. M., Johnson, S. D., Bowers, K. J., Birks, D. J., & Pease, K. (2007). Police perceptions of the long- and short-term spatial distribution of residential burglary. *International Journal of Police Science and Management, 9*, 99–111.

Mullis, P. E., Patel M. S., Brickell, P. M., & Brook, C. G. (1991). Constitutionally short stature: Analysis of the insulin-like growth factor-I gene and the human growth hormone gene cluster. *Paediatrics Research, 29*, 412–415.

Newburn, T. (2007). *Handbook of criminal investigation*. Cullompton: Willan.

Oskamp, S. (1965). Over-confidence in case-study judgements. *Journal of Consulting Psychology, 29*, 261–265.

Owens, A., & Ellis, C. (2004). *Killer catchers*. London. Blake Publishing.

Pease, K. (2006). Science in the service of crime reduction. In N. Tilley (Ed.), *Handbook of crime prevention and community safety* (pp. 173–199). Cullompton: Willan.

Petherick, W. (2005). *Criminal profile: Into th0e mind of the killer*. London: Readers Digest.

Reilly, D. (2006, December 8). Autopsy analysis. *New Scientist*, pp. 24–25.

Roach, J. & Pease, K. (2006). DNA evidence and police investigations: A health warning. *Police Professional, 52*. Retrieved June 2006, from http://www.jdi.ucl.ac.uk/publications/journals/journals_2006.php.

Rossmo D. K. (1998). Presentation to NCIS Conference Canada. Retrieved July 12, 2008, from http://www.ecricanada.com/geopro/krossmo.pdf.

Rossmo, D. K. (2000). *Geographic profiling*. Baton Rouge, FL: CRC Press.

Rossmo, D. K. (2006a). Criminal investigative failures: Avoiding the pitfalls. *FBI Law Enforcement Bulletin, 75*(9), 1–8.

Rossmo, D. K. (2006b). Criminal investigative failures: Avoiding the pitfalls (Part two). *FBI Law Enforcement Bulletin, 75*(10), 12–19.

Shah, S. A., & Roth, L. H. (1974). Biological and psychophysiological factors in criminality. In D. Glaser (Ed.), *Handbook of criminology* (pp. 306–379). New York: Rand McNally.

Shojania, K. G., Burton, E. C., McDonald, K. M., & Goldman, L. (2003). Changes in rates of autopsy detected diagnostic errors over time: A systematic review. *Journal of the American Medical Association, 289*, 2849–2856.

Stelfox, P., & Pease, K. (2005). Cognition and detection: Reluctant bedfellows? In M. J. Smith & N. Tilley (Eds.), *Crime science: New approaches to preventing and detecting crime* (pp. 191–207). Cullompton, Devon: Willan.

Taroni, F., Aitken, C., Garbolino, P., & Biedermann, A. (2006). *Bayesian networks and probabilistic inference in forensic science*. Chichester: Wiley.

Wilson, I. J., Weale, M. E., & Balding, D. J. (2003). Inferences from DNA data: Population histories, evolutionary processes and forensic match probabilities. *Journal of the Royal Statistical Society: Series A, 166*, 155–188.

Recommendations and Conclusion 16

D. KIM ROSSMO

Every act of conscious learning requires the willingness to suffer an injury to one's self-esteem. That is why young children, before they are aware of their own self-importance, learn so easily and why older persons, especially if vain or important, cannot learn at all.

Thomas Stephen Szasz (1973)

Recommendations

The preceding three chapters in this section (as well as Chapter 7) presented a number of ideas for preventing criminal investigative failures, minimizing the chances of wrongful arrests and convictions, and improving detective work. Other commentators have suggested reform frameworks, usually focused on modifying the police and prosecution functions in an effort to avoid wrongful convictions. Of course, any system involving human judgment will contain some error, and the only real way to make sure wrongful convictions do not occur is to never convict anyone. Obviously this is impractical. Workable solutions must balance a number of competing interests, including fairness, public safety, and cost.

Findley and Scott (2006) propose reform in the following areas as ways to prevent tunnel vision and avoid wrongful convictions:

- Legal reform of the direct connection and harmless error doctrine; modification of the limitations on admissibility of statements against penal interest; expanded appellate review of the facts underlying guilt determination
- Education and training of police, prosecutors, and judges
- Improved procedures and protocols for collecting and assessing physical and testimonial evidence
- Better management and supervision of investigations by:
  - Police—selection of police investigators and investigative supervisors, posing alternative case theories, approaching from an ignorance perspective, apportioning investigative responsibilities, using advisory investigators, presenting the case to the prosecutor, disclosing information to the media

- Prosecutors—demanding full disclosure from police, maintaining independence from police investigators, employing multiple levels of case review, counter-arguing
- Transparency
- Institutional reforms of police crime laboratories and prosecution offices.

Epp (1997) suggests establishing a legislated rule system, similar to the police investigative code of practice adopted in the United Kingdom, along with improvements in training, supervision, and discipline. He sees little hope in preventing wrongful convictions through the use of sanctions:

> Attempts to eliminate or significantly reduce police malpractice in the investigation of crime through solutions centered on measures such as the exclusion of evidence, criminal or civil proceedings, and internal discipline or citizen complaints are likely to be ineffective. … Each proposed solution suffers from the inability to impact the "cop culture" and "working personality" in investigation. Self-interest in defending allegations of malpractice diverts energy away from the search for the actual perpetrator. Each proposed solution involves a lapse of time which tends to make it more difficult to detect and convict the actual perpetrator of the original crime once the proceedings against the wrongfully accused, or errant police officer, are finally concluded. (p. 109)

Unfortunately, defining the problem as one of police malpractice or wrong-doing does not properly recognize the cognitive and organizational influences involved. Failures in investigations are not so much a problem of a particular occupational group as they are a problem of human nature.

Finally, the following strategies—derived in consideration of the problems of cognitive bias, organizational traps, and probability errors—are from my original presentation on criminal investigative failures. All are achievable within the context of a police organization and do not require legislative reform or significant cost.

- Ensure that investigators and their managers are aware of these problems through case study-based training (see Cory, 2001).
- Encourage an atmosphere of open inquiry, and ensure investigative managers remain impartial and neutral.
- Defer reaching conclusions as much as possible until sufficient data have been collected.
- Avoid tunnel vision. Consider different perspectives and encourage cross-fertilization of ideas.
- Follow the evidence and the data. Explore hunches but do not become wedded to them.
- Organize brain-storming sessions and seek creativity rather than consensus.

- Ensure that investigative managers are willing to accept objections, doubts, and criticisms from team members.
- Encourage investigators to express alternative, even unpopular, points of view. Assign the role of devil's advocate to a strong team member.
- Consider using subgroups for different tasks, and facilitate parallel but independent decision making.
- Recognize and delineate assumptions, inference chains, and points of uncertainty. Always ask, "How do we know what we think we know?"
- When appropriate, obtain expert opinions and external reviews and give them proper consideration.
- Conduct routine systematic debriefings after major crime investigations, and organize a full-scale "autopsy" after an investigative failure.[1]
- Encourage and facilitate research into criminal investigation failures and how they might be prevented (see Stelfox & Pease, 2005).

Police investigations can significantly benefit from the thoughts and opinions of independent experts. The British Home Office, frustrated over the lack of progress in the Yorkshire Ripper murder inquiry, formed an external review committee that included a civilian. Forensic scientist Stuart Kind, adopting an analytical approach, studied the locations and times of the crimes and correctly concluded that the killer lived in Bradford (Kind, 1987, 1999). Up to that point, the task force believed the offender was from the distant Sunderland area.

Outside review can play an important role in major crime investigations. Police procedures in the United Kingdom require an independent review of unsolved homicide cases after one year.[2] This produces two results. First, as the assigned detective is aware of this policy, he or she is more likely to be thorough and less likely to leave possibilities unexplored. Second, external reviewers, for all the psychological and organizational reasons discussed earlier, are more apt to notice mistakes and omissions overlooked by the original investigators. This is the basis for scholarly peer review, a foundation of scientific research publication.

Training is an important first step, but insufficient by itself. Effort and vigilance are required. Law enforcement agencies need to create formal organizational mechanisms to prevent these subtle hazards from derailing criminal investigations. A final warning—research suggests that, even when individuals are aware of these problems, they may still find them difficult

---

[1] The Vancouver Police Department assigned Deputy Chief Constable Doug LePard to thoroughly review what happened—and failed to happen—in the Missing Women/Pickton Pig Farm Serial Murder case (see Chapters 3 and 13).

[2] Although several factors are involved, it is perhaps worth noting that the homicide clearance rate in the United Kingdom is over 90%, compared to 63% in the United States.

to overcome (Heuer, 1999). The dangers are especially great in high-profile cases of horrific crimes, such as sex or child murders.

Police officers are not the only ones at risk; prosecutors and judges can also fall prey to these traps (Cory, 2001; FPT Heads of Prosecutions Committee Working Group, 2004). A recent and powerful example was the false rape complaints by a black stripper against three white members of the Duke University lacrosse team in March 2006. Right from the beginning, it was clear the case had all the elements of a disastrous investigative failure—intense media interest, a problematic "victim," race tensions, an upcoming district attorney election, and stereotyped suspects (rich college kids). Although the police investigation was flawed,[3] it was the Durham County district attorney Mike Nifong who took the brunt of the blame. After it became clear the victim had lied, North Carolina Attorney General Roy Cooper dropped all the charges and declared the accused players were innocent victims in "a tragic rush to accuse" by a rogue prosecutor. Among other unethical actions, Nifong withheld exculpatory DNA evidence, gave false statements to the media, and manipulated the police investigation. He was eventually disbarred from the North Carolina Bar and convicted of criminal contempt. Although Nifong's behavior was not totally the result of honest errors in judgment, it appears he had convinced himself the lacrosse players were guilty. And he was not the only one—various Duke faculty groups, members of the media, politicians, and civil rights activists blithely followed along.

Concluding Thoughts

Errors in criminal investigations appear to follow reasonably predictable patterns. The following, admittedly unscientific, error theorems are presented for the reader's consideration:

1. One mistake, one coincidence, and one piece of bad luck can produce an investigative failure.
2. Once one mistake has been made, the likelihood of further mistakes increases.
3. Usually the biggest problem is refusing to acknowledge the original mistake.

---

[3] Police investigators showed the Duke University lacrosse team photograph to the complainant, Crystal Gail Mangum, so she could identify her alleged assailants. As most of the team was present at the house party where Magnum said she had been raped, this virtually guaranteed she would pick out somebody present at the scene as a suspect.

It is the third point that appears to result in the most egregious miscarriages of justice. Once the system has made a decision and branded a person guilty, it often appears only a truly massive effort will undo that decision.

In February 2008, Justin Johnson was arrested for the rape and murders of two young girls in rural Noxubee County, Mississippi (Dewan, 2008). He confessed to both crimes; one from 1990, the other from 1992, after his DNA was linked to crime scene evidence. It turned out that Johnson was an early suspect in both cases. The murders were not linked at the time, and few realized that Johnson lived near one victim, while his former wife lived next door to the other.

The only problem with Johnson's arrest is that the courts had already convicted two other men for these murders on the basis of a now discredited bite mark expert. One of them, Kennedy Brewer, a mildly retarded black man originally sentenced to the death penalty, had been exonerated in 2001 by a DNA test. He was kept in prison until August 2007, however, because the district attorney, Forrest Allgood, said he planned to retry Brewer. "Almost no effort was made by county officials to find the person responsible for the rape, and Mr. Allgood said he still believed Mr. Brewer was involved in the murder, perhaps as an accomplice" (Dewan, 2008). The Innocence Project, which helped free Brewer, calls this the unindicted co-conspirator—an amorphous theory almost impossible for a wrongfully convicted person to disprove. A Noxubee County sheriff's deputy said, "there had not been enough money to conduct a thorough investigation" of the case (Dewan, 2008). Apparently, however, there *was* enough money to keep Brewer imprisoned.

It is very difficult to understand this behavior, so hard to accept such an oblivious attitude toward another human being by an officer of the court. But typically in such cases our justice system officials honestly believe the wrongfully convicted party is actually guilty. The problem is that organizational and political pressures can produce distorted judgments. The smallest puddle of doubt becomes a large lake on which a freighter of excuses and rationales can be floated. Also, reviewing a closed case requires a significant effort, one that must fight against organizational inertia. Travis County (Texas) District Attorney Ronnie Earle provides some honest insight into the hurdles of reopening a conviction:

> Cases in which the evidence proves the defendant's guilt beyond a reasonable doubt are difficult to put together, harder to hold together, and happily left behind once a conviction is obtained. The ongoing onslaught of current cases and opposition from victims certain of the identity of the perpetrator add to the pressure to let sleeping dogs lie. (Earle & Case, 2002, p. 73)

Complicating the situation is the difficulty in separating legitimate claims of innocence from the noises of the truly guilty (see Chapter 12). Still, prosecutors and police investigators who preserve the status quo had better be certain they have made the right decision; the consequences of flawed judgment in these circumstances are truly considerable.

Perhaps there is something we can learn from the fictional police detective. Rarely do these individuals jump to conclusions, and the identity of the offender is not known until the end of the story. Although this is often a plot device to help heighten suspense, we can still benefit from the important lesson of keeping all our options open. The potential benefits of advanced forensic techniques, comprehensive criminal databases, and highly skilled police personnel will be undermined by the wrong mindset and a limited organizational approach.

Thankfully, most criminals are not masterminds, and in many cases the criminal investigation is a straightforward process. However, a major crime "whodunit" can be challenging and difficult. Certain factors identified with cognitive and organizational failures—low information levels, limited resources, and pressure to obtain quick results—are all too common in these investigations (Janis, 1982; Stelfox & Pease, 2005). Some of the brightest scientists, judges, politicians, and detectives have fallen victim to these traps. No one is immune. It is a mistake to attribute lack of investigative success to offender cleverness before determining if any internal problems exist.

The criminal investigation process plays an important and special role in countries governed by the rule of law. Its function is to seek the truth, "without fear or favor." That task, integral to both public safety and justice concerns, must be conducted in an unbiased and professional manner. When it is not, the results are unsolved crimes, unapprehended offenders, and wrongful convictions. Understanding what can go wrong is the first step toward preventing criminal investigative failures.

References

Cory, P. de C. (2001). *The inquiry regarding Thomas Sophonow*. Winnipeg, MB: Queen's Printer.

Dewan, S. (2008, February 8). New suspect is arrested in 2 Mississippi killings. *New York Times*, Retrieved July 12, 2008, from http://www.nytimes.com/2008/02/08/02/08dna.html.

Earle, R., & Case, C. B., Jr. (2002, September–October). The prosecutorial mandate: See that justice is done. *Judicature*, p. 73.

Epp, J. A. (1997). Penetrating police investigative practice post-Morin. *U.B.C. Law Review, 31*, 95–126.

Findley, K. A., & Scott, M. S. (2006). The multiple dimensions of tunnel vision in criminal cases. *Wisconsin Law Review, 2*, 291–397.

FPT Heads of Prosecutions Committee Working Group. (2004). *Report on the prevention of miscarriages of justice*. Ottawa: Department of Justice.

Heuer, R. J., Jr. (1999). *Psychology of intelligence analysis*. Washington, DC: Center for the Study of Intelligence, Central Intelligence Agency.

Janis, I. L. (1982). *Groupthink: Psychological studies of policy decisions and fiascoes* (2nd ed.). Boston: Houghton Mifflin.

Kind, S. S. (1987). *The scientific investigation of crime*. Harrogate: Forensic Science Services.

Kind, S. S. (1999). *The sceptical witness*. Harrogate: Hodology.

Stelfox, P., & Pease, K. (2005). Cognition and detection: Reluctant bedfellows? In M. J. Smith & N. Tilley (Eds.), *Crime science: New approaches to preventing and detecting crime* (pp. 191–207). Cullompton, Devon: Willan.

Szasz, T. S. (1973). *The second sin*. New York: Anchor Books.

Bibliography

Axelrod, A. (2008). *Profiles in folly: History's worst decisions and why they went wrong.* New York: Sterling Publishing.

Barak, G. (1996). *Representing O.J.: Murder, criminal justice and mass culture.* Guilderland, NY: Harrow and Heston.

Bell, J. G., Clow, K. A., & Ricciardelli, R. (2008). Causes of wrongful conviction: Looking at student knowledge. *Journal of Criminal Justice Education, 19,* 75–96.

Blair, I. V. (2002). The malleability of automatic stereotypes and prejudice. *Personality and Social Psychology Review, 6,* 242–261.

Blair, J. P. (2005). A test of the unusual false confession perspective: Using cases of proven false confessions. *Criminal Law Bulletin, 41,* 127–144.

Bruner, J. S., & Potter, M. C. (1964). Interference in visual recognition. *Science, 144,* 424–425.

Burkell, C. J., & Wood, H. (1999, March). Make the right call. *Fire Chief.* Retrieved July 12, 2008, from http://firechief.com/mag/firefighting_right_call/index.html.

Chen, M., & Bargh, J. A. (1997). Nonconscious behavioral confirmation processes: The self-fulfilling consequences of automatic stereotype activation. *Journal of Experimental Psychology, 33,* 541–560.

Collie, A. J. (2007, January). Phil Simms. *US Airways Magazine,* 40–44.

Damer, T. E. (2001). *Attacking faulty reasoning: A practical guide to fallacy-free arguments* (4th ed.). Belmont, CA: Wadsworth.

Daugherty, R. (2004). *Murder on a horse trail: The disappearance of Chandra Levy.* Lincoln, NE: iUniverse.

Dror, I. E. (2006). The psychology of police performance and decision making. *Police Professional, 58,* 37–39.

Eck, J. E. (1983). *Solving crimes: The investigation of burglary and robbery.* Washington, DC: Police Executive Research Forum.

Egger, S. A. (1990). *Serial murder: An elusive phenomenon.* New York: Praeger.

Eysenck, M. W. (1997). *Anxiety and cognition: A unified theory.* Hove, UK: Psychology Press.

Faigman, D. L. (1999). *Legal alchemy: The use and misuse of science in the law.* New York: Freeman.

Feynman, R. P. (1988). *"What do you care what other people think?": Further adventures of a curious character.* New York: W. W. Norton.

Fischhoff, B. (1999). What do patients want? Help in making effective choices. *Effective Clinical Practice, 2,* 198–200.

Forst, B. (1993). *The representations of uncertainty in expert systems: An application in criminal investigation.* Ann Arbor, MI: UMI.

Forst, B. (1996). Evidence, probabilities, and legal standards for the determination of guilt: Beyond the O.J. trial. In G. Barak (Ed.), *Representing O.J.: Murder, criminal justice and mass culture* (pp. 22–28). Guilderland, NY: Harrow and Heston.

Forst, B. (2004). Problem-oriented criminal investigation. In Q. C. Thurman & J. Zhao (Eds.), *Contemporary policing: Controversies, challenges, and solutions* (pp. 266–273). Los Angeles: Roxbury.

Forst, B., & Planty, M. (2000). What is the probability that the offender in a new case is in the MO file? *International Journal of Police Science and Management, 3,* 124–137.

Frankel, G. (2006, May 14). Burden of proof. *Washington Post Magazine,* pp. 8–13, 19–24.

Gehlbach, S. H. (2002). *Interpreting the medical literature* (4th ed.). New York: McGraw-Hill.

Gigerenzer, G. (2007). *Gut feelings: The intelligence of the unconscious.* New York: Viking.

Gill, P. (2000). *Rounding up the usual suspects? Developments in contemporary law enforcement intelligence.* Aldershot, Hants: Ashgate.

Gladwell, M. (2003, March 10). Connecting the dots. *New Yorker,* pp. 83–88.

Gladwell, M. (2005). *Blink: The power of thinking without thinking.* New York: Little, Brown.

Grisham, J. (2006). *The innocent man: Murder and injustice in a small town.* New York: Doubleday.

Holyoak, K. J., & Simon, D. (1999). Bidirectional reasoning in decision making by constraint satisfaction. *Journal of Experimental Psychology: General, 128,* 3–31.

Horvath, F., & Meesig, R. (1996). The criminal investigation process and the role of forensic evidence: A review of empirical findings. *Journal of Forensic Sciences, 41,* 963–969.

Huber, P. W. (1991). *Galileo's revenge: Junk science in the courtroom.* New York: Basic Books.

Kahneman, D., & Renshon, J. (2007, January/February). Why hawks win. *Foreign Policy, 158,* 34–38.

Kahneman, D., & Tversky, A. (1972). On prediction and judgment. *ORI Research Monograph, 12*(4), 10.

Kassin, S. M. (2005). On the psychology of confessions: Does innocence put innocents at risk? *American Psychologist, 60,* 215–228.

Katkin, E. S., Wiens, S., & Öhman, A. (2001). Nonconscious fear conditioning, visceral perception, and the development of gut feelings. *Psychological Science, 12,* 366–370.

King, L., & Appleton, J. A. (1997). Intuition: A critical review of the research and rhetoric. *Journal of Advanced Nursing, 26,* 194–202.

Klein, G. A., & Hoffman, R. (1993). Seeing the invisible: Perceptual-cognitive aspects of expertise. In M. Rabinowitz (Ed.), *Cognitive science foundations of instruction* (pp. 203–226). Mahwah, NJ: Erlbaum.

Krippendorff, K. (1986). *Information theory: Structural models for qualitative data.* University paper series on quantitative applications in the social sciences, 62. Beverly Hills, CA: Sage.

LeBourdais, I. (1966). *The trial of Steven Truscott.* Toronto: McClelland and Stewart.

LeGault, M. R. (2006). *Think!: Why crucial decisions can't be made in the blink of an eye.* New York: Simon and Schuster.

Martin, R. M. (1992). *There are two errors in the the title of this book: A sourcebook of philosophical puzzles, problems and paradoxes.* Peterborough, ON: Broadview Press.

Matlin, M. W. (2004). *Cognition* (6th ed.). New York: Wiley.

Matthews, R. (2004, March 13). Opposites detract. *New Scientist*, p. 38.

Nordby, J. J. (2000). *Dead reckoning: The art of forensic detection.* Boca Raton, FL: CRC Press.

O'Hara, P. (2005). *Why law enforcement organizations fail: Mapping the organizational fault lines in policing.* Durham, NC: Carolina Academic Press.

Perry, J. M. (1996). *Arrogant armies: Great military disasters and the generals behind them.* New York: Wiley.

Peterson, M. B. (2004). Applying Heuer's analysis of competing hypotheses (ACH) in the law enforcement intelligence environment. *IALEIA Journal, 16*(1), 1–14.

Petroski, H. (1992). *To engineer is human: The role of failure in successful design.* New York: Vintage.

Philpin, J. (2006). *Shattered justice: A savage murder and the death of three families' innocence.* New York: Avon Books.

Pinizzotto, A. J., & Davis, E. F. (1999). Offenders' perceptual shorthand: What messages are law enforcement officers sending to offenders? *FBI Law Enforcement Bulletin, 68*(6), 1–4.

Rabinowitz, M. (Ed.). (1993). *Cognitive science foundations of instruction.* Mahwah, NJ: Erlbaum.

Read, S. J., Snow, C. J., & Simon, D. (2003). Constraint satisfaction processes in social reasoning. *Proceedings of the 25th Annual Meeting of the Cognitive Science Society.* Boston, MA.

Rensink, R. A. (2004). Visual sensing without seeing. *Psychological Science, 15*, 27–32.

A Review of the FBI's Handling of the Brandon Mayfield Case. (2006). Office of the Inspector General, Oversight and Review Division, U.S. Department of Justice. Washington, DC: U.S. Government Printing Office.

Reyna, V. F. (2004). How people make decisions that involve risk: A dual-processes approach. *Current Directions in Psychological Science, 13*, 60–66.

Sabini, J., & Silver, M. (1993). Destroying the innocent with a clear conscience: A sociopsychology of the Holocaust. In N. J. Kressel (Ed.), *Political psychology: Classic and contemporary readings* (pp. 192–217). New York: Paragon.

Schiller, L. (1999). *Perfect murder, perfect town.* New York: HarperCollins.

Simon, D., & Holyoak, K. J. (2002). Structural dynamics of cognition: From consistency theories to constraint satisfaction. *Personality and Social Psychology Review, 6*, 283–294.

Simon, D., Pham, L. B., Le, Q. A., & Holyoak, K. J. (2001). The emergence of coherence over the course of decision making. *Journal of Experimental Psychology: Learning, Memory, and Cognition, 27*, 1250–1260.

Slovic, P., Finucane, M. L., Peters, E., & MacGregor, D. G. (2002, December). *Risk as analysis and risk as feelings: Some thoughts about affect, reason, risk, and rationality.* Paper presented at the Annual Meeting of the Society for Risk Analysis, New Orleans, LA.

Smith, M. J., & Tilley, N. (Eds.). (2005). *Crime science: New approaches to preventing and detecting crime.* Cullompton, Devon: Willan.

Starbuck, W., & Hodgkinson, G. (Eds.). (In press). *Handbook of organizational decision making.* Oxford: Oxford University Press.

Sullivan, L. (2004, January 27). Sept. 11 hijacker raised suspicions at border: Investigation panel is told of clues linking suspects. *Baltimore Sun,* p. 1A.

Sutcliffe, K. M., & Weick, K. E. (In press). Information overload revisited. In W. Starbuck & G. Hodgkinson (Eds.), *Handbook of organizational decision making.* Oxford: Oxford University Press.

Sweeney, J. (1994, September 18). Why the police hunters took aim at Stagg. *The Observer,* p. 21.

Taroni, F., Aitken, C., Garbolino, P., & Biedermann, A. (2006). *Bayesian networks and probabilistic inference in forensic science.* Chichester: Wiley.

Thaler, R. H., & Sunstein, C. R. (2008). Nudge: Improving decisions about health, wealth, and happiness, New Haven, CT: Yale University Press.

Tracy, P. E. (2003). *Who killed Stephanie Crowe?: Anatomy of a murder investigation.* Dallas: Brown Books.

Tucker, J. C. (1997). *May God have mercy: A true story of crime and punishment.* New York: Dell.

Tufte, E. R. (2006a). *Beautiful evidence.* Cheshire, CT: Graphics Press.

Tversky, A., & Kahneman, D. (1987). *Can normative and descriptive analysis be reconciled?* Manuscript, University of Maryland, Institute for Philosophy and Public Policy, College Park, MD.

Using DNA to solve cold cases. (2002). *NIJ special report* (NIJ Publication No. NCJ-194197). Washington, DC: U.S. Government Printing Office.

van Koppen, P. J. (In press). Blundering justice: A case study of the Schiedam Park Murder. In R. N. Kocsis (Ed.), *The psychology of serial violent crimes and their criminal investigation.* Totowa, NJ: Humana.

Watts, D. J. (2003). *Six degrees: The science of a connected age.* New York: W. W. Norton.

Wecht, C. H., & Kaufmann, D. (2008). *A question of murder: Compelling cases from a famed forensic pathologist.* Amherst, NY: Prometheus Books.

Weeks, L. (2004, February 3). Gut reaction: A customs officer's instinct paid off. *Washington Post,* pp. C1, C8.

Williams, S. (1996). *Invisible darkness: The strange case of Paul Bernardo and Karla Homolka.* Toronto: Little, Brown.

Willmer, M. A. P. (1970). *Crime and information theory.* Edinburgh: Edinburgh University Press.

Zabell, S. L. (2005). *Fingerprint evidence.* Unpublished manuscript, Northwestern University, Mathematics Department, Evanston, IL.

Index